DATE DUE

			PRINTED IN U.S.A.

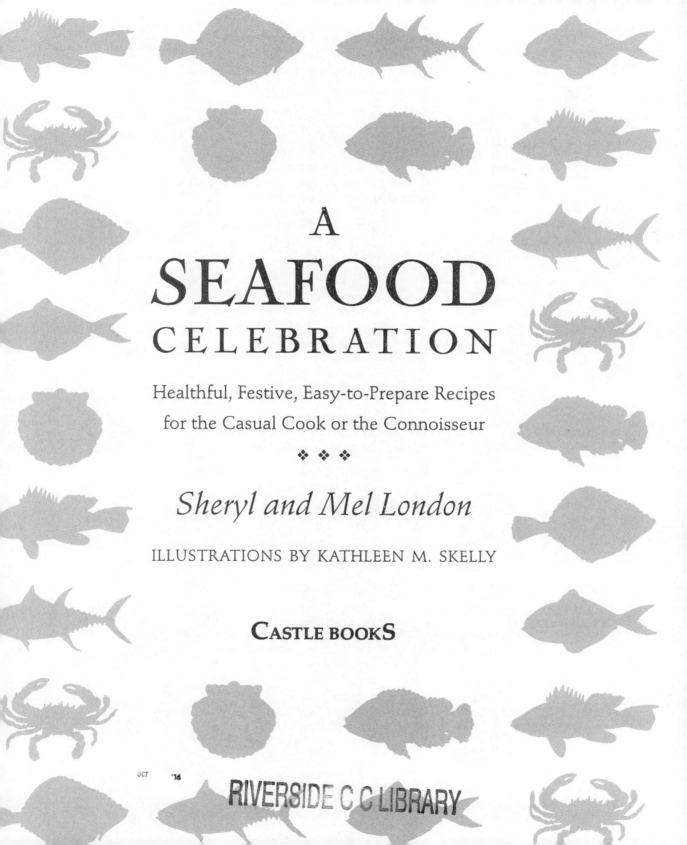

A
SEAFOOD
CELEBRATION

Healthful, Festive, Easy-to-Prepare Recipes
for the Casual Cook or the Connoisseur

❖ ❖ ❖

Sheryl and Mel London

ILLUSTRATIONS BY KATHLEEN M. SKELLY

CASTLE BOOKS

THIS EDITION PUBLISHED IN 1998 BY CASTLE BOOKS, A DIVISION OF BOOK SALES, INC.
114 NORTHFIELD AVENUE, EDISON, NEW JERSEY 08837

CASTLE BOOKS IS A REGISTERED TRADEMARK OF BOOK SALES, INC.

PUBLISHED BY ARRANGEMENT WITH AND PERMISSION OF SIMON & SCHUSTER

SIMON & SCHUSTER
SIMON & SCHUSTER BUILDING
ROCKEFELLER CENTER
1230 AVENUE OF THE AMERICAS
NEW YORK, NEW YORK 10020

DESIGNED BY MARYSARAH QUINN
MANUFACTURED IN THE UNITED STATES OF AMERICA

LIBRARY OF CONGRESS CATALOGING-IN-PUBLICATION DATA

LONDON, SHERYL.
A SEAFOOD CELEBRATION : HEALTHFUL, FESTIVE, EASY-TO-PREPARE RECIPES
FOR THE CASUAL COOK OR THE CONNOISSEUR / SHERYL AND MEL
LONDON ; ILLUSTRATIONS BY KATHLEEN M. SKELLY.
P.   CM.
INCLUDES INDEX.
1. COOKERY (FISH) 2. COOKERY (SEAFOOD)   I. LONDON, MEL.
II. TITLE.
TX747.L664   1993
641.6'92—DC20   93–19727
CIP

ISBN: 0-7858-0927-9

ACKNOWLEDGMENTS

No book is ever done alone—be it a novel, a work of nonfiction, or a cookbook—and as always, along the way, we have been blessed with many helpers. And then there are the testers, the friends and acquaintances who are asked to taste and to give constructive criticism based upon their personal affinities, for as some wise person once said, "There's no accounting for other people's tastes!"

But with a book about fish and seafood cookery, the road becomes particularly difficult, since we also had to depend on suppliers, the seasons of the year, the availability of the catch, and the regional species that appear in the marketplace one day only to be gone the next. And so, we would like to pay tribute to the great many people who have helped to make this book complete, easy to follow, and accurate. Various individuals, as well as the organizations across the country that deal in seafood information and promotion, and the local fishmongers in our teeming city, both in ethnic neighborhoods and in upscale enclaves, have been more than wonderful. We trust that we have not omitted anyone in this list, and if we inadvertently have, we extend our apologies.

We especially would like to give thanks to Ken Gall of the Sea Grant Extension Program of New York, Richard Lord of the Fulton Fish Market, and all the wonderful men and women who gave such vocal support when we arrived at that bustling market at 3 A.M. Also to Russ Meredith, Tony Di Dia, and Leo Gaudin of the National Maritime Fisheries Service, and to our dear sister-in-law, Elaine London, who did our surveys out in the Midwest.

We are also indebted to Nicholas Lemann for allowing us to use his perfect quote with which to begin this book, and to Kathleen Skelly, who once again has provided the perfect and delightful illustrations, and to whom we have dedicated this work, a long overdue salute.

Of course, there are the organizations who offered both telephone advice and an overwhelming outpouring of printed research materials:

National Fisheries Institute
Alaska Seafood Marketing Institute
Fisheries Council of British Columbia
International Pacific Halibut Commission
Pacific Salmon Commission
Gulf and South Atlantic Fisheries Development Foundation
North Atlantic Seafood Association
Catfish Farmers of America
The Catfish Institute
American Heart Association

Center for Science in the Public Interest
The New England Journal of Medicine
U.S. Department of Health and Human Services
Simply Seafood Magazine

And finally, a bow and a genuine word of thanks to our friend and agent, Madeleine Morel, who has been supportive and delightful (as well as being a taster) for several of our books, and to our editor Toula Polygalaktos, with whom we have had the pleasure of working together on three of our cookbooks. The list is long, but we thank each and every one of you.

For our illustrious illustrator
Kathleen M. Skelly,
who not only swims like a fish
but loves the sea and all
its creatures

ABOUT THE AUTHORS

MEL AND SHERYL LONDON are the authors of fifteen other books, including nine cookbooks, as well as books on subjects that range from travel to lifestyle, gardening, and film and videotape career guides. Their *Fish Lovers' Cookbook* was first-prize winner in its category in the Tastemaker Awards, and their *The Versatile Grain and the Elegant Bean* was nominated for the James Beard book award.

As documentary film makers, Mel and Sheryl have worked in more than sixty countries on every continent, producing films for foundations and corporations on the environment, travel, energy, training, fund raising, and health. Mel's documentary on aging and chronic disease was a nominee for the Academy Award and together Mel and Sheryl hold more than 250 other awards for their film work.

They make their home in New York's East Village but create and test recipes at their house on Fire Island.

CONTENTS

Metric Equivalencies

LIQUID AND DRY MEASURE EQUIVALENCIES

Customary	Metric
¼ teaspoon	1.25 milliliters
½ teaspoon	2.5 milliliters
1 teaspoon	5 milliliters
1 tablespoon	15 milliliters
1 fluid ounce	30 milliliters
¼ cup	60 milliliters
⅓ cup	80 milliliters
½ cup	120 milliliters
1 cup	240 milliliters
1 pint (2 cups)	480 milliliters
1 quart (4 cups, 32 ounces)	960 milliliters (.96 liters)
1 gallon (4 quarts)	3.84 liters
1 ounce (by weight)	28 grams
¼ pound (4 ounces)	114 grams
1 pound (16 ounces)	454 grams
2.2 pounds	1 kilogram (1000 grams)

OVEN TEMPERATURE EQUIVALENCIES

Description	°Fahrenheit	°Celsius
Cool	200	90
Very slow	250	120
Slow	300-325	150-160
Moderately slow	325-350	160-180
Moderate	350-375	180-190
Moderatly hot	375-400	190-200
Hot	400-450	200-230
Very hot	450-500	230-260

INTRODUCTION

Bemused members of my family often ask me, What is it with you and fish, Nick? I like the compactness, the efficiency of a fish, and also the feeling that during its life it was wild, elusive, hidden. Cooking a fish is particularly satisfying because it is the closest a casual cook can get to what the business historians call vertical integration: you can personally execute every step, from choosing the live animal to serving the dinner. It confers a sense—obviously illusory, but nonetheless satisfying—of pioneer self-sufficiency. All these reasons to cook fish work for me, but if you require more rational ones, they certainly exist.

Nicholas Lemann
"Me and My Fish Fetish"
Esquire, September 1989
(Used with permission)

A well-educated friend of ours, no doubt an English major, would have dubbed Nicholas Lemann an *ichthyophagist*—one who eats or subsists on fish—and probably the same appellation would apply to us. For we have had a love affair with the sea since we were "tadpoles" and, given half a chance, Mel will tell "fish stories" that date back to his Izaak Walton days, when he was just thirteen. Sheryl, a trained artist, has doodled fish through her telephone conversations for just as many years.

In our later years, our work on documentary films took us to countries that before only had existed in our imaginations—sixty in all. Wherever possible, visits to the markets of the towns and villages and seaside harbors became an important part of each trip. We have been lucky enough to visit the bustling Tsukiji Fish Market in Tokyo, the largest in the world, as well as the harbor at Portimão in Portugal where dockside restaurant chefs grill just-caught sardines for their customers. We have been out on shrimp boats in the Gulf of Mexico and have stood in the dawn fog of Nazaré in Portugal to wait for the arrival of the returning fishing boats, painted in their bright traditional colors, while the women sit on the beach, wrapped tightly in their black shawls like wraiths in the eerie morning mist.

Fresh-caught swordfish (*kiliç baligt*) on the shores of the Bosphorus in Turkey, gala and festive lunches of tiny *calamaretti* and clams no bigger than our thumbnails on the Amalfi Drive in Italy, as well as whitefish netted in the Caspian Sea have all been duly photographed—and then eaten. We've met lobstermen, crabbers, fish farmers, and festival cooks. We've been to fish markets, fish fries, fish dinners, and too many fish restaurants to count. We've listened to fish stories and we've swapped fish recipes and fishing tips.

And so, it was probably preordained that we would write our first fish cookbook about twelve years ago, after having built our house on a barrier island, continuing our love for the sea and for fresh-caught fluke and flounder and blackfish early in the season, and bluefish, little tunny, and striped bass late in the autumn. We also might have predicted that this book would follow that many years later, for not only have *we* changed in our thinking, cooking habits, and nutritional beliefs, but so has the rest of the country. The seafood industry itself has changed radically in that short period of time as a direct result of consumer education and buying habits.

During the early part of this century, the annual per capita consumption of fish and shellfish in this country hovered around eight to eleven pounds a year. For some it was "fish on Friday," for others it was a weekly or monthly menu addition of the most common fish available: flounder or cod near the sea or perch and trout farther inland.

Certainly the harvesting, freezing, and shipping techniques at that time were not sophisticated enough to guarantee freshness, but this began to change at about the beginning of the 1970s. Gradually the per capita consumption of fish and shellfish began to creep up. By the beginning of the 1990s, the annual figure began to reach about sixteen pounds per person. Of course, this was still far below the consumption figures of places like Japan (about four times what we eat), or Hong Kong, Iceland, and Guyana. Nevertheless, it was a trend that was duly noted.

In the home and out in restaurants, more and more menus began to feature seafood, while the consumption of beef and other meat products began a slow decline. At the time that consumers began to show a new awareness of nutrition, the seafood industry began to reflect that awakening and it, too, started to change to meet the growing demand and sophistication of the general public. It is difficult to determine just which change came first—consumer awareness or industry awareness—for somehow it all seemed to happen within the space of a few short years.

Those of us who read the daily newspapers and the major magazines were reminded too often that our diets were not particularly good for our health. We used too much saturated fat, salt was a major contributor to hypertension, we used too much butter and cream (which all agreed made things taste very good!), and the fast-food craze was all but destroying our muscle tone. Words like "cholesterol" became a part of our everyday vocabularies, and most of us waited anxiously for the sometimes startling results of the tests that our doctors ordered each year, with "HDL," "LDL," and "triglycerides" becoming a part of our lunchtime conversations.

At the same time, just about the beginning of the seventies, the price of meat began to rise and people started to look for alternatives. Fish became an economical choice, especially if the shopper could find unusual and underutilized species such as tilefish or skate lying on the fishmonger's bed of ice.

In those days, the restaurant "catch of the day" might be flounder or sole, or some fillet masquerading as the latter, for the choice was limited, as were the tastes of the customers, and regional preference and *availability* strongly dictated what was in the marketplace. Cities such as Dallas and even Chicago might have boasted only a few seafood restaurants, since most of the customers who lived in that vast area between the coasts much preferred a large cut of beef, in any case.

To use just one measuring stick, in the last ten years, Dallas has gone from four to almost fifty restaurants specializing in the catch from the sea. At fish markets and even supermarkets around the country, customers have been treated to an incredible range of new names, with over a thousand varieties now available. Local fishmongers feature lobster-holding tanks, many of them thousands of miles from the cold Maine and Canadian waters.

Restaurant diners even have accepted some of the more unusual (and uglier) fish as easily as they once did their rare or medium T-bone steaks. Sushi bars, once very rare and as empty as the Sahara, are now more crowded than ever, and some cities like New York seem to flaunt them two to a block. The daily special or catch of the day might well be orange roughy, monkfish, wolffish, skate, tilapia, or opah. And although cod and flounder still hold reign as the most popular selections, the use of former "junkfish" like Alaska pollack has increased the annual per capita consumption through its use in imitation crab called *surimi*, now ubiquitous in seafood displays.

During the sixties and seventies, we also saw a huge jump in foreign travel. People tasted the original and authentic bouillabaisse right in Marseilles. They discovered the delicious and tempting *anguillas* (elvers or baby eels) and *percebes* (gooseneck barnacles) in Spain, while the more adventurous (and suicidal) came home boasting of a night with *fugu*, a potentially poisonous blowfish used in sashimi, in the heart of Tokyo. Indeed, not only are our eating habits different from those of just ten or fifteen years ago, but even the condiments and spices in our pantries and the availability of fresh herbs have drastically changed.

To meet this new demand, the commercial fishing industry developed more intricate, high-tech, efficient systems. Huge factory ships now flash-freeze the catch so that the more perishable species of fish can be shipped to the markets. Air transportation has meant that cities and towns across the entire country can sample diversity and quality never thought possible before. The handling of seafood products has improved to the point where much of what is caught at sea and immediately flash-frozen might well be considered "fresher" than the bounty that we fisherpeople bring home from the beach or the lakes.

The growing demand for seafood has been called a revolution by some food writers, and certainly the word comes very close to describing what has been happening. However, it has not been without cost. Several problems have arisen at the same time.

As demand has grown, the price of fish has also slowly climbed until most varieties are no longer an economical substitute for red meat. Overfishing by large fleets of ships, many of them floating drift nets as long as 40 miles, has seriously affected the supply of some species. Dire predictions have been made that some species, such as the bluefin tuna, may entirely disappear.

Yet another problem has begun to plague those of us who love to fish and who love to eat our catch. Worse still, it has sorely affected those who make their living from the catch of the sea. A series of events, many of them attributable to the growth of industry and lax environmental controls, has created a pollution problem that has opened up a Pandora's box of dangers and diseases in our most popular species. We shall have more to say about this later on in this book.

There are, however, two rather bright lights on the horizon, even as we overfish and pollute our seas and rivers with seeming abandon. First of all, we have become *aware* that our supply of fish is in dire straits if we don't do something about it soon. Thus, there has been some movement toward limiting overfishing by foreign flag vessels as well as our own, and we have begun to crack down in some of the more polluted areas, such as New York's Hudson River.

The other optimistic sign is the tremendous growth of aquaculture, farm-raised fish and seafood that carry no pollutants or parasites. In addition, aquaculture is slowly filling the gap as supplies of some species begin to dwindle, as well as offering us a larger supply of "underutilized" species, once unfortunately known as "trash fish." We now find farm-raised catfish all across the country, as well as salmon, shrimp, trout, mussels, and tilapia, which was an experimental African variety when we first wrote about it twelve years ago and now frequently is found at our local fish market.

Taking all of these things into consideration, we found that the writing and testing of a cookbook such as this presents some interesting problems. As the number of species proliferates, we find that the *names* of many of these fish also change with the region, marketing creativity, and just plain local folklore. It is not at all unusual to find green-lipped New Zealand mussels being sold as "kiwi clams." The Israeli aquaculturists call tilapia "St. Peter's fish," and if you've tasted the popular John Dory in England, you'll find it on the menu in Italy as San Pietro and in France as St.-Pierre. Pollack has been marketed as blue snapper, and hake as white snapper. The common Northeast striped bass is called rockfish down around the Chesapeake Bay area, while our own weakfish is sea trout up and down the Atlantic Coast. There are over forty different varieties of flounder, not to mention its summer cousin, the fluke. And, to make matters even more confusing, lingcod is not even a cod; it is a member of the greenling family.

Just a few weeks ago, we visited the Chinese markets in lower Manhattan, a place in which we love to shop and where we feel that we have returned to Hong Kong. The fishmongers overflow onto the narrow streets, displaying the catch on beds of ice. The blue crabs are still alive, as they should be, and the holding tanks show off live carp, so popular with the local restaurants. Some shoppers spend as many as ten or fifteen minutes before making their final selection—examining the eyes and gills of the fish for brightness, subjecting the scales to a closer look, and testing the texture with a tentative probing of the index finger.

To make all of our lives easier, we have loosely grouped the fish in this book so that they are quite interchangeable, each one within its group. Should you find that one variety is just not at your fish market that day, or more important, that a particular fish looks tempting and fresh and you buy it impulsively (a correct choice, we might add), it should fit easily into a category of mild- or stronger-flavored fish or into a family, such as flatfish, for example. You'll even find a category in which to place the more unusual fish in a chapter that we've called "The Bizarre Bazaar" (frogs' legs, sea urchins, octopus, monkfish). Thus, in whichever category your catch of the day falls, all of the accompaniments and the sauces will serve nicely for a broad range of species.

We also have tried in our recipes to punch the *flavor* button rather than the *fat* button. Wherever possible, we have substituted mono-unsaturated oils (e.g., olive oil) for saturated fats (butter or lard). When cream is used, we have kept it to a minimum or we have diluted it with milk for a lighter texture. We have relied upon flavorful marinades, fresh herbs, aromatic vegetables, fruits, and nuts. Salt has been kept to a minimum, for we feel that the naturally briny flavor of fish requires less salt, particularly when we can use citrus instead.

Most of all, we have tried to create a range and a balance in our recipes, both with national favorites such as shrimp and flatfish, which are always available, as well as with the more unusual choices in the marketplace, such as seasonal shad or species like wolffish and superb Arctic char.

We hope to encourage and tempt you and especially to help you gain confidence in expanding your culinary repertoire by trying new varieties of fish and seafood or preparing the more common ones in new and interesting ways. For, while beef is always beef to us ichthyophagists, fish come in a vast range of sizes, colors, shapes, and tastes. We hope we can inspire you to try them all.

Sheryl and Mel London
Fire Island, New York

I.
BOUGHT OR CAUGHT
And Keeping Fish Fresh at Home

Hanging on the wall in our office at Fire Island is an old, battered, tin sign that once graced the stand of a fishmonger, probably about the turn of the century. In the shape of a whole fish of unknown lineage, the fading letters read: FRESH FISH. Almost ninety years later, the signs are in neon or more contemporary graphics, but the words are just the same. FRESH FISH still brings us to our local fishmonger or to the fishing grounds of stream, lake, or beach in the quest for the freshest fish of our choice. It could well be that the fish today are fresher than those of the old fishmonger with the tin sign, but, even so, there can be many a slip 'twixt boat and customer, and it pays to know just how to choose your own personal catch of the day and how to keep it fresh.

Whether the fish is caught by a professional who travels hundreds of miles into the ocean or by an amateur fisherperson, its care at the very beginning has a lot to do with whether or not we really can give it the label of "fresh." An intrepid reporter once traced his red snapper from fishing boat to fishmonger and found that the trip took twelve days. Yet the handling of the fish was such that it could actually be labeled as fresh on the day that he bought it, since it was in perfect shape, the vital signs that we've listed below all checked out, and the end result was a perfect dinner.

Consumer demand is such that the catch must be kept better than ever before. There was a time when fish were dumped in the bottom of the boat with a bed of ice. The next day's catch was dumped right on top, bruising the bottom layer, and then all were unloaded using unsophisticated tools like pitchforks or lifts. However, the competition from countries such as Norway, Iceland, New Zealand, and others has forced the American fishing industry to reconsider. Adding even more pressure is that fish raised by aquaculture reach the marketplace free of bruises and blemishes and are consistent in quality.

For the consumer, there are some very easy rules to follow that will guarantee that the fish you choose can be called "fresh," even though it was caught twelve days ago by a trawler that had been out to sea for over two weeks. The critical parameter is how the fish has been treated rather than where it was caught or how long ago it was dropped into the flash-freezer hold.

BOUGHT: AT THE FISHMONGER

Possibly the best guarantee of quality fish is the choice of a trusted fishmonger. One of our guidelines is to check the shop itself, making sure that the hygiene is up to standards and, most important of all, that it doesn't smell of fish. We find that our favorite places have the fragrance of the sea or fresh seaweed.

Then the ultimate guideline is to get to know the fishmonger over a period of time so that his suggestions can be taken with confidence.

Your fishmonger knows what is in season, and therefore the catch will probably be more plentiful and possibly less costly. Ask for recommendations before you buy, and know how to substitute the various species for the recipe that you'd like to try. Many times we find that we go to our local fishmonger with one variety in mind, only to find on our arrival that another type has just come in and looks sparklingly fresh. The menu changes at that very instant. It makes good sense when it comes to fish to remain flexible when you shop, and this is where the fishmonger generally can give excellent advice.

What to Look For When You Buy Fish

In spite of your relationship (or lack of it) with your fishmonger, there are several simple rules that can be learned in order to help you choose your own fish:

WHOLE FISH: This is the most accurate way to tell if your selection is fresh. After choosing the fish, you can then have the fishmonger prepare it in any way you choose—fillets, drawn, or dressed (see page 15).

❖ *Eyes.* Never buy a fish that you can't look straight in the eyes. They should be bright, clear, and protruding with a noticeable gleam. Fish eyes should never be milky gray or sunken into the sockets. The only exceptions are deep sea varieties, such as grouper, which may have cloudy eyes due to the pressure change going from the depths of the sea to the surface.

❖ *Odor.* The only noticeable smell should be the characteristically briny fragrance of the sea. Fresh fish just does not have a strong, fishy odor. If a fish has been kept at too high a temperature, the bacteria will multiply to produce an odor that closely approximates ammonia if it has gone too far. If the fishmonger has a thermometer in the refrigeration section of the store, it should register 33°. Every 10° higher will double the spoilage rate of the fish. A consistently cold temperature is another key for freshness.

- ❖ *Flesh.* The flesh should be elastic and firm to the touch. If you poke it, the flesh should spring back immediately without leaving an indentation. Since you may not be allowed to touch the displayed catch, watch carefully as the fishmonger picks up your choice. The same rule applies.

- ❖ *Gills.* When fish are fresh, the gills are a bright, healthy red. They fade quickly to pink or grayish pink and then brownish green when they have begun to lose their sparkle.

- ❖ *Skin and Scales.* The fish should be glisteningly shiny and bright with tightly attached scales. Since constant spraying with cold salt water can deceive the consumer by brightening up the skin, use the other tests to make certain. Even the most recent wash with brine will not mask an odor or change the color of the gills or eyes.

PRE-CUT FISH: Many of the fish in the local fishmarkets already have been cut into fillets or steaks. This may be due to the honest fact that the fish is too large to display, or the other honest fact that the fishmonger may be saving the heads and carcasses for making fish stock. Whatever the reason, make sure that you never buy a pre-wrapped fish or a fish that seems to be located in a too warm spot in the display.

- ❖ *Flesh.* The flesh should be firm in texture with a shiny translucent glow and never watery or spongelike. If the flesh has yellow or brown edges or seems bruised, move on to another selection.

- ❖ *Odor.* The same rule of smell applies to pre-cut fish as it does to whole fish: Fresh fish do not smell fishy!

- ❖ *Display.* Fish should always be displayed on fresh crushed ice, never in water, never pre-wrapped.

Some Guidelines for Buying Shellfish

When it comes to buying shellfish, especially raw oysters, clams, scallops, or mussels, it is perhaps even more important that you abide by the first cardinal rule of thumb: *Know your seafood seller!* The National Fisheries Institute and the Food and Drug Administration strongly recommend that you buy only from approved, reputable sources to be certain that the shellfish have come from certified growing waters. If you're in doubt, ask to see the certified shipper's tag that accompanies "shell-on" products. Make certain that they are kept well refrigerated or on a bed of ice while on display. Here are some other suggestions:

- ❖ Shellfish and particularly mollusks (clams, oysters, mussels, scallops) should never be eaten raw. We will expand on this in the chapter on shellfish (page 262).

- ❖ Live shellfish, bivalves as well as lobsters and crabs, should be stored under well-ventilated refrigeration and not in airtight containers or plastic bags.

- ❖ Cover the live shellfish with damp paper towels. Do not place them in a bath-tub filled with water or (believe it or not) they'll drown! However, you may put a bed of ice under them and cover the ice with damp paper towels. As the ice melts, drain off and discard the water every few hours.

- ❖ If lobsters, crabs, clams, oysters, or mussels have died while in storage, discard them at once.

SOME GOOD ADVICE FOR FISHERPEOPLE

Possibly the best publication on handling fresh-caught fish, as well as some tips on how to handle your catch at home, is published by the New York Sea Grant Extension Program. It's called *Handling Your Catch* and although the subtitle reads *A Guide for Saltwater Anglers,* the advice holds for any of us who fish, whether in lake, stream, or on the seashore. It was written by Ken Gall, the seafood specialist at the Sea Grant Institute, and it's listed as a Cornell Cooperative Extension Program Information Bulletin #203.

For further information, write to:

New York Sea Grant
125 Nassau Hall
SUNY at Stony Brook
Stony Brook, NY 11794–5002

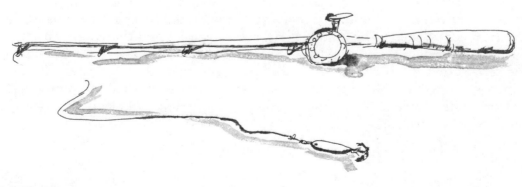

CAUGHT: IN THE BOAT OR
ON THE BEACH

Anglers sometimes wonder why the fish they catch don't taste as fresh as the fish served in their favorite restaurants . . . fish is a highly perishable food . . . handling the catch is as important as tackle and other gear.

Handling Your Catch
Ken Gall
New York Sea Grant Extension Program

At one time or another, most people who fish are guilty of ignoring the rules on keeping the catch fresh. As dedicated fisherpeople ourselves, we have been just as errant as most other anglers. It is difficult, to say the least, to find our beach churning with schools of thrashing bluefish, to spend hours casting and hitting large fighting fish with others standing shoulder to shoulder and whooping with the glee of an autumn run, to be swept up in the screeching of flocks of diving terns, and to even think of how we might *handle* the fish once they've been beached.

Nevertheless, the reality is that fish change rapidly from the moment they are hooked until the time that we get them home to the refrigerator or the stove. The fish that we treasure because of their fight are the ones that begin degenerating most quickly, and the physiological changes that take place begin to affect texture and quality almost at once.

Once landed, the thrashing that occurs can damage the texture, and when the fish dies, severe enzyme reactions take place and the natural barriers that protect the living fish break down, with bacteria both inside and outside the catch beginning an immediate deterioration toward spoilage.

Following a few simple rules can retard this reaction, but for those fisherpeople who would like more specific details, we suggest that you check the sports fishing sections of your bookstore or write to the local extension programs that deal with the subject (see box, page 4).

❖ The prime rule is to keep the catch *cool.* Nothing creates spoilage more quickly than the warm temperatures of summer, with a fish lying in the sun. Take an ordinary ice cooler with you, and put a layer of crushed ice on the bottom. Even in the midst of a churning fish run, it is a simple matter to drop the catch into the cooler and go right back to casting.

❖ Another method that works well is to use chilled, clean sea or lake water and crushed ice to make a slush. This can last for several hours.

❖ Don't let the fish jump around in the bottom of the boat or on the dock after it's been landed. Also try to avoid bruising the fish when the hook is removed. Most of us now take with us a heavy object with which the fish can be stunned immediately. It is both practical and humane.

- ❖ One of the best ways to handle a freshly caught fish is to bleed it, since the fish loses heat as it bleeds, which decreases the cooling time and slows rancidity. A deep cut along the tail or the throat will sever the blood vessels. The fish then should be immersed in clean water.

- ❖ Another method of retarding spoilage is to gut the fish, then rinse the gut cavity with clean water. After gutting, keep the fish in a shady spot or in the ice cooler. If either is not available, wrap the catch in a damp cloth or wet newspaper.

Our readers who are also fisherpeople have probably shared this amusing postscript. There are only so many fish that our freezer will hold, and we have been raised to never waste food. Thus, there is nothing more rewarding than to come home at dusk after a successful day out on the beach and to share our bounty with our neighbors. Unfortunately, most of America does not recognize that fish come complete with heads, and several times we have been turned away with words such as "Don't let my daughter see it with a head. She'll scream!" or the response of one of our otherwise favorite people, "Can't you catch me a fillet?"

Our favorite recipients are two neighbors (Charles and Jane Martin) in our Fire Island community, who accept the gift enthusiastically and *whole.* Not scaled. Not filleted. Not dressed in any way. Just a whole beautiful fish. Certainly we greatly appreciate it, since cleaning twelve or thirteen fish as night begins to fall and mosquitoes emerge can be quite enervating, however joyful and lucky we feel at having had a successful day with nature's generosity.

Some Guidelines for Harvesting Shellfish

Some of us are lucky enough to either live near waters that offer us a fresh harvest of shellfish or vacation near the coastlines and bays that offer us clams or scallops or mussels. Our own island is one such place, and for years we have sent our guests out with clam rakes, buckets, and boundless energy to scoop up the evening meal (which we also "allow" them to clean on the deck while sipping a pre-dinner drink).

However, we have noticed that in the past few years a change has taken place. We are not alone. People all across the country have also noticed—our environment is changing. The mussels, once so plentiful on our bulkheads, have all but disappeared. We have not seen scallops in five years. Clams are harder to find and more difficult to harvest. Worst of all, much of our offshore water is closed from time to time by the supervisory environmental state agencies because of pollution. Therefore, if you do harvest your own shellfish from local waters, make certain that those areas are approved for harvest. The simplest way is to check with your local office of the EPA (Environmental Protection Agency) or with your state or local health department.

After getting your shellfish home, follow the instructions that we've given on the previous pages. Refrigerate them properly and discard any that have died in the interim: shellfish that have opened before cooking or those that refuse to open during cooking.

BOUGHT OR CAUGHT: AT HOME

Whether purchased at your fishmonger's or taken from lake or ocean, for the best possible nutrition and taste, fish should be eaten within twenty-four hours. When you've bought it from a reliable market, fish can generally be kept in the refrigerator for up to two days. Three days would be the limit if caught by you and treated properly. Keep in mind that the rules of temperature hold true at home just as they do on the boat or on the beach.

Experts tell us that for every 10° of temperature rise, the spoilage rate doubles. Conversely, a 10° drop halves the deterioration rate.

- ❖ Rinse the whole fish, fillets, or steaks under cold running water.

- ❖ Place a cake rack or roasting rack in a shallow pan. Then place lots of ice on the rack and put a paper towel on the ice. The rack will allow the melting ice to drip down into the pan to be poured off as it collects.

- ❖ Put shellfish on the ice, cover it with damp paper towels to prevent surface dehydration, and then store it in the coldest part of the refrigerator.

- ❖ Empty the water and replenish the ice twice daily.

COLD FACTS ABOUT FREEZING FISH

Certainly we all may be partial to fresh fish or some varieties that are flash-frozen at sea, but there are other times when freezing our catch becomes a necessity. During the fall run of fish off our shores, we freeze enough of our catch to last us most of the winter. Anyone who has been given a gift of fish or has been lucky enough to return home with a bonanza on a string has also been in the position of making room in the freezer for future meals.

Generally, the local fishmonger is handling fish that has been frozen once and then thawed. Some species such as New Zealand orange roughy certainly have arrived here frozen. Therefore, unless you are absolutely certain that the fish is really "fresh," it should not be frozen again. However, near the sea and freshwater fishing, some species are available from the market just caught, truly fresh, and reasonable in price. These would be the likely candidates for the freezer. Bluefish, fluke and flounder, and shad are good examples. Halibut, with its very short season, is another one that you might buy in bulk to lay in a supply for the next few months. And, of course, truly fresh fish such as wild salmon should be frozen before cooking so that any possible parasites will be eliminated. (Aquacultured salmon do not have the same potential problem.)

There are several easy steps to freezing fish. Some people with large freezers go to the trouble of freezing their catch in milk cartons filled with water, but unfortunately, we, as do most of our readers, have a small "kitchen-size" freezer atop our refrigerator, so that the milk carton trick is not very practical for us.

❖ Before wrapping any fish for the freezer, rinse the whole fish, fillet, or steak under cold running water and keep it wet. Freezing tends to dry out the fish, but water will give it a protective barrier as it freezes, slowing "freezer burn."

❖ Each fish or fillet or steak should be frozen in its own separate package. Otherwise when it comes out of the freezer, a package of fillets will be in a block of ice and impossible to separate. We write this with friends in mind who ended up with a congealed lump of fish fillets.

❖ We find that keeping the fish quite wet when it is packaged does the job fairly well. However, you may want to go one step further and ice glaze your fish. Simply dip the fish in cold water and place it on a pan in the freezer. In a short time, a glaze will form. Dip the fish a second time and repeat the process, and then a third time. After the glaze has formed, the fish can be wrapped for storage.

❖ Some people prefer to wrap their fish in plastic or cling wrap. We prefer aluminum foil, since we find that it handles better. Whichever wrap you use, make sure that it is tight and that all the excess air is squeezed out of the package.

❖ Label each packet with the information you'll need later when you take it from the freezer:

    * Name of fish and how it's cut
    * Date frozen
    * Weight or number of servings

BUYING FROZEN FISH

Although we truly cannot say that we never buy frozen fish, since many species are flash-frozen on the fishing boats, we really mean to say that we have never tried the cod, haddock, or pollack fish sticks that populate the freezers of our supermarkets. Whether plain, breaded, or browned, these portions or sticks generally are cut from solidly frozen blocks of fish fillets. If you live in an area where this is your primary supply of seafood, here are some tips that might help in choosing the right package:

❖ We strongly suggest that you buy only portions or sticks that are plain rather than breaded or with a ready-to-cook batter. By making your own breading, you'll know exactly what goes into it, and you can increase food value with whole grains, as well as seasoning to your taste with fresh herbs.

❖ Supermarkets have a line on the inner side of the freezer, above which food should not be stacked. Do not buy anything stacked above the load line.

❖ Choose packages that feel solid and keep them that way until you get them to your freezer. Also make certain that the package is not broken or damaged and that the contents are not discolored with freezer burn.

❖ If you see any dripping or ice on the outside of the package, choose another one. Chances are that it has been accidentally thawed and then refrozen.

❖ Once you thaw the fish, make sure that you do not hold it in your refrigerator for more than twenty-four hours. And, if your freezer does not go down to 0°, don't keep the package more than a week.

TIP: When you place the packet in the freezer, keep the folded edges on top. Until the fish freezes, the water will have a tendency to ooze out of the edges and on to the freezer floor. Once the fish is completely frozen, the packet can be turned right side up to show the label.

Bought or Caught

Some Storage Guidelines
When Freezing Fish

We've always been fascinated with the conflicting guidelines for the length of time that a fish can be frozen properly and then thawed for use. Although one chef actually suggests that fish cannot be frozen for more than one week, the general opinion and our own experience tells us that the process actually can work for as long as several months. The question, of course, is "How long is long?"

Organizations such as the New York Sea Grant Program and The National Fisheries Institute recommend that fatty fish (i.e., herring, mackerel, salmon, lake trout, bluefish) can be frozen for up to three months. Lean fish (i.e., cod, flounder, fluke, halibut, haddock, red snapper) hold up fairly well at 0° for up to six months. If you have wrapped your fish well, and in spite of the fact that most species lose some moisture while in a freezer, we have found these guidelines to be quite acceptable.

Our own experience tells us that the fish that we land in the autumn will hold up very well into the following spring, when the smaller bluefish, winter flounder, weakfish, and fluke come into our bay and we can replenish our freezer supply. The time lapse is six to seven months. However, after about three months, we generally use the fillets only for such dishes as fish salad, since we find that they do tend to become a bit dry. If any are left after that time, we usually unwrap them and throw them back into the bay as sustenance for crabs. For all this, however, note that the freezer temperature should be as close to 0° as possible.

Thawing Frozen Fish

Our own preference for thawing is to place the frozen fish, wrapper and all, in a shallow dish under gently running cold water. Allow between 20 and 45 minutes for thawing a one-pound package, depending upon the coldness of the water and the thickness of the cut. Another method is to thaw the fish in the refrigerator overnight or for several hours before cooking it. However, whichever method you choose:

❖ Never thaw fish at room temperature or under warm water.

❖ Never refreeze fish once it has been thawed.

Play safe and thaw the fish completely so there will be no question as to just how long to cook it. If you must cook fish that's still frozen, the length of cooking time given in the recipe generally should be doubled.

SOME WORDS TO THE WISE ON SEAFOOD SAFETY

Essentially there are two major factors involved in discussing the safety of seafood. We have covered the first factor—handling—in the previous pages. All other things being equal, how the fin fish or shellfish are treated from the moment of the catch through distribution to your fishmonger and then our care and handling at home is the prime element in seafood safety.

However, there is a second element that goes beyond the reputation of your fishmonger and the rules about refrigeration and/or freezing. There has been a growing concern that some of the fish being harvested today are not perfectly pure and, indeed, may be heavily contaminated with pesticides, heavy metals, and organic chemicals such as PCBs (polychlorinated biphenyl).

Some species, especially some fresh-water fish and fish that spawn in fresh water, may contain parasites. For the lover of seafood, the profusion of newspaper and magazine articles about contamination presents a very real problem, since one must constantly weigh the benefits of seafood against the risks. What are the chances of becoming ill? What can we do to protect ourselves? Can we continue to eat our beloved sashimi?

On the one hand, the entire safety issue must be put into perspective. Even though the consumption of seafood has increased substantially over the years, the number of people who have been the victim of seafood-related illnesses has actually decreased relative to the consumption. The Food and Drug Administration has stated that the food poisoning cases linked to fin fish and shellfish represent only a very small portion of all food poisoning statistics.

According to the U.S. Centers for Disease Control in Atlanta, shellfish accounted for only 2.8 percent and fin fish only 2.2 percent of all statistics. Pound for pound, chicken is 200 times more likely to cause illness than seafood and 100 times more likely to result in death. Put another way, there is one case of illness for every 25,000 servings of chicken and only one case for every 250,000 servings of fish.

On the other hand, the FDA does warn that *raw or undercooked* shellfish are 100 times more likely to cause illness than chicken and 250 times more likely to result in death, although limited almost exclusively to people with liver disease. However, the problem can be eliminated almost entirely with proper cooking.

Certainly we strongly suggest that our readers do as we do and take the warnings seriously. Our own island waters have been victim to PCB contamination in our local fish, both the bluefish and the striped bass. The latter, spawning in the Hudson River, have large amounts of contamination and have been put on the "do not eat" or "eat only once a week" lists for the past few years.

As with everything else, there are good, common sense rules to follow:

❖ In addition to getting seafood from a reliable source (whether caught or bought), try to eat a variety of both fin fish and shellfish.

❖ Fish that are taken far out at sea are much more likely to have fewer, if any, contaminants. On the other hand, fish that spawn in rivers or lakes and, especially, fresh-water fish are the most susceptible to parasitic infection.

❖ On the same note, never use fresh-water fish for sashimi or sushi. Freeze salt-water fish for two days if they are carriers of parasites: salmon in particular, but also cod, haddock, mackerel, herring, and rockfish.

❖ The other obvious tip is one that we have mentioned before: Cooking the fish to a temperature of 145° will destroy any parasitic infestation.

❖ Areas such as California have quarantined bivalves for the part of the year when they are most affected by the red tide and are therefore inedible (May through October). Check with your fishmonger if you live on the West Coast and find out the origin of any shellfish displayed during that time.

❖ Do not eat the dark meat in oily fish such as bluefish. The same holds true for the "mustard" in blue crabs and the tomalley in lobsters, because PCBs concentrate in these organs.

❖ There have been warnings about the possible concentration of mercury in both swordfish and tuna. Thus some doctors suggest that pregnant or breast-feeding women strike them from their diets.

On a positive note, aquaculture has solved a great many problems of contamination, and we have begun to see labels in fish markets for those species that were farm raised. Although wild salmon may contain parasites, the fish raised in farm waters are free and clear (as are the imports from Norway). These days rainbow trout, striped bass, sturgeon, tilapia, redfish, crayfish, oysters, scallops, and even abalone are all being raised commercially through aquaculture and business is booming.

Possibly the greatest success story has been with bottom-feeding catfish. Catfish nearly lost its popularity because of pollution but has come back as the giant of the aquaculture industry. This fish is raised throughout the South on grain and shipped now to every section of the country. Actually the entire aquaculture industry has seen incredible growth, rising in sales from less than $200 million in 1980 to close to $1 billion at the beginning of the 1990s.

Is the benefit of eating seafood worth the small risk? Richard Lord of the Fulton Fish Market Information Services in New York has stated that fish are the safest of flesh foods; Lee Weddig, executive vice president of the National Fisheries Institute, says that cooked fin fish "are probably the safest source of muscle protein available." While there is still no mandatory federal inspection program for seafood as there is for meat (although several bills are now waiting in Congress), we both feel that seafood will continue to play an important role in our diets. Throughout this book, where there are concerns about seafood safety, as in the section on shellfish, we have given more specific information about findings and rules.

It just takes a little more time to become familiar with seafood products and their safety, to choose them wisely, to handle them sensibly, and cook them properly. Certainly they are nutritious, easy to prepare, and very, very tasty. The only thing we have yet to prove is that fish are really "brain food" as the sages used to tell us!

II.
BOUGHT: THE MARKET FORMS FOR FIN FISH
The Well-Dressed Fish

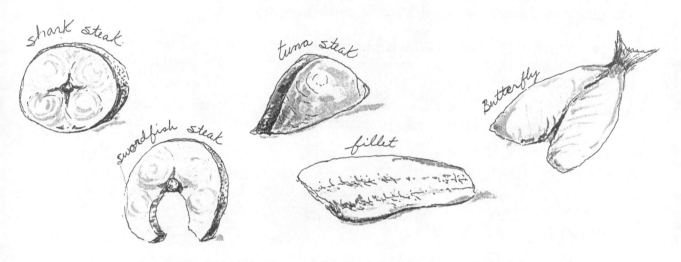

Some of the market forms are already cut and displayed on beds of ice. Others are cut to order from the whole fish. Your fishmonger generally is expert at knowing the cut that might be best for your recipe and recommending a particular species for its freshness, quality, or availability. The market forms are fairly simple and quite logical.

WHOLE: The fish as it comes from the water, and one of the best forms to tell whether or not the fish is fresh (see page 2). This form is sometimes called "round," although the term applies to both roundfish and flatfish.

DRAWN: The fish is whole with only the entrails removed.

DRESSED: The fish is whole but has been gutted and scaled and the gills have been removed. Occasionally the fins are also cut off, but the head is left intact.

PAN-DRESSED: The fish is scaled and gutted, with head and fins cut off, and the tail has been trimmed. This form is generally used for smaller fish so that they can fit easily into a moderate-size pan.

STEAKS: This cut is perfect for larger species of fish—halibut, cod, salmon, tilefish, or even smaller mackerel or kingfish. The cut is made across the fish against the grain, and the resultant steak includes the center backbone. Most fishmongers cut their steaks well in advance, and displays are arranged for easy selection. To keep the steaks from drying out while cooking, we suggest that they be about 1 to 1¼ inches thick for the larger fish and about ½ inch thick for the smaller species.

- *Steaks from Loins:* With large tuna, the fillets ("loins") are cut from the central bone of the fish and then the fillets are cut across the grain for steaks after the skin is removed.

- *Steaks from Center Cuts (or "Wheels"):* This is specifically used for shark and swordfish, with steaks cut across the grain.

CHUNKS: With very large fish—such as grouper, bluefish, bass, salmon, and tilefish—the fishmonger cuts across the heaviest part of the fish along with the bone. He or she can either bone it for you so that it can be stuffed or steaks can be cut from the large section.

FILLETS: For quick, easy cooking, the fillet is probably the most popular market form. It also solves the problem for those who prefer not to see the whole fish lying on their counter or who prefer all their fish boneless.

Fillets are cut from both sides of the fish and can be either skinned or unskinned, depending upon personal preference and recipe choice. Some fillets, such as salmon, have tiny pin bones down the length of the fish. A good fishmonger generally will remove them for you, but you can also do it yourself with a pair of tweezers or a clean pair of long-nose pliers.

You also can cut fillets further into medallions or scallops (see page 23).

BUTTERFLIED: A butterflied fish is simply two fillets connected by the uncut belly skin. The fishmonger will scale and remove the head of an ungutted fish and then split it open from the back, bone it, gut it, and lay it out flat. You can cook them exactly as you would single fillets. Although a butterflied fish is usually grilled or broiled, it can also be stuffed and skewered closed.

III.
CAUGHT OR BOUGHT: THE ANATOMY OF A FISH
Cleaning, Scaling, Cutting, and Dressing Fin Fish

Although most of us have the fishmonger prepare the fish, there are times when we prefer to do it ourselves or we absolutely must. The gift of a fresh fish delivered by a local fisherperson is one such time that the fish lies waiting for us to do the honors. As we've mentioned, our favorite recipients are the neighbors who greet us at the door with filleting knife in hand.

There are times, though, when dressing your own fish is your choice, even if you buy it from a fishmonger. Coastal fish markets usually display whole fish, just landed by the fishing boats docked right outside the doors. The fish are fresh, reasonably priced, and shining with the promise of a very special dinner. The cost per pound is much less than it would be if you were to buy the fillets or the steaks already cut.

And, of course, there are those fisherpeople who consider the late-evening cleaning and dressing a very important part of the quest and its success.

The basic forms are exactly the same as those described in the previous section. Following are some suggestions and instructions about doing it all yourself.

A few general tips:

❖ The key to successful fish preparation is a very sharp filleting knife, used only for that purpose and for nothing else.

❖ Also have at hand a small sharpening tool (there's an excellent one about three inches long called Zip Zap). The blade of the knife should be run over the sharpening tool after every five or six cuts. This is especially important if you are going to skin the fish as we describe below.

❖ When preparing the fish, cut it while it's on newspaper or an easily cleaned cutting board. If you use newspaper, the pages can be peeled off as they get wet, leaving a clean working surface for the next stage.

ROUNDFISH OR FLATFISH

With the exception of the more unusual fish such as skate or eel, most species can be broken down into two major categories in terms of their anatomy: roundfish and flatfish. Of course, roundfish are not all round. Some are oval, some are rounder than others, and head sizes vary. However, their bone structure is much the same, and this is the most important factor to consider when preparing fish.

Flatfish, on the other hand, truly can be called flat, since they have compressed bodies. They lie or swim close to the bottom of the sea to avoid detection, and their eyes eventually move from both sides of their heads to one side or the other. Among fisherpeople, the constant discussion is whether winter flounder have their eyes on the right or left side (right) as compared with the summer fluke (left). A whole range of fish fall into this category, many of them favorites with home cooks: halibut, plaice, the sole family (although gray sole is really a flounder), and turbot. Here, too, once you understand the basic anatomy of the flatfish, home preparation is an easy job.

Scaling, Gutting, and Removing the Gills

Fish Scaler

The preparation of the fish, of course, depends upon your eventual method of cooking it. If you are going to prepare skinless fillets, the fish does not have to be scaled or, if freshly caught and filleted immediately, it also does not have to be gutted or the gills removed. This holds true for both roundfish and flatfish. On the other hand, if the fish is to be left whole and refrigerated overnight or cooked in several hours, then it should be gutted and the gills removed.

SCALING: If you are going to cook the fish whole or stuff it, then scale it first. Some fish need not be scaled because of their smooth skin (catfish, for example, with its own particular skinning methods, and monkfish or wolffish). Tiny fish such as the bluefish snapper caught late in summer or the small butterfish need only be scraped lightly.

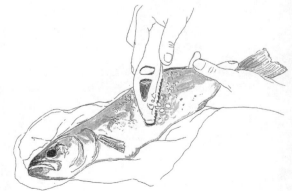

If you decide that the fish must be scaled, place a large plastic bag in the sink and put the fish inside. Use a scaler with toothlike ridges or a flat, short knife and remove the scales by scraping lightly from the tail toward the head. Be careful not to damage the skin. The plastic bag will keep the scales from showing up on the kitchen floor for weeks afterward. Most of us who fish prefer to scale our catch down at the dock.

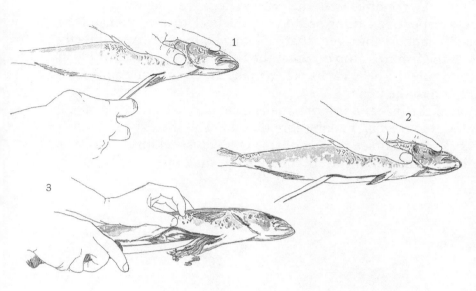

GUTTING: This process should take place just as soon as possible, since the fish decomposes more quickly when the entrails remain. Many of us, given the time, gut the fish while still in the boat or on the dock. However, if the catch is given to you intact, gutting is a simple process.

Place the fish on a board or on a newspaper and, using a sharp filleting knife, cut the belly up from the anal fin to the head of the fish. Then, scraping with the knife, remove all of the contents of the cavity, making sure that nothing remains. This is the best time to remove the gills as well.

REMOVING THE GILLS: Since leaving the gills in the fish for any length of time leads to quicker degeneration of the flesh, they must be removed. With smaller fish, we find that merely reaching up through the gill opening and pulling sharply will detach them for easy removal. With larger fish, use a sharp knife or a pair of scissors to cut the gills and the membrane that is attached to them by severing them at the muscle that holds them to the inside of the cheek. If the gills seem sharp, handle them with a piece of paper towel to keep from being scratched.

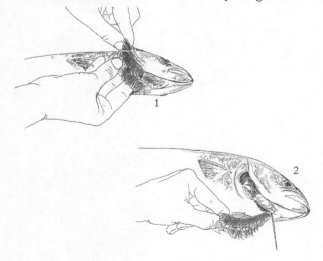

Caught or Bought: The Anatomy of a Fish

Cutting Fillets: Roundfish

If you are going to fillet the fish, there is no need to scale or gut it or remove the gills. However, if the end result is to be a fillet with skin intact (which some cooks prefer), then scale the fish first and then continue with the process described below.

Place the fish on a newspaper or a cutting board with the back toward you and the head facing toward your left hand. Using a very sharp filleting knife, make a cut directly behind the gills and across the fish from top down to the belly. Don't cut too deeply at the bottom or you may puncture the belly cavity. Then make a cut across the flesh right behind the tail, cutting down to the bone.

Keeping the backbone of the fish toward you, make a cut about 1 inch deep along the fish from the head down to the tail, making sure that you feel the flat bone structure as you do so. The trick for making a perfect fillet is to always feel for the bone as you cut. It keeps the knife flat and takes most of the meat off the bone.

Using a sliding motion with the knife and feeling the bone beneath it, cut down as far as the center bone from head to tail. Use long strokes rather than tiny sawing movements. As you cut, you can lift the flesh slightly with your other hand so that you can see just where you are cutting. Then, lifting the flesh so you can see the center bone, cut the bottom half of the fillet with the same slicing motion. The fillet will still be attached to the belly flesh. Do not remove it. Leave the first fillet attached so that the fish will not become concave when you turn it over to do the other side, making the second fillet much more difficult to cut.

Turn the fish over, still with the backbone toward you, and repeat the process. Both fillets will now be ready to be removed. Cut the fillets away. You should have two lovely looking pieces of fish, the skin still attached, and, if done properly, with little or no meat still clinging to the skeleton. Discard the carcass unless you plan to keep it for fish soups or for fish stock. (In that case, you will have to remove the entrails and the gills as well as the eyes.)

If you have more than one fish to clean, you'll find it much easier if you repeat this process with each one rather than continuing on with the next steps. It makes for sort of a one-person "assembly line" and saves time.

Cutting Fillets: Flatfish

Flatfish have top and bottom fillets, with the bottom fillets being much thinner than the top. The procedure for filleting flatfish varies somewhat from that of the roundfish, but the principle of keeping the sharp knife close to the bone still holds true.

If the fish is fairly large, we find the best method is to make four fillets. The fish is put on the newspaper or board with the top side up. The knife is inserted behind the gills to make the same cross cut as with the roundfish. Then make a cut across the tail.

Insert the sharp knife at the center bone near the head and begin to cut down toward the tail, keeping the knife flat so that one half the fish will be filleted. Leave it attached to the fish.

Then turn the fish around and do the fillet right next to the first one. Again, do not remove it. Turn the fish over on its back and fillet both sides of the bottom just as you did the top. Then remove all four fillets.

With smaller flatfish, you may want to end up with only two fillets instead of four. In that case, make the cross cuts behind the head and near the tail and then, starting on the side opposite the belly cavity, cut along the fin, slicing down to the center bone. Lift the cut fillet and continue slicing with the flat knife on the other side until you reach the other side. Again, do not remove the fillet so that it provides a firm base for the second stage.

Turn the fish over and repeat the process with the thinner side of the flatfish. Then remove both fillets. You are now ready to skin them.

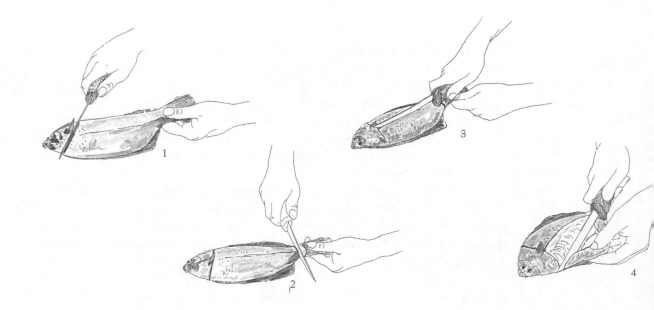

Skinning the Fillets

Clean the board or remove one layer of the newspaper to make a clean surface. We find that we prefer a board for the step of skinning the fish, since the knife must lie very flat while doing it. This step also answers the question as to just why you don't have to scale the fish if you're planning to cook skinless fillets.

Place the fish skin side down on the board. Hold the tail firmly at the very edge by using your fingernail or a small fork. At the point right past your finger, insert the filleting knife and make a cut down to the skin. Then turn the knife to its flat side and begin to saw it back and forth between skin and flesh. As you progress, flip the fillet up and over to reveal the skin and keep sawing, grasping the skin firmly to let the knife move toward the other end. This also prevents the knife from cutting through the skin itself.

If you've done the job properly, the fillet should be clean-looking with no skin clinging to it. Trim any rough edges on the fillets and then feel for any pin bones that might still be there. Some fish have a prominent bone at the head end of the fillet, and we remove it by cutting out a small triangle to leave a "V" shape on the edge. Other fish have a long string of firm pin bones that can be removed by cutting them out with a filleting knife. Still others, such as salmon, have a string of tiny bones that can be felt with the tip of your finger; they can be removed with a pair of tweezers or long-nose pliers.

Rinse the fillets thoroughly under cold running water and either store them in the refrigerator, pack them for freezing, or continue on with your recipe.

Fanciful Fillets

Generally flatfish fillets are of more even thickness than those of the roundfish. As a result, they are easier to handle in recipes since they cook evenly and timing is not disturbed.

❖ If flatfish fillets cut from the bottom of the fish seem too thin, they can be rolled up and fastened with a toothpick or folded into thirds before you prepare them.

Roundfish fillets may be of varying thickness, with the part near the head much larger than the tail section. After the pin bones have been removed and depending upon your chosen method of preparation, roundfish fillets can be cut into various forms for both aesthetics and cooking practicality. Whether the fillets are skinned or unskinned will also depend on your chosen cooking method (see page 31).

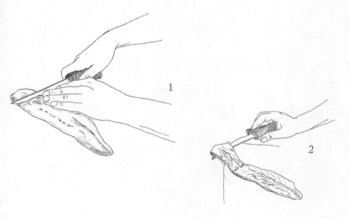

❖ *Leveling a fillet.* If one end is much thicker than the other end, cut crosswise into the fillet horizontally, almost but not quite through the thickest part. Then fold back the flap to level the fillet to make it slightly wider than it was at the beginning.

❖ *Diagonal cutting.* Hold the knife at an angle and cut diagonal slices 1½ or 2 inches apart, working toward the tail and cutting wider slices as the fillet gets thinner. This will give you serving portions of equal weight.

❖ *Perpendicular cutting.* Cut thin slices, about ¼ to ½ inch wide, to make *escalopes* (a very thin, flattened slice of fish that requires just a few seconds of sautéing on both sides).

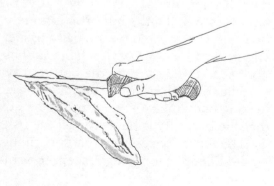

We call them "scallops" here, but the term may be confused with bay or sea scallops, and the shapes are not at all the same. After cooking, you can arrange the slices artistically on the plate as desired.

❖ *Cutting medallions.* Cut crosswise into the thickest part of the fillet, making slices about 1 inch thick. Cut against the grain of the fillet. Curl the thinner part of the slice around the thicker part. Insert a toothpick to hold them together and stand them on end.

Butterflying

This only can be done with roundfish, because flatfish anatomy doesn't quite allow it. Roundfish generally have a piece of connecting belly tissue, while flatfish fillets are separated by a row of bones. Essentially the butterfly is merely two fillets connected by the belly tissue, and it must be done with a fish that has not been gutted through the bottom cavity, for obvious reasons.

Fillet the fish from the top, making sure that the knife goes no further than the connecting belly meat. Then turn the fish over and fillet the other side. At the same time that the butterfly is being made, the fish is also being boned.

The butterfly cut is perfect for grilling or broiling, and it works well for smaller fish, where fillet portions might seem too small to serve to your guests.

Steaks

For the most part, steaks are already cut at your fishmonger's, and it is fairly rare to be given a fish large enough from which to make steaks (which doesn't stop us fisherpeople from dreaming of catching one!).

With flatfish, halibut is one of the few that is large enough to be cut into steaks. With roundfish, however, large striped bass, bluefish, salmon, or cod are a very practical choice for steaks.

The fish should be scaled and gutted first. Mark off the steaks with small guiding cuts of the knife 1 to 2 inches apart. Then put a sturdy knife into each cut and begin to slide. At the backbone, you may have to tap the knife with a hammer or wooden mallet to cut through.

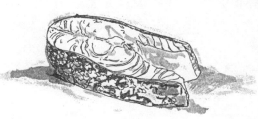

The Cheeks

When a whole fish is served at a Chinese banquet, the honored guest is offered the succulent meat of the cheeks as a token of esteem. Called the "filet mignon" of the fish, the cheeks are an often overlooked delicacy. If the fish is large enough, you'll find these little morsels right behind the mouth. They can be removed and cooked along with the fillets, or if the fish is prepared whole, the cheeks can be scooped out at the table. Either way, we suggest that you try it.

OTHER FIN FISH—OTHER FORMS

There are other ways of preparing fish for the table, but for the most part they are the domain of the fishmonger or expert fisherperson. To include them all here would require an encyclopedic section that most home cooks would do well to ignore.

For example, the tasty shad, in season only in early spring, has a bone structure that is both complex and difficult to remove. We prefer to let our fishmonger do it for us. Some fisherpeople who catch the smaller varieties, such as 3-inch-long bluefish snappers, prefer to gut and pan fry them, while others actually fillet them with one quick sweep of the knife, cooking them for only seconds on each side. Blowfish, eel, skate, shark, and tuna all have their own techniques, but we realize that very few of our readers will be hauling in a 1,000-pound tuna and then cutting it up for the freezer.

IV.
HOW MUCH TO BUY, HOW MUCH TO SERVE

This is an area in which it pays to have a fishmonger whom you can trust. As with all rules, there are no hard and fast ones when it comes to buying the perfect amount of fish, and any chart given by a cookbook author or a so-called fish expert must be taken as approximate (as in our chart, see box, page 28). Your instincts will play a large role, as will the fishmonger's suggestions when you discuss your needs:

- ❖ Individual appetites, of course, dictate the selection and the weight.

- ❖ Whether the fish is to be served as an appetizer or an entrée will also help you in making your choice.

- ❖ If the fish is rich or if it is to be served with a rich sauce, smaller portions may be indicated.

- ❖ Keep in mind what is going to be served before and after the fish course. The rest of the meal may help determine the size of the purchase.

- ❖ Some whole fish have larger heads (red snapper, for example), some lose more liquid than others when cooked (such as monkfish), some have a heavier bone structure than others (i.e., halibut) so that purchase weight may have to be adjusted.

- ❖ If the fish is going to be stuffed, you will probably need less weight per serving.

And after all this, you arrive at the fishmonger to discover that the fish you had in mind for that night's dinner is not available, or that another species has just arrived and it looks absolutely sparklingly fresh and tempting. And, suddenly, the menu for that evening has changed!

SUBSTITUTING FISH IN RECIPES

Popularity, regional and seasonal availability, color, flavor, fat content, texture, and more than 600 edible species of fish off the coasts of the United States (with over 3,000 worldwide) frequently will convince you to substitute one fish for another. Quite often, we have arrived at the fishmonger with sole or red snapper on our list, only to depart with a delicious Arctic char. If by force or by choice you must substitute, here are some tips to keep in mind:

FIN FISH: BUYING AND SERVING	
Market Form	*Amount Per Person*
Whole	12 to 16 ounces
Whole (dressed or drawn)	8 to 12 ounces
Fillets	4 to 6 ounces
Steaks (allowing for bones)	6 to 8 ounces
Chunks	10 to 12 ounces

❖ The type of preparation and the sauce should be compatible with the flavor of the fish.

❖ The cut (fillet or steak), the type of fish (flatfish or roundfish), and the texture of the fish—whether lean and dry or moist and oily—also should serve as a guide.

We have organized our recipes to allow for substitutions, and here are just a few examples that can help you to make your choice:

❖ Fillets or steaks from lean, mild-flavored fish can be interchanged: cod, scrod, haddock, pollack, whiting, the basses.

❖ Monkfish, tilefish, and mahi-mahi can be used in the same recipes.

❖ Use snappers or rockfish, seabass or tilefish, or you may choose grouper as a substitute.

❖ The flatfish (fluke and flounder) are interchangeable with orange roughy and are usually filleted. Their delicate, sweet flavors are quite similar. The larger flatfish (halibut or turbot) are also interchangeable and can be cut into steaks.

❖ Stronger-flavored fish can be substituted one for the other: tuna, swordfish, mako, bluefish, and mackerel.

❖ Steaks: halibut, tilefish, turbot, or salmon steaks can be treated in very much the same way.

It all comes back to the basics: If it's in season and looks irresistible, buy it and then find a recipe for it!

V.
COOKING YOUR FISH
The Basic Methods

General Advice

Poaching

Steaming

Braising

En Papillote

Pan Frying, or Sautéing

Blackened Fish

Stir Frying

Deep Frying

Oven Frying

Baking, or Roasting

Broiling

Grilling

Microwaving and Smoking

Boning and Serving a Whole Fish

The Whale that wanders round the Pole
Is not a table fish.
You cannot bake or boil him whole
Nor serve him in a dish.
     "The Whale"
      Hilaire Belloc
      A Bad Child's Book of Beasts

GENERAL ADVICE

Except for Hilaire Belloc's whale, all seafood cooks quickly and quite easily. The biggest sin in fish cookery, we think, is the overcooking of both fin fish and shellfish. They are tender to begin with and thus do not need a great deal of cooking to make them ready for the table. Fish should be cooked only long enough to develop their individual flavors and to change their color and texture from translucent to pearly opaque. For the beginner, of course, the question again arises, "How long is long enough?"

The three things that you control in fish cookery are time, temperature, and the method of cooking, all three dependent upon the thickness of the fish. We have always been partial to what has become known as the "Canadian Method," developed by the Canadian Department of Fisheries and Oceans. This method recommends 10 minutes cooking time for each inch of thickness, and we have found it to be a pretty good guide. However, since most fish are not even in thickness but rather slope from thick down to very thin, we suggest 8 minutes per inch at the thickest part, testing several minutes before the end of the estimated cooking time.

Test for doneness at the part nearest to the bone or at the thickest part of the fillet by sticking a metal skewer or the tip of a sharp paring knife into the fish. The very center should have just a touch of translucence remaining, and since the fish will continue "cooking" after the heat is off, the result should be just perfect at that moment.

We prefer nonreactive oval pans in which to cook all fish: nonstick coated aluminum, enamel-covered cast iron (such as Le Creuset), stainless steel, ovenproof glazed earthenware or ceramic, or tempered glass.

THE TWO MAJOR COOKING METHODS: As a rule of thumb, the basic methods by which most fish are cooked can be divided into two major categories, depending upon whether the fish are lean or fatty:

❖ *Moist Heat:* e.g., poaching, steaming, braising, sautéing, and frying, is best for lean fish such as flounder, halibut, haddock, etc.

❖ *Dry Heat:* e.g., broiling, baking, and grilling, is preferred for fattier fish such as mackerel, tuna, salmon, etc.

Of course, there are always exceptions to any rule, and the key to flavor lies in making the most of the natural juices and natural fats in the fish. Here are some other tips to keep in mind:

❖ When cooking fish steaks, do not remove the bones. They help to retain the natural succulence of the fish while it cooks.

❖ No matter which method you use, do not turn thin fillets over, and use a wide spatula when turning other fish.

❖ If fillets are covered with sauce while baking, allow an additional 3 minutes per inch at the thickest part, but watch carefully and test often, since most stoves are quirky and the heat they give off is uneven.

POACHING

All fin fish and shellfish can be poached, but lean fish especially will profit from this cooking method. Poaching is done in a mild aromatic liquid such as a court bouillon (see page 37) or fish stock (see page 402). Fattier fish (such as salmon) also can be poached, but they require an acidic liquid containing either wine, vinegar, or citrus juice added to the water to help firm the fish and to act as a foil for its richness. Aromatic fish broths with milk in them help keep the flesh white.

In poaching, the fish is immersed in a simmering broth that just covers the fish and is poached at a bare simmer until it is cooked through, then removed at once to prevent further cooking. The slow cooking process allows the herbs, vegetables, and wine, vinegar, or citrus juice to infuse the fish with flavor. In turn, the aromatic poaching liquids are enhanced by the fish and can be reused for poaching, steaming, or for soups and sauces. They also freeze well for future use.

Selecting the Proper Poaching Pot

The size of the fish determines the poaching equipment to use. If you're poaching a small fish (rather than steaks or fillets), a nonstick skillet or baking pan with 4-inch sides will do for pan poaching. Or, lacking a proper fish poacher, you can improvise with a covered poultry roaster that has a bottom rack on which to place the fish.

Although an oval fish poacher with a lift-out tray for easy removal of a whole fish is costly, it is a good investment. They typically stand between 4 and 8 inches tall, and the larger ones will cover two stove burners. These poachers come in various materials; so if you decide to invest in one, avoid the ones that are made of aluminum since they discolor both the poacher and the fish (due to the acidic reaction of the poaching liquid and the metal). They also come in various sizes (see box, page 34), so consider your needs when purchasing.

Cooking Your Fish

POACHING PANS

A 20-inch poacher (with 17½ inches inside measurement) will hold an entire fish weighing 4 pounds with head and tail intact.

A 24-inch poacher will hold a 4- to 6-pound fish.

A 36-inch poacher will hold an 8- to 10-pound fish.

For smaller fish or fillets, any nonstick pan or skillet with high (4-inch) sides will do nicely.

Basic Poaching Method

Prepare the poaching liquid (see page 35) and then cool it to lukewarm.

Wrap the larger fish in a double layer of cheesecloth moistened in the poaching liquid to allow for easy handling as the fish is cooked. Allow about 10 extra inches of cheesecloth on each end to facilitate handling. Twist the ends of the cloth to make knots, which you can then use as handles. If you're using a fish poacher, place the wrapped fish on the tray, twist the ends of the cheesecloth around the handles of the insert tray, and then remove the tray along with the wrapped fish when you are finished poaching.

Bring the aromatic liquid to the boiling point over moderate heat. Lower the heat to simmer and immerse the wrapped fish on the tray. If the liquid does not cover the fish by 1 inch, add additional water. When the liquid begins to simmer again, cover the pan and begin timing. The poaching time will depend upon the size of the fish—anywhere between 20 and 45 minutes. For example, a 3-pound whole fish will serve 4 people and take approximately 20 minutes. A 6-pound fish, which serves 8, will take about 45 minutes.

Test the fish about 5 minutes before the end of the suggested poaching time. Chunks of fish or thinner pieces will take less time, of course. Never allow the liquid to boil actively or the more delicately textured fish can break apart. The poaching technique is always the same, regardless of the liquid that you use.

When the fish is cooked through, remove it from the broth, keeping it on the tray and still wrapped in the cheesecloth to keep it moist and to let it firm up a bit. Place 2 chopsticks or knives crosswise over the top of the poacher, place the tray on top, and allow the excess liquid to drain back into the pan.

When the fish is cool to the touch, transfer the wrapped fish along with the tray to a work surface. Open the cheesecloth, but let the fish rest on the cloth while you remove the skin.

To remove the skin, make a shallow cut at the base of the tail and pull the skin off toward the head. Using the cheesecloth as an aid, roll the fish over onto a serving platter, skinned side down (see box, below), and remove the cheesecloth and the skin from the second side.

Cover the fish with plastic wrap and refrigerate it if you want to serve it cold. Strain the poaching liquid and put it in a plastic container in the freezer for future use.

Oven Poaching

Rather than using two burners of the stove top, you may prefer to poach the fish in the oven. Preheat the oven to 450°. Place the fish flat in a nonreactive pan and add just enough poaching liquid to cover the fish. Cover the pan and poach just until the flesh of the fish becomes opaque.

FOR A LARGE POACHED FISH . . .

If the fish is a large one, you'll probably need a second person to assist you in supporting the midsection of the fish while transferring it to a serving platter. Use a very broad spatula or a plate to support the fish, otherwise the weight of the center will cause the fish to break apart.

Poaching Liquids

There are three basic poaching liquids: court bouillon, fish stock, and fish fumet.

❖ *Court Bouillon.* A blend of water, wine, or other acidic liquid, aromatic herbs, and vegetables (see recipe, page 37). When fish bones and other scraps are added, it becomes:

❖ *Fish Stock.* This also can be used for poaching, but its primary use is for soups, stews, and sauces. When fish stock is cooked down to a concentrated form, it is:

❖ *Fish Fumet.* This is used mostly as a base for sauces. Any fish stock that does not contain vinegar can be cooked down for a fumet. (See pages 402 and 403 for fish stock and fumet recipes.)

Many times, a fish skeleton and head contain enough poached fish from which you can prepare a cold salad. So pick off the meat, cover it with a bit of poaching liquid, and freeze to use another time.

COURT BOUILLON

7 cups water

1½ cups dry white wine

1 large onion, coarsely chopped (about 1 cup)

1 large carrot, coarsely chopped (about ¾ cup)

1 large leek, rinsed well and trimmed, white and green parts, coarsely chopped (about 1½ cups)

2 ribs celery with leaves, coarsely chopped (about 1 cup)

1 bay leaf

3 sprigs parsley

3 sprigs thyme

8 whole black peppercorns

1 whole clove

Salt to taste

To a large 6- to 8-quart nonreactive pot, add the water, wine, onion, carrot, leek, celery, bay leaf, parsley, thyme, peppercorns, and clove. Bring to a boil over medium heat, then lower the heat and simmer, covered, for 15 minutes. Add the salt and continue to simmer for 15 minutes more. Strain and discard the vegetables and herbs before using the liquid to poach the fish.

After poaching the fish, save the stock and freeze it for poaching other fish or for use as a fish stock.

Cooking Your Fish

AROMATIC MILK BROTH

MAKES 6 CUPS

This milk-based court boullion is best for poaching delicate-tasting white-fleshed fish such as cod, haddock, and halibut. After using it, reduce it by half and freeze it to use as a base for velouté or other sauces (see page 55).

5   cups water
1   medium onion, thinly sliced (about 6 ounces)
1   large carrot, quartered
4   sprigs parsley
3   sprigs thyme
1   small rib celery with leaves, quartered

1   large bay leaf
¼   teaspoon whole black peppercorns
⅛   teaspoon cayenne pepper
2   whole cloves
    Salt to taste
3   cups milk

In a 12-inch sauté pan, bring all the ingredients except the milk to a boil over medium heat. Lower the heat and simmer, covered, for 15 minutes. Add the milk and simmer for 10 minutes more. Strain, pressing the vegetable and herb solids against the strainer to extract as much liquid as possible.

STEAMING

Steaming preserves the delicate and natural taste of fish and, as with poaching, it's an excellent choice for those on low-fat diets, provided that the fish is not accompanied by an overly rich sauce. Crustaceans—that is, crabs, shrimp, and particularly lobsters—take well to steaming, since they do not get waterlogged. Bivalves—for example, mussels and clams—also can be steamed in a bit of wine or water (without a rack), producing delicious broths as they open (see the individual chapters on these shellfish for specifics).

Basic Steaming Method

Steaming equipment can be any large pot that has a tightly fitting lid. There should be room for a steaming rack or a Chinese basket steamer. Or you can improvise a steamer by placing a plate at least 1 inch smaller than the width of the pot (to make it easy to put in and take out) on two small heatproof custard cups.

Place a whole fish or pieces of fish on the oiled rack or plate that rests *above,* not immersed *in,* gently boiling liquid. The liquid may or may not be flavored. The tightly fitting lid on the pot will create the steam that cooks the fish. The fish will steam quickly over moderate heat at a medium boil, and depending upon the thickness, it should turn opaque in anywhere from 3 to 12 minutes.

If you wish, when using a plate as an insert, you can add finely julienned aromatic vegetables and fresh herbs under and over the fish.

BRAISING

Braising is really a combination of two methods, sautéing and steaming. Firm-textured large pieces of fish or whole fish, e.g., tilefish, catfish, monkfish, or lobster, take well to braising.

Basic Braising Method

The fish is first briefly seared in a small amount of fat for just a few seconds and then combined with aromatic herbs and vegetables, which exude a bit of their own liquid. A touch of wine or fish stock is included for extra moisture. The fish "steams" as it cooks in a tightly closed vessel, forming a natural sauce in the process.

Braising can be accomplished on top of the stove or, after searing and adding the remaining ingredients, popped into a preheated oven.

The braising pan or casserole should be of earthenware or another heatproof material that can tolerate both stove top and oven heat. All the ingredients should fit snugly into the dish, and the cover should be tight to prevent moisture loss.

EN PAPILLOTE

The name is derived from the Latin word for butterfly, *papilio,* which emerges from its cocoon in much the same way that the fish comes forth from its paper wrapper.

The same ingredients used for braising are tightly enclosed in either oiled or buttered parchment paper and then baked in the oven (see Note). The packets inflate with steam while cooking and then are slashed open when served, releasing a puff of perfumed steam. The packets can be filled and wrapped well ahead of time if you wish.

Basic Method of Cooking en Papillote

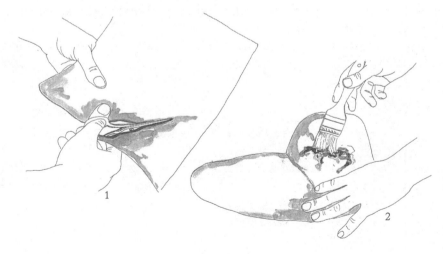

The procedure is quite simple. Fold a 24- by 16-inch piece of parchment paper in half lengthwise and draw a half heart on the paper 3 inches larger than the food to be enclosed. Cut along the outline, then unfold the paper to reveal a full heart shape. Brush half of the heart with melted butter.

Arrange the fish on the buttered half of the heart along with finely diced or julienned vegetables, herbs, and a few tablespoons of wine, citrus juice, or fish stock. Then drizzle melted butter over all.

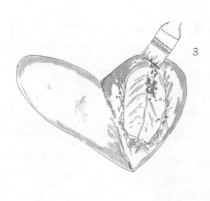

If you wish, you can lightly beat an egg white, then brush it over the edges of the heart as well as the empty side. (This helps to make a tighter seal.) Then fold and press the edges over twice in quarter-inch folds and crimp to seal, working toward the "tail" end.

Fasten a paper clip on the tail end to make sure that the packet is airtight. When ready to bake, place the packet on a baking sheet in a preheated 400° oven and bake for 20 minutes. When the paper has puffed up and started to brown, remove the packet to a warm serving plate. Be careful when opening the oven door for the first time, since a sudden draft of cold air may collapse the packet.

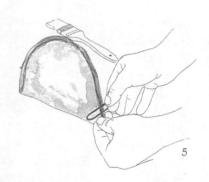

NOTE: We recommend parchment paper rather than aluminum foil, since the latter reflects the heat and keeps the fish from browning properly. It is also difficult to trust the timing. Note also that the fish cannot be tested while it cooks without deflating the package and releasing the steam.

PAN FRYING, OR *SAUTÉING*

This popular method, sometimes referred to as shallow frying, is achieved with a dry coating and a minimum amount of fat—just enough to leave a crisp, brown, light crust and a moist, tender interior. The fish best suited for this method are whole or pan-dressed small fish, usually under 10 to 12 inches, the perfect size for most skillets. Pan-frying or sautéing is also perfect for firm-fleshed fillets and fish that are cut into medallions or butterflied.

The Cajun method of blackening highly seasoned, dry, spiced fish that is rubbed in oil and char-cooked in a red-hot cast-iron skillet is merely another way of pan frying or sautéing

---

A TIP FOR PAN FRYING OR SAUTÉING

It's a good idea to keep one pan for frying or sautéing fish, preferably one made of heavy cast iron for even cooking.

Don't wash it—ever. Just wipe it well after each use by covering the surface with abrasive kosher salt and rubbing it thoroughly with paper towels. Rub a thin film of oil onto the surface to keep the pan well seasoned, and you'll need much less fat when either pan frying or sautéing.

Basic Pan-Frying Method

To pan-fry properly, the fish must be completely dry or it will splatter when it's placed in the hot fat. To allow the dry ingredients to adhere, the fish is sometimes dipped into a seasoned liquid such as milk, yogurt, or buttermilk and then, to seal in the juices, dredged lightly with a dry protective coating. Any one of these can be used: cornmeal, flour, dried bread crumbs, pulverized crackers, oat or wheat bran, sesame seeds, chopped nuts, dried herbs, or other seasonings. Thus, the fish will remain dry enough to pan-fry or sauté, yet will retain its inner moisture.

Use only enough oil or clarified butter (see page 65) to cover the bottom of the pan. This will give the fish a wonderful nutlike flavor. Clarified butter also does not burn as readily as regular bar butter. You may also try the half-oil, half-butter combinations that are sold under various trade names.

Heat the fat to a temperature that is hot but not smoking (about 350 to 360°) before adding the fish. Don't crowd the pan or the fish will not brown properly or cook quickly enough.

Cook the fish over moderate heat, sliding the pan back and forth once or twice so that it doesn't stick. Cook the fish until it's golden on one side (about 2 to 3 minutes). Then turn it once, using a wide spatula, and fry or sauté the other side, testing with a skewer after 2 to 3 minutes if the fish is thin, a bit longer if it is thicker.

BLACKENED FISH

Although this has not been our favorite way of preparing fish, we cannot argue with its popularity in the past few years. The diminishing catch of red drum has been attributed to the demand for the species for blackening, and blackened fish preparation has spread to tuna, catfish, and even bluefish. Be warned, however, that properly prepared blackened fish is made in a super-hot ungreased iron skillet, which ruins the skillet for any other kind of cooking.

BASIC CAJUN BLACKENED FISH

MAKES 4 SERVINGS

Here is a simple Cajun blackened fish recipe.

DRY CAJUN SPICE MIXTURE:
1   tablespoon each garlic and onion powder
2   teaspoons each white, black, and cayenne peppers
2   teaspoons each dried thyme and oregano
4   teaspoons salt
1   teaspoon paprika

4   ½-inch-thick red drum fillets (6 to 7 ounces each)
¼   cup olive oil, vegetable oil, or clarified butter
Lemon wedges for serving

In a bowl, whisk the ingredients for the spice mixture together to combine them.

On the top of the stove, heat a dry cast-iron skillet *upside down* over high heat for 10 to 15 minutes. It will be a pale bluish gray in color when it's ready to use. Using your fingers, rub the fillets with the oil or butter, coating both sides. Then dip them into the dry spice mixture, coating them evenly but not too thickly.

Using a heavy potholder or oven mitt, turn the hot pan right side up and add the fish. Cook the fillets a total of 2½ to 3 minutes, turning only once during the process. There will be a lot of smoke, so turn on the exhaust fan. The fish should be singed but not burned. Serve with lemon wedges.

NOTE: If you wish to avoid the smoke in your kitchen, you can try heating the skillet outdoors on a grill.

STIR FRYING

This is basically a rapid form of sautéing that employs a Chinese wok rather than a skillet, although the latter is quite acceptable if you lack the Asian cooking utensil. The similarity in the two methods is that a small amount of fat is used, but the difference is that a higher heat is needed in order to stir-fry properly.

In stir frying, bite-size pieces of fish or seafood are kept moving constantly as they cook in the fat, with sauces, thickeners, and vegetables added to moisten the fish near the end of the cooking time.

DEEP FRYING

There are two simple elements that give consistently good results when deep-frying fish or seafood: an adequate supply of fresh, good-quality oil and maintaining the proper temperature of the oil. Fish that is deep-fried correctly should not be greasy or soggy.

Unlike pan frying, in which a dry coating and a small amount of fat are used, deep-frying requires that the fish be immersed completely in hot oil to cover. In addition, when deep-frying, *moist* batters as well as dry batters can be used.

The batter or coating on the fish should be light enough to seal the moisture in, and it should keep the fat from penetrating to the inside. The result is a dry, crisp exterior with a tender, moist interior. The superb taste makes it well worth the additional calories, although impeccable frying will minimize the amount of oil the fish will absorb during cooking.

The preferred oils for deep-frying are vegetable, corn, grapeseed, or peanut oil, which can reach higher temperatures without smoking or burning easily. They are preferable to safflower or canola oil. Because most fats and oils smoke and burn at 400°, maintain the temperature of the oil between 365° and 375°. Check the oil with a deep-fry thermometer or use an electric deep-fryer with a temperature control. Tiny whole fish (e.g., whitebait), lean, firm fish or skinned catfish fillets, and small clams, oysters, and squid take well to deep frying. Many species—e.g., squid rings or small clams—should take no more than 30 seconds to cook.

Basic Deep-Frying Method

Use a deep heavy pot or an electric deep-fryer—or a wok, which is shaped to minimize the amount of oil needed. Use at least 3 inches of oil in the cooking pot and bring it to the proper temperature.

In the meantime, dry the fish well and dip in either the dry coatings, or moist batters (see below for recipes) just before frying. Using tongs, dip the piece of fish first into the batter, letting the excess drip off, then lower it carefully into the hot oil. Or, if you are using a wire basket, lower the basket. Maintain the temperature of the oil by not overcrowding the pot—have no more than 4 or 5 pieces cooking at a time. Fry only until crisp and golden brown, which may take just a few minutes, depending upon the thickness of the fish.

After the fish is fried, lift it out with tongs or a slotted spoon—or raise the basket—and drain on paper towels. Keep the deep-fried fish warm in a preheated 200° oven while frying the next batch.

Before putting the next batch of fish into the oil, skim the surface of the oil with a small wire sieve, removing any floating pieces. Repeat this process between each batch.

After cooking, the oil can be strained through a fine sieve and returned through a funnel to the same bottle, which allows you to reuse it once or twice more if it is not too dark. Remember to label the bottle so that the oil is not mistakenly used for salad dressing.

Also, if kitchen ventilation is not adequate and you find the greasy odor objectionable, simmer ½ cup vinegar in a small pot to help clear the air.

Here are two moist batters that make excellent blankets for deep-frying. They help seal in moisture while keeping the fat out. All three should yield enough for 2 pounds of fish or seafood (4 servings).

CLUB SODA LEMON BATTER

MAKES ABOUT 1½ CUPS

2	tablespoons lemon juice	¾	teaspoon salt
1	cup low-fat milk	¼	teaspoon cayenne pepper
¾	cup all-purpose flour	½	teaspoon baking soda
2	teaspoons finely minced lemon peel	1	egg
¼	teaspoon freshly ground black pepper	2	tablespoons club soda or seltzer

Combine the lemon juice and milk in a cup and let it stand for 5 minutes. In a large bowl, add all the dry ingredients, including the lemon peel, and whisk them together to blend. Whisk in the milk mixture and then the egg and club soda; whisk until smooth. Let stand for 30 minutes at room temperature and stir before using.

HERBED BEER BATTER

1 cup all-purpose flour

¼ cup stone-ground white cornmeal or rye flour

1 teaspoon salt

½ teaspoon white pepper

1½ teaspoons sweet paprika

¼ teaspoon cayenne pepper

½ teaspoon dried oregano

¼ teaspoon ground cumin

2 large eggs, separated

1½ cups light beer, at room temperature

1 tablespoon olive oil or corn oil

In a large bowl, whisk all the dry ingredients together to blend. Make a well in the center and add the egg yolks. Start beating with the whisk, stirring in the beer and the oil. Blend well.

Cover the bowl and let stand for 1 hour. Just before the fish is to be fried, beat the egg whites until they are stiff and fold them into the batter.

OVEN FRYING

The term is misleading. Although it's called "oven frying," the fish is actually baked in the oven. However, unlike deep-fat frying, less fat is used.

Basic Oven-Frying Method

The procedure is simple. The oven is preheated to 500°. The fish, usually thick fillets, are dipped in melted butter or oil and then covered with a dry coating, usually seasoned bread crumbs. The fish is baked in a well-buttered baking dish, with additional butter or oil trickled over the surface. The high temperature cooks the fish quickly and results in a moist center with a crisp, brown crust. The fish needs no turning and no sauce—only a squeeze of lemon juice to enhance the flavor and the crispy treat.

BAKING, OR ROASTING

The terms are interchangeable, although the word "roast" conjures up meat rather than fish. In the past, meat was roasted, fish was baked. However, these days, the menus in many upscale restaurants list "roasted fish" as an excellent choice. No matter which term you use—bake or roast—this dry heat, slower cooking method keeps just enough moisture on the bottom of the pan to prevent the fish from sticking.

Basic Baking Method

You may use wine, water, or a bed of moistened vegetables on the bottom of the pan and only enough butter or oil for flavor and to give the fish a brown, glazed surface. Almost any fish of any size, shape, or form can be baked or roasted. Fatty fish such as shad or mackerel, butterflied trout, or a central chunk of the tail of a large salmon or tough-skinned mahi-mahi are particularly good choices, since the skin keeps the flesh moist and flavorful.

Thin fillets can be stuffed and rolled before baking; colorful red snapper lends itself well to this treatment. Or you can stuff an entire whole fish for a delicious and festive treat.

We suggest retaining the head on a whole fish for baking to seal in the juices, although there are still those faint of heart (particularly in the United States) who are offended by seeing the head of a fish when it's served. To each his own. We personally feel that without the head, the fish looks incomplete.

The best oven temperature is 400° and the baking time depends, of course, on the fish's thickness. Figure about 8 to 10 minutes per inch at the thickest part. Thick fillets will take about 15 to 20 minutes and a 3-pound whole fish about 35 to 40 minutes.

How to Stuff a Fish

All fish—pike, bass, trout, salmon, weakfish, flounder, sole, mackerel—have different size body cavities and, indeed, all fish are different sizes. Thus, the amount of stuffing needed will vary. If you have any stuffing left over when using the recipes that follow these instructions, you can bake it either around the fish as a garnish or in a separate baking dish to be served with the fish as a side dish.

STUFFING A WHOLE ROUNDFISH

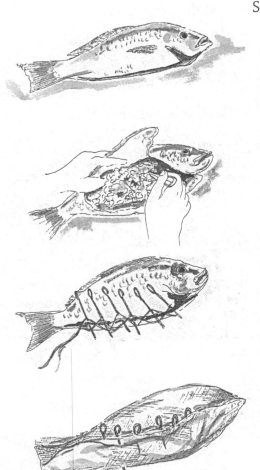

❖ Rinse and dry the scaled, gutted whole fish with paper towels. Cut a still deeper pocket in the body cavity by slicing almost to the tail section.

❖ Prepare the stuffing.

❖ Drizzle lemon juice and sprinkle salt and pepper to taste in the cavity of the fish, then add the stuffing.

❖ Insert small oiled metal skewers through both sides of the fish and use a heavy white cord to lace and tie the skewers like a boot.

❖ Brush the entire fish lavishly with melted butter or oil, then place it on a long, doubled piece of cheesecloth.

❖ Wrap the cheesecloth around the fish, allowing the skewers to pierce the cloth. Fold the ends over to encase the fish.

❖ Poach or bake the fish according to specific recipe instructions.

STUFFING FILLETS

❖ Pan-dress the fish (see page 16) and use the thickest center cut. This is best for long, thin fish that won't fit in the pan, such as mackerel, pike, or pompano.

❖ Stuff the fillets like a sandwich and skewer both sides closed with oiled metal skewers.

❖ Tie with string in several places across the fish to keep the stuffing encased in the fish.

FISH MOUSSE STUFFING

MAKES ABOUT 3½ CUPS

1 cup soft sourdough bread crumbs
½ cup milk
1 pound skinned pike fillets (or any other white-fleshed fish, such as ocean perch or sole)
1 whole egg
3 egg whites

¼ teaspoon crushed dried tarragon
½ teaspoon dried thyme
2 or 3 drops Tabasco
¼ teaspoon white pepper
Salt to taste
2 to 4 tablespoons heavy cream, very cold

In a deep bowl, soak the bread crumbs in the milk until the crumbs absorb all the liquid. Purée the fish in a food processor until pastelike in consistency. Add the wet bread crumbs, egg and egg whites, and all the seasonings to the fish and process with only enough cold cream to give the mixture a smooth and very fine texture. You may use this mixture to stuff a whole fish or, if you wish, you may wet your hands, form it into tiny fish balls, and poach them in court bouillon (see page 37). Use also to spread thickly on a fish fillet such as flounder or sole, then roll the fillet up, secure with a toothpick, and either bake or poach.

CUCUMBER, MUSHROOM, AND DILL STUFFING

MAKES ABOUT 3 CUPS

2 medium scallions, cut in pieces
¼ pound white mushrooms
2 to 3 large cucumbers, peeled, seeded, and cut into chunks (about 2 cups)
2 tablespoons melted butter
1 cup soft bread crumbs

2 eggs, lightly beaten
1 tablespoon lemon juice
1 tablespoon finely minced fresh dill
½ teaspoon black pepper
Salt to taste

In a food processor, process the scallions, mushrooms, and cucumbers together until finely chopped. Add the melted butter, bread crumbs, and eggs, then stir in the lemon juice, dill, and salt and pepper to combine.

Use with any whole fish or as a filling between two fillets.

MIDDLE EASTERN STUFFING

MAKES 1½ TO 2 CUPS

2 tablespoons olive oil
1 large onion, finely chopped (about 1¼ cups)
1 cup cooked white rice
2 tablespoons toasted pine nuts
2 tablespoons currants, soaked in boiling water and drained

½ teaspoon ground allspice
1 tablespoon lemon juice
1 tablespoon minced parsley
1 teaspoon finely minced fresh mint, or ½ teaspoon dried mint
¼ teaspoon black pepper
Salt to taste

In a medium skillet, heat the oil over medium-high heat. Add the onion and sauté until wilted, stirring frequently, about 5 minutes. Add to the rice along with the toasted pine nuts and drained currants, then stir in the remaining ingredients. Let cool for 20 minutes to allow the flavors to develop before stuffing the fish.

Use with any whole fish or as a filling between two fillets.

BROILING

When broiling, the intense, dry heat comes from above, in contrast to grilling and barbecuing, where the heat comes from below. Broiling is the best method for moderately fatty or very fatty fish, or the thicker, leaner fish such as mackerel, bluefish, mahi-mahi, or shark. During broiling, the fish should be basted to keep it from drying out. Large fish cut into kebobs as well as boned and butterflied fillets and steaks can be broiled only if the fish is between ½ and 1¼ inches thick.

Basic Broiling Method

In addition to the timing, the thickness of the fish dictates the distance from the heat source: 3 inches for fish ½ to ¾ inch thick, 4 inches for fish 1 to 1¼ inches thick. Preheat the broiler. Oil or butter a perforated rack, preferably nonstick and one that fits over another pan. Do not use a wire rack that will not support the fish properly—the fish will probably break and fall through or stick to the wires.

If the fish is less than ½ inch thick, don't turn it during the broiling process; just cook it on one side. The same holds true for butterflied fish, which are placed skin side down after the rack is oiled. If, however, the fish is more than ¾ inch thick, it can be turned just once during broiling. A half inch of water added to the pan under the perforated rack will help to keep the fish moist by creating steam.

Allow about 8 minutes per inch but test with a skewer after about half the time has elapsed. The fish is done when the skewer reveals just a tiny bit of translucent flesh at the thickest part. The approximate broiling time for thinner fish will be about 3 to 6 minutes, and 6 to 10 minutes for thicker fillets.

GRILLING

Judging from the number of people across North America who own barbecue grills and who spend many Sunday afternoons in their backyards preparing what we've laughingly called "the burnt meat offering," we've decided there must be something basic and primeval about this method of cooking. The scent of burning wood or charcoal, the basic simplicity, the fresh air, and the arrival of the first spring breezes seem to arouse us, and the fever spreads throughout the land during the entire summer and into autumn. While most of what is grilled is meat—the ubiquitous steaks or hamburgers—those who have never tried fish on the grill have missed a sublime experience. The smoky flavored result of grilling lends itself admirably to a whole range of fish and seafood.

Firm-fleshed fish, meaty steaks, fillets, and kebobs, whole fish and even smaller fish, as well as almost every crustacean will grill nicely: swordfish, mako, mahi-mahi, tuna, grouper, monkfish, salmon, trout, bluefish, lobster, and shrimp are all candidates. And although the more delicate fish such as flounder, fluke, and sole are generally not considered suitable for the grill, even they can be handled by placing them on a perforated rack with small holes (sometimes called a Griffo Grill) so that they don't fall through the grill and onto the coals.

Basic Grilling Methods

Far be it from us to be giving grilling instructions to the millions of America's "experts." However, there are some grilling tips that may help with your preparation of fish, since the timing may vary considerably from that of the traditional meats, and the delicacy and flavor of fish are affected much more easily by intense grilling heat.

The basic heat source, of course, comes from the bottom (in contrast to broiling), and open fire or direct-heat grilling is done with the food placed on a rack over some sort of charcoal or wood. With fish and seafood, an oiled or nonstick perforated rack will prevent them from falling through the grill. We think the rack is a must. There are also basket-style racks that enclose an entire fish to make for easy turning, and it's a good investment if you plan to grill whole fish. It's also quite necessary if you plan to grill over an open campfire or even if you own one of the new high-tech gas or electric grills with the covered hood.

Actually, the use of a covering, be it a hood, a piece of aluminum foil, or a disposable aluminum foil roasting pan, will induce *indirect* heat that's quite similar to a convection oven, allowing the heat to circulate around the food and to instill the flavor of the grilling process.

Grilling fish or seafood to perfection has only a few rules, both for proper cooking and for safety. Once mastered, we guarantee success every time:

❖ Use only hardwood (e.g., maple or hickory) or hardwood charcoal and know where it comes from. Don't use wood from known pesticide-treated areas. We feel that charcoal briquettes that contain petroleum products give an off taste to food. We feel the same way about starter fluids, but if you do use a chemical fluid to start your fire because it's more convenient, let it soak into the coals before lighting and then let the coals burn for at least 30 to 45 minutes before cooking. We advocate the use of an electric starter or a metal chimney-type canister with paper on the bottom and coals on the top. Try going natural.

❖ Check the direction of the wind before you light the fire and choose a well-ventilated spot so that the smoke can waft away.

❖ When you're building the fire, arrange the coals so there are hot and cool spots by piling up the coals near the back or sides of the grill and spacing them out toward the center or front to control the heat.

❖ Success in cooking fish and seafood on the grill depends upon timing. So light your charcoal fire 30 to 45 minutes before you're ready to cook. The charcoal fire will reach a temperature of about 425° within 30 minutes and then remain at about 350° or more for at least an hour more. The coals should be at least 80 percent covered with ash before you begin.

❖ To obtain a smoky flavor, soak a few aromatic wood chips in water for several hours before grilling and then throw them on the coals. They will also slow the rate of combustion. Mesquite, cherry, apple, or grapevine trimmings, fennel stalks, or fresh or dried herbs dipped in water and sprinkled over the coals also give additional fragrance.

❖ If you're using bamboo skewers for kebobs, be sure to soak them also and do it well before you begin to cook, so they don't burn.

❖ Useful tools include one or two wide spatulas with insulated handles, a long-handled basting brush, and elbow-length, heavy, fire-resistant gloves. Another safety rule is that you do not wear flowing clothing or sleeves that can ignite.

❖ For the sudden flare-ups that occur when oil or fat drips onto the hot coals, we keep a filled water pistol on hand for quick dousing, without affecting the rest of the fire.

❖ Grilling is one preparation for which we strongly suggest marinades to add flavor and moisture. We also highly recommend basting liquids for any fish or seafood grilling. For a basting brush, we use a sprig of rosemary or another fresh herb to impart a slight hint of the herb along with that of the basting mixture.

Grilled fish and seafood are tested for doneness in exactly the same way they are with other methods by inserting the tip of a knife or skewer into the middle. For seafood, a small cut into one piece will tell you if it's finished. The timing for seafood is also about the same as for fish—about 4 to 5 minutes on each side or about 8 minutes per inch. Just remember that fish cook quickly and that there's nothing more disappointing than an overdone fillet, particularly if it's one that you have personally landed in the boat or on the beach. Don't walk away from the fire. Watch carefully and test frequently beginning several minutes before the allotted cooking time. When the fish is slightly translucent at the thickest part, it's done.

MICROWAVING AND SMOKING

There are those who use their microwave ovens for everything, and we even know one young friend who boils her coffee water every morning by using her microwave oven! Very frankly, those who have read our cookbooks before know that we consider the microwave just another burdensome piece of equipment rather than a *method* of cooking fish. More importantly, fish cook so quickly by conventional methods that we've never had the desire to use one, nor do we own one. If you insist upon microwaving fish, we strongly suggest Barbara Kafka's book on the subject.

As for smoking fish, we have spent many labor-intensive hours doing just that after a large catch at the shore. But no matter how successful we've been, we find that our results are not nearly equal to those professionals who do nothing but smoke fish with the proper equipment, the time, the patience, and the expertise to achieve a moist, flavorsome end result. We love smoked fish—but we leave it to the pros. However, if you do decide to try it, all smokers come with clear, concise instructions. All you need provide are the fish and the fuel.

BONING AND SERVING A WHOLE FISH

There is nothing more festive than offering your guests an entire fish lying on its platter, surrounded by a bouquet of vegetables or decorated with fresh herbs. The choice then becomes one of taking it back to the kitchen to dismantle it or performing the necessary operation right at the table.

The flesh of the cooked whole fish is quite fragile, and care is needed when boning and serving, but the process is really quite basic and very much like filleting a freshly caught fish.

BONING ROUNDFISH. Place the fish on a platter and, using a fork to hold it steady, use a knife to gently peel the skin off, working from the tail up toward the head. Pull out the fins as you go along. Then slice the fish down the length of the backbone along the center line. Using a fish serving knife, you can lift off portions of the fish (if it is a large one) or the entire fillet (if you are serving that portion to your guests).

Lift the tail of the fish and the spine will begin to come up with it, taking the head off at the end. Discard it or put it aside. The bottom half of the fish will be revealed and the fillet can be served exactly the same way.

BONING FLATFISH. The procedure is exactly the same: Remove the skin, cut along the center line, and remove the fillets by using the spine as a guide against which to cut. After the skeleton is removed along with the head, the bottom half of the flatfish will be revealed, but remember that these fillets are smaller than those on top.

VI.
SAUCES
Transforming the Ordinary into the Sublime

When we looked back at our fish cookbook of about twelve years ago, we were aghast at our prodigious use of cream as well as butter, cheese, and oils—all the "no-no's" of today. The rich sauces of yore now are recognized as imprudent for our health and should be offered sparingly, if at all.

Certainly we have kept this in mind in the writing of our other more recent books, and this one is no exception. We have changed the balance of our sauces by using more herbs, citrus, fruits, and vegetables and keeping cream, butter, and oil to a minimum. But we have never lost sight of the fact that *sauces* are important to the enjoyment of fish and seafood.

Sauces not only add visual appeal but also color while complementing and enhancing the flavors of the fish and shellfish. In addition, they enlarge the repertoire of basic recipes, transforming the ordinary to the sublime.

When you select a sauce, try to choose one that will not overpower the fish. For example, for the lean, mild-tasting fish such as sole, orange roughy, and whiting, more delicately flavored sauces should be used. Fish that declare their own natural flavors are usually the fattier ones such as mackerel or bluefish and can take more assertive and highly spiced sauces or marinades that are based upon citrus, wine, vinegar, tomatoes, or fruit and vegetable salsas. Poached fish are usually complemented with herb-based sauces, while cold seafood benefits from those that are piquant and mayonnaise based.

Simply put, most sauces evolve from a basic foundation with the addition of several variations. And, if you like, you may use your own ingenuity to put your personal imprint on the sauce of your choice. We have divided the basic foundations into seven major categories:

Hot Butter Sauces and Compound or Cold Butter Sauces
Cream, Sour Cream, and Yogurt Sauces
Mayonnaise-Based Sauces
Acidic, Citrus, and Vinegar-Based Sauces
Velouté Sauces
Tomato-Based Sauces
Fruit, Vegetable, and Herb Sauces

HOT BUTTER SAUCES AND COMPOUND OR COLD BUTTER SAUCES

LIGHT BEURRE BLANC (WHITE BUTTER SAUCE) WITH VARIATIONS

MAKES 4 TO 6 SERVINGS

This beurre blanc is made without cream and is a more fragile, lighter sauce as a result. The rosy hued beurre rouge variation is lovely with most lean fish such as sole. The addition of arugula gives a sharp enough bite to go well with firm fish such as red snapper, wolffish, or tautog.

2 medium shallots, finely minced (about 2 tablespoons)	¼ pound butter, cold, cut into 8 pieces
½ cup dry white wine	Salt and pepper to taste
1 tablespoon white wine vinegar	

In a small saucepan, combine the shallots, wine, and vinegar over medium-high heat and boil until the liquid is reduced to about 3 tablespoons. Remove from the heat, add the first piece of butter, and whisk until it is almost but not completely emulsified. Quickly whisk in the next piece of butter, then return the saucepan to very low heat. Whisking rapidly and continuously, add the butter a piece at a time, keeping the texture creamy and not allowing the butter to melt before it emulsifies.

When all the butter has been incorporated, whisk in the salt and pepper, remove from the heat, and spoon over the fish (see Note).

Variation 1: Beurre Rouge
Replace the white wine and white wine vinegar with dry red wine and red wine vinegar for a shell-pink–colored sauce.

Variation 2: Arugula Beurre Blanc
Stir in 1 cup finely chopped arugula just before adding the last piece of butter.

Variation 3: Tomato Basil Beurre Blanc
Add 1 large plum tomato, peeled, seeded, and finely diced (about ½ cup), along with 2 tablespoons basil cut into a very fine chiffonade after the last piece of butter has been added.

NOTE: The sauce can be held for 5 minutes before serving if you keep it barely warm (98°) using a flame tamer and low heat to prevent it from breaking down.

ENRICHED BEURRE BLANC (WHITE BUTTER SAUCE) WITH VARIATIONS

MAKES 4 TO 6 SERVINGS

To our way of thinking, almost every fish and shellfish (except for mackerel and tuna) goes well with a bit of beurre blanc. Try the ginger-flavored variation with sautéed skate or the fines herbes *sauce spooned over steamed clams. This beurre blanc, made with cream, is richer than the previous recipe and, as a result, holds up quite well.*

2	large shallots, finely minced (about ¼ cup)	¼	cup heavy cream
2	tablespoons water	¼	pound butter, cold, cut into 8 pieces
3	tablespoons white wine vinegar		Salt and pepper to taste

In a small saucepan combine the shallots, water, and vinegar over medium-high heat, and boil until the liquid is reduced to about 2 tablespoons. Add the cream and continue to cook for 1 to 2 minutes until reduced by half. Remove from the heat and whisk in the butter one piece at a time, as each piece is almost but not completely incorporated. Return the pan to very low heat after 2 or 3 pieces of butter have been added.

Season with salt and pepper and strain, pressing the solids against the strainer. Keep the sauce warm on a flame tamer over very low heat until ready to serve, up to 5 minutes.

Variation 1: Ginger Beurre Blanc
Substitute ¼ cup finely minced fresh ginger for the shallots and follow the same procedure as above.

Variation 2: Beurre Blanc aux Fines Herbes
Remove the finished beurre blanc from the heat but do not strain. Add 1 tablespoon each finely minced chives and parsley, 1 teaspoon finely minced tarragon, and 2 teaspoons finely minced chervil. If you wish, add 1 tablespoon Pernod for a licorice flavor.

ORANGE BUTTER AND CHIVE SAUCE

MAKES 6 TO 8 SERVINGS

This golden citrus sauce flecked with bits of chive complements fish such as grilled king mackerel and can also be used as a basting mixture. Try it with almost any fish that has an assertive flavor, such as bluefish or mahi-mahi.

¼ pound butter

2 tablespoons orange juice

1 teaspoon finely minced orange peel

1 tablespoon finely minced chives

Salt and white pepper to taste

In a small saucepan, melt the butter over low heat, then whisk in the orange juice, peel, chives, salt, and pepper and heat the sauce until hot, stirring frequently.

LEMON AND PARSLEY BUTTER SAUCE (MAÎTRE D'HÔTEL BUTTER) WITH VARIATIONS

The marriage of lemon juice and parsley in a butter sauce is a delicate way to bring out the flavors of any lightly poached fish or shellfish without overpowering them. Try it with lobster, orange roughy, or sole.

¼	pound butter	⅛	teaspoon cayenne pepper
2	tablespoons lemon juice		Salt and pepper to taste
1	tablespoon finely minced lemon peel	2	tablespoons finely minced parsley

In a small saucepan, melt the butter over low heat. Add the lemon juice, peel, cayenne, salt, and pepper and continue to heat until warm. Stir in the parsley just before serving.

Variation 1: Lemon and Mint Butter Sauce
Replace the parsley with 2 tablespoons finely minced fresh mint or 1 teaspoon crushed dried mint.

Variation 2: Tarragon and Lemon Butter Sauce
Replace the parsley with 1 tablespoon finely minced fresh tarragon or ½ teaspoon dried tarragon.

NOTE: By creaming the butter in a food processor instead of heating it, this recipe can be made into a compound butter, formed into a log, and refrigerated, to be sliced and placed on hot fish, where it melts into a sauce.

PIRIPIRI BUTTER

This spicy butter sauce is used in tropical countries for fish or shellfish that are grilled or baked. Try it with red snapper just as they do in the Caribbean.

1 to 3 small fresh or dried hot chiles, such as serrano or Thai (see Note), seeded	1 teaspoon paprika
	Salt to taste
2 large cloves garlic, peeled	¼ pound butter, softened
1 teaspoon lime juice	
¼ teaspoon cumin	

In a blender, add the chile, garlic, lime juice, cumin, paprika, and salt and blend to a purée. Add the butter and blend until well mixed. Taste to see if more lime juice is needed and, if so, add it. Place the butter on a piece of plastic wrap and roll into a log 1 inch in diameter. Chill or freeze or use at room temperature.

NOTE: These small chiles are very hot to our taste so we are prudent and use but one. However, our friends from the Caribbean prefer 2 or even 3, and they still don't call the fire department.

SHALLOT AND GARLIC "SNAIL" BUTTER

Here is a versatile butter: In its softened form, it's spread in the openings of snail shells before baking or over fish before baking or broiling. Melted, it can be drizzled over shrimp, crab, lobster, steamed clams, or mussels.

¼ pound butter, softened

2 small shallots, finely minced (about 1½ tablespoons)

2 large cloves garlic, finely minced (about 1 tablespoon)

1 teaspoon lemon juice

2 or 3 drops Tabasco

3 tablespoons finely minced parsley

Salt and pepper to taste

In a food processor, blend the butter until soft and creamy. Add the shallots, garlic, lemon juice, Tabasco, parsley, salt, and pepper and blend to incorporate. Scrape out with a rubber spatula onto a piece of plastic wrap. Use the butter softened, or form into a log about 1 inch in diameter and chill or freeze, cutting off slices as needed.

LEEK AND *SAFFRON* COMPOUND BUTTER

Sunny and flavorful like many Spanish dishes, this sauce lends itself to cod, haddock, or whiting with delicious results. Or toss a piece of this butter with some rice, add peas and pimientos, and you have a marvelous side dish.

2	tablespoons dry white wine	2	teaspoons lemon juice
½	teaspoon saffron threads, crumbled	1 or 2	drops Tabasco
¼	pound butter, softened		Salt and pepper to taste
1	small leek, white part only, finely minced (½ cup)		

In a small saucepan, combine the wine and saffron over low heat and heat for 1 minute. Remove from the heat and reserve.

In a small skillet, melt 1 tablespoon of the butter over low heat. Add the leek and sauté, stirring frequently, until softened. Add the saffron mixture and cook for 1 minute more. Remove from the heat and let cool. Then stir in the lemon juice, Tabasco, salt, and pepper. Add the remaining butter to the bowl of a food processor and process until creamy. Add the leek mixture and process with just a few strokes until combined. Scrape the butter out with a rubber spatula onto a piece of plastic wrap and form into a log 1 inch in diameter. Chill or freeze and slice as needed.

GREEN PEPPERCORN COMPOUND BUTTER WITH VARIATION

The vibrant bite of green peppercorns in this butter gives a lift to simply poached trout or salmon. With the addition of a bit of cream and fish fumet (see Variation), voilà! *another flavor realm is reached.*

¼	pound butter, softened	Salt to taste
1	teaspoon lemon juice	
1	tablespoon drained water-packed green peppercorns, mashed	

In the bowl of a food processor, add the butter and process until creamy. Add the lemon juice, green peppercorns, and salt and process with a few strokes until combined. Transfer the butter to a piece of plastic wrap and form into a log 1 inch in diameter. Chill or freeze to be used as needed.

Variation: Green Peppercorn and Cream Sauce
Add a frozen cube of Fish Fumet (see page 403) and 2 tablespoons heavy cream to a saucepan. Bring to a boil and stir in ¼ cup of the green peppercorn butter and heat until warm.

LEMON CAPER BUTTER WITH VARIATION

A piquant butter with a bonus: Softened, it can be used as a spread on small pieces of pumpernickel or rye bread and topped with smoked fish such as eel, trout, or salmon. Or use it for a final flavorful glossing by melting a cube over grilled swordfish, tuna, mackerel, or opah.

¼ pound butter, softened	⅛ teaspoon white pepper
1 teaspoon lemon juice	¼ cup nonpareil capers, rinsed and dried
½ teaspoon finely minced lemon peel	

Either with a fork or in a food processor, beat the butter until creamy, adding the lemon juice, peel, and pepper. Scrape it out if using a food processor and stir in the capers. Wrap with plastic wrap and chill for 2 hours to allow the flavors to blend.

Bring the butter to room temperature before using as a spread, or form into a log 1 inch in diameter and freeze it. Slice off pieces as needed or cut out a fanciful shape (such as a heart) and melt it over a grilled swordfish or other steak.

Variation: Caper and Anchovy Butter

To the same amount of butter, add 1 clove garlic, finely minced, 3 flat anchovies, rinsed and dried, and only 1 tablespoon rinsed and dried capers. Follow the recipe above.

CLARIFIED BUTTER

Once clarified, butter may be kept for several weeks in a bowl or crock, covered with plastic wrap. This is the butter served in most seafood restaurants to accompany boiled lobsters. It's also excellent for sautéing at high temperatures, since it does not spatter or burn as easily as unclarified butter.

1 pound butter

In a medium saucepan, slowly melt the butter over low heat. Skim off the surface foam and then pour the clear yellow liquid into a bowl, leaving and discarding the milk solids that have sunk to the bottom of the saucepan.

Cover the bowl with plastic wrap and use as needed. If refrigerated, bring to room temperature or melt before using. This is also the *ghee* that is used in Indian cuisine, although it is usually kept unrefrigerated because it is used so frequently. We do not use it as often, and probably neither will you, so we suggest keeping it in the refrigerator.

When we serve it with lobster, we usually perk it up with a bit of salt, a few grains of cayenne, and a squeeze of lemon juice.

CREAM, SOUR CREAM, AND YOGURT SAUCES

BASIC CRÈME FRAÎCHE

MAKES 1¼ CUPS

One of the greatest things about this slightly tart, thickish cream is that it will not curdle when stirred into a sauce. It is now available in some gourmet food shops, but it is ridiculously easy to make at home. Use it not only for fish sauces but also to spoon over fresh berries or other fruit desserts as well. Just remember, it cannot be whipped.

1 cup heavy cream (*un*sterilized)   1½   tablespoons buttermilk

Combine the cream and buttermilk and pour into a sterilized glass jar. Cover loosely with a piece of waxed paper and let stand at room temperature for 10 to 14 hours, depending upon the heat of the room. Stir, cover tightly with the jar lid, and refrigerate. It will keep for 2 weeks refrigerated.

MUSSEL AND SAFFRON SAUCE

This sunny, saffron-tinted, light cream sauce is afloat with tiny poached mussels. It's perfect with any delicate white-fleshed poached fish.

1 pound very small mussels	1 cup heavy cream
½ cup dry white wine	⅛ teaspoon cayenne pepper
½ teaspoon loosely packed saffron threads, crumbled	1 tablespoon butter, softened
2 to 3 large shallots, finely chopped (about ⅓ cup)	Salt, if needed

Scrub the mussels with a nylon scrub pad and rinse in several changes of cold water. Pull off the beards and put the mussels in a wide sauté pan along with the wine. Cover and cook over high heat for 3 to 5 minutes, sliding the pan back and forth once or twice while cooking. When the mussels have opened, lift them out with a slotted spoon to a bowl to cool. Discard any that do not open.

Strain the broth into a small bowl through a dampened coffee filter or a doubled piece of cheesecloth. Add the saffron to the broth and let steep for 10 minutes.

In a medium saucepan, combine the shallots, cream, and mussel broth and cook, uncovered, over medium-high heat for about 10 minutes until slightly thickened and reduced.

While the sauce is simmering, remove the mussel meat from the shells, then add it to the sauce along with the cayenne and butter. Taste to see if additional salt is needed. Cook for 1 minute or less until the mussels are hot and the butter is melted.

SORREL SAUCE

MAKES 4 TO 6 SERVINGS

Either abhorred or adored, the slightly acidic, tart sorrel leaves poke their heads through the earth just when the first shad come into market in the spring. Try this sauce then with shad, salmon, or Arctic char and use it sparingly.

1   pound fresh sorrel leaves

1   cup heavy cream

1   cup Fish Fumet (see page 403)

2   tablespoons butter

Salt and pepper to taste

Rinse and dry the sorrel leaves. Fold the leaves in half lengthwise and cut out and discard the rib of the leaf and the stem. Then cut the leaves into a thin chiffonade and set aside.

In a medium saucepan, add the cream and bring to a boil over medium heat, then lower the heat and simmer until reduced by half, about 10 minutes. Add the fish fumet to the cream and continue to simmer for 5 minutes.

In a medium nonreactive skillet, melt 1 tablespoon of the butter over medium-high heat. Stir in the sorrel and cook, stirring frequently, only until the leaves have wilted and turned from bright to olive green. Stir the sorrel into the sauce, then add the remaining 1 tablespoon butter. Season with salt and pepper and serve at once.

SHRIMP AND SCALLION SAUCE

This rich sauce should be used sparingly to enhance delicately flavored, lean fish such as sole.

3 tablespoons butter

6 medium scallions, green part only, finely minced

½ cup dry white wine

1 cup Crème Fraîche (see page 66)

¼ pound raw shrimp, shelled, deveined, and coarsely chopped

1 tablespoon lemon juice

2 tablespoons finely minced parsley
   Salt to taste

¼ teaspoon white pepper

In a medium skillet, heat the butter over medium heat. Add the scallions and sauté, stirring, for 30 seconds. Add the wine and cook until it has evaporated and the scallions are tender. Stir in the crème fraîche, bring to a boil, and cook for 1 to 2 minutes until slightly thickened. Stir in the shrimp and continue cooking for 30 seconds until the shrimp are cooked. Remove from the heat and stir in the lemon juice, parsley, salt, and pepper. Serve hot.

YOGURT, CUCUMBER, AND DILL SAUCE

A quickly prepared, uncooked cold sauce for the calorie and cholesterol conscious. Try it with poached halibut or salmon.

1 cup plain yogurt, low fat or no fat if you wish

2 tablespoons dry white wine

2 tablespoons olive oil

2 small Kirby cucumbers, peeled, seeded, and diced

1 small clove garlic, finely minced

1 tablespoon finely minced fresh dill

Salt and white pepper to taste.

In a small bowl, combine all the ingredients. Cover with plastic wrap and refrigerate for at least 2 hours. Stir before using.

HORSERADISH AND SOUR CREAM SAUCE

MAKES 4 TO 6 SERVINGS

This sauce is traditionally served with smoked fish such as trout, mackerel, bluefish, and eel.

4 to 5 tablespoons drained prepared horse-radish

1 cup sour cream (see Note)

1 tablespoon lemon juice

2 or 3 drops Tabasco

⅛ teaspoon white pepper

Salt, if needed

Combine all the ingredients in a small bowl. Cover and chill before serving.

NOTE: If you prefer, whip 1 cup heavy cream and substitute it for the sour cream for a lighter *mousseline* sauce.

SAUCE DUGLÈRE
(CREAM AND TOMATO SAUCE)

MAKES 6 TO 8 SERVINGS

This lovely silken tomato and cream sauce can lightly nap an airy fish mousse or an orange roughy.

2 cups Fish Stock (see page 402)

½ cup dry white wine

1 tablespoon butter

2 large shallots, finely minced (about ¼ cup)

½ pound ripe tomatoes, peeled, seeded, and diced (about 1½ cups)

1 tablespoon lemon juice

⅛ teaspoon cayenne pepper

1 cup Crème Fraîche (see page 66)

Salt to taste

1 tablespoon finely shredded fresh basil (optional)

In a small saucepan, combine the fish stock and wine and bring to a boil over high heat. Boil, uncovered, until reduced to ¼ cup and set aside.

In a medium skillet, heat the butter over moderate heat. Add the shallots and sauté, stirring frequently, until wilted, 3 to 4 minutes. Add 1 cup of the tomatoes, the lemon juice, and cayenne and bring to a boil; lower the heat and simmer for 8 to 10 minutes. Stir in the reduced fish stock, remove from the heat, and purée in a blender.

Return the tomato mixture to the saucepan, add the crème fraîche, and cook over moderate heat, stirring occasionally until hot. Stir in the remaining ½ cup tomato and add salt if necessary. Add the basil, if you wish, just before serving.

CILANTRO, CHILE, AND CUMIN SAUCE WITH YOGURT

This Indian sauce is tart, cool, and hot all at the same time. Try it with grilled mackerel or bluefish or any other assertive-tasting fish that can hold up to a strongly flavored sauce.

1   cup loosely packed cilantro leaves
1   fresh green chile, stemmed
3   tablespoons water
1   tablespoon lemon juice

¼   teaspoon ground cumin
    Salt and pepper to taste
1   cup plain yogurt

In a blender, add the cilantro, chile, water, lemon juice, cumin, salt, and pepper and whirl until puréed. Add the yogurt and blend. Scrape into a bowl, cover with plastic wrap, and keep at room temperature for 1 hour before using.

COCKTAIL SAUCE WITH CREAM AND BRANDY

MAKES 6 TO 8 SERVINGS

Chilled shrimp cocktails are popular as a first course throughout the country, but the sauce—usually ketchup and horseradish—is a bore. If you'd like a change of sauce with your chilled shrimp, try this one. It's good, too, with lump crabmeat or cold lobster.

1 hard-cooked egg yolk	¼ teaspoon white Worcestershire sauce
1 teaspoon strong Dijon mustard	⅛ teaspoon cayenne pepper
3 tablespoons olive oil	2 tablespoons heavy cream
1 teaspoon lemon juice	1 tablespoon brandy
6 tablespoons bottled chile sauce	Salt and pepper to taste

To the bowl of a food processor, add the egg yolk and mustard and pulse to combine. With the motor running, add 2 tablespoons of the oil very slowly, as if you were making mayonnaise. Gradually add the lemon juice and then the remaining tablespoon oil. Transfer to a small bowl and stir in the chile sauce, Worcestershire, cayenne, cream, and brandy. Season with salt and pepper. Cover and chill for at least 30 minutes before serving.

❖ 73 ❖ *Cream, Sour Cream, and Yogurt Sauces*

MAYONNAISE-BASED SAUCES

TARTAR SAUCE

MAKES 6 TO 8 SERVINGS

This classic sauce is served with many simply broiled or fried fish; but it's particularly good with codfish cakes (see page 116).

1   cup mayonnaise
1   medium shallot, finely minced (about 2 teaspoons)
2 to 3   cornichons, finely minced
1   tablespoon nonpareil capers, rinsed and dried
1   tablespoon finely minced parsley
¼   teaspoon dried tarragon, crushed

1   teaspoon lemon juice
⅛   teaspoon Tabasco
1   teaspoon Dijon mustard
½   teaspoon anchovy paste (optional)
   Black pepper to taste
   Salt, if needed

In a small bowl, mix all the ingredients until smooth. Cover with plastic wrap and refrigerate for several hours or overnight before using.

RUSSIAN DRESSING

This old-fashioned dressing dates back to when it literally was spooned over a wedge of iceberg lettuce. Mom served it with cold poached halibut. We loved it then, and recently after trying it again, we found we love it still!

1 cup mayonnaise	2 teaspoons olive oil
⅔ cup bottled chili sauce	1 teaspoon lemon juice
¼ cup drained sweet pickle relish	1 small clove garlic, lightly crushed
1 teaspoon drained prepared horseradish	Salt and pepper to taste

In a small bowl, mix all the ingredients until smooth. Cover and chill for at least 1 hour or overnight. Remove the garlic clove before serving.

DILL SAUCE

MAKES 4 TO 6 SERVINGS

As with most mayonnaise sauces, this one is also a cold sauce and, therefore, goes best with cold seafood, smoked fish, or poached fish.

¾ cup mayonnaise	⅛ teaspoon cayenne pepper
½ cup sour cream	2 tablespoons finely minced dill
1 tablespoon lemon juice	Salt and white pepper to taste
½ small clove garlic, finely minced	1 to 2 tablespoons dry white wine (optional)

In a small bowl, mix all the ingredients except the wine until smooth, cover with plastic wrap, and chill for at least 1 hour. If you wish a thinner sauce, dilute with the wine.

TOMATO, CAPER, AND
JALAPEÑO SAUCE

MAKES 4 TO 6 SERVINGS

Somewhat like a tartar sauce, but the tomato and jalapeño give it additional zap. Try it with cold crab legs or other chilled seafood or as a dip for fried clams or oysters.

6 cornichons (French gherkins)

1 medium jalapeño chile, stemmed and seeded

¼ small onion

1 ripe large tomato, peeled, seeded, and finely diced

1 tablespoon nonpareil capers, rinsed and dried

1 cup mayonnaise

2 tablespoons lemon juice

Salt and pepper to taste

In the bowl of a food processor, finely chop the cornichons, jalapeño, and onion together. Transfer to a small bowl and stir in the tomato, capers, mayonnaise, lemon juice, salt, and pepper. Cover and chill for 1 hour or overnight before serving.

SAUCE VERTE

This verdant sauce can be served with crisply fried squid or cold shrimp, crab, or lobster. It's particularly marvelous with freshly poached whole salmon that has been cooled to room temperature.

1	small clove garlic	¼	cup finely snipped fresh chives
½	cup loosely packed fresh dill leaves	1	cup mayonnaise
½	cup loosely packed parsley leaves	2	tablespoons lemon juice
½	cup stemmed watercress leaves	1	teaspoon finely minced lemon peel
½	cup stemmed spinach leaves		Salt and pepper to taste
1	tablespoon fresh tarragon leaves		
2	medium scallions, green part only, finely minced (about ½ cup)		

In the bowl of a food processor, finely mince the garlic. Add the dill, parsley, watercress, spinach, and tarragon and process until very finely chopped. Scrape the mixture into a medium bowl and stir in the scallions, chives, and mayonnaise, then add the lemon juice, lemon peel, salt, and pepper. Cover with plastic wrap and chill for 1 hour before serving.

ACIDIC, CITRIC, AND VINEGAR-BASED SAUCES

MIGNONETTE SAUCE WITH BALSAMIC VINEGAR

MAKES 4 TO 6 SERVINGS

The Oyster Bar Restaurant in New York's Grand Central Station has served this sauce with their raw shellfish for many, many years. We changed the red wine vinegar to balsamic vinegar to give it a more mellow flavor.

2   medium shallots, finely minced (about 2 tablespoons)

½   cup balsamic vinegar

½   cup tarragon vinegar

1   teaspoon freshly ground black pepper or more to taste

Put all the ingredients into a jar and shake to combine. Keep at room temperature until ready to serve.

NOTE: Although this sauce traditionally is served with *raw* shellfish, we suggest that clams and mussels be steamed and oysters broiled lightly if their origin is unknown.

GINGER-LIME VINAIGRETTE

MAKES 6 TO 8 SERVINGS

This vibrant ginger-laced sauce is ideal for a mixed seafood salad, or use it as a marinade and basting mixture for mackerel or shrimp when grilling.

2 to 3 large scallions, thinly sliced (1 to 1¼ cups)

1 large jalapeño chile, roasted, peeled, seeded, and finely minced

¼ cup peeled and finely minced ginger

½ cup lime juice

¼ cup tamari

¼ cup Oriental sesame oil

¾ cup canola oil

In a medium bowl, combine the scallions, jalapeño, ginger, lime juice, and tamari; gradually whisk in the sesame oil and then the canola oil. Cover with plastic wrap and refrigerate overnight to allow the flavors to blend.

BLACK OLIVE AND LEMON SAUCE

MAKES 6 TO 8 SERVINGS

An olive lover's delight, this inky colored lemon-scented sauce can be spread over almost any kind of fish before or after broiling.

⅛ cup lemon juice

2 tablespoons black olive paste (olivada) or 24 to 30 oil-cured olives, pitted and finely minced

½ teaspoon dried thyme

½ cup olive oil

1 tablespoon finely minced parsley

Black pepper to taste

Salt, if needed

In a small bowl, whisk the lemon juice, olive paste, and thyme together to combine (or purée the pitted olives in a food processor along with the lemon juice). Whisk in the olive oil, parsley, and black pepper. Taste for salt.

SWEET AND HOT PEPPER VINAIGRETTE

A sort of Mexican mignonette, this is a vinegar-based sauce with confetti colors of red, yellow, and green peppers. Try some spooned over a platter of lightly steamed shellfish served on the half shell.

½ cup dry white wine

½ cup white wine vinegar

2 tablespoons lime juice

1 medium shallot, finely minced (about 1 tablespoon)

1 or 2 small jalapeño or serrano chiles, seeded and very finely diced

1 tablespoon each very finely diced red, green, and yellow peppers

1 tablespoon finely minced cilantro

⅛ teaspoon ground cumin

Salt to taste

In a small bowl, combine all the ingredients.

SAUCE PIQUANT

A lively sauce that's perfect to mix with cold poached fish, crayfish, or cooked shrimp.

3 tablespoons Creole mustard, such as Zatarain's, or imported French grainy mustard

2 tablespoons tarragon wine vinegar

2 tablespoons lemon juice

2 tablespoons drained prepared horseradish

1 tablespoon paprika

½ teaspoon black pepper

⅛ teaspoon cayenne pepper

2 anchovies, rinsed and coarsely chopped

1 small clove garlic, finely minced (about ½ teaspoon)

1 hard-cooked egg, quartered

½ cup canola oil

½ cup olive oil

1 large rib celery, finely diced (about ½ cup)

3 large scallions, finely minced (about ⅔ cup)

⅓ cup finely minced parsley

Salt to taste

Tabasco to taste

In the bowl of a food processor, add the mustard, vinegar, lemon juice, horseradish, paprika, pepper, cayenne, anchovies, garlic, and egg and process until well combined. With the motor running, slowly add the oils until a thickish emulsion is formed. Scrape the mixture into a bowl and stir in the celery, scallions, and parsley. Taste for salt and add Tabasco for an extra peppery taste if you wish. Cover with plastic wrap and chill for 1 to 2 hours before using.

SESAME, GARLIC, AND HOT CHILE OIL

MAKES 4 TO 6 SERVINGS

This Oriental hot sauce is delicious as a dip for crisply fried fish or seafood. It's also excellent tossed with julienned cold chicken.

¼ cup tahini (sesame paste)	4 to 5 cloves garlic, finely minced (about 2 tablespoons)
3 tablespoons cold water	1 tablespoon Oriental sesame oil
3 tablespoons light soy sauce	Salt to taste
3 tablespoons rice vinegar	3 teaspoons hot chile oil or more to taste
1 teaspoon sugar	
¼ cup canola oil	

In a medium bowl, whisk the tahini and water together, then whisk in the remaining ingredients except the hot chile oil. When all the ingredients are well blended, whisk in the chile oil, a teaspoon at a time, and taste to determine just how hot you wish the sauce to be.

CILANTRO, SCALLION, AND TOMATO VINAIGRETTE

MAKES 4 SERVINGS

This is a particularly good sauce for fattier fish, such as bluefish and mackerel, or with grilled tuna or swordfish.

3 tablespoons white wine vinegar
1 teaspoon Dijon mustard
Salt and black pepper to taste
¼ cup Spanish olive oil
4 to 5 thin scallions, finely minced (about 1 cup)

¾ pound ripe plum tomatoes, finely diced (1½ to 2 cups)
½ cup coarsely chopped cilantro leaves

In a small bowl, whisk the vinegar, mustard, salt, and pepper together. Slowly add the oil, whisking constantly, until a thin emulsion is formed. Stir in the scallions, tomatoes, and cilantro and spoon over the fish.

SWEET-AND-SOUR HOT SAUCE

With a touch of hot chile and ginger, sweet peppers and honey, then a counterbalance of tart rice vinegar, a wonderful Chinese blend of flavors is achieved in this sauce. Serve over simply steamed whole sea bass or snapper.

¾ cup pineapple juice	1 small dried hot chile
¼ cup rice vinegar	2 teaspoons finely minced ginger
1 tablespoon soy sauce or tamari	2 tablespoons cornstarch
2 tablespoons mild honey	⅓ cup water
½ cup Fish Stock (see page 402)	2 medium scallions, green part only, sliced diagonally ½ inch thick.
1 small red pepper, cut into julienne (about ⅔ cup)	

In a medium nonreactive saucepan, mix the pineapple juice, vinegar, soy, and honey. Add the fish stock, pepper, chile, and ginger and bring to a boil over medium heat. Mix the cornstarch and water together in a cup and slowly add to the boiling sauce, stirring constantly with a wooden spoon. Lower the heat and cook for 1 minute until the sauce has thickened and is clear. Discard the chile before serving. Spoon the hot sauce over the fish and scatter the uncooked scallions over the surface.

VELOUTÉ SAUCES

BASIC FISH VELOUTÉ

MAKES 4 SERVINGS OR 1 CUP

A velouté is a mild basic sauce that is thickened with flour and enriched with a bit of butter. Its delicate flavor is derived from good stock (or fumet for a more intense flavor). This sauce, just as it is or enriched with egg and cream, is the basis of a repertoire of sauces that are only limited by your imagination.

2   tablespoons butter, softened

2   tablespoons all-purpose flour

Salt and white pepper to taste

1   cup Fish Fumet (see page 403) or Fish Stock (page 402)

In a small nonstick saucepan, melt the butter over medium heat. Add the flour, salt, and pepper and whisk for 1 minute. Lower the heat and gradually whisk in the fish fumet, stirring constantly. Simmer over low heat, stirring frequently, for 10 minutes. Taste to adjust the seasoning.

NOTE: Reduced aromatic milk broth (see page 38) that has been used as a poaching liquid can replace the fish fumet.

ENRICHED FISH VELOUTÉ
WITH VARIATION

We used 3 egg yolks and 1 cup heavy cream for this sauce in our days of cholesterol innocence. Now we find that this pared-down version is even better and certainly is still rich enough. How tastes do change!

1	cup Basic Fish Velouté (see page 85)	⅛	teaspoon cayenne pepper
1	egg yolk	⅛	teaspoon nutmeg
½	cup heavy cream		

In a small nonstick saucepan, bring the basic velouté to a simmer. Combine the egg yolk and cream in a small bowl. Whisk ¼ cup of the hot velouté into the egg mixture, then return to the saucepan over low heat. Stir in the cayenne and nutmeg and whisk constantly until the sauce is smooth and thick and the egg is cooked, about 3 minutes. *Do not let the sauce boil.* Remove from the heat and continue to stir for 1 to 2 minutes more.

Variation: Sauce Mornay
To the hot enriched velouté, stir in ½ cup grated Gruyère cheese and thin the sauce with ¼ cup milk. Simmer until the cheese is melted. Taste for additional salt or cayenne. Spoon the Mornay sauce over the fish and slip under the broiler until it's bubbly and dappled with brown.

SHRIMP AND CHIVE VELOUTÉ

The velouté base with the addition of a few chopped shrimp and some chives is a luxurious sauce for sole or orange roughy.

1   cup Basic or Enriched Fish Velouté (see
    page 85 or 86)
½   cup shelled, deveined, and finely chopped
    raw shrimp

1   tablespoon finely minced chives
    Pinch of cayenne pepper

Heat the velouté over low heat. *Do not boil.* Add the shrimp and stir constantly until the sauce is hot and the shrimp are cooked, about 1 minute. Stir in the chives and cayenne and serve.

SAUCE CARDINALE (LOBSTER VELOUTÉ)

So little lobster is required for this sauce that a small lobster tail would be sufficient. Or save a claw from your next poached lobster and use the flesh in this sauce to top tilefish, turbot, or grouper.

1   cup Basic or Enriched Fish Velouté (see
    page 85 or 86)
½   cup coarsely chopped cooked lobster meat
1   teaspoon dry sherry

⅛   teaspoon paprika
⅛   teaspoon cayenne pepper
1   teaspoon finely minced scallion green

Heat the velouté over low heat. Stir in the lobster, sherry, paprika, and cayenne and simmer until hot. Stir in the scallion and serve.

SPANISH SAFFRON AND TOMATO VELOUTÉ

*A golden sauce with tiny bits of tomato, perfect for spooning over
poached hake or haddock.*

½   teaspoon saffron threads, crumbled

1   tablespoon dry white wine

1   cup Basic Fish Velouté (see page 85)

2   tablespoons heavy cream

1   teaspoon grated onion

1   large tomato (about 4 ounces), skinned and
    finely diced (about ¾ cup)

1   teaspoon lemon juice

⅛   teaspoon cayenne pepper

Mix the saffron and wine together in a small cup and let stand for 10 minutes. Heat the velouté over low heat, whisk in the saffron mixture, cream, and onion, and simmer for 5 minutes until hot. Stir in the tomato, lemon juice, and cayenne and simmer for 1 minute more. Serve hot.

TOMATO-BASED SAUCES

TOMATO CHILE SALSA

MAKES 4 TO 6 SERVINGS

The freshest, most flavorful ingredients should be used, and the sauce made just before serving. It's a good accompaniment for grilled fresh sardines, mackerel, or bluefish.

¾ to 1   pound ripe tomatoes (about 5 medium)

1   small red onion, finely minced (about ½ cup)

1   jalapeño chile, roasted, seeded, and minced (about 1 tablespoon)

2   tablespoons lime juice

2   tablespoons olive oil

2   tablespoons finely minced cilantro leaves
Salt and pepper to taste

In a food processor, coarsely chop the tomatoes with a few strokes. Put the tomatoes in a strainer, drain, and discard any liquid. In a small bowl, combine all the remaining ingredients with the tomatoes. This salsa is best eaten fresh for it can become watery if left to stand.

CHUNKY TOMATO SAUCE WITH FENNEL

Licorice-scented fennel seeds and a hint of orange flavor this quickly prepared sauce. Spoon it over black sea bass or red snapper.

2	tablespoons olive oil	2	2½- by 1-inch strips orange peel
½	large onion, thinly sliced	¼	teaspoon fennel seeds
1	28-ounce can Italian plum tomatoes, drained and tomatoes cut in half	⅛	teaspoon hot pepper flakes
			Salt and pepper to taste
¼	cup dry white wine		

In a medium skillet, heat the oil over medium-low heat. Add the onion and sauté, stirring occasionally, for 5 to 8 minutes until the onion is soft but not brown. Add the remaining ingredients, raise the heat to medium, and bring to a boil. Lower the heat and simmer to reduce the sauce for 10 to 12 minutes. Remove the orange peel before serving.

SAUCE PROVENÇALE (TOMATO, GARLIC, AND BLACK OLIVE SAUCE)

Lightly sautéed frogs' legs and sauce Provençale are an old-fashioned French bistro dish, still popular and enjoyed by all who sample it. The sauce is good, too, with swordfish, tuna, or mahi-mahi.

¼ cup olive oil

4 cloves garlic, coarsely chopped (about 1½ tablespoons)

3 pounds ripe tomatoes (6 to 8), skinned and cut into large pieces

⅓ cup pitted Niçoise olives

2 whole basil leaves

Salt and black pepper to taste

2 tablespoons coarsely minced parsley leaves

In a large skillet, heat the oil over medium-low heat. Add the garlic and sauté, stirring constantly, for 1 to 2 minutes without browning the garlic or it will turn bitter. Stir in the tomatoes, olives, basil, salt, and pepper and bring to a boil. Then lower the heat, cover the skillet, and simmer for 15 minutes. Remove and discard the basil leaves and stir in the parsley.

GAZPACHO SAUCE (TOMATO AND RAW VEGETABLE SAUCE)

MAKES 6 TO 8 SERVINGS

A lusty fresh tomato and raw vegetable sauce with a touch of oil and vinegar—perfect for sparking up a delicate fish mousse or saucing a grilled swordfish or bluefish. Prepare the sauce one hour before serving.

1	small green pepper, seeded	2 or 3	drops Tabasco
1	medium Kirby cucumber	2	teaspoons red wine vinegar
2	thin scallions	1	tablespoon olive oil
3	ripe large plum tomatoes, skinned and quartered	⅛	teaspoon ground cumin
1	small clove garlic	⅛	teaspoon dried oregano
			Salt and pepper to taste

Finely mince about 2 tablespoons each green pepper, cucumber, and scallions, and 1 tomato. Cover with plastic wrap and refrigerate. Add the remaining pepper, cucumber, scallions, tomatoes, and garlic to a blender and blend until smooth. Add the Tabasco, vinegar, olive oil, cumin, oregano, salt, and pepper and blend again. Pour into a bowl, cover with plastic wrap, and keep at room temperature for 1 hour or longer if necessary. When ready to serve, stir in the reserved minced vegetables.

FRUIT, VEGETABLE, AND HERB SAUCES

MANGO AND BLACK BEAN RELISH

MAKES 6 TO 8 SERVINGS

A hearty, sweet, hot relish that's great with mahi-mahi, yellowfin tuna, or grilled salmon.

1 ripe large mango, peeled and cut into ¼-inch dice (about 2 cups)

½ small red onion, finely diced (about ¼ cup)

¼ cup drained cooked black beans

1 teaspoon ground cumin

1 medium jalapeño chile, seeded and finely minced

2 tablespoons coarsely chopped cilantro

2 tablespoons lime juice

1 tablespoon olive oil

⅛ teaspoon chile powder

Salt and pepper to taste

In a medium bowl, combine all the ingredients just before preparing the fish. Do not let the relish stand too long or it will get watery.

MIXED FRUIT SALSA

MAKES 6 TO 8 SERVINGS

A fruit salsa with a Latin accent. Try it with Arctic char, grilled salmon, or swordfish.

1 ripe medium papaya, peeled and cut into ½-inch dice (about 1 cup)

2 kiwi fruits, peeled and cut into ½-inch dice

1 cup diced (½ inch) fresh pineapple

1 cup diced (½ inch) honeydew melon

1 small red pepper, seeded and cut into ½-inch dice

¼ cup coarsely chopped cilantro

½ teaspoon hot pepper flakes

¼ cup rice wine vinegar

Salt and pepper to taste

Combine all the ingredients in a medium bowl just before preparing the fish.

SICILIAN EGGPLANT SAUCE

This chunky sauce is typical of the Arab or Saracen influence on Sicilian food. Prepare it two to three days ahead and try it with strongly flavored fish such as tuna, bluefish, swordfish, or mackerel.

1½ pounds eggplant, peeled and cut into ¾-inch cubes

2 teaspoons coarse or kosher salt

½ cup olive oil or as needed

1 large onion, coarsely chopped (about 1¼ cups)

2 ribs celery, coarsely chopped (about 1 cup)

3 large plum tomatoes, diced (about 1 cup)

⅓ cup Kalamata olives, pitted and sliced

⅓ cup green olives, pitted and sliced

1½ tablespoons capers, rinsed

3 tablespoons golden raisins

2 tablespoons red wine vinegar
    Black pepper to taste

2 tablespoons pine nuts, toasted
    Salt to taste

Place the eggplant in a large bowl, sprinkle with coarse salt, and let stand for 30 minutes. Then rinse in cold water and dry well on paper towels. Heat 2 tablespoons of the oil in a skillet over medium-high heat and sauté the eggplant in several batches until tender, about 7 minutes for each batch. You'll need 2 tablespoons oil for each batch. Place the sautéed eggplant in a bowl and set aside. Add 2 tablespoons more oil to the skillet and sauté the onion until soft, stirring frequently, about 5 minutes. Add the celery, tomatoes, both kinds of olives, capers, raisins, vinegar, and pepper. Cover the skillet, lower the heat, and simmer for 15 minutes.

Stir in the reserved eggplant and the pine nuts, then return the sauce to the bowl, cover, and refrigerate for 2 to 3 days. Bring to room temperature before serving and taste for salt and pepper.

SWEET-AND-SOUR PINEAPPLE VEGETABLE SAUCE

Spooned over a whole poached bass or grouper, this tart-and-sweet Chinese sauce laced with fresh ginger is a colorful treat.

1 tablespoon canola oil

1 medium clove garlic, finely minced (about 1 teaspoon)

1 tablespoon finely minced ginger

1 cup plus 2 tablespoons water

¾ cup rice vinegar

½ cup mild honey

¼ cup tamari or light soy sauce

¼ teaspoon black pepper

2 small white onions, peeled and cut into quarters

2 small plum tomatoes, peeled and cut into quarters

1 small green pepper, seeded and cut into ¾-inch strips

½ cup drained canned pineapple chunks

3 tablespoons cornstarch

In a medium saucepan, heat the oil over medium heat. Add the garlic and sauté for 1 minute, stirring. Add the ginger and sauté for 1 minute more. Remove from the heat. Combine 1 cup water with the vinegar, honey, tamari, and pepper and add to the saucepan. Cook, stirring constantly, over medium heat, then add the onions, tomatoes, green pepper, and pineapple and cook for 2 minutes. Mix the cornstarch with the remaining 2 tablespoons water and add it to the sauce. Cook, stirring constantly, until the mixture is thickened and the vegetables are tender but still slightly crisp.

SWEET RED PEPPER AND GARLIC COULIS

MAKES 4 TO 6 SERVINGS

A vibrantly colored, thick sauce, particularly delicious with grilled swordfish, shrimp, or crab.

3 to 4   large red peppers (about 1½ pounds)
2   large shallots, peeled
1   large garlic, peeled
1   bay leaf
1   whole clove
6   whole peppercorns

4   parsley stems
½   cup chicken stock or water
¼   cup olive oil
    Salt and pepper to taste
1   teaspoon lemon juice

Char the peppers over an open flame or under a broiler. Let them steam in a closed paper bag for 10 minutes. Scrape off the charred skin, then cut them in half and remove the seeds and whitish inner veins. Cut the peppers into 2-inch pieces. Combine the peppers, shallots, and garlic in a medium saucepan. Tie the bay leaf, clove, peppercorns, and parsley stems in a piece of cheesecloth and add it to the pot along with the chicken stock. Bring to a boil over medium heat, stirring, then lower the heat and simmer for about 15 minutes. Most of the liquid will have evaporated and the peppers will be soft.

Remove and discard the cheesecloth bag. Place the peppers, shallots, garlic, oil, salt, and pepper into the bowl of a food processor and process until smooth. Add the lemon juice and process to blend.

CHILE AND MELON RELISH WITH MINT AND BASIL

Sweet-fleshed juicy melon is combined with cooling herbs and fired with a touch of hot serrano or jalapeño chile. It's just right with pan-seared tuna or grilled swordfish.

3 cups diced honeydew melon or can-
  taloupe, or combination of both

1 small red onion, finely diced (about ½ cup)

1 small serrano or jalapeño chile, seeded and
  finely minced (about 2 teaspoons)

¼ cup coarsely chopped fresh basil

1 tablespoon coarsely chopped fresh mint

3 tablespoons lime juice

1 tablespoon canola oil

2 teaspoons finely minced lime peel
  Salt to taste

In a medium bowl, combine all the ingredients and let stand for 15 minutes before serving.

THE
FISH
RECIPES

We've divided this next section of the book into what seems to us the most logical way to meet a variety of parameters: some fish and seafood carry a profusion of names for exactly the same species, regional designations further complicate the process, and many fish easily can be substituted for others that are not available in a given area or at a particular time of year.

In the end we came up with six major categories of fish and seafood, plus a section for soups and stews and another for sauces. The categories are based upon the specific characteristics of the fish and seafood, so that you can easily substitute one fish or seafood within a category for another. Thus, we have:

❖ *Group A:* Saltwater fin fish that are mildly flavored, such as the bass and grouper family, flatfish, drums, croakers, cod, etc. Almost all of these fish also fall into the category of "lean."

❖ *Group B:* Saltwater fin fish that are more strongly flavored. Some are labeled as "fatty," such as tuna, herring, bluefish, mackerel, while some have stronger flavors but are considered "lean" or "low fat," such as shark and swordfish.

❖ *Group C:* What we call the *anadromous* and *catadromous* fish. Anadromous fish are those that spawn in fresh water and then make their way to saltwater homes (salmon, striped bass, Arctic char, for example). Catadromous fish are those that live, for the most part, in fresh water but go down to the sea to spawn (eel, for instance).

❖ *Group D:* Fresh-water fin fish such as perch, pike, carp, whitefish, and catfish.

❖ *Group E:* Shellfish are the mollusks and crustaceans: lobsters, crayfish, crabs, shrimp, oysters, scallops, and mussels.

❖ *Group F:* We have dubbed this group "The Bizarre Bazaar." It includes everything from frogs' legs to abalone, octopus, gooseneck barnacles, monkfish, and mahi-mahi. Today's "bizarre" sea creature can well become tomorrow's market favorite, given half a chance.

Finally, we have included a section of *Mixed Seafood* recipes, combining tasty combinations of fish and shellfish, as well as a section on *Soups and Stews,* including chowders and bisques.

GROUP A
Mildly Flavored Saltwater Fish

Sea Bass and Grouper Family
- Black sea bass
- Red and black grouper

Cod Family
- Atlantic and Pacific cod
- Scrod
- Dried salt cod
- Haddock
- Whiting (silver hake)
- Atlantic pollack
- Cusk

Drums and Croakers
- Red and black drum
- Croakers
- Weakfish (seatrout)
- Corvina
- White "sea bass" (corbina)

Flatfish Family
EAST COAST FLATFISH
- Winter flounder
- Summer flounder (fluke)
- Gray sole
- American plaice
- Yellowtail flounder
- Southern flounder

WEST COAST FLATFISH
- Petrale sole
- Rex sole
- Dover sole (Pacific flounder)

EAST AND WEST COAST FLATFISH
- Halibut

IMPORTED FLATFISH
- Dover sole
- Lemon sole
- Turbot

Other Mildly Flavored Saltwater Fish
- John Dory
- Lingcod
- Orange roughy
- Porgy (sheepshead)
- Red snapper
- Rockfish (ocean perch)
- Blackfish (tautog)
- Tilefish

SEA BASS AND GROUPER FAMILY

Black Sea Bass

Possibly one of the most popular dishes served in Chinese restaurants on the East Coast is steamed whole black sea bass with fermented black bean sauce and crisp, shredded vegetables. Festive, aromatic, and delicious, this firm, white, flaky, moist fish has been the centerpiece for many of our own feasts.

On the West Coast, however, distant family members of this lean, tasty fish have their own regional names—rockfish, rock bass, or rock cod, and sometimes blackfish, although the latter is not to be confused with the tautog, also called blackfish by some. For our Italian-American friends, black sea bass is also a favorite, for it closely resembles the sea bream of the Italian coast.

Black sea bass has a very distinctive shape, with iridescent black scales and sharp, pointed dorsal fins. It's generally marketed between one and three pounds, although some weigh in at five pounds during the fall months. It's usually sold whole, but the larger fish can be cut into fillets by your fishmonger.

Because this bass has a firm texture due to its diet of mollusks, crabs, and shrimp, it's a choice that some cooks claim just cannot go wrong in the kitchen. We highly recommend it steamed, poached whole, or oven braised. If it's not available, you may substitute red snapper, striped bass, or fresh-water white bass.

Red and Black Groupers

The French call them *mérou,* and they're found in warm coastal waters throughout the world. The entire family is a favorite of scientists, who call them the "chameleons of the sea," because they change color to match their surroundings. They've been known to "paint" their stripes in order to blend in with another school of fish and to turn darker near the bottom of the ocean and lighter when they approach the surface. Marine biologists are fond of them because they're friendly enough to be handled by scuba divers and swimmers. And surf fishermen love them because they take almost any bait trolled over the rocks or coral reefs. Most of all, restaurant chefs and home cooks love them because of their texture and taste. They've become quite popular these past ten years.

Although the red and black groupers are the most commonly available of the family, there are varieties that are better known in other regions. A popular Pacific Ocean grouper is called *cabrilla*, while Nassau grouper is more abundant in the Caribbean. Perhaps the champion of the family is the jewfish or giant sea bass that weighs in between 500 and 800 pounds and can grow to a length of 8 feet!

However, the red and black groupers, found from the southern Atlantic Coast down to Brazil, are much smaller than their giant cousin. Red grouper reaches about 40 pounds, while black grouper can be about twice that size. Both are marketed under 10 pounds, then cut into fillets or steaks or whole dressed. The skin is quite tough and should be removed before cooking, but grouper heads make superb fish stock and are the secret ingredient for many Caribbean fish chowders.

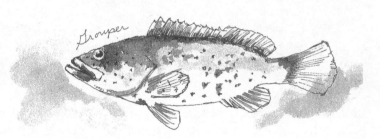

Baking and broiling tend to dry out the fish, so we suggest that they be poached, braised, or deep-fried, or used in chowders. If neither is available, you can substitute striped bass.

OVEN-BRAISED BLACK SEA BASS WITH VEGETABLES, GINGER, AND CILANTRO

MAKES 4 SERVINGS

The attractive black skin of the sea bass helps to retain moisture while it cooks, and its simple bone structure allows the flesh to be lifted off easily when it's served.

3	tablespoons canola oil		Salt and pepper to taste
2	tablespoons thinly sliced garlic (2 medium cloves)	4	sprigs cilantro plus 2 tablespoons whole leaves for garnish
2	tablespoons very thinly slivered ginger	2	small bay leaves
2½	cups halved and very thinly sliced Bermuda, Oso, or Vidalia sweet onion (about ¾ pound)	1½	cups dry white wine
		1	3-pound scaled, gutted black sea bass, with head on (substitute: red snapper or rockfish)
1½	cups fennel cut into julienne (about 6 ounces)		
1	large or 2 medium carrots, cut into julienne (about ¼ pound)	¼	pound sugar snap or snow peas, blanched

Preheat the oven to 425°. On top of the stove, heat the oil in a large oven-to-table baking pan over medium-high heat. Add the garlic and ginger and sauté, stirring, for 30 seconds. Stir in the onion, fennel, carrot, salt, and pepper. Tie the cilantro sprigs and bay leaves together and add. Sauté for 4 to 5 minutes, stirring occasionally, then add the wine and bring to a simmer. Remove the pan from the heat and lay the fish on top of the bed of vegetables. Cover with oiled aluminum foil and bake for 10 minutes.

Uncover the fish, then baste and spoon some of the vegetables over top. Bake, uncovered, basting occasionally, about 20 minutes more until the fish flakes when tested with a skewer at the thickest part. Remove and discard the herb bundle. Scatter whole cilantro leaves and blanched sugar snaps over the surface and serve at once.

BLACK SEA BASS SCALLOPS WITH YELLOW SQUASH, ZUCCHINI, TOMATOES, AND BASIL

MAKES 4 SERVINGS

Paper-thin slices of fish are quickly baked, then topped with a tangle of long strands of vegetables in an emulsified vinaigrette sauce that is based upon a greatly reduced fish fumet.

1½	cups plus 4 tablespoons Fish Stock (see page 402)	1	small yellow squash (about ¼ pound), cut into very thin long julienne
1	pound skinned black sea bass fillets (substitute: red snapper or grouper)	1	small zucchini (about ¼ pound), cut into very thin long julienne
2	teaspoons white wine vinegar	2	plum tomatoes (about ¼ pound), diced (about ½ cup)
¼	cup olive oil		Salt and pepper to taste
2	medium scallions, thinly sliced on the diagonal (about ¼ cup)	1½	tablespoons finely minced basil

In a medium saucepan over high heat, reduce 1½ cups fish stock to 3 tablespoons, about 10 minutes. Cool completely and transfer to the bowl of a food processor. The fumet will be thick and syrupy.

While the fish stock is being reduced, use a very sharp knife to cut thin scallops from the sea bass, slicing at an angle almost horizontally. There should be about 16 scallops. Place the slices between 2 sheets of waxed paper and pound them lightly until they even out. Spoon 2 tablespoons of the remaining fish stock in the bottom of a large oven-to-table baking pan, then arrange the scallops in the pan in one layer, making sure that they do not overlap. Spoon the remaining 2 tablespoons fish stock over the scallops and set aside.

Preheat the oven to 450°. Add the vinegar to the fumet in the bowl of the food processor and combine. With the motor running, slowly add the olive oil through the feed tube to make a thickish emulsion. Scrape this sauce into a medium nonstick skillet and combine with the scallions, squash, zucchini, tomatoes, and salt and pepper to taste. Stir gently to combine and cook over low heat only to warm.

While the sauce is warming, bake the fish for 4 to 5 minutes just until the fish loses its transparency. Lift the fish out with a slotted spatula to warmed serving plates. Spoon equal portions of the vegetable and sauce mixture over the fish, sprinkle each serving with basil, and serve at once.

STEAMED JAPANESE EGGPLANT AND BLACK SEA BASS WITH SCALLION AND GINGER SAUCE

Eggplant fans will love this delightful combination of fish and slim Oriental eggplants in a spicy sauce. Prepare one hour before serving.

6   small slim Japanese or Chinese eggplants, trimmed (4 to 6 ounces each)

2   pounds black sea bass fillets, scaled but with skin intact, cut into 6 equal portions (substitute: red snapper or grouper)

1   2-inch piece ginger, thinly sliced

¼   cup canola or corn oil

1   small clove garlic, finely minced (about ½ teaspoon)

2   teaspoons Oriental sesame oil

1   tablespoon rice vinegar

¼   teaspoon Oriental hot chili oil or Tabasco

2   tablespoons light soy sauce or tamari

½   teaspoon sugar

⅛   teaspoon anise seeds

    Salt and pepper to taste

1½ teaspoons sesame seeds, toasted

    Cilantro sprig for garnish

Place the eggplants and fish on an oiled steaming rack in a steamer. Put 2 inches water in the bottom of the steamer and bring to a boil. Cover tightly and steam both the fish and the eggplants for 5 to 8 minutes until the fish is just cooked through.

Place all the remaining ingredients except the sesame seeds and cilantro in a blender and blend well. Arrange the fish and eggplants attractively on a platter. Spoon the sauce over all and let stand for 1 hour at room temperature. Sprinkle with sesame seeds before serving, then garnish with cilantro. Serve at room temperature.

BAKED GROUPER WITH JULIENNED VEGETABLES AND SPICED TOMATO PURÉE

Firm-textured grouper is quickly sautéed, then transferred to the oven to bake with a tangy tomato purée and long strands of colorful julienned vegetables.

5 tablespoons olive oil	⅛ teaspoon powdered mace
1 medium red pepper, cut into thin long julienne (about ¾ cup)	¼ to ½ teaspoon hot pepper flakes
1 medium green pepper, cut into thin long julienne (about ¾ cup)	Salt and pepper to taste
2 medium carrots, cut into thin long julienne (about 1 cup)	¾ pound tomatoes, skinned, seeded, and puréed in a food processor, or a 15-ounce can tomato purée
1 large onion, coarsely chopped (about 1½ cups)	¾ cup dry white wine
¼ teaspoon whole black peppercorns	1 tablespoon red wine vinegar
½ teaspoon whole allspice	Pinch of sugar
1 large bay leaf	1½ pounds grouper fillets (substitute: parrot fish or snapper)

In a large nonreactive skillet, heat 3 tablespoons of the oil over high heat. Add the peppers and carrots and sauté, stirring constantly, for 1 minute until tender yet slightly crisp. Remove with a slotted spoon to a plate and set aside.

Add the onion to the skillet and sauté, stirring frequently, for 3 to 4 minutes until soft. Tie the peppercorns, allspice, and bay leaf in a cheesecloth bag and set aside. Stir in the mace, hot pepper flakes, salt, and pepper. Add the tomato purée and the spice bag and bring to a boil. Add the wine and continue to cook over high heat for 1 minute. Then lower the heat to medium-low and simmer the sauce for 15 minutes. Remove and discard the cheesecloth bag and stir in the vinegar and sugar. This sauce may be prepared well in advance.

When ready to proceed with the recipe, preheat the oven to 375°. Heat the remaining 2 tablespoons oil in a large skillet over high heat. Season the fish with additional salt and pepper and sauté, turning the fish once, for 2 minutes on each side. Spoon some of the tomato mixture on the bottom of a large oven-to-table baking pan and transfer the sautéed fish to the pan. Top with the remaining tomato mixture, scatter the reserved julienned vegetables on top, and bake only until the fish is cooked through, 7 to 8 minutes. Serve directly from the pan.

GROUPER WITH STIR-FRIED SHIITAKE MUSHROOMS AND SCALLIONS

A simple and quick stir-fry dish that would be lovely with a mixture of crispy, steamed vegetables and rice to make a complete meal.

2 pounds grouper fillets, cut into 2- by 1-inch pieces (substitute: red snapper or wolffish)	¼ cup canola or corn oil
½ cup cornstarch	1 tablespoon finely minced ginger
2 egg whites	1 cup thinly sliced shiitake mushrooms (about ⅓ pound)
¼ teaspoon black pepper	1 cup diagonally sliced scallions (½-inch pieces) (about 4 to 5 scallions)
⅛ teaspoon cayenne pepper	2 tablespoons tamari or light soy sauce
Salt to taste	1 tablespoon dry sherry

Dry the fish on paper towels. Put the cornstarch in a plastic bag, add the fish, and toss to coat the pieces evenly. Whisk the egg whites lightly until foamy, add the black pepper, cayenne, and salt, and set aside.

Heat the oil in a wok until very hot but not smoking. Dip the cornstarch-coated fish into the egg white mixture and fry, a few pieces at a time, until golden, turning with tongs for even frying. Remove the fish, drain on paper towels, place them in a serving dish, and keep warm in a low oven. Repeat with the remaining fish.

In the same wok, stir-fry the ginger, mushrooms, and scallions for about 1 minute. Add the soy and sherry, heat, then pour this mixture over the fish. Serve at once.

COD FAMILY

Atlantic and Pacific Cod

Atlantic Cod

Today, after years of disparagement, the cod is doing swimmingly. Le Bernardin, New York's most acclaimed seafood restaurant, now features cod in as many as three different entrées, including cod fillet served over *escalibada,* made with gently braised eggplant, zucchini, onions, and red bell peppers. This is certainly a far cry from the cod and mashed potatoes of our own school day lunches! Le Cirque, La Colombe d'Or, and Montrachet in New York also have rediscovered this great and versatile fish, as have restaurants like Jasper's in Boston, Z's in Cleveland, and a range of mid-priced restaurants all across the country.

For the home cook, cod has grown in popularity not only because it has a mild taste and a firm, flaky texture and is adaptable to every method of cooking except grilling, but also because it is still, to this day, an economical substitute for more expensive white-fleshed fish such as red snapper. And it is available year round.

Cod is certainly the most widely consumed fin fish in the United States. The North Atlantic Seafood Association reports that an average of 400 million pounds of cod are eaten every year. Atlantic cod can be found in the waters from Virginia to the Arctic but are most abundant off the coast of Newfoundland.

For many years, dating back to 1623, Gloucester was the principal port in Massachusetts from which the fishermen went to sea in their fragile wooden boats. Throughout New England, the "widow's walk" became a fixture of every house that faced the sea, where the wives could pace until the return of the fishing fleets or mourn their loss at sea.

Atlantic cod is so much a part of New England that a huge carving of the "Sacred Cod" has hung in the Massachusetts Hall of Representatives since 1784. Throughout the history of Colonial America, the cod appeared on coins, stamps, legal documents, corporate seals, and weather vanes.

Pacific cod is the Western relative of its Atlantic cousin. Known as "true cod" to distinguish it from rock cod, black cod, and lingcod (which are not in the cod family), it's found in the colder waters of the Pacific Ocean from northern California to Alaska. As with Atlantic cod, the Pacific cod fishing industry is the oldest one on the Pacific coast, dating back to the 1880s when the fishing fleets ranged as far as Siberia in their three-masted schooners. Pacific cod are fished year round, and their flavor is quite like the Atlantic cod—mild with a white meat that flakes apart when cooked.

Although fishermen's tales speak of a 211-pound , 6-foot-long cod caught off Massachusetts in 1895, the average catch today reaches about 2 to 3 feet in length and is marketed between 2½ and 10 pounds. If, for some reason, cod is not available at your fishmonger, hake and haddock make perfect substitutes.

Fresh cod roe is a delicacy that is quite popular in Europe; when salted, it sometimes replaces scarce mullet roe in Greece for *taramosalata,* an hors d'oeuvre spread. For the more adventurous, cod tongues and cheeks are also considered delicacies in some places, while cod liver oil, the scourge of children back in our early days, is still favored in Scandinavian countries.

Scrod

There is a story, possibly apocryphal, that the manager of the famous old Boston restaurant the Parker House used to feature the freshest fish as the special of the day. Never knowing just which fish that would be, he invented the word "scrod" to cover any and all possibilities.

Actually, however, scrod (or schrod) is just the name for smaller cod, usually those under 3 pounds, and frequently covers "baby" haddock or pollack as well. Scrod is usually marketed as fillets and has a sweeter flavor than adult cod. Keeping the skin on the fillets helps keep the delicate meat intact during cooking.

Dried Salt Cod

Drying (or curing) salted cod preserved the catch before such modern conveniences as the refrigerator and the home freezer were invented. Because dried cod can keep for months without refrigeration, it was perfect for the long voyages that took the schooners away from their home ports for extended periods of time.

Split, salted, and then dried, it was one of the first export items sent to Europe from the American colonies. It is still popular in developing countries, although no salted cod is produced in the United States today. Most of the processing takes place in Scandinavia, Iceland, Canada, and parts of the Mediterranean. We've come across it as *bacalhau* in Portugal, *bacalao* in Spain and the West Indies, *baccala* in Italy, and *morue* in France.

Before using dried salt cod, it must be reconstituted by soaking it in several changes of cold water for 12 to 24 hours, and then gently poaching it for 20 minutes, depending upon the amount of salt and the thickness of the cut.

Haddock

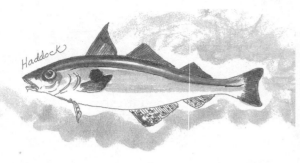

A close relative of cod, haddock looks very much the same except for the black lateral stripe on its body and a black shoulder blotch that fishermen have dubbed the "devil's thumb print" or "St. Peter's mark." Haddock is also smaller than cod, averaging from 2 to 6 pounds when caught. Its habitat is the North Atlantic coast off Newfoundland and Nova Scotia and south to Maine and the Georges Banks, about 200 miles offshore Boston.

Its white, lean flesh is more flavorful and finer in texture than that of cod. Generally it's marketed as fillets. These poach well and can be stuffed or baked or steamed. If haddock is not available, try substituting cod or hake.

Smoked haddock is the basic ingredient for the famous Scottish dish finnan haddie, which gets its name from Finon in Scotland where it was developed more than 100 years ago and "haddie," merely the Scottish term for haddock. Although haddock is, by nature, quite white, the fish is dyed before smoking to give it the characteristic finnan haddie tawny amber color.

Whiting (Silver Hake)

Whiting were generally discarded as another "junk fish" until the 1920s when it finally developed a market in the fried-fish shops that proliferated around St. Louis. However, because its flesh is much softer than that of cod and must be frozen quickly to maintain its texture, it was not until the development of modern freezing methods that the species became an important commercial resource.

Although there are about a dozen species of whiting, the most popular is Atlantic or American whiting (silver hake), which abounds in the coastal waters of the Northeast. Whiting has a delicate, almost bland flavor and requires careful handling, since the lean, flaky flesh is quite fragile and becomes more fragile if not cooked soon after purchase. Because whiting is a thin fish about 1 pound in weight, we recommend purchasing one fish per person.

Popular throughout the world and usually larger than their eastern cousins, the hake family generally are sold as fillets or steaks. Pacific hake is harvested from the Gulf of Alaska to the Gulf of California, while European hake is quite familiar as *merluza* to those who have traveled to Spain.

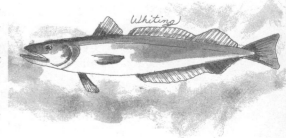

Whiting can be baked, poached, pan-fried, or deep-fried.

Atlantic Pollack

Looking somewhat like a green codfish (making us wonder why it sometimes is called Boston bluefish), pollack is found in the rocky coastal waters from Nova Scotia to Virginia.

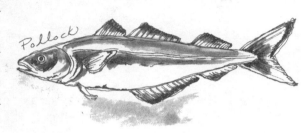

Its flesh is a rosy gray that turns lighter when it's cooked; it generally ranges between 4 and 8 pounds in weight. Pollack is yet another species that remained unappreciated for many years. When the supply of haddock became dangerously depleted, pollack was given its chance at fame. It is now extremely popular, partly because of its excellent taste and texture but certainly because it is much cheaper than both cod and haddock. It can be prepared in exactly the same ways as its two cousins.

A WORD ABOUT SURIMI
(Alaska or Walleye Pollack)

Alaska pollack or walleye pollack is, as its name suggests, harvested in the Gulf of Alaska and the Bering Sea. Sonar-equipped fishing boats report that the schools are so vast and deep that they register on their screens as the size of a downtown office building! The major use for Alaska pollack is for the manufacture of surimi: flash-frozen pollack is minced and formed into a gelatinous, tasteless paste; blended with egg white, salt, sugar, starch, artificial flavor, and sometimes MSG; then forced through an extruder into shapes of shrimp, crabmeat, lobster, and scallops, which are then cooked.

It has been called "pseudo-shrimp" and "quasi-crab," "bogus seafood" and "seafood analogs." By whatever name, the end product is both over-salted and overprocessed. Although United States law requires that all surimi products be labeled "imitation," surimi is frequently passed off as the real thing. Surimi surreptitiously replaces crab in seafood salads, and Japanese restaurants often use it in sushi rolls.

The one advantage of surimi is that it is a good substitute for people allergic to shellfish. But some blends now contain a bit of real crab or shrimp, so it pays to check your source or to read the labels carefully. This caution also applies to those who react badly to MSG, a product that most good Chinese restaurants have done away with but which still is added to surimi as well as other processed products as a flavor enhancer.

Cusk

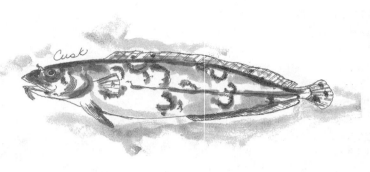

This member of the cod family is little known outside of New England, because it is generally caught off the coast of Maine and consumed right in its own home territory. Because the white flesh has a chewy texture that is quite similar to monkfish, cusk is excellent for chowders and stews. Sold mostly as skinless fillets, it should be cut into 1-inch-thick slices before cooking. If it's not available in your area, you may substitute cod, monkfish, or tilefish in the recipes.

POACHED COD STEAKS WITH MUSTARD AND PARSLEY SAUCE

The poaching liquid helps keep the fish moist and delicate, and the buttery mustard-laced sauce adds just the right touch to the lean, flaky cod.

3 cups water	2 to 3 large shallots, finely minced (about 3 tablespoons)
1 cup milk	2 tablespoons red wine vinegar
10 sprigs parsley, tied together	1 tablespoon cold water
1 large bay leaf	6 tablespoons butter, cold, cut into 6 pieces
1 whole clove	2 tablespoons coarse-grain mustard
10 whole black peppercorns	¼ cup finely minced parsley
Salt to taste	Pepper to taste
4 cod steaks, cut 1 inch thick, about ½ pound each (substitute: haddock)	

In a large, heavy shallow casserole, bring the water, milk, parsley bouquet, bay leaf, clove, peppercorns, and salt, to a boil over medium-high heat; lower the heat and simmer for 5 minutes. Add the cod steaks and simmer for 4 to 5 minutes. Carefully turn the fish over and turn off the heat. Allow the fish to remain in the broth while preparing the sauce.

In a small saucepan, cook the shallots and vinegar over medium-high heat until the vinegar has evaporated. Add the cold water and remove the saucepan from the heat. Using a whisk, add the butter one piece at a time, beating hard after each addition. After 3 or 4 tablespoons of the butter have been added, place the pan on a flame tamer over very low heat, then continue to add and whisk in the remaining butter. The resulting sauce should be smooth, hot, creamy, and slightly thick. Do not allow it to boil or it will curdle. Whisk in the mustard and parsley and add salt and pepper to taste.

Transfer the fish steaks with a slotted spatula to a heated serving platter (see Note). Spoon some of the sauce over the fish. Boiled small red potatoes in their jackets would be a perfect accompaniment.

NOTE: The poaching liquid can be strained and frozen to poach fish another time or as the base for a fish velouté (see page 85).

OLD-FASHIONED CODFISH CAKES
WITH TARTAR SAUCE

MAKES 18 TO 20

These feather-light, tasty fish cakes seem to be everybody's favorite. Prepare them, along with the tartar sauce, the day before serving, and fry them at the last minute before serving as a first course or as a main dish along with some crunchy coleslaw.

Tartar Sauce (see page 74)

2 pounds skinned cod fillets, cut into 2-inch chunks (substitute: haddock or scrod)

Salt and pepper to taste

1¾ pounds russet or other baking potatoes, peeled and cut into 1½-inch chunks

2 tablespoons butter, softened

¼ teaspoon ground ginger

⅛ teaspoon cayenne pepper

2 teaspoons dry English mustard

¼ teaspoon white pepper

½ teaspoon white Worcestershire sauce

3 large scallions, both white and green parts, finely minced (about ¾ cup)

¼ cup finely minced parsley

2 eggs, lightly beaten

½ cup fine dry bread crumbs

¼ cup all-purpose flour

Corn oil for frying

Prepare the tartar sauce and refrigerate until ready to serve. Season the fish with salt and pepper and place in a vegetable steamer in a wide skillet over boiling water. Cover tightly and steam for 7 minutes. Lift out the steamer rack and set aside to allow the fish to cool.

In a medium saucepan, cook the potatoes in boiling salted water until tender, 12 to 15 minutes. Drain the potatoes and return them to the saucepan, then add the butter. Mash the potatoes with a potato masher (do not use a food processor or the potatoes will be gummy). Transfer the potatoes to a large bowl. There should be about 4 cups. Mix the ginger, cayenne, mustard, white pepper, and salt to taste and sprinkle over the potatoes. Beat with a wooden spoon to incorporate. Add the Worcestershire, scallions, parsley, and eggs and beat again to combine.

Break the fish up into smaller pieces with your fingers and fold into the potato mixture. Cover the bowl with plastic wrap and chill for at least 1 hour or overnight. Form the fish cakes into thick ovals, using about 2 heaping tablespoons for each cake, and place them on a piece of waxed paper.

Mix the bread crumbs and flour together on another piece of paper and coat the fish cakes in the crumb mixture. Heat about ½ inch oil in a large nonstick skillet over medium-high heat until hot. Add as many cakes as will fit and fry for about 3 minutes on each side until golden. Drain the cakes on paper towels, then keep them warm in the oven. You will have to fry them in 2 to 3 batches. Serve with tartar sauce.

FOIL-BAKED SCROD WITH GREEN PEPPERCORN BEURRE BLANC

The mild sting of crushed green peppercorns in a creamy textured, buttery sauce enhances the flaky delicacy of the scrod.

1½ to 2	pounds thick scrod fillets, pin bones removed (substitute: tilefish, salmon, or wolffish)	3	tablespoons dry white wine
¼	cup finely minced scallions	3	tablespoons Fish Stock (see page 402)
	Salt and pepper to taste	4	tablespoons butter, cold, cut into 4 pieces
2	teaspoons butter, softened	2	teaspoons water-packed green peppercorns, drained, rinsed, and crushed

Preheat the oven to 400°. Place the fish on a large piece of heavy-weight aluminum foil. Sprinkle with the scallions, salt, and pepper and spread the soft butter over the surface. Fold the foil to enclose the fish tightly, place in a large baking pan, and bake for 20 minutes.

Open the foil carefully and test the fish to see that it is cooked through. If not, return it to the oven and watch carefully so that it doesn't overcook.

Lift the fish out with a wide spatula to a warm serving dish and cover with fresh foil to keep it warm. Pour any accumulated fish juices in the baking foil into a medium saucepan. Add the wine and fish stock and boil rapidly until the liquid is reduced to 2 tablespoons. Remove the saucepan from the heat and quickly add the first piece of cold butter, beating well with a wire whisk. Add the second piece of butter and return the saucepan to low heat. Do not let the butter melt too quickly but whisk it in so that the sauce is creamy. Whisk in the remaining butter, piece by piece, to keep the sauce creamy. Finally stir in the crushed green peppercorns. Cut the fish into equal portions when serving and spoon some of the sauce over each portion.

SCROD AND CLAMS IN PARSLEY SAUCE

MAKES 6 SERVINGS

Meaty, flaky, delicate, tender scrod is paired with briny clams in a heavenly sauce of verdant parsley and garlic.

½ cup olive oil

1½ tablespoons finely minced garlic (3 to 4 cloves)

3 tablespoons all-purpose flour

2 cups coarsely chopped parsley (3 cups loosely packed leaves)

3 pounds scrod fillets, cut into 6 portions, pin bones removed (substitute: cod or haddock)

36 littleneck or Manila clams, scrubbed well

1½ cups Fish Stock (see page 402)

⅓ cup dry white wine

¼ teaspoon hot pepper flakes

Salt and pepper, if needed

In a large heavy skillet, heat the oil over medium-high heat. Add the garlic and sauté for 30 seconds, stirring constantly. While still stirring, sift the flour over the garlic and oil and stir in 1 cup of the parsley. Continue to stir and cook for 2 minutes. Arrange the fish in the skillet in one layer. Tuck in the clams, hinge side down, and add the fish stock, wine, and hot pepper flakes over all. Bring to a simmer over medium heat, then cover tightly and cook for 3 minutes.

Using 2 slotted spatulas, turn the fish over, then cover again and cook for 2 minutes more. Carefully remove only the fish to a large, deep serving dish; cover and keep warm.

Add the remaining 1 cup parsley to the clams, cover the skillet, and raise the heat to high. Cook 1 or 2 minutes more until the clams open, sliding the pan back and forth a few times. Add salt and pepper if needed. Spoon the clams and the sauce over the fish. Serve with crusty bread for dipping up the sauce or with orzo or small pasta shells.

scrod & clams in parsley sauce

BAKED HADDOCK WITH GARLIC, RED PEPPER, PEAS, AND SAFFRON

This delicately flavored white-fleshed fish is enhanced by a vibrantly colored red pepper sauce and sweet, tiny green peas. The garlic is gentled by first sautéing, then baking, as it mingles with the sauce.

¼ teaspoon saffron threads	Salt to taste
2 tablespoons boiling water	2 tablespoons dry sherry
4 tablespoons olive oil	1½ pounds haddock fillets (substitute: cod or scrod)
2 medium red peppers (about ½ pound), seeded and cut into ½-inch strips, then cut diagonally to form diamond shapes (about 1 cup)	1 teaspoon dried thyme
	Black pepper to taste
4 to 5 large cloves garlic, cut crosswise into slices (about 1½ tablespoons)	½ cup frozen petit peas, cooked for 2 minutes
⅛ teaspoon cayenne pepper	1 tablespoon finely minced parsley

In a small cup, combine the saffron and boiling water and set aside to steep for 10 minutes. Preheat the oven to 400°.

In a medium skillet, heat 2 tablespoons of the oil over medium-high heat. Add the peppers and sauté for 2 minutes. Stir in the garlic and sauté, stirring frequently, for 1 to 2 minutes more. Add the cayenne and the salt.

Add the saffron and sherry and bring to a boil. Lower the heat and cook for 30 seconds. Spread this mixture on the bottom of a shallow oven-to-table casserole, large enough to hold the fish in one layer. Add the fish and turn to coat both sides. Drizzle the remaining 2 tablespoons oil, the thyme, and salt to taste over the fillets. Cover with aluminum foil and bake for 12 to 15 minutes until the fish flakes when tested with a skewer.

Tilting the pan, baste the fish with the pan juices and spoon some of the peppers over the top as well. Scatter the peas among the peppers and sprinkle with parsley. Serve with hot cooked rice if you wish.

MILK-POACHED HADDOCK WITH SWEET PICKLE BEURRE BLANC

MAKES 6 SERVINGS

Meaty, large-flaked haddock is delicately poached and then napped with a buttery sauce that has the tingle of sweet pickle relish.

Aromatic Milk Broth (see pagee 38)

2½ pounds haddock fillets (substitute: scrod or cod)

3 large shallots, finely minced (about 3 tablespoons)

⅓ cup dry white wine

8 tablespoons butter, cold, cut into 8 pieces

¼ cup India pickle relish, preferably B&G brand, drained, with 2 teaspoons relish liquid

⅛ teaspoon Tabasco

⅛ teaspoon black pepper

Salt, if needed

*S*train the milk broth into a 12-inch sauté pan or fish poacher, bring it to a boil, add the fish, and cover. Lower the heat to low and poach for 10 to 12 minutes. Test with a skewer at the thickest part after 10 minutes.

While the fish is poaching, bring the shallots and wine to a boil in a nonreactive saucepan over medium-high heat. Lower the heat to medium and reduce to 1 tablespoon of liquid. Off the heat, whisk in the cold butter, 1 tablespoon at a time, returning the pan to very low heat after 2 or 3 tablespoons of the butter have been incorporated. Continue to add the remaining butter until 1 piece is left, then whisk in the relish and liquid, Tabasco, pepper, and salt. Add and incorporate the remaining piece of butter. The sauce should be creamy in consistency and warm, not hot.

When the fish is poached, carefully lift it out with two slotted spatulas to a warm serving platter. Blot up any excess liquid with paper towels. Spoon the sauce over the fish and serve, dividing it into portions at the table.

BAKED WHITING WITH POTATOES, TOMATOES, OREGANO, AND FETA CHEESE

MAKES 4 SERVINGS

Brightened with sprightly bursts of lemon, this baked whiting and potato dish has a decidedly Greek accent that it receives from a touch of oregano and a bit of briny feta cheese.

3 tablespoons olive oil

2 1½-pound whitings, butterflied, boned, and heads removed (substitute: trout)

Salt and pepper to taste

2 medium baking potatoes (about 1 pound), scrubbed and sliced paper thin

2 medium sweet white onions (about ½ pound), thinly sliced and separated into rings

2 large tomatoes (about 1 pound), peeled and cut into eighths

1 clove garlic, finely minced (about 1 teaspoon)

1½ teaspoons dried oregano, preferably Greek

1 small lemon, peel and white pith removed, pitted, thinly sliced, and cut into tiny pieces

¼ cup coarsely minced parsley

¼ pound feta cheese

Preheat the oven to 350°. Oil a large oven-to-table baking pan with 1 tablespoon of the oil. Season the fish with salt and pepper and fold them over into their original shape. Place them in the center of the pan and set aside.

In a saucepan, parboil the potato slices in water to cover for 3 to 4 minutes. Lift them out with a slotted spoon and arrange them in overlapping slices around the fish. Trickle 1 tablespoon of the olive oil over the potatoes and sprinkle liberally with salt and pepper.

In a bowl, place the remaining 1 tablespoon oil, add the onions and tomatoes, and toss gently to coat with the oil. Scatter the tomatoes and onions over the fish and potatoes. Sprinkle the garlic, oregano, and lemon over the top, then sprinkle the parsley over all.

Bake for 30 minutes, tilting the pan and basting with the pan juices occasionally. Test the fish and potatoes with a skewer for tenderness. Scatter the feta cheese on top and return to the oven for 1 minute to heat the cheese. Divide the fish into 4 portions, along with the potatoes, tomatoes, and onions at the table.

FRICASSEE OF POLLACK WITH CAPERS, TOMATOES, AND OIL-CURED OLIVES

Firm, flaky poached pollack is tossed with capers, tomatoes, onions, and oil-cured olives and served at room temperature. This dish is perfect to pique a waning summer appetite.

1½	pounds skinned pollack fillet (substitute: cod or cusk)	4 to 5	large plum tomatoes, diced (about 1½ cups)
	Salt to taste	2	anchovies, rinsed and cut into small pieces (optional)
3	sprigs thyme	3	teaspoons coarsely chopped parsley
4 or 5	whole black peppercorns		Black pepper to taste (optional)
1	lemon wedge	1	tablespoon large capers, rinsed
3	tablespoons olive oil	9	oil-cured black olives, pitted
2	large onions, coarsely chopped (about 1½ cups)		
2 to 3	medium cloves garlic, finely minced (about 2 teaspoons)		

Sprinkle the fish with salt to taste and set aside. To a medium skillet, add water up to 1 inch from the top of the pan. Add the thyme and peppercorns, then squeeze the lemon and drop in the wedge as well. Bring to a boil, add the fish, and cover the pan. Lower the heat and simmer gently for about 8 minutes. Test for doneness at the thickest part. Remove the fillet with a slotted spatula to a plate, cover with aluminum foil, and set aside. Discard the poaching water.

Wipe out the skillet, add the oil, and heat over high heat. Add the onions and sauté, stirring frequently, until wilted. Stir in the garlic and sauté for 1 minute, then add the tomatoes, anchovies, 1 teaspoon of the parsley, and pepper if you wish. Lower the heat and cover the pan. Simmer for 5 minutes. Stir in the capers and olives and simmer for 1 minute more.

Break the fish into 1-inch chunks and gently combine with the sauce. Transfer to a serving dish and sprinkle with the remaining 2 teaspoons parsley. Serve hot or at room temperature.

MUSTARD-MARINATED FRIED CUSK WITH DILL

Cusk is another delicious member of the cod family, similar in appearance to hake but with a firmer texture. Because the cusk puts up a fight when caught, it is a favorite with sports fisherpeople, and we have treated it here as they prefer to cook their catch.

2   tablespoons lemon juice

2   tablespoons dry English mustard (e.g., Coleman's)

2   pounds cusk fillets, 1 inch thick, cut into pieces 2 to 3 inches long (substitute: Atlantic pollack)

Salt and pepper to taste

2   eggs

2   tablespoons cold water

¾   cup stone-ground cornmeal

Corn oil for frying

2   lemons, cut into wedges, for serving

1   tablespoon finely minced fresh dill

In a small bowl, mix the lemon juice and mustard together and let stand for 10 minutes to develop flavor. Place the fish on a piece of aluminum foil and season with salt and pepper. Spread the mustard mixture on the fish fillets and let marinate at room temperature for 30 minutes.

In a tempered glass pie pan or shallow bowl (do not use a metal pan or bowl), lightly whisk the eggs and water together. Spread the cornmeal on a piece of aluminum foil. Heat 2 to 3 inches oil in a deep cast-iron skillet to 375°. When the oil is hot, dip the fish first in the egg and then the cornmeal and fry in the hot oil, doing a few pieces at a time without crowding the pan.

Drain on paper towels and keep warm on a serving platter placed in a low oven while frying the remaining fish. Dip the lemon wedges in minced dill and serve with the fish.

DRUMS AND CROAKERS

Red Drum and Black Drum

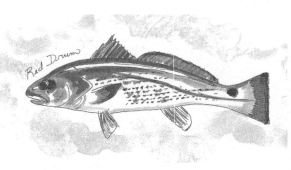

This entire family of fin fish gets its name from the fact that they have a drumming muscle that contracts against an air bladder to make a distinctive sound that can actually be heard on shore on a quiet night. Some have called it the noisiest fish in the sea. The smaller relatives of the drum make a croaking sound, and thus are called croakers.

Red drum, the most popular fish in the family, was the innocent victim of a fad for a Cajun dish called "blackened redfish" that spread across the country in the eighties, decimating the fish until its harvest was limited to sports fishermen throughout the Southern Atlantic and Gulf states. It has disappeared almost completely. The good news is that Americans quickly move to other fads, and the red drum has begun to make a comeback, gently assisted by intensive aquaculture.

Of the two major members of the family, red drum (also known as red sea bass and channel bass) is the more flavorful, with a moist, lean white meat and a heavy flake. It can be baked whole or prepared as fillets, then broiled, baked, poached, or fried. And, because it has a firm flesh, it works well on the barbecue grill. Its weight ranges between 3 and 10 pounds.

The black drum has a coarser flesh and is not quite as flavorful as the red drum, although during the "redfish drought" of some years ago, it was not uncommon to find black sold as red drum fillets, since it is difficult to tell the difference when the fish is not whole. Black drum can be prepared in the same way as its cousin, but because of its coarser flesh, it's generally preferred for fish chowders, especially in the South.

There is one family relative called freshwater drum that is found in the lakes and rivers from the Hudson Bay down to the Gulf of Mexico and into Central America. Sometimes sold as sheepshead or gaspergou, it has a lean white meat that is quite coarse and thus is not too popular.

Croakers

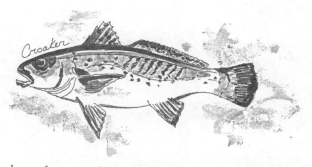

We first heard the distinctive sounds of this unusual fish when we were filming near Padre National Park in Texas and a fisherman and his young son had landed about ten croakers. Sometimes called golden croaker because it takes on a rich golden color on the upper half of the body during spawning season, it's also called hardhead because of its broad, smooth forehead. The croaker is a fairly small fish, usually sold whole dressed at 1 to 1½ pounds. The flesh is moist, firm, and moderately lean.

Weakfish (Seatrout)

As any fisherperson knows, weakfish gets its name from its very fragile mouth structure; too much pressure on the hook will cause it to break free, giving rise to still more tales of "the one that got away." A hooked, fighting weakfish is always brought in very gently and the net lowered very carefully to finally win the battle. We think they are one of the most exciting of gamefish.

On our island, the slim, iridescent fish comes into the bay about the middle of spring, with an average size of 5 to 6 pounds but occasionally topping the scale at 8 to 10 pounds. In the commercial marketplace, weakfish is usually sold at weights of 2 to 5 pounds.

For those of us who also take pride in eating our catch, the weakfish proves to be the exception to the rule that a freshly caught fish is far better than one that has been frozen. Because the flesh of the weakfish is slightly soft and watery, we have found that it's best to freeze the fish overnight to firm it up. The next day, thawed and prepared, it's quite perfect for cooking whole or stuffed or as a fillet: sautéed, broiled, baked, steamed, or pan-fried. If you need to turn the fillet in cooking, do it carefully, since it has a tendency to break easily.

In the southern Atlantic, the relative of our northern weakfish is the spotted seatrout (or speckled trout). Just as the lingcod is not a cod, the seatrout is not a trout but a member of the drum and croaker family. It's available most of the year in Louisiana and around the Gulf of Mexico.

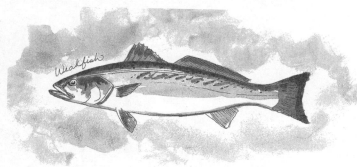

Corvina

Through many trips to Latin America, we made note of a fish, called corvina, that tasted just marvelous and seemed to be ubiquitous through most of the area. We discovered about twenty years ago that it was actually a relative of the drum and croaker family and an excellent substitute for striped bass. However, it is not to be confused with the West Coast sports fish called *corbina* (see below), yet another example of fish nomenclature that can drive a fish lover to distraction.

White "Sea Bass" (Corbina)

Not a true bass, corbina is also a member of the drum and croaker family that hails from the southern California coast down as far as Mexico and Chile. It's a large fish and a favorite with West Coast sports fisherpeople. Although it can weigh in at as much as 80 pounds, market size generally ranges from 10 to 15 pounds.

The larger fish can be cut into steaks or thick fillets, and the smaller fish can be poached or baked whole. Its lean, white meat is comparable to that of striped bass or grouper, excellent substitutes if corbina is not available.

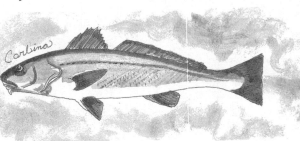

NOTE: No member of the drum and croaker family should be eaten raw. The species is prone to parasitic infection but is quite harmless if the fish is cooked. It should never be used for seviche, sushi, or sashimi.

STEAMED RED DRUM WITH FRESH TOMATO, GINGER, THYME, AND VINAIGRETTE

An intensely flavored fresh ginger and herb vinaigrette perks up a delicately steamed fish.

3	tablespoons rice vinegar
1	tablespoon Dijon mustard
⅓	cup olive oil
1	tablespoon light soy sauce
2 to 3	drops Tabasco
2	tablespoons finely minced ginger
1	thin scallion, finely sliced (2 tablespoons)
1	tablespoon minced parsley

1	tablespoon fresh thyme leaves or 1 teaspoon dried thyme
2 to 3	plum tomatoes, peeled and diced (about ¾ cup)
	Salt and pepper to taste
1½	pounds red drum fillets, cut into 4 pieces about 6 ounces each (substitute: blackfish, tilefish, or weakfish)
4	sprigs fresh thyme

In a small mixing bowl, whisk the vinegar and mustard together, then slowly add the olive oil, whisking vigorously. Whisk in the soy sauce, Tabasco, and ginger. Stir in the scallion, parsley, thyme, tomatoes, salt, and pepper and set aside.

Bring 2 inches water in any sort of steamer to a boil and place the fish on the steaming rack. Season with salt and pepper to taste and place a sprig of thyme on each fillet. Tightly cover the steamer and steam for 4 to 5 minutes. Test with a skewer so the fish doesn't overcook. Remove and discard the thyme sprigs and transfer the fish to a warm serving platter. Spoon the sauce over the fish and serve.

SAUTÉED ATLANTIC CROAKER WITH CAYENNE, PECANS, AND LEMON

MAKES 4 SERVINGS

Cayenne-spiked pecans are very popular as a cocktail nibble in the South and are just as good when spooned over simply sautéed fish.

¼ cup fine dried bread crumbs

¼ cup all-purpose flour

Salt and black pepper to taste

4 pan-dressed croakers, about ¾ pound each (substitute: catfish fillets or pan-dressed catfish)

4 tablespoons butter, softened

2 tablespoons olive oil

½ cup coarsely broken pecans

¼ teaspoon cayenne (or less if you prefer less heat)

¼ cup lemon juice (about 2 lemons)

1 tablespoon finely minced parsley

Combine the bread crumbs, flour, salt, and pepper on a piece of waxed paper and roll the fish in the mixture. Heat 3 tablespoons of the butter and the oil in a large heavy skillet over medium-high heat until hot. Add the fish and sauté until golden brown, turning carefully after 5 minutes and testing after 3 to 5 minutes more with a skewer. When the fish just flakes, remove to a warm serving platter.

Wipe out the skillet with paper towels, return to the stove, and melt the remaining 1 tablespoon butter in it. Stir in the pecans, cayenne, and salt and pepper to taste and toast the pecans over medium heat, shaking the pan frequently so they don't burn.

Spoon the pecans over the fish and pour the lemon juice over all. Sprinkle with parsley and serve.

BAKED WEAKFISH FILLETS WITH A GROUND HAZELNUT CRUST

MAKES 4 SERVINGS

A thick, nutty, crunchy golden crust tops delicate weakfish that has been marinated in spiked lemon sauce to enhance its flavor.

1½ pounds weakfish fillets, cut into 4 equal portions (substitute: striped bass, pollack, or catfish)

¼ cup lemon juice (2 to 3 lemons)

1 tablespoon white wine Worcestershire sauce

2 or 3 drops Tabasco

Salt and pepper to taste

1 tablespoon olive oil

4 tablespoons melted butter

½ cup ground toasted hazelnuts

1 tablespoon all-purpose flour

1 tablespoon minced parsley

Place the fish in one layer in a nonreactive dish. Mix the lemon juice, Worcestershire, Tabasco, salt, and pepper and pour over the fish. Marinate the fish for 30 minutes at room temperature, turning once.

Preheat the oven to 450°. Brush a shallow oven-to-table baking pan with the oil. Lift the fish out of the marinade and place it in the pan.

In a small skillet, place the butter, nuts, and flour; cook, stirring constantly, over medium heat for only 1 minute so that it doesn't burn. Spread this mixture over the fish with a spatula. Bake in the upper part of the oven for 10 to 15 minutes. Test with a skewer to see if the fish flakes. Sprinkle with parsley just before serving.

BROILED WEAKFISH WITH SAFFRON BUTTER, BAY LEAVES, PEARL ONIONS, AND PIMIENTO-STUFFED OLIVES

MAKES 6 SERVINGS

A sunny and colorful presentation inspired by the flavors of Spain. It would be delicious served with black beans and white rice.

12	tiny pearl onions	2½	pounds weakfish fillets, cut into 6 portions (substitute: striped bass)
¼	teaspoon saffron threads, crushed		Salt and pepper to taste
2	teaspoons boiling water		
1	tablespoon lemon juice	2	tablespoons sliced pimiento-stuffed Spanish olives
6	tablespoons butter, softened		
6	small bay leaves		Lemon wedges for garnish

Parboil the onions in water to cover in a small saucepan for 5 minutes. Let cool and slip off the skins. In a small cup steep the saffron in the boiling water for 5 minutes, then stir in the lemon juice and set it aside.

Put the butter in the bowl of a food processor and process until light and fluffy. Add the saffron mixture a few drops at a time and process until incorporated.

Preheat the broiler. Choose a baking pan large enough to accommodate the fish in one layer and line it with aluminum foil. Spread some of the saffron butter on the foil, then arrange the bay leaves on the butter and place the fish over them. Spread the remaining saffron butter over the fish, scatter the pearl onions around, add salt and pepper to taste, then sprinkle the olives over the surface. Broil 2 to 3 inches from the heat until the fish turns opaque and the top has browned. Baste frequently and test with a skewer after 6 to 8 minutes. Carefully transfer the fish to a warm serving platter with a spatula. Discard the bay leaves and spoon any sauce and onions in the pan over all. Garnish with lemon wedges.

FLATFISH FAMILY

We came across an old, crumbled, yellowed newspaper clipping in our files the other day that succinctly answered the major question always asked about the flatfish family. The anonymous writer had queried: "When I buy sole from my local fish market, it seems to me that the fillets are almost always a bit different in size and texture. Is there more than one fish dubbed as sole?" The answer is "Yes!" It went on to explain, correctly, that any flatfish from either Atlantic or Pacific waters may be sold as sole, including yellowtail or winter flounder, fluke (summer flounder), lemon or gray sole, dab or any other uncle, cousin, or aunt in the vast and tasty family.

Actually, there is no *true* sole caught in American waters, either on the East or West Coast. The only legitimate member eligible to be called by that name is Dover sole or Channel sole, harvested in the waters off England, Belgium, the Netherlands, and Denmark. Nevertheless, both restaurants and fishmongers have found it convenient to include almost every white-fleshed flatfish that can be cut into fillets.

All flatfish begin life by swimming in the normal, upright manner. Soon, however, their skulls begin to twist and one eye moves toward the opposite side to join the other. The shape of the fish becomes that of a flying saucer, with the white underside turned toward the bottom and the darker, pigmented top closely resembling the floor of the ocean or bay. To camouflage themselves even further, they flip sand over their backs as they lie in wait for passing prey. Sometimes both eyes are on the right (as with winter flounder) and sometimes on the left (as with fluke), but the mouth is always slightly distorted, which makes them look either clownlike or pained.

The one thing that is certain is that the white, translucent, delicate-tasting flesh has made them one of the most versatile and popular of fish. The smaller ones are perfect for cooking whole, while the simple bone structure of the larger ones allows the fisherperson or fishmonger to fillet them easily. Most sole, fluke, and flounders are interchangeable in recipes.

Because of their mild flavor, they are generally best prepared simply. Indeed, one of the simplest recipes that we've come across has what must be the longest name in fish cookery. In his beautiful book *Seafood* (Simon & Schuster, New York), Alan Davidson offers a simple Finnish recipe for sole rolls in dill titled *Tilliliemessäkeitetytlalakääryleet!*

EAST COAST FLATFISH

Winter Flounder

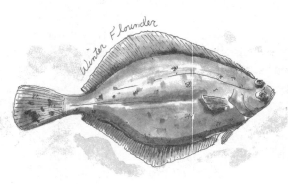

One of the most popular and important of all the eastern flatfish, winter flounder, sometimes called blackback flounder, is generally marketed at under 3 pounds. When its weight goes above that, it is marketed as lemon sole. Most sports fisherpeople accept the fact that it is not a fighting fish (such as the bluefish) and liken it to a doormat when caught, but we accept it for its superb taste and texture.

Summer Flounder (Fluke)

The left-eyed relative of the winter flounder—fluke—is generally larger than winter flounder, with market size averaging from 3 to 5 pounds. However, some have been landed at up to 20 pounds. The smaller ones are sold whole, while the larger fluke make excellent fillets and, occasionally, steaks. They're popular with vacationing fisherpeople, since they are most prevalent during the summer months, from Maine down to the Carolinas.

Gray Sole

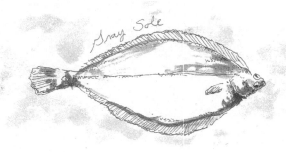

Also known as witch flounder, gray sole has dark gray skin rather than the brown mottled skin of the winter and summer flounders. It grows to about 25 inches in length and is fast becoming known as a premium flatfish with thick, white fillets. At the marketplace, gray sole is generally more expensive than the other flounders.

American Plaice

American plaice is reddish brown and called in the marketplace dab, sanddab, or seadab. It is not the same fish as European plaice, which many travelers have sampled all over the Continent, although both are of the flatfish family. It is generally marketed at 2 to 3 pounds and is known for its firm, thick fillets.

Yellowtail Flounder

Sometimes called dab or rusty flounder, yellowtail flounder should not be confused with the yellowtail, a member of the jackfish family (along with pompano). It's caught in the waters off Canada and the New England coast.

Southern Flounder

Our first taste of this flatfish was on the Gulf Coast in a tiny, marvelous restaurant called Lou's in Pascagoula, Mississippi. Although most are caught commercially off the Carolina and Texas coasts, as well as in the Gulf, a great many sports fisherpeople go out at night with lights and trident-like spears to impale them. This isn't easy. Parallax distortion from the rippling water makes the fish a difficult target, and we have never managed to spear one. The fish are marketed at weights between 1½ and 2 pounds. The closest relative is probably the summer flounder (fluke) of the Northeast.

WEST COAST FLATFISH
Petrale Sole

On the West Coast, petrale sole has the deserved reputation as being the finest and tastiest of the flatfish. It's found from central California up to the coast of Alaska, with average market size between 2 and 5 pounds. As with most flatfish, it is perfect for almost any type of preparation, fillet or whole, baked, steamed, poached, broiled, or sautéed. They are occasionally found at the fishmarket as California sole.

Rex Sole

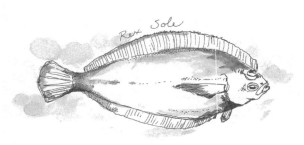

Some of our friends out on the West Coast prefer this smaller sole because of its delicate taste. It's generally sold whole or pan-dressed rather than as fillets because of its small size of about 1 pound.

Dover Sole (Pacific Flounder)

Although it carries the same name as the classic European variety, this sole is by no means its equal. It is slightly mushy and not as tasty as its namesake (or even the petrale or rex sole) and usually found at between 2 and 6 pounds. However, it is the most plentiful of the group, and almost all frozen fillets come from it.

EAST AND WEST COAST FLATFISH
Halibut

If there were a Guinness Book of Fish Records, halibut would certainly top the list for the flatfish family. They are caught in the Atlantic from Virginia up to Greenland and the northern coast of Europe, as well as in the Bering Sea, then the Pacific Ocean down to California and over to Japan. It is not unusual to find the larger females topping the scales at 500 pounds and more! In the terminology of the industry, these fish, as well as others that weigh in at over 80 pounds, are called "whales." The small ones are demeaned as "chickens."

However, most halibut are marketed at about 10 pounds or slightly more, making them quite perfect for preparation as steaks or as cubes for brochettes. The firm, white meat also lends itself to grilling, baking, or poaching, but halibut is so lean that it dries out quickly if it's not watched. Most Atlantic halibut can be purchased fresh, but almost all Pacific halibut is frozen, and thereby hangs a most interesting tale.

As early as 1967, the halibut industry began to feel the effects of overfishing by both domestic and foreign trawlers. Many halibut were taken too young, while millions more were trapped in nets by fishermen who were searching for other Pacific species. Since halibut do not spawn until the age of 8 to 16 years, the catches dwindled sharply. Out of this came the "fishing frenzy" of Alaskan waters.

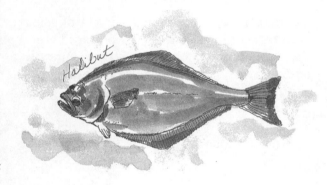

Canada now restricts its fleet to several trips of four to eight days. In Alaska, the fleet is so large that halibut is fair game three times a year for 24 hours only. Hundreds of boats, thousands of hooks baited with octopus and herring, and hundreds of tough fishermen go out to sea at the starting gun, and the word "frenzy" is too tame to describe the action, especially if the waters are rough. In those 24 hours, the fishermen have been known to land between 75 and 100 million pounds for the three "openings." All of the fish is flash frozen aboard the trawlers, but since halibut is one fish that freezes superbly if handled properly, it still remains one of our favorites.

There is also a large flounder called California halibut with a market name of Greenland turbot. It is not a true halibut nor a true turbot, is less flavorful than the Atlantic and Pacific halibuts, and dries out quickly under direct heat.

IMPORTED FLATFISH
Dover Sole

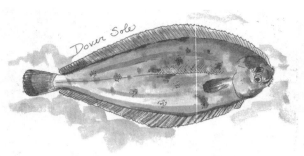

If ever we were to dub a flatfish "sole food," it would be this European relative. Although the Pacific flounder carries the same name (see page 134), the two should not be confused, since the import is a much better tasting fish and is generally considered to be the only *true* sole. It is, by far, the choicest of all soles and is generally found in waters from the Mediterranean Sea up to the coastline of Scandinavia. At one time, the only Dover sole to reach our shores was frozen, but modern transportation has allowed some of the better restaurants and fishmongers to offer the thick, tasty fillets truly fresh.

Lemon Sole

A smaller member of the flatfish family, it generally weighs no more than ¾ to 1 pound. Lemon sole is the market name in France for true sand sole, as well as in Great Britain for lemon dab. However, although the European designation is given to the smaller fish, you may find lemon sole at your fishmonger in larger fillets; it's probably North Atlantic winter flounder over 3 pounds in weight.

Turbot

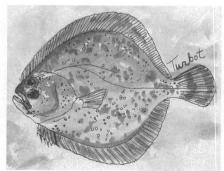

Although several Pacific flounders also carry the name of "turbot," there is only one true and highly regarded turbot, which is harvested in European waters and frequently compared in quality and taste to Dover sole. The turbot is diamond shaped and swims in waters as far south as the Mediterranean Sea and as far north as the Arctic Circle. It can weigh as much as 25 to 30 pounds, but the market sizes are generally much smaller. Its delicate, firm, white meat is far superior to the Pacific coast flounders that masquerade under names that are quite similar, such as diamond turbot or Atlantic/Pacific Greenland turbot, which, as we've mentioned earlier, is neither a turbot or a halibut. If turbot is not available at your fishmonger, the best substitute is grouper.

FLOUNDER SEVICHE WITH SWEET AND HOT PEPPERS, CILANTRO, AND KIWI

MAKES 4 SERVINGS

Spring-green, sweet kiwi forms the core of this star-shaped flounder seviche set in a ring of delicate alfalfa sprouts with a confetti of hot and sweet peppers showered over all. Flounder seviche makes a lovely first course or light summer luncheon.

1 pound flounder fillets, skinned and cut diagonally into 1-inch diamonds (substitute: ocean perch)

½ cup lime juice (3 to 4 limes)

¼ teaspoon ground cumin

Salt and pepper to taste

3 tablespoons very thinly sliced scallion greens

¼ cup finely diced green pepper

¼ cup finely diced red pepper

2 teaspoons finely minced seeded jalapeño chile (1 medium)

2 tablespoons finely minced fresh cilantro

3 tablespoons orange juice

1 tablespoon cider vinegar

Alfalfa sprouts

2 kiwis, peeled and cut into ¼-inch slices

Place the fish in a glass or ceramic bowl. Mix the lime juice, cumin, salt, and pepper together and pour over the fish. Cover with plastic wrap and marinate in the refrigerator at least 6 hours or up to 12 hours.

About 2 hours before serving, drain the fish. In a small bowl, mix the scallions, peppers, jalapeño, cilantro, and additional salt and pepper if you wish. Add the orange juice and vinegar. Place the alfalfa sprouts on the outer rims of 4 serving plates. Place a slice of kiwi in the center of each plate and arrange the slices of fish around the kiwi to form a star. Spoon some of the peppers and cilantro in a circle over the fish and then trickle any remaining liquid over all. Cover with plastic wrap and chill. Return to room temperature before serving.

FLOUNDER FILLETS LAYERED WITH SHRIMP, BASIL, AND TOMATOES

MAKES 6 SERVINGS

These are no-fuss, stuffed and baked fillets that have a sandwich layer of tiny shrimp. A fresh tomato and basil sauce and the natural pan juices that form as the fish bakes are thickened with bread crumbs.

6   skinned flounder fillets, about 6 ounces each (substitute: sole or orange roughy)
    Salt and pepper to taste
1   tablespoon mayonnaise
1   tablespoon Dijon mustard
2   tablespoons butter, softened
½   pound small shrimp, shelled and deveined

3   fresh large tomatoes, skinned and quartered
1½ tablespoons finely minced basil, plus 6 small basil leaves for garnish
½   cup soft fine bread crumbs
2   tablespoons melted butter

Preheat the oven to 350°. Oil a large oven-to-table baking pan and place 3 of the fillets in the pan. Dust them with salt and pepper. In a small bowl, beat the mayonnaise, mustard, and softened butter together and spread half over the fillets. Lay the shrimp in one direction on top of the fillets, then spread the remaining mustard mixture on the other three fillets and place them spread side down over the shrimp, like a sandwich.

Surround the fish with the quartered tomatoes and the basil. Mix the bread crumbs with the melted butter and sprinkle over all. The bread crumbs absorb and thicken the juices that form during cooking.

Butter a piece of aluminum foil and place it butter side down over the fish. Bake for 20 minutes. Remove the foil after 15 minutes; baste and test the fish before returning to the oven, uncovered, for any additional cooking. Cut each sandwich crosswise to make six portions and top them with the sauce, tomatoes, and a fresh basil leaf for garnish.

WINE-POACHED SOLE WITH HERBED BUTTER

MAKES 6 SERVINGS

The delicacy of sole is enhanced but not overpowered by a light, verdant sauce that forms as the fish is poached. A small pasta, such as orzo or conchigliette, served with the fish will utilize any extra sauce in a delicious way.

6 sole fillets, about 6 ounces each (substitute: orange roughy or flounder)	1 tablespoon finely minced parsley
1 tablespoon lemon juice	2 teaspoons finely minced fresh dill
Salt and pepper to taste	1 teaspoon finely minced fresh tarragon
6 tablespoons butter, softened	½ cup Fish Stock (see page 402) or ½ cup water
2 tablespoons finely minced chives	½ cup dry white wine

Lay the fillets on a piece of waxed paper. Sprinkle with the lemon juice, salt, and pepper. In a food processor, beat the butter and herbs until creamy and smooth. Spread the herb butter evenly on the fish with a spatula, then fold the fillets in half crosswise and secure with a toothpick if necessary.

Place the fish in a single layer in a shallow, heavy flameproof oven-to-table baking dish. Pour the fish stock and wine around the fish. Butter a piece of waxed paper to fit the dish and place it butter side down over the fish. Pierce the paper once in the center to allow the steam to escape. Cover the waxed paper with a piece of heavy aluminum foil. Poach the fish over very low heat for about 15 to 20 minutes until the fish offers no resistance when pierced with a skewer. Remove both papers, spoon some of the herb sauce over the fish, and serve directly from the pan.

FILLETS OF SOLE WITH MUSHROOMS EN PAPILLOTE

MAKES 6 SERVINGS

The term en papillote *refers to the cocoon of the emerging butterfly (papillon)—just as the enclosed parchment pouch which puffs up with steam as it bakes, upon opening, reveals the beautiful fish inside.*

3 lemon sole or flounder fillets, about 12 ounces each, cut lengthwise in half for 6 portions

6 tablespoons lemon juice

¼ pound white mushrooms, thinly sliced

4 tablespoons butter

1 large clove garlic, finely minced (about 1½ teaspoons)

1 tablespoon coarsely chopped fresh tarragon or 1 teaspoon dried tarragon

Salt and pepper to taste

6 tablespoons sour cream

3 tablespoons finely minced chives

Place the fillets in a nonreactive dish and toss with half the lemon juice. Let stand for 30 minutes, turning once.

In a bowl, mix the mushrooms with 1 tablespoon of the lemon juice and let stand while preparing the fish. Melt the butter in a small skillet over medium-low heat. Add the garlic and sauté for 1 minute, stirring frequently so it doesn't burn. Remove from the heat and stir in the tarragon, salt, and pepper; set aside to cool a bit.

Cut six 24- by 12-inch sheets of parchment paper into large heart shapes, making a lengthwise center crease as a guide. Open the hearts and brush them lightly with some of the tarragon butter. Dip each fillet into the same butter mixture, coating both sides, and place each fillet near the center fold and slightly toward the wider part of the heart.

Add 1 tablespoon sour cream, some mushrooms, and additional salt and pepper if you wish to each serving. Fold the fish fillets crosswise in half to enclose the mushrooms. Top with any remaining butter, the chives, and the remaining 2 tablespoons lemon juice.

Then fold the paper over at the crease and bring the edges together. Starting at the widest part of the paper, seal by folding over the edges a ¼ inch at a time. Crimp the edges as tightly and neatly as possible. The paper folds should be very tight so that the steam that forms during cooking will not escape. The fish can be prepared up to this point and refrigerated for several hours.

When ready to bake, bring the packets to room temperature and preheat the oven to 400°. Place the packets on a baking sheet and bake for 20 minutes until the paper is puffed up. Don't open the oven during this time since cold air might collapse the packets.

Serve one packet to each person as quickly as possible. Slash an "X" in the paper with a razor blade or sharp knife and peel the paper back. The fish is eaten right from the packet.

LEMON SOLE PINWHEELS FILLED WITH SALMON IN A DILL AND LEMON CREAM

MAKES 6 SERVINGS

For those of us who are cholesterol watchers—and it is certainly prudent to be one—this richly sauced fish is for the occasional splurge when caution gets thrown to the winds.

6 lemon sole fillets, about 6 ounces each (substitute: flounder)

6 thin slices salmon scallops, cut into 4- by 2-inch pieces

Salt and pepper to taste

5 tablespoons butter, softened

2 medium shallots, finely minced (about 2 tablespoons)

½ cup dry white wine

½ cup Fish Stock (see page 402)

1 cup Crème Fraîche (see page 66)

⅓ cup lemon juice

2 tablespoons finely minced fresh dill

Preheat the oven to 425°. Place the fillets on a flat surface and with a sharp knife, trim and remove the central bone line, dividing the fillet in half lengthwise. Lay one piece of salmon on each fillet, sprinkle with salt and pepper, and roll up, fastening each with a toothpick.

In a large, shallow ovenproof skillet melt 4 tablespoons of the butter and sprinkle with the shallots. Roll the fish in the butter and shallot mixture and arrange them flat side up to show the pinwheel design.

Cut a piece of waxed paper to fit the skillet and butter one side heavily. Add the wine and fish stock to the fish, cover with the buttered paper, butter side down, and bring to a boil over medium heat. Transfer to the oven and bake for about 10 minutes. Remove and discard the paper and test the fish with a skewer. Baste and continue to bake until the fish almost flakes, another 5 to 10 minutes. Transfer the fish pinwheels to a large plate with a slotted spatula. Remove the toothpicks and cover the fish with aluminum foil to keep warm.

Place the skillet pan on top of the stove, and boil over medium-high heat for about 3 minutes until the liquid is reduced a bit. Whisk in the crème fraîche and bring to a boil again. Turn the heat down to very low and stir in the lemon juice and dill. Pour any accumulated liquid on the fish plate into the sauce and then warm it, stirring constantly. Return the fish to the sauce. Tilting the pan, spoon some sauce over the top of each roll, then serve.

GRILLED HALIBUT STEAKS WITH ARTICHOKE SAUCE, TOMATO, AND HERBS

A pale, cool green artichoke sauce floats tiny pieces of tomatoes, a diced artichoke bottom, and a few briny olives, and is then pooled around flaky white halibut. A shower of herbs tops it off.

3 large artichokes

¼ cup lemon juice

½ cup olive oil plus 1 tablespoon for brushing fish

1 head garlic, separated into cloves but unpeeled

½ teaspoon ground coriander seeds

3 sprigs thyme

½ teaspoon black peppercorns

1¼ cups chicken stock

Salt and pepper to taste

6 halibut steaks (from the narrow end of the fish) or fillets, 2 to 2½ pounds total (substitute: tilefish)

GARNISH:

2 medium tomatoes, peeled, seeded, and cut into ½-inch pieces

16 Niçoise olives, pitted and sliced

2 tablespoons finely minced parsley

2 tablespoons finely shredded fresh basil

Trim the artichokes of leaves and chokes, leaving only the bottoms. Brush them with lemon juice to keep them from discoloring and set them aside. In a small saucepan, heat ¼ cup of the olive oil over low heat. Add the garlic cloves, coriander, thyme, and peppercorns. Cook over very low heat, stirring occasionally, until the garlic is softened, 12 to 15 minutes.

Raise the heat to medium-high, add the chicken stock, and bring to a boil. Lower the heat and add the artichoke bottoms and simmer, covered, until tender, 10 to 15 minutes. Lift out the artichoke bottoms with a slotted spoon. Cut 1½ artichoke bottoms into ½-inch cubes and set them aside. Strain the liquid into a blender and add the remaining artichoke bottoms. Reserve 2 cooked garlic cloves and discard the rest. Blend the chicken stock and artichoke bottoms until puréed. Then, with the machine running, slowly add about ¼ cup of the olive oil until the sauce is the consistency of heavy cream. Add salt and pepper to taste and some of the lemon juice, tasting to adjust the acidity. Squeeze the 2 cooked garlic cloves from their skins into the blender and purée again. Then transfer the sauce back into the saucepan to be reheated after the fish is cooked.

Preheat a ridged grill pan or an outdoor grill. Brush the fish with the remaining 1 tablespoon oil and season with salt and pepper. Grill over moderately high heat for 3 to 4 minutes on each side. Transfer each portion to a warmed serving plate. Warm the sauce and spoon some around the fish. Scatter the diced artichokes, tomatoes, olives, parsley, and basil over the sauce and serve.

OVEN-ROASTED HALIBUT WITH VEGETABLES

Four kinds of allium are used, onions, shallots, leeks, and scallions, and these aromatic vegetables roast along with potatoes, carrots, and zucchini, providing moisture and succulence to this wonderful one-dish meal.

3 medium carrots, sliced ½ inch thick (about 1½ cups)

1 pound small red potatoes, scrubbed and cut in half or quartered if larger

3 medium leeks, white part and 1 inch green, sliced diagonally ¼ inch thick (about 3 cups)

1 medium onion, diced (about ¾ cup)

3 large shallots, halved

Salt and pepper to taste

3 tablespoons olive oil

4 halibut steaks (6 to 8 ounces, cut from the narrow end of the fish) or fillets (substitute: tilefish or blackfish)

3 tablespoons lemon juice

3 small thin zucchini (about 1 pound), sliced diagonally ¼ inch thick

1 large scallion, thinly sliced on the diagonal (about ¼ cup)

Preheat the oven to 400°. In a large bowl, combine the carrots, potatoes, leeks, onion, and shallots. Sprinkle with salt and pepper and the olive oil. Toss to coat the vegetables with the oil and transfer them to a large oven-to-table baking pan. Roast the vegetables, stirring them 2 or 3 times, for about 40 minutes until the potatoes and carrots are tender.

While the vegetables are roasting, sprinkle the fish with 1 tablespoon of the lemon juice and season with salt and pepper.

Season the zucchini lightly with salt and pepper and stir them into the vegetables along with the remaining 2 tablespoons lemon juice and half the scallion. Push the vegetables away from the center of the pan to make room for the fish. Arrange the fish in the center and spoon some of the leeks, onion, and shallots (not the other vegetables) over the surface of the fish. Return to the oven and roast for 8 to 10 minutes more until the fish flakes when tested with a skewer or knife point. Sprinkle with the remaining scallion just before serving.

HALIBUT SEVICHE WITH RED ONIONS, ORANGES, AND CILANTRO

Seviche can be prepared with many firm, white-fleshed fish or scallops, but we are partial to the naturally sweet flavor and firm texture of halibut, one of our favorite fish, unfortunately with a regrettably short season.

1   cup lime juice (6 to 8 limes)

½   small onion, finely minced (about 2 tablespoons)

1   small clove garlic, finely minced (about ½ teaspoon)

2   large tomatoes, skinned and diced

1   large jalapeño chile, roasted, peeled, seeded, and finely minced

4   tablespoons olive oil

½   teaspoon dried thyme or 1 teaspoon fresh thyme leaves

1   teaspoon nonpareil capers, rinsed

½   cup coarsely chopped cilantro

2   pounds halibut steaks, skinned, boned, and cut into 1-inch cubes (substitute: tilefish or sea scallops)

Salt and pepper to taste

Leaf lettuce

1   small red onion, thinly sliced

1   medium orange, peeled and thinly sliced

In a large nonreactive bowl, combine well all the ingredients except the lettuce, red onion, and orange. Cover with plastic wrap and marinate in the refrigerator for at least 8 hours or overnight. Stir the mixture once or twice during that time.

When ready to serve, make a bed of lettuce leaves on a platter. Surround it with alternating overlapping slices of red onion and oranges, then heap the fish in the center. Serve chilled.

TURBOT BAKED IN MILK WITH BAY LEAVES, CARROTS, AND LEEKS

A chive-laced creamy and delicate sauce with tart, small pieces of lemon is prepared from the highly flavored poaching liquid.

4	tablespoons butter, softened	2	pounds turbot fillets (substitute: grouper)
1	small leek, thinly sliced (about ½ cup)	½	cup dry white wine
1	medium carrot, thinly sliced (about ½ cup)	2	tablespoons all-purpose flour
2	large bay leaves	2	tablespoons finely minced chives
1	teaspoon whole black peppercorns	1	lemon, peeled, seeded, thinly sliced, and cut into small pieces
	Salt, to taste		
1	cup milk		

Preheat the oven to 350°. Butter a large, heavy, shallow roasting pan with 1 tablespoon of the butter and make a layer of the leek and carrot on the bottom. Crumble the bay leaves over the vegetables and scatter the peppercorns and salt over the surface. Pour the milk over and bring to a boil on top of the stove. Lay the fish on the vegetables, tilt the pan, and baste the fish with some of the liquid. Bake for 8 to 10 minutes, basting 2 or 3 times.

Lift the fish out with a spatula, transfer to a warm serving platter, and cover with foil to keep warm. Strain the poaching liquid into a nonstick saucepan, pressing the solids against the sides of the strainer. Discard the vegetables and spices. Add the wine to the saucepan and bring to a boil over medium-low heat.

Mix the remaining 3 tablespoons butter with the flour until smooth and whisk it gradually into the sauce. Simmer, stirring constantly, for 3 to 4 minutes until slightly thickened. Stir in the chives and the lemon, then spoon the sauce over the fish.

OTHER MILDLY FLAVORED SALTWATER FISH

John Dory

Known in Europe as St. Pierre or St. Peter's Fish, John Dory is a most unusual creature. Almost painfully thin by fish standards, this import might be called a "vertical flatfish" because of its odd, compressed body. On its sides, it carries black spots that look somewhat like a full eclipse of the sun with the corona of the sun circling the dark center of the moon. By legend the spots were left by the thumb and forefinger of Peter (Matthew 17:26–27), when he held the fish too tightly in his search for the money that Jesus had promised would be in the mouth of the first fish that he caught.

Although John Dory is caught up to 12 pounds, only about one-third of the fish is usable because of its large head and body cavity. However, it is one of the tastiest fish in the sea, and its popularity in European restaurants attests to that fact. It's moist, very flaky and has a sweet taste. It is fished in the Mediterranean and into the Atlantic Ocean. A near relative is imported from New Zealand and sometimes marketed as oreo dory.

Lingcod

Lingcod are not really cod. Lingcod actually are a member of the *greenling* family, native to the West Coast from California up to British Columbia and Alaska.

Friends of ours in California consider it one of the finest fish in their marketplace, and it's available year round. Before cooking, the flesh is a light blue-green, but it turns white during cooking. Because of its dense flesh, it may take a bit longer to prepare than other lean fish. Although the fish can weigh in at 30 to 50 pounds, most market fish range from 8 to 10 pounds whole and about 2 pounds as fillets.

Orange Roughy

Orange roughy was not even mentioned in our original book on fish cookery, nor can it be found in the encyclopedias of marine life that were published before that time. However, it has since taken its place alongside the more common household purchases of cod and flounder. Discovered in deep waters off the New Zealand coast about 1975, the fish began to be exported to the United States and Canada about four years later. Today it's a popular export fish because it does not lose its delicate flavor when flash frozen at sea and shipped so many thousands of miles.

Our frank opinion about orange roughy is that it is quite mild, almost bland tasting, although its firm, flaky texture is excellent for soups and stews and it poaches and braises quite well. For those who prefer a very mild, lean fish to the stronger-tasting species such as bluefish or mackerel, orange roughy is a perfect choice. If it's not available, you can substitute red snapper in our recipes.

Porgy (Sheepshead)

If you've traveled down the coastal highways of the eastern United States, you probably have wondered, as have we, just what all those fisherpeople were doing dropping their lines into the saltwater inlets that run under the bridges or along the seawalls and the piers. Probably one of the fish they were after was the porgy, called sheepshead the further south you go, or sometimes convict fish, because of its distinguishing striped markings. Actually about 25 percent or more of the porgy catch here in the United States

is landed by sports fisherpeople. Northern porgy (or scup) is one of the favorites on our island during the late spring and early summer months, when they crowd the docks in search of tiny bait fish.

There are probably hundreds of varieties of porgy to be found all around the world, all of them members of the sea bream family. The Atlantic coast alone boasts about 15 varieties, the scup being the most plentiful and the most popular. Porgies are prized for their excellent taste, a result of their feeding on crustaceans, young squid, barnacles, and other invertebrates. And although they sometimes reach a weight of 4 pounds, the average catch is generally ¾ to 1 pound.

They have a tough skin and their size makes them impractical to fillet, so that they generally are found at the fish market pan-dressed or butterflied—perfect for grilling, pan-frying, or steaming. The skin should be removed *after* cooking.

Red Snapper

When fish lovers say "snapper," the chances are that they are speaking of red snapper—or possibly yellowtail snapper if they live in Florida or the Caribbean. There are over 250 species of snappers around the world, 14 in Hawaii alone, but none quite as popular or as tasty as the American red snapper, harvested throughout the Gulf of Mexico. The fish is so popular that the National Maritime Fisheries service frequently sets a quota on the catch to keep the species from disappearing. This, and the fact that the American red snapper is generally available fresh, is handled more carefully than imported varieties, and arrives in the marketplace more quickly usually makes it the most expensive snapper at the market and the restaurant.

This handsome, pink-red fish with startling red eyes is marketed between 2 and 6 pounds whole, and, although it can be prepared in almost any way, there is nothing quite as beautiful as seeing the whole fish on a platter. It is also a sure way to make certain that it is *red* snapper that you are buying, since many other snappers are passed off as the real thing. For example, red rockfish is occasionally sold in California as "red snapper," and skinned fillets may come from a range of other snappers that hail from as far away as Indonesia and South and Central America. This is one more time where it pays to have a fishmonger you can trust—especially when you see the price.

The flesh is firm, moist, sweet, and tender. Once you taste true red snapper, you will realize why the demand is always far greater than the supply. Black sea bass can be substituted if red snapper is not available.

Rockfish (Ocean Perch)

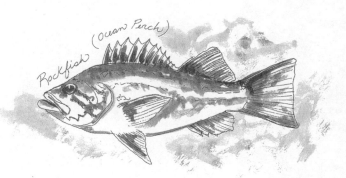

This is yet another species that can boggle the mind of the fish lover and where a trusty fishmonger is again a necessity. The term "rockfish" can be applied to about 300 species worldwide, with at least 50 of them swimming off the Pacific coast and 1 lone deep-sea relative in the Atlantic Ocean (ocean perch). They range through a kaleidoscope of colors: yellow, blue, orange, and red, with patterns and stripes, spots and mottled scales. And they have names that can tickle an etymologist: chilipepper, splitnose, rougheye, semaphore, fourbeard, widow, and boccacio, just to name a few.

Although most rockfish have fine, flaky, mild flesh, each one in the marketplace can be handled slightly differently from another—thus the reminder once again that the fishmonger can always help. On the Pacific coast, rockfish (or one of its numerous relations) is the most common species and a major industry. It's harvested as far north as British Columbia and Alaska, with market weights that range from about 1½ pounds to 5 pounds. In the West, the Chinese use them for steamed or fried whole fish (while their Eastern brethren use black bass). The Mexican community in the U.S. uses rockfish for their famous Veracruz-style seafood dish wrapped in banana leaves, since the original red snapper is much too expensive to be shipped.

As we've cautioned earlier, the red-colored rockfish on the Pacific coast is often falsely sold as Pacific red snapper. However, where recipes specifically call for West Coast rockfish, East Coast cooks can substitute the American red snapper, ocean perch, or black sea bass.

Blackfish (Tautog)

Of the fish often described as "almost like lobster," this member of the wrasse family is yet another candidate. Because blackfish feeds on crustaceans, its flesh is mild and very firm, making it perfect for stews, soups, and chowders.

It's found from as far north as Nova Scotia down into the Carolinas, and we are quite familiar with it on our island. Since blackfish like to haunt old shipwrecks, a perfect habitat exists near a Coast Guard buoy right off shore on the bay. Each spring and well into the summer, a flotilla of boats gathers around the wreck—rowboats, small motor boats, party boats, and sophisticated small yachts that even sport radar dishes and outrigger booms. Using clams as bait, the fisherpeople plumb the depths for black- fish, losing countless rigs amidst the out- cropping timbers, the rocks, and the barnacled remains of the wreck. The re- sults are well worthwhile, however, for the catch generally runs from 3 to 5 pounds per fish, and all of us agree that they are one of the best-tasting species on the Atlantic coast.

Whether you are given a blackfish as a gift, have caught one yourself, or purchased it at your local fishmonger, keep in mind that the skin is quite tough and should be removed either before or after cooking. If blackfish is not available, you may substitute any other firm-fleshed fish in the recipes: red snapper, black sea bass, grouper, tilefish, or monkfish.

Tilefish

Another good example of just how much the seafood industry (and the consumer) have changed is tilefish, which twelve short years ago we listed in our book as "underuti- lized." Now this is no longer an accurate description. Currently one of the most popu- lar of lean saltwater fish, tilefish has become quite common on both the menus of seafood restaurants and in home cooking.

It's unfortunate that consumers can- not see a tilefish right after it's been landed, for it is one of the most colorful fish in the sea. Dotted with yellow spots on the side and ranging from blue-green to blue along the back with a silvery, al- most white underbelly, the fish quickly loses its brilliance after death, turning an almost dull blue gray.

However, the change of color does not affect the absolutely marvelous taste of tile- fish, a species that feeds on small crustaceans to give it the firm, sweet, mild, and flaky meat that has become so popular with fish lovers. It's found all along the Atlantic coast and is usually available all year round. And, because it's firm and holds its shape so well, it's perfect for almost any kind of preparation. If you're so inclined, ask your fishmon- ger for any tilefish heads he has available; the head makes great fish stock and its large cheeks are a treat.

HERB-CRUSTED
OVEN-FRIED LINGCOD

Makes 6 servings

*A crisp and crunchy herb-scented cornmeal crust forms while the lingcod bakes
quickly in a very hot oven.*

¾ cup stone-ground yellow cornmeal

¼ cup plus 2 tablespoons grated Parmesan
    cheese

2 tablespoons sesame seeds, toasted

1 teaspoon finely minced parsley

1½ teaspoons dried thyme

¾ teaspoon dried sage

1 large clove garlic, finely minced (about 1½
    teaspoons)

¾ teaspoon freshly ground black pepper

Salt to taste

2 eggs, lightly beaten

2 teaspoons light cream or half-and-half

2½ pounds lingcod fillets, cut into 2 or 3
    pieces (substitute: grouper or Atlantic
    pollack)

1½ tablespoons corn oil

4 tablespoons butter

Lemon wedges dipped in minced parsley

Place the cornmeal, Parmesan, sesame seeds, parsley, thyme, sage, garlic, pepper, and
salt in a large plastic bag and shake the bag to mix well. Preheat the oven to 450°.

In a wide shallow bowl, whisk the eggs and cream with a bit of salt. Dip the fish a
few pieces at a time into the egg mixture, then add to the bag and shake to coat evenly.
Put the oil and butter in a 15- by 10-inch jelly-roll pan and place it in the oven just long
enough to melt the butter.

Turn the pieces of fish in the butter and oil to coat evenly and arrange on the pan.
Bake for 3 minutes, then turn the fish over to the other side to brown. Bake 4 to 6 minutes more until done when tested with a skewer. Serve on a warm platter with parsley-
dipped lemon wedges to be squeezed at the table.

PAN-GRILLED ORANGE ROUGHY WITH WARM GREEN LENTILS

If you are not particularly partial to fish, orange roughy is the candidate to win you over.
It has a very mild, somewhat bland taste that takes well to almost any sauce.

¾ cup green lentils, picked over and rinsed

½ cup finely diced red onion

2 medium tomatoes (about ¼ pound), finely diced (about ¾ cup)

1 small green pepper, finely diced (about ⅔ cup)

¼ cup coarsely chopped cilantro, plus a few leaves for garnish

4 tablespoons olive oil

3 tablespoons red wine vinegar

Salt and pepper to taste

4 orange roughy fillets, about 8 ounces each (substitute: pan-dressed whiting, or catfish or flounder fillets)

All-purpose flour for dredging

In a medium saucepan, cover the lentils with tepid water plus 2 inches. Bring to a boil, then lower the heat and simmer for about 20 minutes until the lentils are tender but still maintain their shape. Drain and rinse the lentils under warm water, drain again, and transfer them to a mixing bowl. Add the onion, tomatoes, green pepper, cilantro, 3 tablespoons of the olive oil, the vinegar, salt, and pepper; stir to combine. Cover the bowl with foil to keep warm and set aside.

Dry the fish well on paper towels, season with salt and pepper if you wish, and dredge lightly with flour. Heat the remaining 1 tablespoon oil in a heavy, ridged grill pan over medium-high heat. When the oil is hot, pan-grill the fish about 4 minutes on each side until it flakes when tested with a skewer. Using a slotted spoon, divide the lentils among four plates, top each serving with a fish fillet, and garnish with cilantro leaves.

WINE-POACHED PORGY WITH SAFFRON, LEMON, AND MINT, MOROCCAN-STYLE

MAKES 4 SERVINGS

Flavorful, firm-fleshed porgies are poached in a lemon-and-wine brew made golden with saffron. A touch of hot cayenne and a bit of cool mint balance the flavors. Couscous laced with tiny cubes of vegetables would be a good accompaniment.

½ teaspoon loosely packed saffron threads, crumbled

2 tablespoons boiling water

1 cup dry white wine

1 cup water

2 cloves garlic, thinly sliced

¼ cup olive oil

2 pan-dressed porgies, about 1½ pounds each (substitute: sheepshead steaks or king mackerel steaks)

Salt to taste

⅛ teaspoon cayenne (or more to taste)

2 small lemons, peel, white pith, and seeds removed, thinly sliced

2 tablespoons coarsely chopped fresh mint

In a small cup, steep the saffron in the boiling water for 10 minutes. In a 12-inch sauté pan or skillet, combine the wine, water, garlic, oil, and saffron and bring to a boil. Season the fish with salt and cayenne and add them to the skillet. Lower the heat to low, cover the surface of the fish with lemon slices, then cover the pan and poach for 10 to 12 minutes. After 10 minutes, test the thickest part of the fish with a skewer to see if it flakes.

Lift the fish and the lemon out with a slotted spatula and place on a serving platter. Spoon 3 to 4 tablespoons of the poaching liquid over the fish. Sprinkle with the mint. Serve at once or cool and serve at room temperature.

BRAISED RED SNAPPER WITH BLACK OLIVES, TOMATO, AND FENNEL

MAKES 2 SERVINGS

An impressive dinner for two—easy, yet colorful and delicious. The addition of small new potatoes and sugar snap or green peas would make a gorgeous plate.

Butter for baking pan

1 2-pound red snapper, scaled, gutted, gills removed, head left on (substitute: black sea bass or Pacific rockfish)

1 tablespoon lemon juice

Salt and pepper to taste

2 teaspoons olive oil

2 large shallots, finely minced (about 3 tablespoons)

1 small fennel bulb, thinly sliced, feathery tops reserved for garnish

1 large plum tomato, thickly sliced

4 to 6 black olives, such as Greek Kalamata, pitted and thickly sliced

⅔ cup dry white wine

2 teaspoons butter, cut into small pieces

Butter an oven-to-table baking pan that can also be used on top of the stove. Place the fish in the pan, pour the lemon juice over it, and season with salt and pepper. In a small skillet, heat the oil over low heat. Add the shallots and fennel and sauté, stirring frequently, for about 2 minutes, then spoon over the fish. Arrange the tomato slices in a row over the top. Scatter with the olives and slowly pour the wine around the fish. Dot with the butter and cover tightly with aluminum foil.

Braise the fish over medium heat for 15 to 20 minutes. Remove the foil after 15 minutes and test the fish with a skewer. Baste, and continue to cook if necessary until the fish tests done. Remove the foil and scatter the feathery fennel tops over the surface.

RED SNAPPER VERA CRUZ–STYLE, STUFFED WITH LIMES

The fish marinates in lime juice and the shells from the limes are stuffed into the cavity of the snapper to perfume it while it bakes in a blend of Mexican herbs and spices.

1   5-pound red snapper, scaled, gutted, gills removed, head left on (substitute: black sea bass or Pacific rockfish)

2   large limes

Salt and black pepper to taste

3   tablespoons olive oil

1   large sweet Bermuda onion, thinly sliced (about 1½ cups)

2   large cloves garlic, finely minced (about 1 tablespoon)

¾   pound plum tomatoes, skinned and diced (about 2 cups)

2   tablespoons nonpareil capers, rinsed

1   large jalapeño chile, seeded and finely minced (about 1 tablespoon)

½   teaspoon dried oregano, preferably Greek

½   teaspoon ground cumin

1   small bay leaf

Lime wedges for garnish

Cilantro sprigs for garnish

Put the fish into a shallow nonreactive baking pan large enough to accommodate it. Cut the limes in half and squeeze the juice over the fish, then stuff the cavity of the fish with the lime shells. Season with salt and pepper and cover with plastic wrap. Marinate in the refrigerator for 3 to 4 hours.

Preheat the oven to 400°. In a large skillet, heat the oil over medium heat. Add the onion and garlic and cook, stirring frequently, until the onion is transparent, about 4 minutes. Stir in the tomatoes, capers, jalapeño, oregano, cumin, and bay leaf and simmer for 5 minutes. Remove the lime shells from inside the fish and spoon the sauce over the fish. Bake, uncovered, basting frequently and adding water if necessary, for 40 to 50 minutes or 10 minutes per inch of fish measured at the thickest part. Test and then garnish with lime wedges and cilantro. Remove the bay leaf before serving.

ROASTED RED SNAPPER WITH CRABMEAT-AND-THYME STUFFING

MAKES 6 SERVINGS

What could be more elegant and festive than a bright red fish filled with snowy crabmeat and pungent with the sting of cayenne and mustard?

2   2½-pound red snappers or 1 5- to 6-pound fish, scaled, gutted, gills removed, head left on, boned and split open for stuffing (substitute: black sea bass or Pacific rockfish)

2   tablespoons olive oil

3   tablespoons lemon juice

¾   pound lump crabmeat, picked over to remove any stray bits of cartilage

¼   cup soft bread crumbs

2   teaspoons fresh thyme leaves or 1 teaspoon dried thyme

1   teaspoon Dijon mustard

2   scallions, finely minced (about ½ cup)

4   tablespoons melted butter

¼   teaspoon cayenne pepper

    Salt and pepper to taste

½   cup dry white wine

½   cup water

Preheat the oven to 400°. Oil a shallow oven-to-table baking pan large enough to accommodate the fish without crowding. Rub the remaining olive oil and 2 tablespoons of the lemon juice over and inside the fish and lay the fish open, skin side down in the baking pan.

In a medium bowl, combine the crabmeat, bread crumbs, thyme, mustard, scallions, 2 tablespoons of the melted butter, the cayenne, salt, pepper, and the remaining 1 tablespoon lemon juice. Spread the stuffing on half the fish, fold the fish over like a book, skewer, and tie (see page 48). Pour the remaining 2 tablespoons butter over the fish and pour the wine and water in the bottom of the pan.

Roast, basting several times and adding water if necessary to increase the basting liquid and keep the fish moist. Depending upon whether you are roasting 2 smaller fish or 1 larger fish, the baking time will vary. As a guide, measure the fish at the thickest part and allow 10 minutes per inch of thickness. Test with a skewer after 20 minutes for the smaller fish and 30 to 35 minutes for the larger one. Allow additional time if the skewer meets resistance.

NOTE: A meat thermometer inserted into the thickest part of the large fish should register 135°.

ROCKFISH (OCEAN PERCH) MOUSSE WITH GAZPACHO SAUCE

A pristine white feather-light mousse flecked with tiny bits of green and surrounded by a sprightly fresh-tomato-and-raw-vegetable sauce. Serve it as a first course or light summer luncheon dish accompanied by garlic-rubbed sourdough toasts.

Gazpacho Sauce (see page 92), prepared 1 hour before serving

1 tablespoon butter, softened

⅔ pound skinned rockfish fillets, pin bones removed, cut into 1-inch pieces (substitute: catfish or sole)

4 egg whites

¼ teaspoon Tabasco

1 teaspoon lemon juice

2 tablespoons very finely minced scallion green

1 tablespoon finely minced fresh dill

¼ teaspoon salt

⅛ teaspoon white pepper

1 cup heavy cream, cold

Place 1 of 6 ½-cup ramekins upside down on a piece of aluminum foil and trace and cut 6 circles to fit the top. Butter one side of the foil circles and the insides of the 6 ramekins.

Preheat the oven to 350° and boil a kettle of water. In the bowl of a food processor, purée the fish for about 10 strokes. Add the egg whites and process for about 10 more strokes. Add the Tabasco, lemon juice, scallions, dill, salt, and pepper, and process 1 or 2 strokes more to combine. With the motor running, slowly add the cream through the feed tube and process until the mixture is smooth and thick. Spoon equal amounts into the prepared ramekins. Place the buttered foil rounds over the surfaces and put the covered ramekins in a larger pan.

Pour boiling water halfway up the sides of the molds. Bake for 20 to 22 minutes until the mousse is set. Remove the foil and cool for 10 minutes, then run a sharp knife around the sides of the ramekins and unmold each mousse onto a serving plate. Spoon the gazpacho sauce around the mousse.

ROCKFISH (OCEAN PERCH) SALAD

A refreshing and satisfying weekend summer luncheon or light supper dish that can be prepared in the morning and chilled until needed. Serve it on a bed of mixed salad greens for crunch.

SAUCE:

1¼	cups mayonnaise
1	tablespoon Dijon mustard
½	teaspoon powdered mustard
2	teaspoons nonpareil capers, rinsed and drained
5 to 6	small gherkins or cornichons, rinsed and coarsely chopped (about 2 tablespoons)
1	small shallot, finely minced (1 teaspoon)
1	plum tomato, finely diced (about 2 tablespoons)
1	tablespoon lemon juice
1	tablespoon finely minced chives
1	tablespoon finely minced parsley
¼	teaspoon crushed dried tarragon
¼	teaspoon paprika

2	teaspoons anchovy paste
½	clove garlic, finely minced (about ¼ teaspoon)
¼	teaspoon black pepper
	Salt to taste

POACHED ROCKFISH (OCEAN PERCH)

½	cup dry white wine
1	cup water
1	large onion, thickly sliced
1	bay leaf
3 or 4	whole peppercorns
	Salt to taste
2½	pounds rockfish or ocean perch fillets (substitute: halibut steaks)

FOR THE SAUCE: In a medium bowl, combine all the ingredients, cover well with plastic wrap, and chill for 2 hours to allow the flavors to blend.

FOR THE POACHED FISH: In a large skillet, bring the wine, water, onion, bay leaf, and peppercorns to a boil. Lower the heat and simmer for 15 minutes. Add the fish and additional boiling water if necessary to cover the fish. Cover the skillet, and poach for about 5 to 8 minutes. Test with a skewer to see if the fish flakes. Using a slotted spoon, transfer the fish to a bowl and tear it into large chunks. Discard the poaching liquid. Cover the fish with plastic wrap and chill until serving time.

When ready to serve, spoon about 1¼ cups of the sauce (or more if necessary) over the fish and stir gently. Serve on a bed of mixed salad greens if you wish.

CHILLED BLACKFISH (TAUTOG) WITH CITRUS, HOT PEPPER FLAKES, AND LOVAGE

A hot citrus marinade briefly poaches the fish and then the blackfish is marinated and chilled for several hours in its sweet onion, hot pepper, and citrus bath. It easily can be prepared the day before. Serve as a cold summer luncheon dish.

1	large sweet Bermuda, Oso, or Vidalia onion, thinly sliced (½ to ¾ pound)	⅛	teaspoon black pepper
2	pounds blackfish (tautog) fillets, cut crosswise into ¾-inch strips		Salt to taste
		1	tablespoon white wine vinegar
2	bay leaves	½	cup lime juice
¼	teaspoon crushed dried tarragon leaves	½	cup orange juice
1	medium clove garlic, finely minced (about 1 teaspoon)	1	orange, thinly sliced, for garnish
½	teaspoon hot pepper flakes	¼	cup coarsely chopped lovage or celery leaves

Place the onion slices in a nonreactive skillet, layer the fish over the onions, and add the bay leaves, tarragon, garlic, pepper flakes, pepper, and salt.

In a small bowl, combine the vinegar and lime and orange juices and pour over the fish and onions. Cover the skillet and bring to a boil. Remove from the heat at once and transfer to a large serving bowl. Cover with plastic wrap and chill in the refrigerator for at least 6 hours or overnight.

When ready to serve, remove and discard the bay leaves. Garnish with the orange slices and a sprinkle of lovage just before serving.

BROILED BLACKFISH (TAUTOG) WITH CREAM, LEEKS, AND MUSTARD

Creamy leeks are combined with mustard to perk up the flavor of delicate, meaty fleshed tautog.

Butter for baking pan

2 pounds blackfish (tautog) fillets (substitute: tilefish or striped bass)

6 tablespoons Dijon mustard

2 teaspoons dry white wine

½ cup water

2 tablespoons butter

3 leeks, white and pale green parts only, thinly sliced ½ inch thick (about 1½ cups)

Salt and pepper to taste

½ cup heavy cream

4 lemon wedges

Small parsley bouquets for garnish

Preheat the broiler. Butter a shallow baking pan large enough to accommodate the fish in one layer. Arrange the fish in the pan. Combine the mustard and wine in a small cup and brush the fish with this mixture. Broil for 5 minutes on each side, testing with a skewer to see if the fish flakes. Cover with aluminum foil to keep warm.

In a large skillet, bring the water and butter to a boil. Add the leeks, salt, and pepper and cook, uncovered, over medium-high heat, stirring occasionally, for 5 minutes. Stir in the cream and cook for 2 minutes more. Divide the fish into 4 portions on the plates and spoon some of the sauce over. Place a lemon wedge on each plate and garnish plate with a small parsley bouquet.

MARINATED AND BROILED TILEFISH STEAKS WITH SPICED YOGURT

A hot, spiced yogurt marinade flavors these simply grilled fish steaks, which are then served with a cooling dish of yogurt mixed with refreshing cucumber and mint.

6 tilefish steaks, 1¼ inches thick and 7 to 8 ounces each (substitute: halibut or black-fish [tautog])

2 cups plain yogurt

1 teaspoon paprika

1 teaspoon ground cumin

1 teaspoon ground coriander

⅛ teaspoon cayenne pepper

⅛ teaspoon black pepper

Salt to taste

1 tablespoon coarsely chopped fresh mint

1 small Kirby cucumber, shredded

Place the steaks in a nonreactive shallow dish. Using a blender, combine 1 cup of the yogurt with all the spices and the salt. Pour over the fish, cover tightly with plastic wrap, and marinate in the refrigerator for at least 4 hours up to 8 hours, turning the steaks over once or twice.

When ready to cook, preheat the broiler or prepare the grill. Lift the fish from the marinade, put them on an oiled grill, and place 4 inches from the heat source. Broil or grill, turning once, for about 8 to 10 minutes. Test with a skewer.

Mix the remaining cup yogurt with the mint, cucumber, and additional salt and pepper if you wish, and serve as an accompaniment to the fish.

TILEFISH CARPACCIO WITH PINK AND GREEN PEPPERCORNS

A light and unusual appetizer inspired by a dinner at the famous New York restaurant Le Bernardin.

⅓ cup olive oil

1 small red onion, very thinly sliced and separated into rings

⅛ teaspoon ground cloves

Salt to taste

1 thick 1½-pound tilefish fillet (substitute: only farm-raised salmon)

¼ cup dried mixed green and pink peppercorns

1 tablespoon lemon juice (about ½ lemon)

Buttered thin whole-grain toast triangles

In a medium bowl, mix the oil, onion, cloves, and salt, and set aside for 30 minutes, stirring once after 15 minutes. Place the fish in the freezer for 15 minutes, just long enough to firm it up sufficiently to slice easily. Then, with a very sharp knife, cut the fish into very thin slices. Place the slices between 2 sheets of clear plastic and pound, using a heavy flat mallet, until they are paper thin, taking care not to make holes in the slices.

Arrange the fish slices slightly overlapping on the center of 8 chilled plates. Crush the peppercorns between 2 pieces of aluminum foil, using the same flat mallet. Distribute the crushed peppercorns equally over the fish. Sprinkle each serving with a few drops of lemon juice. Lift the onion rings out with a slotted spoon and distribute a few along one side of each plate; place the toast triangles on the other side. Trickle the clove-scented oil over all. To eat, lift a slice of fish onto a piece of the toast and top with onion if you wish.

GROUP B
More Strongly Flavored Saltwater Fish

Tuna Family
Albacore
Yellowfin
Blackfin
Bluefin
Big-Eye tuna
Little tunny
Skipjack tuna
Bonito

Mackerel Family
Atlantic mackerel
Chub mackerel
Spanish mackerel
King mackerel
Cero mackerel
Wahoo

Jack Family
Pompano
Yellowtail (amberjack)
Pacific jack mackerel
Crevalle jack

Shark Family
Mako
Bonito
Thresher
Dogfish
Soupfin
Blacktip

Swordfish

Bluefish

Mullet

Sablefish

Small Fish
Smelt
Silversides
Butterfish
Anchovy
Herring
Sardines

THE TUNA FAMILY

If we look only at the statistics of consumption, then tuna is by far the most popular fish in the United States. However, most of the tuna purchased is canned rather than fresh, over 1 billion cans a year. On the other hand, in Japan, the consumption pattern is just the reverse, with fresh tuna, particularly in sashimi and sushi, far outstripping any other fish.

In the last ten years, however, fresh tuna has found a place on the menus and in the kitchens of the United States and Canada; if it's grilled quickly to seal in the juices, it has a rich, pink-red center when cut.

Tuna is a member of the mackerel family, and so is related through a vast and diverse family tree to bonito. The distinguishing features for all family members are the sharply pointed, distinctively split tail and the smooth, remarkably designed, streamlined body—built for speed and endurance. However, the family members are really quite different, although all belong to the fatty saltwater fish group.

Tuna are found all over the world in both temperate and subtropical waters, and since they are so widespread, the flavor of the major varieties can vary considerably, as can the texture and color of the flesh. Flavor and texture also change from season to season and from month to month, varying from very light and almost white to a very dark, rich red.

But all tuna is firm and dense, with the market forms available as fillets, loins, thick steaks, cubes, and thin medallions. We generally suggest removing the very dark lateral strip of meat, since it has a tendency to be bitter. We also usually undercook tuna to prevent it from drying out.

The Japanese also cook tuna, but their choice preparation method is the use of raw tuna for sashimi and sushi, with the prime, fatty parts of the bluefin (see below) commanding the highest prices.

Albacore

Albacore has the lightest flesh of the family and is the only tuna that can legitimately be called "white." When canned, it's usually the most expensive on the supermarket shelves. However, it can also be prepared fresh. It's found, for the most part, in the Pacific Ocean all the way to Japan but is also caught in the Atlantic. It usually weighs between 10 and 50 pounds and seldom reaches as much as 80 or 90 pounds.

Yellowfin Tuna

With a slightly stronger flavor than the albacore variety and slightly lower in fat, yellowfin tuna roams the world in tropical and subtropical waters. It is also the most abundant of the species and certainly the most colorful, with a long yellow stripe on its side and golden dorsal and anal fins. The yellowfin has been caught at sizes that measure close to 7 feet and its weight can run well over 350 pounds. However, most commercial catches range from 30 to 150 pounds.

When yellowfin is canned, it goes under the label of "light." However, it currently is the favorite for the fresh tuna steaks that have become so popular in restaurants.

Blackfin Tuna

A smaller tuna and a favorite of some of our fishing friends, the blackfin tuna runs up to 40 pounds, although market sizes and sports catches rarely top 10 pounds. It's found in the Atlantic, ranging all the way from New England down to the coast of Brazil, but is not too well known in the American marketplace and frequently not even mentioned as a market choice. This is unfortunate because the meat of the blackfin has a delicate flavor that makes it quite distinctive.

Bluefin Tuna

Bluefin tuna has been compared to a baby elephant and is, by far, the largest member of the family, weighing as much as 1,500 pounds. But the bluefin seems to be in serious trouble, another victim of greed. A bluefin of about 300 pounds can bring up to $1500 in Japan, where it is highly prized for sushi and sashimi; the fatty section of belly flesh (*toro*) brings more than $20 per pound. Fishermen have been known to catch the fish, bleed and gut it, and then quickly get it on a plane to Japan, all at inflated, premium prices. As a result, even with fishing quotas, bluefin is fast disappearing from North Atlantic waters. In fact, the National Audubon Society has proposed that the bluefin be listed as an endangered species.

The color of the flesh varies, depending upon the time of year. The fat content also varies, depending upon feeding habits or the time of spawning. Although the oiliest flesh is perfect for sushi and sashimi, it becomes rather strong when cooked.

Big-Eye Tuna

With the bluefin catch limited, thus driving up the price, the big-eye has become the next favorite, especially for use in sashimi and sushi. It's found all over the world, especially in tropical and subtropical waters, and weighs in at up to 400 pounds. It's moderately fatty, somewhere between albacore and bluefin tuna.

Little Tunny

This may well be our favorite, if only because it runs off our beach during the fall fishing season and to catch one is to be dragged down the beach for at least half a mile before being able to land it. And yet, by tuna standards, it is a smaller variety, averaging from 4 to 6 pounds. It sometimes goes by the name of false albacore or bonito, and

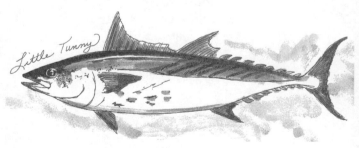

it has a very strong flavor. We find that it's quite perfect when eaten raw as sashimi but requires an overnight soaking in brine before cooking. It also smokes quite well. Generally, the major part of the catch is done by sports fisherpeople along the Atlantic coastline.

Skipjack Tuna

One of the smaller members of the tuna family, the skipjack averages in size from about 4 to 8 pounds, rarely topping 40 pounds. They are sometimes called striped tuna because of the dark stripes on the lower part of the body and occasionally can be found as ocean bonito, a relative they closely resemble. Although it can be prepared for sashimi, it also can be cooked; some chefs recommend soaking it in brine overnight first because of its strong flavor.

Bonito

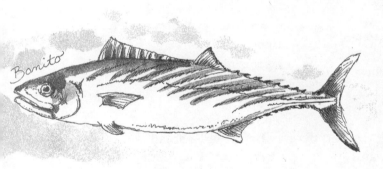

With stripes on the upper half of its body to identify it, bonito is found both in the Pacific and the Atlantic, generally weighing under 25 pounds but at market weights of 3 to 10 pounds.

One fact about bonito that has always fascinated us is that technically it is a full-fledged member of the mackerel (and tuna) family, but it cannot be sold as tuna, only as bonito. Still, it is generally included in the tuna category, as we have done, since it is so similar in shape, taste, and texture, but frequently quotation marks are put around the word "tuna" to separate it from its cousins.

The Japanese dry bonito until the pieces are as firm as what one writer described as "dried boomerangs." They then shave off thin slices to make *dashi,* an ingredient that is used in many traditional Japanese soups. Many find fresh bonito among the strongest flavored of the family; it should be soaked in brine overnight before cooking.

TUNA TAPENADE WITH GRILLED TUNA

MAKES 4 SERVINGS

Tapenade, the flavorful condiment from Provence, is derived from the word "caper" or "tapeno," one of the ingredients in it. We lavish it here on thyme-scented grilled tuna steaks.

TAPENADE:

- 2 teaspoons olive oil
- ½ small red onion, finely minced (about ¼ cup)
- 1 small garlic clove, finely minced (about ½ teaspoon)
- ⅛ teaspoon sugar
- ¼ pound Niçoise olives, pitted
- 1 or 2 flat anchovy fillets, rinsed and dried on paper towels
- 1 tablespoon capers, rinsed and dried on paper towels
- ½ teaspoon white wine Worcestershire sauce

- 1 tablespoon balsamic vinegar
- 1 tablespoon lemon juice
- ¼ cup mayonnaise
- ½ teaspoon Dijon mustard
- ¼ teaspoon black pepper
- 1 3¼-ounce can water-packed white tuna, drained

- 4 tuna steaks, ¾ to 1 inch thick and 6 to 8 ounces each (substitute: swordfish)
- 1 teaspoon canola oil
- ½ teaspoon dried thyme
- 4 lemon wedges

Prepare the tapenade several hours or even the day before: In a small skillet, add and combine the olive oil, onion, garlic, and sugar over very low heat. Sauté, stirring occasionally, for 10 to 12 minutes, until very soft but not brown. Set aside to cool.

In a food processor, add the olives, anchovy, capers, and onion mixture. In a small cup, combine the Worcestershire, vinegar, lemon juice, mayonnaise, mustard, and pepper and add to the food processor. Process for only 2 to 3 seconds until a coarse purée is formed. Scrape into a bowl. Break the canned tuna into small flakes and gently stir in. Cover with plastic wrap and refrigerate until needed but no longer than overnight.

When ready to serve, bring the tapenade to room temperature and preheat the broiler or prepare a very hot grill. Coat the fish with the oil to prevent it from sticking to the grill. Rub the thyme on the surface and place the fish on the hot grill. Grill for approximately 3 to 5 minutes on each side. After turning the fish over, test for doneness with a skewer after 3 minutes (see Note). Remove to a serving platter and spoon about 1 tablespoon of the tapenade over each portion. Serve with lemon wedges.

NOTE: Some people prefer the center of their tuna slightly raw. If you prefer it that way, grill the fish for only 3 minutes on each side.

PAN-GRILLED PEPPERCORN-CRUSTED TUNA STEAKS WITH LIME

MAKES 4 SERVINGS

A spicy, peppery, crusty surface encases quickly pan-seared tuna. Serve with simply steamed tiny new potatoes with a dab of minted yogurt for contrast to cool your palate.

2　teaspoons each dried black, white, green, and pink peppercorns

2　teaspoons mustard seeds

1　teaspoon fennel seeds

1　teaspoon finely minced lime peel

½　teaspoon lime juice

1　very small clove garlic, finely minced (½ teaspoon)

4　tablespoons butter, softened

4　tuna steaks, cut ¾ inch thick and about 6 ounces each (substitute: swordfish)

Salt to taste

Small lime wedges

Put all the peppercorns and mustard and fennel seeds in a spice grinder or mortar and pestle and grind or crush until a coarse mixture is formed. Transfer to a small bowl, add the lime peel, lime juice, garlic, and butter, and beat with a wooden spoon until well combined. Season the tuna with salt and spread the spice mixture on both sides of the steaks. Place the tuna steaks on waxed paper and refrigerate them for 15 to 20 minutes until the butter hardens.

Preheat a cast-iron skillet or ridged grill pan until very hot. Add the steaks in one layer and sear them for 2 minutes. If you are using a ridged grill, turn the steaks 90° to create a crisscross pattern. Continue to grill for 1 to 2 minutes more. Turn the steaks over and repeat the process, testing with a skewer for doneness after 2 minutes if you prefer a slightly rare center. Serve with wedges of lime.

TUNA TARTARE

Raw, very fresh tuna belly is used for this appetizer, one that will more than please any lover of sashimi. It even may convert those who think they don't like raw fish.

12 ounces fresh tuna in one piece, preferably *toro* (the marbled flesh from the tuna belly)

2 small Kirby cucumbers (about 6 ounces), cut into ¼-inch cubes

2 tablespoons pickled Japanese ginger, drained and cut into very fine julienne

1 large scallion green, finely shredded on the diagonal (about 2 tablespoons)

6 tablespoons tamari

1 teaspoon sugar

2 tablespoons rice vinegar

1 teaspoon wasabi paste (Japanese mustard) or more to taste (see Note)

6 paper-thin slices lemon for garnish

Trim the tuna of any very dark flesh. Cut into ¼-inch dice, removing any whitish membrane you may come across. Put the tuna in a medium bowl and combine with the cucumber, ginger, and scallion.

In a small cup, whisk together the tamari, sugar, vinegar, and half the wasabi. Taste and add the remaining wasabi until there is a sharp pungency. Pour over the tuna mixture and combine lightly. Transfer with a slotted spoon to chilled serving plates (preferably glass). Slash each lemon halfway across, twist, and use to garnish each plate.

NOTE: Wasabi sometimes comes in powder form and a bit of water is needed to prepare a thick paste.

MACKEREL FAMILY

Probably one of the richest-tasting fish to swim the seas, the mackerel was quite unappreciated for many years, because it is very perishable and has a fatty flesh that varies greatly depending upon season and geography. It took modern methods of catching, bleeding, flash freezing, and rapid transportation to bring the mackerel to the attention of consumers as a remarkable and flavorful fish.

Indeed, mackerel has had a poor reputation for centuries, which was eloquently stated in this nineteenth-century attack by Representative John Randolph of Virginia on Edward Livingston: "He is a man of splendid abilities, but utterly corrupt. He shines and stinks like rotten mackerel by moonlight."

Mackerel is the family to which the tuna belong, although mackerel generally are of a much smaller size than their cousins. They're a favorite with sports fishermen, with characteristics quite similar to tuna in their jolting strikes, breakneck runs, and a struggle that closely approximates that of large bluefish. Traveling in packs and capable of lightning runs for their food, they have been called the "wolves of the sea." It is not unusual, for example, to see the Spanish mackerel leap up from the water as much as ten feet into the air and then descend like a missile to try to shake the hook.

Because of their fatty flesh, mackerel are probably one of the best fish for grilling, with a choice of whole or pan-dressed fish, steaks, or fillets. One of the reasons that they have become so popular is that they have no small bones and are very easy to cook, no matter which method you choose.

Atlantic Mackerel

From a market point of view, Atlantic mackerel is probably the most important of the species. Found both in the Atlantic coast off Newfoundland down to Cape Hatteras as well as in the waters off most of Europe down into the Mediterranean, it has a shiny body with a series of characteristic wavy bands on the upper part. It has a large amount of red meat, which can be found fresh or frozen, as well as smoked, air-dried, or peppered.

Chub Mackerel

Although more plentiful in the Pacific and thus sometimes called Pacific mackerel, chub is also caught in the Atlantic Ocean. It is a smaller fish than the Atlantic mackerel, seldom weighing over a pound or two. It has a rich distinctive flavor and generally is sold whole. Pacific jack mackerel, which is not a mackerel at all (see page 178), is sometimes confused with chub, since they are quite similar in appearance. Fishmongers on the West Coast occasionally will sell either or both as mackerel, but the jack has a milder flavor.

Spanish Mackerel

Spanish mackerel is the most delicately flavored of the mackerel family, and many consider it the culinary champion. It's magnificently colored with a dark blue upper body that gradually pales to a silvery belly with small yellow or olive spots on its sides. Although it can grow to nearly 20 pounds, most market weights are 2 to 4 pounds. Their high fat content makes them ideal for broiling, grilling, baking, or smoking.

King Mackerel

Sometimes called kingfish, king mackerel should not be confused with the fish of the very same name in the drum family. King mackerel is one of the larger members of the group, ranging in size from 5 to 20 pounds, although it has been known to reach nearly

100 pounds. Because it is so large, it is one of the few mackerels that can be bought as steaks, although fillets and pan-dressed or whole fish are more usually found at the fishmonger. It has a fatty flesh with a quite fine texture and more intense flavor than most of its cousins. Its blue-tinged flesh whitens when cooked.

Cero Mackerel

Found mostly in Florida waters, the cero also swims in the Caribbean and from New England down to the coast of Brazil. Market sizes range from 5 to 10 pounds, although the fish can reach weights of over 30 pounds. It more closely resembles the Spanish mackerel than the other members of the family in that it is delicately flavored. The cero makes excellent steaks and takes well to grilling or smoking.

Wahoo

Somehow it is a name that has always delighted us, particularly when said aloud. Unlike most of its cousins, the wahoo has a white, delicately textured flesh, and some consider it one of the great delicacies of the oceans. In fact, the Hawaiians call the fish *ono,* which means "sweet." Wahoo are caught throughout most of the tropical and subtropical waters of the world, with most of the catch coming from the Pacific and the Caribbean islands. The average market weight runs about 25 pounds, and the fish is excellent for broiling or baking, either as fillets or as steaks.

Mackerel Family

GRILLED MOROCCAN MACKEREL WITH CHARMOULA VINAIGRETTE

Mackerel, one of the richest-tasting fish in the sea, always needs to be counterbalanced with enough acidity to cut its richness. The Moroccans cook fish with a more pastelike charmoula, but we have added some olive oil to this fragrant, lightly spiced mixture, allowing it to be used as both a marinade and a sauce.

2 cups cilantro leaves (about 1 large bunch)	½ teaspoon cayenne pepper
½ cup parsley leaves	½ teaspoon ground saffron powder (see Note)
3 large cloves garlic, peeled	Salt and pepper to taste
1 small red onion (about 3 ounces), quartered	½ cup olive oil
¼ cup lemon juice (about 1 large lemon)	6 whole Atlantic mackerel, 1 to 1¼ pounds each, gutted and scaled, with heads on (substitute: jackfish or bluefish)
1 tablespoon red wine vinegar	
2 teaspoons ground cumin	
¼ teaspoon ground ginger	

In a food processor, finely mince the cilantro and parsley leaves. Add the garlic and onion and continue to process until very fine. Add the lemon juice, vinegar, cumin, ginger, cayenne, saffron, salt, and pepper and process until combined. With motor running, slowly add the oil through the feed tube until a thickish emulsion forms. Transfer to a small bowl. There should be about 1¼ cups.

Place a piece of heavy aluminum foil on a counter and place the fish on it. With a small spatula, spread some of the vinaigrette evenly on both sides of the fish and marinate in the refrigerator for 1 hour. While the fish is marinating, prepare a grill. When the grill has no flame but only hot glowing embers, place the fish on an oiled perforated rack and grill 4 to 6 inches from the heat for 4 to 5 minutes on each side. Test with a skewer to see if the fish flakes easily. Or broil the fish about 4 inches from heat for about 5 minutes on each side.

Serve the fish with a small amount of sauce either on the side of the plate or in a small shell or dish. Grilling some eggplant slices, brushed with the same marinade, along with the fish can provide a side dish.

NOTE: Ground saffron, which has some turmeric in it, can be found in Middle Eastern or Spanish specialty shops.

WHOLE SPANISH MACKEREL BAKED WITH SUMMER VEGETABLES

A colorful assortment of summer vegetables and herbs bake along with the beautiful, silvery skinned Spanish mackerel in a sort of ratatouille mixture. Serve it with rice or tiny pasta if you wish.

6   tablespoons olive oil

1   whole 3½- to 4-pound Spanish mackerel, gutted and with head intact (substitute: bluefish)

     Salt and pepper to taste

1   medium onion (about 6 ounces), cut and separated into ¼-inch-thick rings

1 or 2   medium green peppers (about ¾ pound), cut into ¼-inch rings

1 or 2   small zucchini (about ¾ pound), trimmed and cut into 1-inch pieces

1   small yellow squash (about ½ pound), cut into 1-inch pieces

2   slim Japanese eggplants (about ¾ pound), peeled and cut into ¾-inch pieces

3   tablespoons coarsely chopped fresh basil, plus a few extra leaves for garnish

½   teaspoon dried oregano, preferably Greek

2   tablespoons finely minced parsley

2   cups tomato juice

¼   teaspoon Tabasco

1   medium lemon, peeled, thinly sliced, and pitted, for garnish

Preheat the oven to 425°. Add 3 tablespoons of the olive oil to an oven-to-table baking pan large enough to accommodate the fish and vegetables. Add the fish and turn to coat evenly with the oil. Season with salt and pepper and set aside.

In a large bowl, add the remaining oil, the onion, pepper, zucchini, squash, eggplants, basil, oregano, parsley, and additional salt and pepper. Toss to coat the vegetables with the oil, then arrange around the fish. Mix the tomato juice and Tabasco together and pour over the vegetables and fish. Bake for 30 to 40 minutes, basting both the fish and vegetables every 10 minutes. Test the thickest part of the fish with a skewer after 28 minutes to see if it flakes easily. Garnish the fish with the lemon slices and basil leaves. Serve hot.

GRILLED KING MACKEREL STEAKS WITH FENNEL BUTTER AND GRILLED FENNEL

The intense licorice flavor of fennel seeds, Pernod, and grilled fennel are the perfect triple whammy for flavorful kingfish steaks. Grayish in color when raw, kingfish turns white when cooked.

3   small fennel bulbs, about ½ pound each, trimmed and halved, feathery tops reserved for garnish

6   king mackerel (kingfish) steaks, about ¾ inch thick and 6 to 8 ounces each (substitute: other mackerel, bluefish, or amberjack)

½   teaspoon black pepper

Salt to taste

5   tablespoons butter

2   teaspoons fennel seeds, pulverized in a blender

2   tablespoons Pernod or Ricard liqueur

1   tablespoon lemon juice

2   tablespoons grated Parmesan cheese

Lemon wedges

In a medium saucepan, drop the fennel into enough boiling salted water to cover. When the water returns to the boil, lower the heat and simmer for 8 to 10 minutes until the fennel is almost tender, then drain and set aside on paper towels.

Preheat and oil an outdoor grill or broiler. Season the fish steaks with pepper and salt. In a small skillet, melt the butter over low heat. Add the fennel seeds, Pernod, and lemon juice and stir to combine. Brush the fennel butter generously over the steaks and fennel and grill the steaks on one side, basting frequently, for about 4 to 5 minutes. Carefully turn the fish with a wide spatula and add the fennel to the grill. Continue to baste and grill the fish and fennel for 3 to 4 minutes more, turning the fennel frequently so that it's charred slightly all over. Test the fish with a skewer to see if it is cooked through.

Using a wide spatula, transfer the fish to a serving platter and surround the steaks with the grilled fennel. Sprinkle only the fennel with the Parmesan; if there is any basting butter left, spoon it over the fish. Scatter the reserved fennel tops over all and tuck in the lemon wedges.

JACK FAMILY

With the exception of pompano and to a lesser extent yellowtail, the jack family is not particularly widespread on the ice beds of our fish markets. There are some states, such as Hawaii and Florida, where the prevalence of some jacks during certain seasons makes them more available. Hawaii, for example, has ten family members swimming off its shores. But, for the rest of the country, the most familiar is without doubt the pompano.

There are nearly 200 members of the family found throughout the world in most tropical and subtropical waters. Their culinary qualities run the gamut from very poor to delicious and sublime. Some have softer textures and others are quite firm; some have flesh that is a gentle pink white, while others are rich and red. We have listed the most common (or popular) jacks below.

Pompano

Somehow, we've always had the feeling that pompano is like the rich relative who doesn't want to be associated with the "poor trash" of its immigrant family and has moved uptown to pursue a life of its own. We rarely remember that pompano is a member of the jack family. Indeed, we frequently find that most fish cookbooks give the fish its own listing, as if it were a separate species. We have moved it back to where it belongs.

Pompano, especially those caught off the Florida coast, have a remarkable reputation, and rarely does a visitor to that state ever leave without having tasted the fish in some restaurant. Pompano generally runs between ¾ and 2 pounds and is fine textured, moderately fatty, with a mild and delicate flavor. Given its reputation, the demand often exceeds the supply and, thus, it can be fairly expensive. Whether the fish is overrated or not, we cannot judge. We also nod when someone dubs pompano "the aristocrat of fish."

For pompano lovers outside of Florida, there is no need to travel to Florida to taste it. It's now shipped all over the country and is available in most places fresh and generally sold whole to show off its almost flat, shiny, silvery skin. It need not be scaled, although it can be filleted by the fishmonger. We strongly suggest that you avoid already cut "pompano fillets," since they probably come from imported relatives that are not quite as tasty as the Florida variety. Pompano takes well to almost all types of preparation, although the preferred method is *en papillote*.

Yellowtail (Amberjack)

Although actually two different members of the family, amberjack and yellowtail are generally marketed interchangeably, with yellowtail being the name of choice. As Japanese restaurants have proliferated here, and people generally have overcome their prejudices about eating raw fish, the yellowtail has become more familiar, especially in the preparation of sashimi and sushi. In fact, the Japanese have been farming an amberjack called yellowtail for centuries, and it is found on menus as *hamachi*.

The fish can grow to the weight of 100 pounds, but market sizes are much, much smaller, ranging from 5 pounds to 20. The smaller fish are preferable, since the larger jacks are sometimes subject to parasites. However, the problem is more prevalent in the Caribbean than in northern countries.

Pacific Jack Mackerel

We have already mentioned this fish on page 172 as closely resembling the chub mackerel, even though it is not a member of the chub family. And even though it carries the appellation of mackerel, it is still a true jack. It is a mild-tasting fish and is generally quite small, usually between 1 and 5 pounds. Although some jack mackerel is available fresh on the Pacific coast, most of the catch goes to the canning factory where it frequently is mixed right along with chub mackerel.

Crevalle Jack

Crevalle

Although crevalle jack is found in waters around the world, it is most common in Florida, where it appears in large schools, running as high as 20 pounds, but generally within the 2- to 4-pound range. There is a story, possibly apocryphal, that the early Florida settlers found them so numerous that they hunted them from the shoreline with rifles! If you're ever lucky enough to fish for them in Florida, make certain to bleed your catch before taking it home (see page 19).

BROILED POMPANO WITH TOMATO, ORANGE, AND HERB VINAIGRETTE

MAKES 4 SERVINGS

Silvery-skinned pompano and Florida restaurants were once almost synonymous. This once local specialty now can be enjoyed all over the country, thanks to fast shipping and better handling.

4 6- to 8-ounce pompano fillets, with skin (substitute: mahi-mahi or ocean perch)

1 teaspoon dried thyme

1 teaspoon finely minced ginger

1 tablespoon lemon juice

2 tablespoons light soy sauce or tamari

6 tablespoons olive oil

   Salt and pepper to taste

2 tablespoons red wine vinegar

1 large scallion green, finely minced (about ¼ cup)

2 medium cloves garlic, finely minced (about 2 teaspoons)

¼ cup coarsely chopped fresh basil

2 teaspoons finely minced orange peel

⅛ teaspoon cayenne pepper

2 large plum tomatoes, cut into ¼-inch cubes (about ¾ cup)

Place the fillets skin side down in one layer in a nonreactive pan. In a small bowl, mix the thyme, ginger, lemon juice, soy, 2 tablespoons of the olive oil, the salt, and pepper, and pour over the fillets. Cover with plastic wrap and refrigerate for 1 hour, turning the fish once after 30 minutes.

While the fish is marinating, place all the remaining ingredients except for the tomatoes into a mixing bowl and blend well with a whisk. Stir in the tomatoes and additional salt and pepper if needed. Keep the sauce at room temperature.

When ready to cook, preheat the broiler or prepare an outdoor grill. Lift the fish out of the marinade and place it skin side down on an oiled grill or pan. Discard the marinade. Grill or broil 4 inches from the heat about 3 minutes on each side until a skewer inserted into the thickest part of the flesh will flake the fish. Pompano is a thin fish, so watch it carefully while grilling so that it doesn't overcook.

When ready to serve, place a fillet off center on each plate and spoon a bit of the sauce over the fish and a bit more on the side of each plate.

POMPANO EN PAPILLOTE WITH GIN AND CHERVIL

MAKES 4 SERVINGS

As each pocket is slashed open, the handsome silver-skinned pompano sparkles like sequins, then tastes divine in its bath of gin and chervil.

4 tablespoons melted butter

4 whole 1-pound pompano, gutted, with heads intact (substitute: 6-ounce ocean perch fillets with skin)

2 large shallots, finely minced (about ⅓ cup)

4 large mushrooms (¼ pound), preferably cremini, trimmed and thinly sliced

Salt and pepper to taste

4 tablespoons gin

2 tablespoons finely minced fresh chervil or parsley

4 thin slices lemon, peeled and pitted

Preheat the oven to 400°. Cut 4 large sheets of parchment paper and fold each piece in half. Place one fish on one half to test for the size of the paper. Cut a heart shape around each fish, allowing a 2-inch border. Open the parchment paper and brush it with melted butter, avoiding the border. Place a fish on half of each paper heart, top with ¼ of the shallots, the mushrooms, the salt, the pepper, a trickle of the remaining butter, the gin, the chervil, and finally the lemon. Fold the paper over and bring the edges together, allowing room for steam to expand the paper.

Starting at the widest part of the paper and working down to the narrowest end, fold the paper over twice, ¼ inch at a time, in order to firmly seal the package; twist the paper at the end to fasten it. If necessary, you can fasten the ends with paper clips or brush them with egg white (see page 40). The packets of fish can be prepared in advance and refrigerated until baking. However, if you do prepare them in advance, make sure to bring them back to room temperature.

When ready to bake, place the packets on a baking sheet and bake for 20 minutes. The paper will be lightly brown and puffed up. Serve one packet per person. Slash with an "X" at the table and peel back the paper to eat.

SHARK FAMILY

Although current perception has it that the notoriety of the shark as a wild, thrashing killer dates only to the popular film *Jaws*, it actually has had its frightening reputation long before that. We remember as children seeing the early 1930s film *Tiger Shark* in which a shipwrecked sailor (whom we recall as Edward G. Robinson) drifted in a lifeboat through shark-infested waters, his arm dangerously dangling overboard. In a terrifying instant, his arm was gone, taken by a tiger shark, and horrifying the audience not yet inured to motion picture blood and gore.

However, we, and many like us, have said that it is high time that the tables were turned, since many more sharks have been eaten by humans than vice versa. In fact, shark has been consumed for centuries in Europe and the rest of the world; it is only within the last ten or fifteen years that North Americans have discovered it as a culinary treat.

There are over 300 species of shark worldwide. It is popular in Africa and is an important ingredient for shark fin soup in the Orient. For many years, it has been the traditional ingredient for what A. J. McClane calls the "hamburger of England," fish and chips. We're also certain that, for years, many unsuspectingly have been eating shark sold as swordfish, fillet of sole, or even halibut. During World War II, shark was reportedly dyed and sold as salmon and tuna! But, all this has changed. For the most part, now shark is *shark,* either sold generically or as shark or, for more sophisticated shoppers, by their specific names, some of which we've listed below.

The larger the shark, the coarser the texture, and if they are not handled properly aboard ship or by those who love to catch them, the quality deteriorates rather quickly. Shark must be bled, usually by cutting off the tail, then decapitated, gutted, and iced at once. Since they contain urea, they will begin to produce a strong, ammonia-like smell if the procedure is not followed. In fact, when buying a shark at the fishmonger, you can quickly determine freshness by the smell—or lack of it. If you should catch a shark while on a fishing trip or you buy one on the dock, you may want to first soak the meat in ice water with some salt, lemon juice, or cider vinegar. Then let it marinate for about 2 to 4 hours in the refrigerator to eliminate what some have called the "wild taste." Shark purchased at the fishmonger should not need this treatment.

Shark flesh is solid and holds its shape well, making it particularly good for stews, broiling, deep-frying, grilling as kebobs, or with any other high-heat method. Although shark will vary in flavor and texture depending upon the species, they are usually lean and slightly moist with a taste that is quite pronounced. And that they are not bony—except for the cartilaginous spine—makes them even more popular.

We have listed some of the more popular members of the family below, but the list is by no means complete. Other areas of the world may offer even greater diversity—including the terror we described at the outset, the tiger shark.

Mako

Mako shark

Mako is one of the most popular of the species and a large fish, sometimes weighing up to 1,000 pounds. It's available year round and, because of its size, is usually sold in steaks or cubes. Mako is highly prized not only by home and restaurant chefs but also as a fighting game fish. Mako is caught in the Atlantic and down in tropical waters. The fine-grained, moist flesh often is cut into steaks, when it most closely approximates swordfish, one of the reasons that it may occasionally be sold as such. Yet another reason for having a fishmonger you can trust.

Bonito

No relation to the bonito in the tuna family (see page 167), bonito shark is the closest-tasting Pacific Coast relative of the East Coast mako. It also has the distinction of being one of the larger species, as well as closely resembling swordfish, as does the mako.

Thresher

Thresher Shark

Found in temperate and subtropical waters around the world, thresher can reach the size of bonito and mako, but the average catch is closer to 100 pounds, still a large fish by any standards. The flesh is quite dense and firm with a slightly pink tinge. It turns whiter when cooked and it is most often found at the fish market as steaks.

Shark Family

Dogfish

Despite the unfortunate name, dogfish is a most fortunate choice for dinner. Unfortunately you may be hard pressed to find it at the local fish market, since it is regarded as a nuisance by most fisherpeople in our area, who throw them back immediately. On the other hand, it has long been a prime ingredient in the ever-popular British fish and chips.

The dogfish and some of its relatives such as the spiny dogfish or sand shark are the smaller of the family, generally running no more than 10 pounds. They are slightly softer in texture than the larger members of the family and somewhat fattier with a very distinctive taste. We'd strongly suggest, if one of your fishing friends happens to land a dogfish, you grab it at once and try it as a fillet. We hope that the commercial fish markets also take note that this is really a very underutilized species. The British have tried dubbing it rock salmon, and the Italians have called it veal of the sea, while up in Maine our friends call it harbor halibut. Unfortunately, none of this seems to have helped its popularity.

Soupfin

If you look carefully at the name, you realize at once that this is the original shark of shark-fin soup. However, other varieties are now used. A West Coast species, the soupfin ranges in size from 30 to 50 pounds and can usually be found as fillets and steaks.

Blacktip

Blacktip Shark

Usually found in the Atlantic off the coast of Florida and in the Caribbean, blacktip shark can also be found in temperate waters in other parts of the world. They usually weigh somewhere around 70 pounds, with commercial catches between 30 and 40 pounds. Their flesh is somewhat drier than that of the other species (such as mako) and therefore should be brushed with oil or butter when cooked.

SHARK
Rough skin like sandpaper. Slate-colored skin. Rounder swirls on dark meat. Mako has pale, pink flesh.

SWORDFISH
Smooth, gray-brown skin. More compact, dense flesh. Coral-colored meat.

shark steak

swordfish steak

WARM POTATO-CRUSTED SHARK SALAD ON PUNGENT GREENS

MAKES 6 SERVINGS

Crusty, golden shreds of potato embrace cubes of firm, sweet mako, served with sharp greens for contrast.

2 tablespoons balsamic or red wine vinegar
1 teaspoon Dijon mustard
1 medium clove garlic, finely minced (about 1 teaspoon)
   Salt and black pepper to taste
6 tablespoons light olive oil
6 cups assorted sharply pungent salad greens, such as arugula, mizuna, curly endive, watercress, red mustard, Belgian endive, escarole, young dandelion greens, or radicchio, torn into bite-size pieces

1½ pounds shark (preferably mako), boned, skinned, and cut into 1½-inch cubes (substitute: monkfish)
⅛ teaspoon cayenne pepper
1 large egg, lightly beaten
¾ cup all-purpose flour
1½ pounds russet potatoes, peeled
1 small wedge lemon
   Corn oil for frying

In a small bowl, whisk the vinegar, mustard, garlic, salt, and pepper together, then slowly add the oil, whisking constantly. Set aside.

Combine the greens in a large bowl and keep chilled. Season the cubes of fish with salt, pepper, and cayenne. Put the egg in a bowl and the flour on a piece of waxed paper. Shred the potatoes, using the shredder blade of a food processor and adding a few drops of lemon juice to each batch to prevent the potatoes from discoloring. Add the potatoes to a strainer as they are shredded, then press them against the strainer to extract any excess liquid. (Some potatoes will be more watery than others.) Season the potatoes with additional salt and pepper.

In a large cast-iron skillet, heat about 1 inch oil over medium-high heat. Dip the fish cubes first in the egg, then in the flour, and then the shredded potatoes, pressing lightly with your fingers so that the potatoes adhere. Fry a few pieces at a time for about 4 to 5 minutes on each side until the potatoes are crisp and golden, turning to brown evenly.

While the fish is cooking, toss the greens with one-third of the dressing and distribute among 6 plates. As the fish is cooked, arrange it alongside the greens and drizzle some of the remaining dressing over the fish and greens on each plate.

CHINESE SHARK AND VEGETABLE PANCAKES

These crisp little pancakes, filled with fish and vegetables, easily can become addictive. Try them as a first course or serve them with rice as a main course.

⅓ cup plus 1 teaspoon soy sauce or tamari

2 teaspoons rice vinegar

1 teaspoon finely minced ginger

1 pound shark fillet, preferably mako, cut into 1-inch cubes (substitute: ocean perch)

1 cup all-purpose flour

½ teaspoon baking powder

2 eggs, lightly beaten

¼ teaspoon cayenne pepper

1 small carrot, finely minced (about ⅓ cup)

5 to 6 medium scallions, finely minced (about ¾ cup)

1 tablespoon finely minced cilantro

2 ounces green beans, finely chopped and blanched

Corn oil for frying

In a small cup, combine ⅓ cup of the soy, the vinegar, and ginger; distribute among 4 tiny dishes or sake cups to use as a dipping sauce.

Put the fish in a food processor and process only until coarsely chopped. There should be about 1¼ cups. Transfer to a large bowl, add the remaining ingredients, including 1 teaspoon soy but excluding the oil, and stir to combine. The batter should be thick.

Heat about 1½ inches oil in a skillet or wok over medium-high heat until very hot (about 370°). Drop the batter by tablespoons into the oil. Flatten each pancake slightly with the back of a spoon as you drop it into the oil. Fry until golden brown, turning to cook evenly. With a slotted spoon, transfer the pancakes to paper towels to drain. Repeat with the remaining batter. Serve with the dipping sauce.

SWORDFISH

Found in temperate waters throughout the world and one of the most popular of trophy game fish, swordfish is the lone member of its family, although others boast the same weapon: billfish, marlin, spearfish, and sailfish, for example. They're quite distinctive and certainly recognizable because of their lethal sword, which is used both offensively and defensively, letting them rise from below to skewer or swat their prey. Shaped like a huge mackerel, the swordfish can weigh close to 1,000 pounds, with averages between 200 and 400 pounds not at all uncommon.

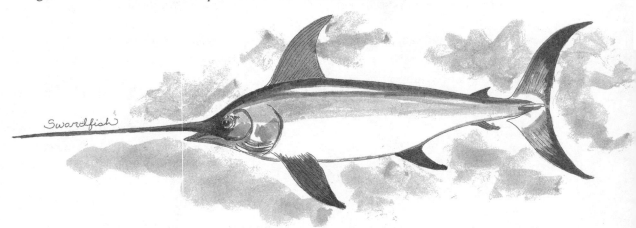

Swordfish

Incredibly fast and powerful, swordfish are formidable fighters when harpooned or hooked, and tales of the sea tell of their sharply pointed swords piercing the sides of ships. Over the years, they have been quickly gathering importance in the marketplace, and the demand has now begun to exceed the supply. Too often, therefore, mako shark is substituted for swordfish on the beds of ice (see page 185).

As the use of the grill has increased, so has the popularity of this firm-fleshed, full-flavored, lean predator. Although scaleless, swordfish has a thick skin that helps keep the flesh together through almost any kind of cooking, especially over hot coals. However, they can be cooked successfully by almost any other method: sautéing, poaching, frying, broiling, or baking. They're usually cut first in center cuts or wheels and then portioned into steaks or cubes. With only the one bone in the center, they're a delight to eat. We suggest that portions be 1 to 1½ inches thick and that the fish be marinated before cooking, then brushed with oil or butter to keep them from drying out. You'll find that the flesh will vary from pale coral to a gray white, but the fish will turn pure white when it's cooking.

NOTE: Swordfish does not separate into flakes when tested with a skewer. When it is properly done, the flesh will be opaque. Cut into the thickest part of one piece with the tip of a sharp knife after 6 minutes to begin testing for doneness.

BAKED SWORDFISH WITH MUSTARD GLAZE

The bite of mustard plus the additional crunch of mustard seeds and some dill is tempered by a touch of mayonnaise, which forms a puffy golden glaze over the firm-fleshed swordfish as it bakes.

2 tablespoons mustard seeds	1 tablespoon minced fresh dill
2 tablespoons dry white wine	4 swordfish steaks, 1 inch thick and 6 to 8 ounces each (substitute: tuna or mahi-mahi)
⅓ cup coarse-grain mustard	
2 tablespoons lemon juice	
⅔ cup mayonnaise	Salt and pepper to taste
2 to 3 large shallots, finely minced (about 2 tablespoons)	

Soak the mustard seeds in the wine for 30 minutes to soften them a bit. Then drain and discard the wine and add the seeds to a small bowl. Add the coarse mustard, lemon juice, mayonnaise, shallots, and dill and whisk to combine.

Preheat the oven to 425°. Butter an oven-to-table baking pan. Spread about one-third of the mustard glaze on the bottom of the pan and arrange the fish on top. Season with salt and pepper and spoon the remaining glaze over the fish.

Bake for 10 to 12 minutes, until the fish, when tested with the point of a knife or skewer, is opaque all the way through and the glaze has browned a bit. If the glaze is not dappled with brown, slip it under the broiler for about 30 seconds.

GRILLED SWORDFISH WITH TROPICAL FRUIT SALSA

A slightly sweet, fruity sauce is flamed with cayenne and mellowed by mild rice wine vinegar for these grilled swordfish steaks.

½ ripe large papaya, peeled, seeded, and cut into ¼-inch dice (about 1 cup)

1 tablespoon lime juice

½ ripe large mango, peeled, pitted, and cut into ¼-inch dice (about 1 cup)

1 large kiwi, peeled and cut into ¼-inch dice (about ¼ cup)

2 teaspoons rice vinegar

2 tablespoons finely minced cilantro

⅛ teaspoon cayenne pepper

Salt and pepper to taste

4 swordfish steaks, 1 inch thick and 6 to 8 ounces each (substitute: tuna steaks)

1 tablespoon olive oil

1 teaspoon ground coriander

In a food processor, purée half the papaya along with the lime juice. Scrape into a small bowl and add the remaining papaya, the mango, kiwi, vinegar, cilantro, cayenne, salt, and pepper and stir gently to combine.

Prepare a grill. Rub the fish with the oil and season with salt, pepper, and coriander. Grill the fish, turning once, 3 to 4 minutes on each side. Test with a skewer to see if the fish is opaque. Transfer the fish to serving plates and spoon some of the salsa on the other side of the plates.

More Strongly Flavored Saltwater Fish   ❖   190   ❖

BROCHETTES OF SWORDFISH WITH BAY LEAVES AND COUSCOUS SALAD

1½ pounds swordfish steak, skinned, cut into 1½-inch cubes (substitute: tuna or mahi-mahi)

8 bay leaves

6 tablespoons olive oil

3 lemons

½ teaspoon dried oregano, preferably Greek

¼ teaspoon pepper

Salt to taste

1 cup chicken stock

1 cup quick cooking couscous

2 plum tomatoes, finely diced (about ¾ cup)

1 small green pepper, finely diced (about ½ cup)

1 medium carrot, finely diced (about ½ cup)

2 thin scallions, thinly sliced on the diagonal (about ⅓ cup)

2 tablespoons coarsely chopped fresh opal or green basil

2 tablespoons coarsely chopped fresh mint

2 tablespoons red wine vinegar

1 teaspoon finely minced garlic (1 medium clove)

Place the swordfish in a nonreactive bowl and combine with the bay leaves and 3 tablespoons of the oil. Very thinly slice 2 lemons and set them aside. Peel and finely mince the peel of the third lemon, then juice it; add both the peel and juice to the swordfish, along with the oregano, half the pepper, and salt to taste. Let stand at room temperature for 20 minutes while preparing the couscous.

In a large saucepan, bring the chicken stock to a boil, stir in the couscous, lower the heat, and simmer for 5 minutes. Cover the pot and set it aside for 10 minutes. Add the tomatoes, green pepper, carrot, scallions, basil, and mint. Toss with a fork to separate the grains and to stir in the vegetables completely.

In a small bowl, whisk together the vinegar, the remaining 3 tablespoons olive oil, the garlic, the remaining ⅛ teaspoon pepper, and additional salt to taste. Stir into the couscous mixture, then transfer it to a large serving platter and set aside at room temperature.

When ready to serve, prepare a grill or preheat the broiler. Oil 4 metal skewers and thread the swordfish cubes on them, alternating with the bay leaves and lemon slices that are folded in half so that they don't slip off. Reserve the marinade.

Grill 4 inches from the heat, basting with the marinade every 2 minutes and turning once, for 6 to 8 minutes. When done, the fish will be opaque (see page 53). Lay the brochettes over the couscous and serve.

BLUEFISH

For those of us who fish in the roaring surf of the Atlantic Ocean, the bluefish carries a very special place in our hearts. Pound for pound, this battling dynamo is a fisherperson's dream. In the fall, swarms of shrieking terns announce the arrival of a school as it moves down the shoreline, and we can almost feel the pounding of the hearts of the waiting throngs of men and women, casting their lines into the churning water as the fish attack their prey.

As far back as 1874, a report from the U.S. Commission on Fish and Fisheries described the bluefish as "an animated chopping machine, the business of which is to cut to pieces and otherwise destroy as many fish as possible in a given space of time." Indeed, the bluefish has been known to not only chop up its prey—be it menhaden (bunker) or sand eels—but also its own young, disgorging its feast only to start all over again. Actually, it is the constant feeding that makes them grow so quickly from little snappers to 10 to 12 pounders by season's end.

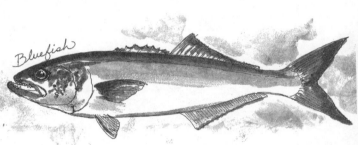

Bluefish

But putting all this aside, we also feel that it is one of the tastiest fish in the ocean, and much of our time is spent in trying to explain to our neighbors that it does not deserve its reputation as too oily. Surfeited with a catch that demands that we give some away, we are often met with a negative response.

Certainly, when compared with flounder or the bland whiting or orange roughy, bluefish does have a very defined, intense flavor, due to its high fat content. At the same time, it is this very fact that makes it imperative that you choose the freshest fish available, assuming that you do not catch your own or are the recipient of a fisherperson's extremely good luck.

Bluefish are plentiful all up and down the Atlantic Coast from New England into the Gulf of Mexico; they move up along the shoreline into the late fall and then back down to warmer waters as winter approaches. Their market weights range from 3 to 5 pounds, with the larger bluefish topping 15 to 18 pounds. In choosing bluefish at your fishmonger's, your nose is the best judge. Also make sure the fish has clear eyes or that the fillets look moist and smell of the sea. If the fillets look milky, pass and choose another fish. Because of its fat content, bluefish spoil quickly if not handled properly, either commercially or when caught by sports people.

There is one other tip that we generally recommend to our friends, and we're sure that you'll find there's a distinct difference if you try it. When the fish is cooked, remove the dark, fatty lateral flesh on the fillet or the skinned whole fish. It is that dark meat that contains most of the fat and not only the "good" omega 3s, but also that strong taste that some find objectionable. With the larger fish, that dark meat also can contain some of the PCBs (polychlorinated biphenyls) found in some of those that spawn in places close to polluted shorelines. Those that spawn at sea are not affected, although they may well feed on other fish that carry PCBs.

You'll also find that the smaller bluefish—about 1½ to 2½ pounds—will have a milder taste than the larger ones, since they have not yet begun to feed on menhaden, an oily prey and a favorite of the blues. For a special treat, if you live near the ocean or a saltwater Atlantic bay, you may see people fishing for snappers, the offspring of bluefish, each weighing about ¼ pound. Quickly scaled and gutted and then just as quickly pan-fried, they are manna from heaven.

GRILLED BABY BLUEFISH (SNAPPERS) AND HERB PACKETS

MAKES 6 SERVINGS

*Outdoor grilling comingles wood smoke with the perfume of summer flowers.
Add packets of baby bluefish (snappers) with fresh herbs, and you have a veritable
festival of scents.*

6 whole baby bluefish, about 1 pound each,
    gutted and scaled (substitute: butterfish
    or pompano)
6 teaspoons butter, softened
1 large onion, very thinly sliced
6 small bay leaves
6 sprigs parsley

6 sprigs dill
1 teaspoon fennel seeds
¾ teaspoon black pepper
    Coarse salt to taste
6 teaspoons lemon juice
6 teaspoons vermouth

Prepare a grill and let the coals get very hot. Tear off 6 sheets of heavy aluminum foil large enough for each one to enclose a fish, allowing about 1½ inches extra. Butter the center of each piece of foil with approximately 1 teaspoon butter. Place a fish on each piece of foil, then top with a few onion slices, a bay leaf, parsley and dill sprigs, a few fennel seeds, some of the pepper, salt, and 1 teaspoon each lemon juice and vermouth. Fold the foil over and crimp the edges tightly. Place the packets on the grill and cook for 10 to 15 minutes on each side. Slash open one packet and test the fish with a skewer after about 25 minutes of total cooking time.

NOTE: If you wish, the packets can be baked in the oven on a baking sheet. Bake at 425° for approximately the same amount of time. The aluminum foil reflects some heat, so that a longer cooking time may be necessary.

MARINATED AND BROILED BLUEFISH WITH ORANGES AND MINT

MAKES 6 SERVINGS

A colorful presentation with enough acidity to cut the richness and enhance the flavor of the bluefish.

½ cup white wine vinegar

¼ cup cold water

3 sprigs thyme or ½ teaspoon dried thyme

1 bay leaf

2 bluefish fillets, about 1½ pounds each, brown strip of fatty meat trimmed (substitute: mackerel, yellowtail, or tuna)

Salt to taste

3 tablespoons melted butter

¾ cup orange juice (2 or 3 oranges)

1 tablespoon finely minced orange peel

1 teaspoon finely minced ginger

½ teaspoon black pepper

2 small oranges, peel, white pith, and seeds removed, thinly sliced

2 small red onions, thinly sliced

1 tablespoon mild honey

2 tablespoons coarsely chopped fresh mint

In a small saucepan, bring the vinegar, water, thyme, and bay leaf slowly to a boil, then let cool completely. Place the fish in a large nonreactive pan, sprinkle with salt, and pour the marinade over the fish. Let stand at room temperature for 30 minutes, turning once.

Dry the fish on paper towels and discard the marinade. Preheat the broiler. In a small bowl, mix the butter, orange juice, orange peel, ginger, and pepper together. Lay the fish in one layer in a large oven-to-table baking dish. Pour the orange sauce over the fish. Place orange slices on top of the fish, then overlap the red onion slices on top. Trickle honey evenly over the onions.

Broil 3 inches from the heat for about 10 minutes until the fish flakes when tested with a skewer. Tilt the pan and baste the fish several times while broiling. If there is not enough liquid for basting, add about ¼ cup boiling water to the bottom of the pan. Sprinkle with the mint just before serving.

BLUEFISH SEVICHE WITH RED ONION, HOT PEPPER FLAKES, AND CILANTRO

MAKES 6 TO 8 SERVINGS

A mixture of hot, cool, and pungent flavors blended together with crisp, sweet onions and mellowed by lime juice. A family favorite of ours for brunch or hors d'oeuvres.

2½ pounds bluefish fillets (substitute: mackerel or tilefish)

Coarse salt

1½ teaspoons hot pepper flakes

1 or 2 medium red onions, thinly sliced

2 tablespoons coarsely chopped fresh cilantro or mint

1 cup lime juice (6 to 8 limes)

Fine lime peel shreds made with a zester tool (optional)

Trim and discard the strip of brown meat on the bottom of the fish fillets, then cut the fish into ¾-inch pieces. Place a layer of fish in a ceramic crock or small soufflé dish (not metal), sprinkle with salt and some of the hot pepper flakes, add a layer of onion rings, and sprinkle with about ½ teaspoon cilantro. Repeat the layers until all the ingredients are used up. Pour the lime juice over to cover the fish. Cover the dish tightly with plastic wrap and refrigerate from 12 to 24 hours. Top with decorative shreds of lime peel, if you wish, just before serving. Serve from the crock with thinly sliced whole-grain or pumpernickel bread.

BLUEFISH "GRAVLAX" WITH CUCUMBER, MINT, AND CAPER SAUCE

MAKES 16 TO 20 SERVINGS

The Scandinavian method of curing fish with salt and pepper draws the moisture out of the fish, firming and preserving it for up to 10 days. Large bluefish are perfect for an untraditional "gravlax," since the original recipe calls for salmon, a fish that should not be eaten uncooked these days.

2 center-cut bluefish fillets, with skin, about 1½ pounds each

⅔ cup coarse or kosher salt

3 tablespoons sugar

3 tablespoons coarsely cracked black peppercorns

1 tablespoon coarsely ground coriander seeds

½ cup coarsely chopped fresh mint

¼ cup coarsely chopped parsley stems only

1 medium leek, white and part of the green, thinly sliced (about ⅔ cup)

1 small onion, coarsely chopped (about ⅓ cup)

¼ cup olive oil

CUCUMBER, MINT, AND CAPER SAUCE:

2 small Kirby cucumbers, coarsely grated

¼ cup coarsely chopped fresh mint

1 cup sour cream

Salt and white pepper to taste

1 teaspoon nonpareil capers, rinsed and dried

Run your fingers over the fish to detect any pin bones and remove them with a tweezers or long-nose pliers. Turn the fillets skin side up and make 4 diagonal slashes, equally spaced, 4 inches long and about ⅛ inch deep, across the width of the fillets.

Mix ⅓ cup of the salt with 1 tablespoon of the sugar and rub over the skin side of the fish. Line a jelly-roll pan with plastic wrap and place one fillet skin side down on the wrap.

In a small bowl, combine the remaining ⅓ cup salt, 2 tablespoons sugar, the pepper, coriander, mint, parsley stems, leek, and onion; spread this mixture thickly over the fillet. Top with the other fillet, skin side up and sandwich fashion, so that the thicker end of the top piece is over the thinner end of the bottom piece. Wrap them tightly in plastic, then place a smaller pan on top and weight with two bricks or other 5-pound weights. Refrigerate at least 2 days and up to 3 days, turning the fish over in its plastic wrap every 12 hours.

When ready to continue with the recipe, unwrap the fish and scrape off the mixture. Place the fillets in a large bowl of cold water to soak for 30 minutes, then fill the bowl and change the water 4 or 5 times. Drain the fillets and dry well on paper towels.

Transfer them to the pan lined with fresh plastic wrap and drizzle them with the olive oil. Wrap again in plastic and refrigerate overnight.

When ready to serve, mix all the ingredients for the sauce together. Slice the fillets very thin across the grain, using a very sharp knife and making almost horizontal cuts right down to the skin. Slide the knife between the flesh and the skin to release the slices. Serve the fish with freshly ground black pepper and thin slices of pumpernickel bread. Pass the sauce in a separate bowl at the table.

MULLET

Mullet has about 100 family members throughout the world (not counting impostors such as the red mullet known as *rouget* in France and *triglia* in Italy, which is really a goatfish). Striped or black mullet and white or silver mullet are the most common in our part of the world.

They're found in both salt and fresh water and have always been one of the most valuable fin fish taken in Florida and Gulf Coast waters, although some range as far north as Cape Cod and there are family members in Hawaii. Since they have a diet of herbs that come from brackish waters, mullet now are being farmed for a taste a bit milder than their normally rich, nutlike flavor. They're a special treat in the Southeast, and mullet roe is particularly prized in that area of the United States.

Traveling in schools, as do bluefish, mullet distinguish themselves by actually jumping out of the water as they move through it. Since most of mullet fishing takes place at night, the splashing can be heard on shore or aboard the boats, signaling that a school is passing through.

Their average market weight is usually less than a pound, so they're generally sold whole since the fillet yield is considered low. They also can be butterflied. Make certain that the scales are removed, since they have a tendency to be quite coarse. Remove the dark, lateral line of flesh after cooking, since the remaining white meat has a more delicate flavor.

CRISP PAN-FRIED MULLET AND ROE

MAKES 4 SERVINGS

A tart buttermilk soak helps the crust adhere and become crisp and golden. In the autumn on the West Coast, spawning female mullet contain the roe, which is highly prized and, as a result, occasionally difficult to come by, but worth it when you can find it.

1	cup buttermilk		Salt and pepper to taste
8	pan-dressed mullet, ⅓ to ½ pound each, with roe (substitute: porgy, see Note)		Corn oil for frying
½	cup all-purpose flour	2	tablespoons butter
1	cup stone-ground white cornmeal	4	lemon wedges
¼	teaspoon cayenne pepper	2	tablespoons finely minced parsley

Pour the buttermilk into a shallow, nonreactive pan and add the fish and roe. Let stand for 20 minutes, turning once during that time. In a plastic bag, combine the flour, cornmeal, cayenne, salt, and pepper. Lift the fish and roe a few at a time from the buttermilk and shake in the bag to coat lightly. Transfer to a piece of waxed paper.

Heat about 1 inch oil in a large cast-iron skillet over medium-high heat until very hot but not smoking (about 370°). Add the fish in two or three batches and pan-fry for 3 to 5 minutes on each side until golden and cooked through. Drain on paper towels as they are cooked and keep them warm in a low oven.

In a medium skillet, melt the butter until foamy over medium heat. Add the roe and sauté for 2 to 3 minutes on each side. Cut into ¾-inch slices and top each fillet with a piece of roe. Dip the wedges of lemon in the parsley and arrange around the fish.

NOTE: If you cannot get roe or you substitute porgy for the mullet, serve the fish without it.

BAKED MULLET SPETSAI WITH FETA CHEESE

MAKES 4 SERVINGS

Mild, nutty striped mullet bakes on a bed of tomatoes topped with garlic, parsley, and spiked bread crumbs, along with slightly briny feta cheese. A specialty of one of the Greek islands.

½ cup olive oil

1 14-ounce can crushed Italian tomatoes

½ cup dry white wine

2 cloves garlic, finely minced (about 1 table-spoon)

2 tablespoons finely minced parsley

½ cup fresh bread crumbs

2 pounds pan-dressed mullet (substitute: sea bass or ocean perch)

Salt and pepper to taste

⅛ teaspoon cayenne pepper

¼ pound feta cheese

Preheat the oven to 400°. Add the olive oil, tomatoes, and wine to a large, shallow oven-to-table baking pan and stir to combine.

In a small bowl, mix the garlic, parsley, and bread crumbs together and set aside. Season the fish with salt, pepper, and the cayenne, place the fish over the tomato mixture, and sprinkle the bread crumbs over the fish.

Bake for 20 to 30 minutes. After 20 minutes, test the fish with a skewer. When the center of the thickest part is not quite opaque, top with the feta cheese and return to the oven for 5 minutes more to heat the cheese and to finish baking the fish. Serve directly from the pan.

SABLEFISH

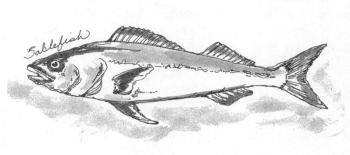

In the marketplace, you may find this fish with another name, a not unusual phenomenon in the world of seafood. It sometimes is sold as black cod (you've probably guessed that it's not a cod and cannot be substituted for true cod), or it is incorrectly sold as butterfish when it's filleted. Sablefish is at its very best when it's smoked, since it is soft and fatty with a mild flavor. Sablefish comes from the deep northern waters of the Pacific Ocean, and much of it is exported to Japan. If you should find it fresh, the market size will range from 1 to 8 pounds, and it takes well to grilling because of its fat content. However, having been raised just a short walk from New York's many appetizing stores, we think of sablefish as a smoked treat along with smoked salmon (lox) and bagels, to help make Sunday brunch a special event.

SMALL FISH

Frankly, we have very mixed emotions about this category. On the one hand, when we think about the very small fish, we think about the food chain and sadly contemplate a world in which small fish are devoured by larger fish, which are in turn devoured by even larger fish. And so, when we see the large schools of small baitfish right off our dock on the Great South Bay, we know that this soon will be followed by a surge in the water and panic as the school tries desperately to avoid capture and certain demise, which then brings us to the second and opposite emotion.

Knowing that a surfeit of baitfish will bring larger fish into nearby waters, we are quite delighted and dash back to get our fishing rods and lures. Part of our delight with small fish is also the knowledge that they are an underappreciated and delicious food source—not only for the bigger fish, but also for us fish lovers.

It is difficult to label small fish very accurately, for some species that start out small grow into monsters of the deep as they mature. The bluefish, for example (page 192), is both delicious as a baby snapper and as an adult gamefish. The fish we have included here are those that generally stay quite small. These are the fish that are so small that the best way to prepare them is to fry or sauté them quickly and, with some species, to consume them whole, without even taking their heads off or gutting them. A prime example is whitebait.

Actually, whitebait is an all-inclusive name for the tiny fried fish consumed by Europeans by the bucketfuls. Sometimes only one or two fish are used, and other times there are combinations, depending upon availability. Generally, Europeans include smelts, sardines, sticklebacks, and pipefish in the mixture. In North America, you will probably find the prime combination a mixture of silversides and sandlance (or sand eels as we call them on our island) along with sardines, herring, and Pacific surf smelts. Of the group, only sandlance generally are not found commercially and have to be netted by the cook.

Those of our readers who visit friends at the seashore or have a vacation home near an ocean or saltwater bay probably have seen millions of silverside swimming near the docks. Next time get a friend, a seine net and two poles, take off your shoes and socks, and wade near the shoreline, holding the net between you. Within a few minutes, you'll have enough whitebait to feed the family along with friends. They deteriorate rapidly, so get them from water to frying pan as quickly as possible, or place them on ice if you don't plan to cook them for a few hours. Don't keep them in water, since they become soggy and tasteless almost at once. If you don't plan to cook them, use them as bait. They're great to use in catching the next fish up the food chain!

Smelt

Although smelts are anadromous, spawning in fresh water but living in salt water (see page 215), they are also very small. Thus, we have chosen to include them here instead of with other anadromous fish. The smallest of the species are marketed at about 3 inches in length, although the fish can reach 7 inches. They are found both on the Atlantic and the Pacific coasts, as well as in the Great Lakes where they have adapted to fresh-water living.

At one time, smelts were even more abundant than they are today. Captain John Smith reported from New England in 1622 that the smelts were so plentiful that the Indians (his word) scooped them out of the water in baskets. To this day, out in California, when the grunion (a smeltlike fish) swarm near shore during the full moon and are stranded, the locals go on a "grunion-hunt" and scoop them up by hand, the only method allowed by law.

Smelts are slender, silvery fish with an olive green coating along their backs. Indeed, the word "smelt" in Anglo-Saxon (*smoelt*) translates "smooth and shining." They're fatty, very sweet, and when they're fresh, they've been described as having the pleasant smell of cucumbers. The smaller fish can be used for whitebait, while those that are slightly larger are perfect for butterflying or pan-dressing.

Silversides

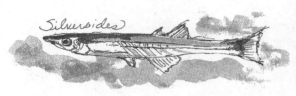

Silversides are the favorite on the East Coast for whitebait, sometimes mixed with sand-lance (sand eels), and also a favorite feast for bluefish, striped bass, and mackerel. As we mentioned earlier, most people think of the silverside only as bait, a most unfortunate decision, since they are delicious when chilled, dried on paper towels, dredged in flour, and fried quickly. They're wonderfully crisp eaten whole and as irresistible as popcorn.

Butterfish

During late summer and early fall, one of our favorite displays at our local fish-monger is that of the butterfish, silver and glistening and shaped somewhat like large coins from the sea. You would not be amiss to tell children who admire them that they are also called silver dollars or dollarfish (as well as shiners and harvest fish).

They're caught in the Atlantic from the Maine coast down to Florida and are particular favorites in the Northeast. Although they are most abundant in the Atlantic, there is a West Coast relative of lesser importance that has been dubbed Pacific or California pompano (although no relative of the popular East Coast pompano).

Butterfish are quite fatty, with a grayish white flesh, and a very delicate, fine, moist, sweet flavor. Because of its delicate skin, there is no need to scale it before cooking. The entire skin with the tiny scales can be lifted off after cooking. Because of their size—usually 4 to 5 inches—they are generally sold whole or pan-dressed, and they're excellent fried, poached, steamed, or smoked.

Anchovy

The only true anchovies are harvested in the Mediterranean Sea and along the southern coastline of Europe; however, there are various family members worldwide, with about sixteen varieties in American waters alone. They're rarely sold fresh in our country, although we have seen them offered at some specialty fish markets. Most of us know them as rolled or flat and packed in oil in cans or in tiny slim jars, or sold loose and dry packed in salt. Anchovies are not naturally salty, but they get that way through the processing that brings them to us.

For fisherpeople, the anchovy is a perfect bait for salmon. For chefs and home cooks, anchovies add a perfect nuance of flavor, both as a garnish or as part of a basic recipe.

Herring

We're not quite certain whether a herring is a grown-up sardine or a sardine is a baby herring. Either would be correct, since they are of the same family but of different ages. In addition, both are marketed somewhat differently, and, thus, we have given sardines their own separate designation (see page 205).

There are hundreds of varieties of herring, swimming in gigantic schools off both the East and West coasts. The Atlantic herring is the most important, with the Pacific herring an important commercial catch in that much of the roe is shipped to Japan, where it is considered a delicacy. They're rarely found fresh, since they tend to spoil rather quickly, but if you find them at your fishmonger in that form, they're perfect for grilling because of their high fat content. Generally, they are sold at about ½ pound each.

The herring is considered one of the oldest fishes, with historical records telling us that they may have influenced the course of history more than any other. They have determined where towns would be located, wars have been fought over them, and they were a major source of barter for Native Americans along the West Coast of the United States and Canada. To this day, the herring plays a role in many cultures. The Dutch make an annual festival during the first herring catch of the season, and the celebrated *smørrebrød* of Scandinavia would not be complete without an endless variety of herring dishes.

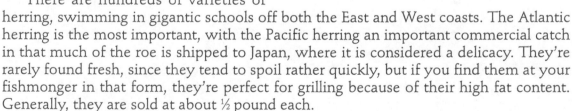

Because herring swim in the sea by the billions, some most ingenious methods of preserving them have been developed over the centuries, some of which are practiced to this day.

- ❖ *Pickled herring* is marinated in spices and vinegar and then immersed in sour cream or a wine sauce.

- ❖ *Kippered herring* is split, then cured by cold smoking, and grilled or baked.

- ❖ *Matjes herring,* named for the first catch of the year (from the Dutch word for "maiden"), is skinned, filleted, and cured in vinegar, spices, sugar, and salt, then sold in bite-size pieces.

- ❖ *Schmaltz herring* is more mature, fattier fish fillets that are preserved in brine.

These are but a few, but herring mavens can look for everything from soused herring to bloaters to Bismark herring, from *fleckerhering* to *rollmops.* All still herring, but each one handled and preserved in a slightly different way.

Sardines

Yes, most of us know canned sardines, but those who have been lucky enough to visit the southern coast of Europe, especially the area around Portugal's Algarve, also know them as a very special treat when fresh and charcoal grilled, served right at dockside as the fishing boats tie up after a long morning at sea. On our last trip to Portimão, we visited those docks as often as we could. Every owner of an outdoor grill restaurant tried to convince passersby that his sardines were fresher, better, tastier, and more memorable. It mattered not. Sitting in the sun, drinking in the activity on the docks and sampling the remarkable grilled sardines, accompanied by a rough peasant bread and a glass of *vinho verde,* made for a day of perfect memories. A far cry from sardines canned in oil, water, or mustard sauce!

Actually, "sardine" is a generic designation, for not one species, but a variety of tiny, soft-boned fish. Our most familiar, the Maine sardine, is a member of the Atlantic herring family, as we have noted above. The European pilchard is also a member of the herring family and thus its young are also called sardines. The same is true of the Japanese pilchard. The name itself probably originated in fourteenth-century Sardinia, where the tiny fish were harvested by the millions.

If you are lucky enough to visit the coast of southern France, Spain, Portugal, or Italy, by all means try them fresh and grilled. On the other hand, if you live on the East Coast and your fishmonger features them one day, try them fresh as a treat. Have the heads removed and the spine bone pulled out and grill them quickly. You may never open a can again.

PORTUGUESE MARINATED SMELT

Smoelt is an Anglo-Saxon word that means "smooth and shining" and that is, indeed, an exact description of these delicate, sweet-flavored fish. Although they are marinated, then sautéed, and marinated again overnight, the recipe itself is easy to do in stages. A crisp salad is all that's needed to accompany this cold dish.

6	pan-dressed smelt, 8 to 10 ounces each (substitute: fresh herring)	1	bay leaf
2	tablespoons lemon juice (½ large lemon)	2	eggs, lightly beaten
4	tablespoons olive oil	1	cup fine dried bread crumbs
1	small clove garlic, crushed		Corn oil for frying
⅛	teaspoon nutmeg	1	cup dry white wine
¼	teaspoon black pepper	2	teaspoons coarsely chopped parsley
	Salt to taste	½	small red onion, finely minced (about 2 tablespoons)

In a shallow nonreactive pan, place the fish in one layer. In a small bowl, whisk the lemon juice, olive oil, garlic, nutmeg, pepper, and salt together. Add the bay leaf and pour over the fish. Cover with plastic wrap and marinate for 3 to 4 hours in the refrigerator, turning the fish over once or twice.

When ready to cook, lift the fish from the marinade and dry well on paper towels. Transfer the marinade to a medium saucepan and set aside.

Using 2 pie pans, place the beaten eggs in one and the bread crumbs in the other. In a large cast-iron skillet, heat 1 inch oil to 370°. Dip each fish first in the egg, then roll in the bread crumbs. Sauté the fish, turning them once, until golden, 3 to 4 minutes, depending upon the size of the fish. You will need to cook the fish in 2 or 3 batches.

Drain the fish on paper towels and place them in one layer in a shallow, nonreactive pan. To the reserved marinade, add the wine, parsley, and onion and bring to a boil. Pour over the fish and let cool, then cover with plastic wrap and refrigerate overnight. Discard the bay leaf and bring the fish back to room temperature before serving.

SMELT AGRI-DULCE

We first tasted this sweet-and-sour combination of vinegar, raisins, and smelt at a seaside restaurant in Palermo and fell madly in love with the flavors. We also have tried bluefish with the same sauce with equally good results.

¾	cup all-purpose flour	1	clove garlic
⅛	teaspoon cayenne pepper	1	sprig rosemary
	Salt and black pepper to taste	4	tablespoons balsamic or red wine vinegar
4	pan-dressed smelt, 8 to 10 ounces each (substitute: small bluefish)	3	tablespoons dark raisins
		3	tablespoons pine nuts, lightly roasted
6	tablespoons olive oil	1	tablespoon coarsely chopped fresh mint

Combine the flour, cayenne, salt, and pepper in a plastic bag. Add the fish and shake the bag to coat the fish lightly. In a large skillet, heat the oil with the garlic and rosemary slowly. When the garlic just begins to brown, remove and discard both the garlic and rosemary. The oil should be very hot and not smoking. Add the fish and sauté for 3 to 5 minutes on each side until golden.

Transfer the fish to a warm serving platter. Discard all but a thin film of the olive oil in the pan and add the vinegar and raisins. Heat, stirring constantly, over medium-high heat for 30 seconds, then pour over the fish. Scatter the pine nuts and mint over the surface and serve at once.

FRIED WHITEBAIT WITH SESAME SEEDS

MAKES 4 TO 6 SERVINGS

These little fish have enjoyed long-standing popularity in Europe, where they are made into a sensational finger food called "whitebait." Just beginning to catch on in the United States, they disappear at the table much like popcorn at the movies.

2 pounds whole silversides or sand lances, no more than 2 to 2½ inches long and absolutely fresh
½ cup milk
2 teaspoons light soy sauce
⅛ teaspoon Tabasco
1 cup all-purpose flour

¼ cup sesame seeds
   Salt to taste
   Corn oil for frying
   Lime wedges for serving
   Malt vinegar mixed with 2 or 3 drops Tabasco for dipping

Rinse the fish in several changes of water until the water is clear, then drain well. In a wide, shallow dish, combine the milk, soy sauce, and Tabasco. Add the fish, stir gently to coat, and marinate for 30 minutes in the refrigerator.

Combine the flour, sesame seeds, and salt in a plastic bag. Remove a few fish at a time from the marinade and shake them in the flour mixture to coat evenly. Place them on a sheet of waxed paper to dry in the refrigerator for 5 minutes while the oil is heating.

Heat 2½ inches corn oil in a large, deep cast-iron skillet to 375° on a fat thermometer. Fry the fish a few at a time keeping the temperature of the oil constant, until golden, usually 1 to 2 minutes. Remove the fish from the oil and drain on paper towels. Keep warm in a low oven until all the fish are cooked. It will take several batches.

Serve the fish in a folded white napkin in a basket or bowl. Pass a plate of lime wedges and a bowl of malt vinegar with Tabasco for dipping at the table.

BACON-FRIED BUTTERFISH

MAKES 4 SERVINGS

The smoky flavor of bacon leaves its imprint on these simply fried, meltingly sweet little fish. This has been a popular recipe at our campfire cookouts and a favorite fish to serve with hominy grits.

4 to 6 strips bacon (depending upon thickness)	Salt to taste
½ cup stone-ground white cornmeal	12 butterfish, ⅓ pound each before pan-dressing (substitute: trout)
¾ cup all-purpose flour	Lemon wedges
½ teaspoon black pepper	Few sprigs parsley for garnish

In a large skillet, fry the bacon until crisp, drain on paper towels, crumble, and set aside. Do not discard the bacon fat.

In a plastic bag, mix all the dry ingredients. Add the fish, a few at a time, and shake to coat well. Reheat the bacon fat until hot but not smoking. Add the fish a few at a time, and fry 3 to 4 minutes on each side. Drain on paper towels, then transfer the fish to an oven-to-table serving dish. Keep warm in a low oven until all the fish are fried. Sprinkle with the crumbled bacon and tuck the lemon wedges and parsley sprigs around the fish before serving.

SPAGHETTINI WITH A SAUCE OF ANCHOVIES, HERBED BREAD CRUMBS, AND FRESH TOMATO

MAKES 4 SERVINGS

This quickly made dish is neither fancy nor trendy—just simple piquant flavors and textures cloaked with the essence of anchovies and perfumed with good olive oil, garlic, and a touch of fresh tomatoes.

¾ pound dried spaghettini

½ cup plus 2 tablespoons olive oil

4 to 6 cloves garlic, finely minced (2 tablespoons)

6 anchovy fillets, rinsed, dried, and cut into pieces

1 small red pepper, finely diced (about ⅛ cup)

1 teaspoon finely minced lemon peel

2 cups coarse fresh bread crumbs (use country French or Italian bread that is not sweet)

½ teaspoon dried marjoram

⅛ teaspoon hot pepper flakes

¼ cup finely minced parsley

Black pepper to taste

Salt to taste, if needed

5 medium plum tomatoes (about ¾ pound), diced

3 tablespoons grated Parmesan cheese

In a large pot, cook the spaghettini in lots of boiling salted water. While the pasta is cooking, heat ½ cup of olive oil in a 12-inch sauté pan over low heat. Add the garlic and sauté for 1 minute, stirring constantly. Add the anchovies and stir until they dissolve. Add the red pepper, lemon peel, bread crumbs, marjoram, and pepper flakes and stir until the bread crumbs absorb the oil. Add the parsley, pepper, and salt and cook until the crumbs become golden.

When the pasta is cooked, drain well in a colander and transfer to the bread crumb mixture in the skillet. Quickly spoon the remaining 2 tablespoons olive oil and the tomatoes over the pasta and toss well. Sprinkle with the Parmesan and additional black pepper if you wish. Serve on individual warmed plates or in bowls.

NOTE: The "sauce" is not a wet sauce but rather dry, with bursts of moisture coming from the tomatoes.

BROILED BUTTERFLIED HERRING WITH ONIONS AND DILL

MAKES 4 SERVINGS

Small red-skinned potatoes would be good with this simply prepared fish. If fresh herring is not available, this recipe is equally good with kippered herring, which are cured and cold-smoked.

4 fresh herring, about 1 pound each, butterflied or filleted with skin (substitute: kippered herring)

4 tablespoons melted butter

¼ teaspoon black pepper

½ teaspoon paprika

2 small red onions, thinly sliced and separated into rings

6 sprigs fresh dill

Balsamic or malt vinegar for serving

Preheat the broiler. Lightly butter a large baking pan and lay the fish, skin side down, in the pan. Brush with half the melted butter, sprinkle with pepper and half the paprika, and place the onion rings over the fish. Sprinkle with the remaining paprika and spoon the remaining butter over the onions.

Broil 4 inches from the heat for about 5 minutes. The onions should be slightly brown and fairly crisp. Test the fish with a skewer to see if it flakes easily and continue to broil until it does. Transfer to serving plates, top with a sprig of dill, and pass the vinegar to be sprinkled over the fish before eating.

PREPARING FRESH WHOLE SARDINES

To prepare fresh whole sardines for cooking, cut the heads off, then cut the underbelly open so that the fish lies flat but is still joined at the spine.

Using your fingers, remove the backbone by pulling and lifting it up from head to tail. It will come out very much like a zipper. Rinse the sardine to remove the viscera, then dry it well with paper towels.

MARINATED AND GRILLED SARDINES WITH PUTTANESCA SAUCE

Try a creamy risotto laced with Parmesan cheese along with these freshly grilled sardines and quickly prepared sauce named after, and popular with, Italian streetwalkers who cook it between assignations.

1½	pounds fresh sardines, 12 to 24 depending on size, boned and heads removed (see page 212) (substitute: smelt)
2	tablespoons nonpareil capers, rinsed and drained
1	small onion, finely chopped (about ⅓ cup)
2	large cloves garlic, slivered
½	cup dry vermouth
2	tablespoons balsamic vinegar
½	cup olive oil
½	teaspoon dried oregano, preferably Greek
¼	teaspoon black pepper
12	black olives, either Gaeta or Kalamata, pitted and halved or quartered
5 to 6	large plum tomatoes, cut into quarters, or 1 14-ounce can Italian plum tomatoes, drained
2 to 3	flat anchovy fillets, rinsed and cut into small pieces
1	tablespoon coarsely chopped parsley

Place the fish in a shallow nonreactive pan in one layer and scatter the capers, onion, and garlic over the fish. In a small bowl, whisk together the vermouth, vinegar, olive oil, oregano, and pepper and pour over the fish. Cover with plastic wrap and marinate in the refrigerator for 1 hour, turning the fish once.

Prepare a very hot grill. Lift the fish from the marinade and place them either in an oiled grilling basket with a handle or on an oiled metal grid, e.g., a Griffo grill. Grill the fish for 3 to 4 minutes on each side, basting frequently with some of the marinade. When the fish is cooked, distribute on serving plates, and keep them warm in a low oven.

Put the remaining marinade in a medium saucepan, add the olives, tomatoes, and anchovies and bring to a boil. Lower the heat and simmer for 2 to 3 minutes. Stir in the parsley, then spoon some sauce over each serving of fish.

BAKED FRESH SARDINES GREEK-STYLE WITH LEMON, OLIVE OIL, AND MARJORAM

MAKES 4 SERVINGS

Surprisingly simple and remarkably good. Try this with a side dish of orzo, the rice-shaped tiny pasta.

1½ pounds fresh sardines, 12 to 24 depending upon size, boned and heads removed (see page 212) (substitute: smelt)

Juice of 2 large lemons (about ½ cup)

½ cup olive oil

1 tablespoon dried marjoram

⅛ teaspoon cayenne pepper

Salt to taste

Preheat the oven to 350°. Arrange the sardines in one layer in a large oven-to-table baking dish. In a small bowl, whisk the lemon juice, olive oil, marjoram, cayenne, and salt together until well blended. Pour over the fish. Bake for 10 to 15 minutes, basting frequently. Test the fish after 10 minutes with a skewer to see if it flakes. Serve hot or refrigerate and serve at room temperature the following day.

GROUP C
Anadromous and Catadromous Fish

Salmon Family
King salmon
Sockeye salmon
Atlantic salmon
Pink salmon
Chum salmon
Silver (Coho) salmon

Arctic Char

Striped Bass

Shad and Shad Roe

Caviars and Roe: "A Roe by Any Other Name"

Eel and Elvers

SALMON FAMILY

The salmon is one of the prime examples of anadromous fish—those which live in the sea and then go back to fresh water to spawn. Nature books, documentary films, and even some cookbooks have covered the fight upriver very well, and most of us are familiar with the sight of the hurtling, shining bodies making their way against the roaring waters in order to reach the spawning grounds upstream, the very place that they were born.

Navigating by sun and their radarlike sense of smell and migrating as much as 2,000 miles in order to reach the fresh-water birthing grounds, the exhausted female finally lays her eggs, lingers briefly, and then dies. The eggs are then fertilized by the male and soon a dull gray mass, known as kelt, gives up the fingerlings, who linger in fresh water for about two years, and by the third year are mature enough to make their way back to the open waters of the Atlantic or Pacific. Many, of course, never make it, victims of natural predators from bears to fisherfolk.

Which brings us to a funny story (at the risk of boring those who have heard it from us before). One of our favorite cities is Seattle, and one of our favorite places in that wonderful city is the aquarium. An exhibit within the building houses a large pool in which salmon were bred in captivity by the scientists of the museum. Underneath the breeding pool is a glass viewing area for the public. Thus, in the experiment to be tried, the public—we among them—waited breathlessly one day for the return of the adult salmon, who would appear right above us to deliver their eggs at the very same spot in which they were born. To say the least, the moment was "pregnant" with expectation.

Suddenly, there was a shout. "Here they come! Here come the fish!" Beside us was the photographer we had brought with us to record the historic ichthyologic moment. He raised his camera and his flash and, as the first fish appeared, he shot the first photo. Which—to the dismay of the assembled gathering—frightened the fish, who turned and swept down the ramp back to sea! In any case, we have not returned in some years, fearful that someone will point to us and say, "There they are! They're the ones who scared the salmon!"

Most of the salmon that come to our tables are fished in the northern waters of both the Atlantic and Pacific, with the coast of Alaska a prime resource. In addition, salmon farming has become more important in many parts of the world, including Scandinavia, Chile, Australia, as well as the United States and Canada. It's important to keep in mind that wild salmon, having spawned in fresh water, quite likely carry parasites. Thus, it is advisable that you never eat raw salmon or use it in recipes such as gravlax or salmon tartare, unless you know for certain that the fish is aquacultured and not from the wild.

Good Japanese restaurants freeze raw salmon for sushi and sashimi for a minimum of 72 hours at 0°. This destroys any parasites that may be lurking. If, on the other hand, you are going to cook the salmon, you need not freeze it first.

We find that some fishmongers remove the tiny pin bones that run down the length of the salmon's body, while others leave them there. We assume that any good restaurant will do the same before serving the fillet or salmon steak, but there are times when we've been disappointed. Run your finger lightly down the center of the fillet to feel for the fine bones. Then, using a pair of tweezers or long-nose pliers, just pluck them out, working from the top of the fillet down to the end. It's a fairly easy process and you and your guests will appreciate the small effort.

Those who love fresh salmon the way we do—whether broiled, poached, baked, or even smoked—will certainly concur with the appellation given by Izaak Walton, author of *The Compleat Angler;* he crowned this delicate, flavorful, colorful species "the king of fish."

King Salmon

Also known as chinook, king salmon is the largest member of the family but also represents the smallest catch, accounting for less than 5 percent of the total harvest. However, king is one of the two prime-tasting salmon. That and the increasing scarcity of the fish also make it the most expensive.

The king is a native of the Northwest, harvested wild in summer and spring from northern California to the Gulf of Alaska, with the major part of the catch coming from the Columbia River. However, in recent years, farm-raised king salmon have also been coming to the marketplace from as far away as Chile, Australia, and New Zealand.

The market sizes range from about 10 to 20 pounds, although king have been caught at over 100 pounds. Depending upon the season, their flesh varies from pinkish white to a deeper red. High in fat content, they take well to almost any kind of cooking, especially the high heat of broiling or barbecuing.

King makes the best cold-cured lox or nova, familiar to many Americans as the perfect accompaniment to a Sunday bagel. They also can be cured in brine and hot smoked to make kippered salmon.

Sockeye Salmon

If king is not available, then sockeye runs a close enough second so that none of us would quibble. Sockeye is sometimes sold as red or blueback salmon, and a great part of the catch is exported to Japan. The best place to taste the sockeye absolutely fresh is during the summer months near Bristol Bay in Alaska, where almost 100,000 tons are caught in just a few days. Considering that the average 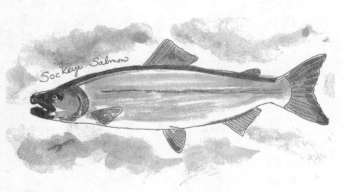 size of the sockeye is 4 to 6 pounds, that's an awful lot of fish. The major part of the catch goes to the canning factories while the remainder is flash frozen for shipment across the country.

The sockeye has the reddest flesh of the species, and it also has a high fat content.

Atlantic Salmon

With almost all major catches of salmon taking place in the Pacific, the Atlantic salmon stands out as the East Coast and European representative of the family. Sometimes sold as Kennebec or New England salmon, it also has the distinction of being able to spawn more than once, unlike its West Coast cousins, who die after doing their duty to continue the chain.

The Atlantic salmon is yet another fish that has suffered from the pollution of both the North Atlantic and the waters off the European coast. As a result, it has been disappearing rapidly from its wild habitat, both at sea and in the East Coast tributaries. The slack has been taken up somewhat through aquaculture, with most of the supply now coming from Canada, and the rapid expansion of fish farming in the Scandinavian countries, Scotland, Australia, the United States, and Chile. In fact, due to European aquaculture, you may find Atlantic salmon at your fishmonger called Norwegian or Irish or Scottish salmon. And, if you've had smoked salmon (or gravlax, which is cured with salt and sugar) in Europe, it was probably Atlantic salmon that you were eating.

It's second in size to the king, although its market weight is generally no more than 5 to 10 pounds. It also has a more orange flesh than the king, and a very high fat content, as do most of its relatives. It's excellent for broiling, smoking, barbecuing, or even poaching or baking.

Pink Salmon

Also known as humpback, pink salmon is the smallest of the Pacific family members and gets its name from the coloration of the males during spawning. They're also among the most abundant of the smaller salmons, with most of the catch taking place from Alaska down to the coast of Oregon. With

an average weight of about 3 pounds, they have a fine-textured, pale flesh. Although most of them end up in cans, they can also be prepared fresh—the pink meat is just a bit softer than other varieties.

Chum Salmon

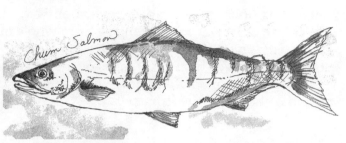

This is the last salmon to run the Pacific rivers late in the fall. At spawning time, the males grow longer teeth, quite similar to those of canines, giving rise to their nickname of dog salmon. (You may also find them called calico or keta when they're canned.)

Chum reach an average length of about 3 feet and can weigh up to 10 pounds or more. Their flesh is lighter than that of the other family members but slightly coarser. They also are not quite as fatty, making them a bit less flavorful than the coho, for example. Until recently, almost all of the catch was canned, but you occasionally can find chum fresh or frozen, making them suitable for poaching, pan-frying, or for use in chowders or casseroles.

Silver (Coho) Salmon

The names "silver" and "coho" are interchangeable, but generally we find this salmon on restaurant menus and at the fishmonger labeled with the latter name. They're a favorite with fisherpeople, generally weighing 6 to 12 pounds and growing up to 3 feet in length when they're in their natural habitat off the coast of California and up to Alaska. Baby cohos are now being farm raised on the West Coast and in Chile, with market weights at about 1 pound, the size of a small trout. Some years back, the Great Lakes were also stocked with coho. We have found the fresh-water varieties somewhat inferior in taste to the saltwater catch, something we have also noticed with other species such as striped bass (see page 226).

Coho are available year round. They have bright red flesh, flake easily, and have a lower fat content than relatives such as the king. If there's a choice, choose the baby cohos over their big brothers and sisters. Each small fish makes a perfect per person portion.

At the Market

Depending upon which variety of salmon is available at the fishmarket, you have a wide choice of market forms, ranging from whole dressed fish to fillets, steaks, chunks, as well as the smoked and kippered fish. As a final note, we should add that even canned salmon has some distinct advantages over other canned fish products. Tuna, for example, is canned in spring water or oil, but the liquid in the cans of salmon is always natural and comes from the fish itself.

SAUTÉED SALMON FILLETS WITH CHIVES AND SMOKED SALMON BUTTER

MAKES 6 SERVINGS

A most delicious, quick, and easy method of preparing salmon. Its simplicity belies its elegance, making it a wonderful dinner party dish for those who are pressed for time.

6 tablespoons butter, softened
2 ounces smoked salmon, cut into large pieces
2 tablespoons finely minced chives

¼ teaspoon lemon juice
6 skinned salmon fillets, 5 to 6 ounces each
Salt and pepper to taste

In a food processor, process 5 tablespoons of the butter and the smoked salmon until smooth. Add the chives and lemon juice and process until combined. Scrape into a small bowl and chill slightly while preparing the fish. The salmon butter can be made well in advance and kept in the refrigerator until ready to cook, but bring it to room temperature before serving.

Heat the remaining butter in a 12-inch skillet over medium-high heat until hot and bubbly. Add the salmon in one layer. Sauté for 3 to 4 minutes on each side, depending upon the thickness of the salmon. Test with a skewer—the salmon should be cooked through with just the slightest bit of resistance at the thickest part.

Transfer the fillets to serving plates and, using a melon baller, place 2 scoops smoked salmon butter on each serving to melt over the fish to form a sauce.

JAPANESE EGGPLANT AND SALMON SCALLOPS

A ravishing color combination of purple eggplant and pink salmon—with an equally ravishing taste.

1½ pounds skinned salmon fillet, pin bones removed (substitute: Arctic char)

¾ cup tamari

⅛ teaspoon hot pepper flakes

1 teaspoon sugar

2 teaspoons rice vinegar

2 tablespoons Oriental sesame oil

1 teaspoon finely minced ginger

6 small long Japanese eggplants (5 to 6 ounces each), trimmed and unpeeled

Corn oil for frying

2 tablespoons sesame seeds, toasted

2 medium scallions, sliced diagonally ¼ inch thick (about ½ cup)

Holding a sharp knife at an angle, cut the salmon into 6 equal slices. Place the slices one at a time between 2 pieces of plastic wrap and, with a rolling pin or a mallet, pound the slices ⅛ inch thick. Divide each slice into 2 scallops weighing about 2 ounces each and place them in a large, shallow nonreactive dish.

In a small bowl, mix the tamari, hot pepper flakes, sugar, vinegar, 1 tablespoon of the sesame oil, and the ginger and pour over the scallops. Cover with plastic wrap and marinate in the refrigerator for 30 minutes, turning them once. Meanwhile, make 4 equally spaced lengthwise cuts 2 inches from the stem end of the eggplants to allow the steam to be released.

In a skillet large enough to hold the eggplants in one layer, heat ½ inch corn oil over medium-high heat to 350°. Add the eggplants and sauté, turning frequently, for 8 to 10 minutes until tender. Drain on paper towels and place one eggplant on the side of each of 6 serving plates. Keeping the tops of each eggplant connected, cut through the slashes to the base of the eggplant and spread them open to make a fan shape. Set the plates aside while cooking the fish.

Wipe out the skillet and add the remaining 1 tablespoon sesame oil. Lift out and dry the salmon scallops on paper towels; reserve the marinade. Heat the oil over medium-high heat. Add the scallops to the pan in a single layer (you will have to cook them in 2 or 3 batches) and cook for 20 to 30 seconds, only until the edges turn opaque. Turn the scallops over and cook the other side for 15 seconds. Transfer the scallops to the plates as they are cooked, allowing two per serving. Add the sesame seeds to the marinade and spoon the scallops over the eggplants. Sprinkle with the scallions and serve.

WHOLE SALMON FILLET WITH LEEK, TOMATO, AND BASIL CREAM

The salmon is poached on top of the stove in wine and shallots, and the sauce is based on a reduction of leeks, wine, cream, and little pieces of lemon and tomato. Aromatic shreds of basil top it all.

3 to 4	leeks, white part with 1 inch pale green (about ¾ pound after trimming and cleaning)
2	tablespoons butter
1	cup dry white wine
1 or 2	large shallots, finely minced (about 2 tablespoons)
1	2-pound center-cut salmon fillet or two 1-pound fillets, with skin, about 1½ inches thick, pin bones removed (substitute: snapper or striped bass)

¾	cup heavy cream
2	thick slices lemon, peel and white pith removed, seeded, and pulp cut into bits
1	large tomato, skinned, seeded, and cut into small bits (about ½ cup)
	Salt and pepper to taste
8	large basil leaves, cut into fine chiffonade

Finely chop the leeks in a food processor. There should be about 3½ cups. In a large skillet, melt 1 tablespoon of the butter over medium heat. Add the leeks and sauté, stirring frequently, for about 3 minutes. Add ⅓ cup of the wine, raise the heat, and bring to a boil. Then cover, lower the heat to moderate, cook for 10 minutes, and set aside.

Meanwhile, with the remaining 1 tablespoon butter, butter a shallow oven-to-table baking pan large enough to hold the fish without crowding. Sprinkle the shallots on the bottom of the pan and place the fish over the shallots. Pour the remaining ⅔ cup wine over the fish, bring to a boil, cover the pan tightly with aluminum foil, and cook on the top of the stove over medium heat for 8 to 10 minutes. Test the fish at the thickest part with a skewer. Transfer the fish to a warm serving platter, using a wide spatula, and cover loosely with foil to keep warm.

Cook the remaining liquid and shallots in the pan until reduced to half the amount. Transfer the mixture to a large saucepan and add the reserved leeks and the cream. Cook over moderate heat about 4 minutes until reduced a bit. Stir in the lemon bits, tomato, salt, pepper, and basil. Cut the fish into serving-size portions at the table and spoon some of the sauce around each serving.

ROASTED FOURTH-OF-JULY SALMON WITH EGG AND CAVIAR SAUCE

Traditionally, the fare of choice for our Fourth of July celebrations has been whole poached salmon and peas in a rich, eggy sauce. Our version roasts a fillet of salmon, glamorizes the sauce with a touch of red caviar, and is served with sugar snap or snow peas.

1 tablespoon olive oil

¼ teaspoon dry mustard

1 2-pound center-cut salmon fillet, with skin, about 1¼ inches thick, pin bones removed (substitute: Arctic char)

1 large scallion, finely minced (about ¼ cup)

2 tablespoons dry white wine

½ cup heavy cream

¼ pound butter, cut into 8 equal pieces

1 hard-cooked egg, peeled and coarsely chopped

2 tablespoons finely minced chives

2 tablespoons finely minced parsley

2 tablespoons lemon juice

1 ounce red salmon caviar

Salt and pepper to taste

1 pound sugar snap or snow peas, strings removed, blanched

Mix the olive oil and mustard and brush over both sides of the salmon. Place on a foil-lined baking sheet. Preheat the oven to 425°.

In a medium saucepan, combine the scallion, wine, and cream. Simmer over medium-low heat until reduced by half, about 10 minutes. Meanwhile roast the salmon in the oven for 12 to 15 minutes. Test with a skewer at the thickest part. There should be just a bit of resistance when trying to flake the fish. If you want the fish to be cooked until it flakes easily, cook for 1 to 2 minutes more and test again.

When the sauce is reduced, take it off the heat and whisk in the butter 1 tablespoon at a time, returning the pan to the heat for the last 2 tablespoons. The butter should form an emulsified sauce and not melt completely. Strain the sauce into a second saucepan and stir in the egg, chives, parsley, lemon juice, and caviar. Keep warm over the lowest possible heat by using a flame tamer until the fish is roasted.

With a wide spatula or two smaller spatulas, transfer the fish to a serving platter and spoon the sauce over it. Surround with sugar snap or snow peas.

ARCTIC CHAR

Although the Eskimos and the people of the northern parts of Scandinavia and the British Isles have enjoyed Arctic char for centuries, it is obviously a secret that they have kept to themselves. Possibly one of the best tasting of the anadromous fish (although some species are also landlocked), this polar-dwelling species is fast becoming more and more popular and, we think, with very good reason. It happens to be one of our favorites, we think surpassing the flavor and texture of salmon.

It is actually more a member of the lake trout or brook trout family than that of the salmon; although it more closely resembles salmon in color and texture, it has the size and shape of trout. Most of the char currently in the marketplace are imported from Canada, with the limited supply of wild saltwater fish being supplemented by successful farming not only in Canada but also in the United States and Scandinavia. The wild fish can run up to 25 pounds in weight, with market weights ranging from about 5 to 10 pounds. However, the farmed fish are generally smaller, closer to the size of trout.

Arctic char has a high fat content. The smaller fish have an orange pink color and the larger ones are bright orange to rich red. If you see it on display at your fishmonger's and have not tried it as yet, we urge you to make it your choice for dinner that night.

ARCTIC CHAR WITH PINK GRAPEFRUIT, CAMPARI, AND MINT

MAKES 4 SERVINGS

Arctic char, which is closely related to trout but looks like salmon, has an unctuous, satiny, pale rosy flesh. Here, the rich intensity is cut with the acidity of pink grapefruit and a bit of refreshing mint.

1½   pounds Arctic char fillets, with skin, cut into 4 equal portions, pin bones removed (substitute: salmon fillets)
    Salt and pepper to taste
2   large pink grapefruits
1   teaspoon ground coriander

1   tablespoon olive oil
2   teaspoons Campari
3   tablespoons butter
⅛   teaspoon cayenne pepper
1   tablespoon coarsely chopped fresh mint

In a shallow nonreactive dish, arrange the fillets skin side down and season with salt and pepper. Squeeze the juice of 1 grapefruit (about ⅔ cup), mix it with the coriander, and pour over the fish. Marinate for 30 minutes, turning once.

Remove just the colored outer skin of the second grapefruit and cut it into very fine julienne strips. Pour boiling water over the julienne and let it steep for 2 minutes. Drain, dry well on paper towels, and set aside. Cut away all the white pith on the grapefruit and then cut the flesh into neat segments, slicing between the fibrous dividing skin. Cut each segment in half, or thirds if large, and set aside.

After the fish has marinated, lift out the fillets and dry them very well on paper towels. Transfer the marinade to a small nonreactive saucepan. Heat the oil in a large skillet over high heat. Place the fish, skin side down, in the skillet and sauté until lightly browned and the edges are opaque, about 3 minutes. Turn the fish over and briefly sear the other side for about 30 seconds. Transfer the fillets skin side down to a warm serving platter and cover with aluminum foil to keep warm.

Bring the grapefruit marinade to a boil over medium-high heat. Add the Campari, then lower the heat and whisk in the butter one tablespoon at a time, almost melting each tablespoon before adding the next one. Add the cayenne, stir in the grapefruit pieces, and simmer until warm. Spoon the sauce over the fish and sprinkle with the mint and reserved julienned grapefruit peel.

STRIPED BASS

Striped Bass

For those of us who love to fish as well as eat fish, the story of the striped bass is one of the most unfortunate examples of environmental indifference. Without a doubt one of the tastiest fish in the Atlantic Ocean, striped bass once ranked close to the cod as a vital food source for the early colonists, who called it "the boldest, bravest, strongest, and most active fish" to dwell in the bays and tidal waters along the Eastern Seaboard. In fact, monies earned from the striped bass catch helped make possible the first free public school of the New World. In 1639, it also was the first fish ever to be subjected to conservation measures; thus it is ironic today that new limitations are in effect because of our own disregard for the future.

The story concerns two prime villains: overfishing by commercial fleets and industrial pollution in the rivers in which they spawn and the bays in which they thrive (mainly the Hudson River and Chesapeake Bay). Thus the commercial catch is either totally banned or severely limited, and sports fisherpeople are limited to fish over 36 inches. Because the catch can be contaminated by industrial pollution, government agencies strongly recommend not eating the wild fish at all. Even on the West Coast, where the striped bass was transplanted some years back, pollution has taken its toll (see "A Word to the Wise," page 11). The only place where pollution and overfishing have not been a factor is off the coast of Europe, where a close relative, the European sea bass (the famous *spigola* of Italy and *bar* or *loup* of France) is still a readily available treat.

However, all of the story is not a sad one. When the fish catch began to be limited and the first warnings about PCB pollution were disseminated, the fish farmers took over, and striped bass again appeared in the marketplace, all plainly labeled as coming from pure and safe environments. In addition, many inland fresh-water lakes have been stocked with stripers (as we fisherpeople call them), and we have even had the pleasure of fishing for them with friends down south. In fact, an amusing incident took place because of one expedition.

We had been fishing with our friends and clients, Ken Clark, Larry Olmsted, and Gene Vaughn of Duke Power down on Lake Norman in North Carolina. The early morning foray into the misty waters had netted two lovely stripers. Since we were to return to New York by plane that same day, Gene and Larry, both biologists, deftly filleted the fish, packed them in ice, and put them in a waterproof box that we were to carry with us.

At the airport, putting our hand luggage through the X-ray machine, the security woman stopped the box and suspiciously peered intently at the contents—four fish fillets lying side by side. She wrinkled her brow, and we asked, "How are our fish doing?" She laughed and said, "I was wondering what they were. I've never seen them on the X-ray machine before!" And we took them back to New York to have for dinner that night.

The stripers that are now on the market are all farm raised, tasty, and incredibly good for baking, stuffing, poaching, filleting, or preparing whole. The larger fish can also be cut into steaks. However, where the wild sea-caught stripers could generally be marketed at 25 to 50 pounds, the farm-raised variety is usually sold anywhere from 2 pounds up to 8 pounds. If you do purchase the fish whole, be sure to use the head and skeleton for one of the best fish stocks you can possibly make yourself (see page 402).

WHOLE STRIPED BASS STUFFED WITH FENNEL AND GARLIC

MAKES 6 SERVINGS

A similar variety of saltwater bass is called loup de mer *in France and is traditionally prepared with licorice-like fennel, as we have done here with its North American cousin, the striped bass.*

1 5- to 6-pound whole striped bass, gutted and gills removed (see Note; substitute: red snapper or two 3-pound striped bass)

Salt and pepper to taste

4 tablespoons butter

2 tablespoons olive oil

4 large cloves garlic, thinly sliced (about 1½ tablespoons)

1 teaspoon fennel seeds

4 small fennel bulbs (1½ to 2 pounds)

2 tablespoons lemon juice

2 tablespoons Pernod or Ricard

⅓ cup Cognac

Preheat the oven to 425°. Season the fish inside and out with salt and pepper and set aside. In a small skillet, heat 2 tablespoons of the butter and the oil, garlic, and fennel seeds over low heat. Do not allow the garlic to color. Remove the garlic with a slotted spoon and pour the mixture into a baking pan large enough for the whole fish. Let cool a bit and add the fish, turning to coat it on all sides with the butter mixture.

Coarsely chop the fennel bulbs and feathery tops and add to a medium bowl. Toss with the lemon juice and season with salt and pepper. Stuff this mixture lightly into the cavity of the fish and dot with the remaining 2 tablespoons butter. Fasten the opening with small metal skewers (or wooden ones that have been soaked in water for 20 minutes). Loosely loop dental floss or string around the skewers as you would lace a boot. Add the Pernod to the bottom of the pan, cover lightly with aluminum foil, and bake for 30 to 40 minutes, basting the fish frequently with the Pernod mixture. Add some boiling water to the bottom of the pan if there is not enough basting liquid and remove the foil after 15 minutes of baking time.

Test the thickest part of the fish for doneness with a skewer. When it's cooked, remove the pan from the oven and cover loosely again with aluminum foil. Let the fish stand for 5 minutes before undoing the laces and removing the skewers. Then, just before serving, heat the Cognac in a small pan over low heat until bubbles form around the edge. Ignite the Cognac with a match and quickly pour the burning liquid over the fish. Serve when the flames die down.

NOTE: Have the fishmonger prepare the fish for stuffing. If the spine is removed, there will be a larger opening to accommodate the stuffing. Sometimes, if the fish is not gutted through the belly, the fishmonger can slit or remove the spine bones and gut through the back of the fish, leaving the head, tail, and abdominal wall intact and allowing you to stuff the entire fish, bake it, and present it boatlike on its stomach.

STRIPED BASS MARECHIARE WITH CLAMS AND MUSSELS

MAKES 4 SERVINGS

Firm, flaky, white-fleshed striped bass is simmered with crushed herb-scented tomatoes and infused with the shellfish broth that is given up as the clams and mussels steam open.

2 striped bass fillets, with skin, about 1 pound each, cut crosswise into 4 pieces of equal weight (substitute: sea bass or red snapper)

½ cup all-purpose flour

Salt and pepper to taste

½ cup olive oil

8 very small littleneck clams or 24 Manila clams, well scrubbed

8 large mussels, well scrubbed and bearded

1 cup canned crushed Italian plum tomatoes, drained

½ cup dry white wine

2 large cloves garlic, thinly slivered

1½ tablespoons finely minced parsley

½ teaspoon dried oregano, preferably Greek

2 tablespoons finely shredded fresh basil leaves

Place the pieces of fish in a plastic bag along with the flour, salt, and pepper, and shake to coat lightly. In a cast-iron skillet, heat ¼ cup of the olive oil over high heat until hot but not smoking. Add the fish and quickly sauté until golden, 1 to 2 minutes on each side. The fish should be mostly undercooked. Transfer to paper towels to drain.

Lightly oil a skillet large enough to accommodate the fish in one layer. Add the fish skin side down and arrange the clams and mussels around it. Spoon the crushed tomatoes over the fish and sprinkle with the wine, garlic, 1 tablespoon of the parsley, the oregano, 1 tablespoon of the basil, and salt and pepper to taste. Pour the remaining ¼ cup oil over all. Cover tightly with aluminum foil and bring to a boil, then lower the heat and simmer for 10 to 12 minutes until the clams and mussels have opened and the fish flakes easily when tested with a skewer. Scatter the remaining parsley and basil over the surface and serve hot.

SHAD AND SHAD ROE

When shad leave their ocean home to make their way upriver to spawn—in the St. Lawrence in Florida and in the Columbia River in Washington and Oregon—"spring has sprung!" In fact, the annual migration of this unusual fish has been a harbinger of spring for hundreds of years of American history. One of the research newsletters of the National Marine Fisheries Service tells it well:

Shad was known as elft, the eleven fish, to the early Dutch settlers. It was on the 11th day of March each year that the first shad were caught and cooked on a plank, a method the settlers learned from the Indians. Shad were so abundant in colonial days . . . that it became quite fashionable among some of the well-to-do. Many of them ate shad on the sly, fearing others would think them unable to afford more expensive foods.

It turns out that George Washington was inordinately fond of shad, while members of both the House and Senate often sailed down the Potomac for the sole purpose of eating shad (and, incidentally, enjoying a few drinks). But the fact that shad had been called the "eleven fish" is what caught our attention about this largest member of the herring family.

Shad is a particularly bony fish. An Indian legend has it that the shad was a discontented porcupine that asked the gods to be changed, following which it was turned inside out. Thus boning a shad has been compared to a surgical procedure that requires a long period of internship before it can be accomplished properly. However, the experts among us—the few remaining fishmongers who are adept at boning a shad properly—do it with *eleven* well-placed strokes, leaving 2 perfect and bone-free fillets. At one time, we tried to learn, even including the procedure in our early book. However, our current advice is to let the experts do it. At the fish market, you will find shad boned. If you are lucky enough to be invited on a fishing expedition, let the veterans fillet your catch.

Shad has a rich, sweet, very distinctive flavor, a high fat content, and a perfect texture for broiling, baking, pan-frying, or poaching. A further harbinger of the advent of spring is yet another special treat given to us by the shad—the delicious and delicate roe.

Shad Roe

Shad roe comes in skeins or sets, joined by a thin membrane. When the fish are brought to the wholesale markets, such as the Fulton Fish Market in New York, the roe is removed at once, with the female fish bringing the highest prices since they are much larger than the males (or bucks). If you happen to catch them on an outing upriver, the roe should be removed as quickly as possible and kept on ice for the trip home, since it is highly perishable.

We've given two of our favorite shad roe recipes in the pages that follow, but, as a general rule, always handle the roe with great care and don't separate the halves until after you've cooked them. Plunging them into iced water before you cook them will firm them up a bit, then always cook them gently only until they're opaque or slightly firm, 8 to 10 minutes at most.

ROE-STUFFED BAKED SHAD IN A LEEK AND SORREL CREAM

Inexhaustible shad work their way up the East Coast from the Carolinas and, as they enter the river estuaries from the sea in order to spawn, fisherpeople are waiting for the first catch of the season. Shad and the fresh, tart, acidic sorrel with which it is paired here are both harbingers of spring.

1 tablespoon plus 1 teaspoon lemon juice	2 shad fillets, with skin, ¾ to 1 pound each, pin bones removed
Salt to taste	4 to 6 large leaves Swiss chard
1 pair shad roe, about ½ pound	3 thin leeks, white part only, finely chopped (about 1½ cups)
1 cup soft fresh bread crumbs	4 tablespoons butter
⅓ cup milk	⅛ teaspoon cayenne pepper
1 tablespoon finely minced parsley	½ cup dry white wine
3 tablespoons finely minced fresh chives	1 cup half-and-half or light cream
1 teaspoon finely minced fresh tarragon	6 ounces sorrel, center stem and ribs removed, leaves shredded
Black pepper to taste	
Butter for baking pan	

Bring a small saucepan of water to a boil, lower the heat, add 1 teaspoon of the lemon juice and salt, then add the shad roe. Simmer over low heat for 3 to 5 minutes only until the roe begins to firm. Lift out the roe with a slotted spoon and, when cool to the touch, tear off the outer membrane and discard it.

In a small bowl, soak the bread crumbs in the milk, then squeeze the excess milk from the bread, keeping the mixture slightly mushy. Add the roe, broken into small pieces, 1 tablespoon lemon juice, the parsley, chives, tarragon, salt, and pepper and combine well.

Preheat the oven to 425°. Butter an oven-to-table baking pan large enough to accommodate the fish in one layer. Season the fillets with salt and pepper. Remove the white part of the center stems of the Swiss chard and save for another use. Lay the chard leaves overlapping on a flat surface. Place one fillet, skin side down, off center on the leaves. Spoon the roe stuffing evenly over the fillet, then top with the other fillet skin side up. Fold over the chard leaves to enclose the fish, then tie securely with string in several places.

Make a bed of the chopped leeks in the bottom of the pan and dot with 2 tablespoons of the butter. Season with cayenne and additional salt and pepper. Place the chard-wrapped fish over this bed and dot with another tablespoon of the butter. Pour the wine and half-and-half over the leeks only. Bake for 30 to 35 minutes, tilting the pan and occasionally basting the fish. Test at the thickest part of the fish with a skewer, right through the chard, to see if it flakes easily. If not, bake 5 to 8 minutes more until it does flake.

Transfer the fish to a large serving platter and cover loosely with aluminum foil to keep warm while preparing the sauce.

Pour the cream and leek mixture through a strainer into a medium nonstick saucepan, pressing the solids against the strainer to extract as much liquid as possible. Discard the contents of the strainer. Cook the sauce over high heat for about 5 minutes to reduce it. While the sauce is reducing, melt the remaining 1 tablespoon butter in a medium skillet over medium-high heat. Add the shredded sorrel and sauté, stirring constantly, only until it wilts and changes color from bright to olive green. Stir into the sauce. Heat over low heat for 1 minute. Cut the strings on the fish and discard them. With a sharp knife, cut the fish into portion-size pieces. Spoon the sauce on the platter around the fish and serve.

"CAVIAR: A ROE BY ANY OTHER NAME . . ."

Caviar comes from a virgin sturgeon.
Virgin sturgeon's a very fine dish.

ANONYMOUS

Sheryl has always had a dream that one day she would sit in a bathtub filled with beluga caviar and eat her way down to the drain, finally getting her fill of the elegant, glistening black jewels. (Mel's dream is the same tub filled with ice cream topped with runny chocolate!) Actually, history tells us that in the early nineteenth century, sturgeon (see page 256) was so plentiful that caviar was served in New York's saloons free along with steins of beer.

Although we generally think of roe as the eggs of the shad (see page 230) and the terribly expensive Russian and Iranian beluga, *sevruga,* and *osetra* caviar from the sturgeon that swims in the Caspian Sea between the two countries, many other types of fish roe make excellent caviar, such as salmon, whitefish, carp, pike, mullet, tuna,

Caviar and Roe

alewife, herring, mackerel, seatrout, and haddock. Only the roe of fresh-water gar and saltwater puffer or blowfish are toxic and should not be eaten.

The roe is sieved to remove the membranes, and the most expensive varieties are done by hand. If the caviar is to be sold fresh, salt is added. The word *"malassol"* on the label is the Russian word for "little salt." Check the labels carefully, since American caviar that comes from the processed and dyed roe of lumpfish or whitefish must be marked clearly as such.

STURGEON ROE

❖ *Beluga:* From the largest of the sturgeon family that swim the Caspian Sea, the roe is also the largest of the caviars, ranging from jet black to slate gray, with the latter, by far, the most expensive of all caviars. For the average palate such as ours, we find that the black is quite acceptable and delicious.

❖ *Sevruga:* From a smaller sturgeon, the roe is smaller, slightly milder, and a bit sweeter than the beluga. Also darker in color, sevruga caviar is about one-quarter to one-third the price of beluga.

❖ *Osetra:* The name comes from a variation of the Russian word for sturgeon. The roe is colored brown or a yellow gold and is about half the price of the most expensive caviars.

For bargain hunters (and aren't we all?), the two best buys in caviar are the pressed or broken roe, the eggs that are at the bottom of the shipment and have been damaged in transit. The prices drop considerably, but the taste is not affected—still perfect for hors d'oeuvres or a special treat.

LUMPFISH ROE: The original color is closer to that of the salmon (below), but it is dyed black in processing so that it closely resembles the more expensive sturgeon roe. Most of the catch comes from Iceland. Quite tiny and very salty, this roe has very little taste by our standards. In addition, we also find that the dye comes off. (If you purchase any dyed caviar, we strongly suggest rinsing them under cold water before using.) Lumpfish roe is, however, moderately priced.

WHITEFISH ROE: Sold as golden whitefish roe, it is another of the less expensive caviars, coming from the Great Lakes and sold fresh without dyeing. It has an excellent flavor with a slightly crunchy texture.

SALMON ROE: Distinguished by an exquisitely golden orange color, salmon roe caviar is about the size of small peas and usually comes from the coho, chum, and pink salmon. It is a reasonably priced caviar, and some of our friends prefer it to the higher priced sturgeon roe. Occasionally, you'll find it sold fresh in bulk rather than in jars. We prefer it that way for it is usually of the best quality.

Other varieties of caviar are now being imported from Japan, and occasionally we have found that a fishmonger's mullet has yielded a bounty of roe, which we promptly took home to devour. In Greece, we were treated to *taramosalata,* a wonderful dip or spread eaten with fish, vegetables, or just bread, made with a smoky gray mullet roe not available in the United States. Whatever roe you happen to buy or discover, all can be used in very much the same way—as hors d'oeuvres, stuffing for a whole fish, or as an elegant touch in a sauce.

The closest we ever came to reaching Sheryl's heaven of bathing in caviar was in the early 1960s when we were doing a documentary in Iran for Alitalia Airlines. As we were leaving the country after ten days of adventure and exquisite scenery, our client came aboard the departing plane right before takeoff and gave the film crew a package that was wrapped in plain newspaper. We all hugged goodbye and the plane departed for Rome. After a few minutes, as excited as children, we opened the package to find eight ½-pound tins of fresh beluga caviar. If ever anything might be described as "pig heaven," it was that plane ride all the way to Italy!

TARAMOSALATA

Our adaptation of this classic Greek fish roe purée is briny and laced with garlic. Besides spreading it on sesame seed crackers or pita bread, try it as a dip for crudités.

3 to 4 slices white peasant bread, such as
        French or Italian, crust removed and
        bread torn into small pieces
2 tablespoons cold water
5 tablespoons tarama (salted carp roe)
   (see Note)
2 tablespoons lemon juice
1 tablespoon grated onion

2 to 3 large cloves garlic, finely minced
⅛ teaspoon cayenne pepper
⅔ to ¾ cup olive oil
1 tablespoon finely minced parsley

Put the bread in a food processor, sprinkle with the water, and process with a few strokes. Add the tarama and process with 2 or 3 more strokes, until just combined. Add the lemon juice, onion, garlic, and cayenne and process until fairly smooth.

With the motor running, slowly add the olive oil through the feed tube and process until thick and creamy. If it's too liquid in consistency, add another slice of torn bread and process until the consistency is better. If too thick, add a tablespoon or two of cold water.

Spoon into a bowl and chill for at least 15 minutes or longer if more convenient. Sprinkle with parsley just before serving.

NOTE: Tarama is available in jars and is found in specialty food shops.

CAVIAR CROWN

An attractive and much less costly way to stretch expensive caviar for a party.

1 8-ounce package cream cheese, softened

1 tablespoon lemon juice

2 or 3 drops Tabasco

½ teaspoon white Worcestershire sauce

2 tablespoons finely minced scallion green

2 ounces salmon caviar

4 ounces black sturgeon, osetra, or sevruga caviar

1 tablespoon finely minced parsley

Lemon wedges for garnish

In a food processor, mix the cream cheese, lemon juice, Tabasco, Worcestershire, and scallion. On a plate make a 3½- by 1-inch-thick circle of the cheese mixture, shaping it in similar fashion to that of a layer cake. Chill for 10 minutes.

In the center of the cream cheese circle, spoon a 2-inch circle of salmon caviar, then cover the remaining rim and sides with black caviar. Place a circle of the parsley around the edge of the salmon caviar, dividing the red and the black with a green border. Surround the base with lemon wedges. Serve with thin toast triangles.

EEL AND ELVERS

The best known member of the species is the American eel, but our most vivid experience with this unique fish took place in Japan, where eel is farmed rather than taken in the wild. We had traveled to Itako, a small town about two hours by rail from Tokyo, to visit the annual Iris Festival, and although we remember the lovely displays of purple, yellow, and white irises planted along the canals, as well as the hundreds of artists who were painting them, it is the lunch that stays with us to this day.

We asked directions and advice from a passing wedding party, and the leader of the group suggested a restaurant that specialized in eel, prepared in forty or more different ways. Seated in a tiny, private, *shoji*-enclosed room, our legs tucked painfully under us, we gorged ourselves on the fish, prepared exquisitely, as only the Japanese can do it.

Popular in Japan as well as Europe, eel was introduced here by immigrants from Italy, Spain, Denmark, and Holland, where the fatty fish is a centuries-old favorite. Once here, however, eel seemed to become an acquired taste, probably because of its looks rather than its culinary attributes. On the other hand, even Irma Rombauer's *Joy of Cooking,* the cookbook that almost every new bride since the 1930s has received as a gift, actually has several recipes for eel and *Larousse Gastronomique,* the bible for professional chefs, lists 48 recipes. We have found, too, that many of our friends newly returned from Europe have suddenly "discovered" eel.

Unlike the anadromous salmon or striped bass, eel is catadromous, spawning in the sea at exactly the same spot where it was born but spending most of its life in fresh-water tributaries and rivers both in Europe and the coast of the United States. All are born in the Sargasso Sea, near the coast of Bermuda, then the newly hatched transparent ribbons, shaped like willow leaves with small pointed heads, drift for one to three years on the currents of the Atlantic until they reach the shoreline and rivers of both Europe and the United States. As they arrive, they undergo a very dramatic transformation to the glass eel stage and finally to that of *elvers,* looking like small, transparent, two-eyed needles and a delicacy for those who have gotten to know them.

In Spain, elvers are known as *angulas,* and they're a seasonal treat in cities like Barcelona, where we got to know them during several film trips at a wonderful restaurant called Can Costa in the Barceloneta section of the city. The noisy, crowded restaurant has been a favorite spot of ours for some years now, and we have continued to visit it in order to eat *angulas,* hundreds of tiny elvers cooked quickly in hot fruity olive oil, garlic, and hot chiles. They're served sizzling in an earthenware dish and eaten with a wooden, rather than metal, fork because they're so slippery.

Full-grown eels are caught throughout the seasonal year, but most eel lovers feel that winter provides the best-tasting catch. The fish range from 10 to 16 inches in length, and they are quite meaty, very rich and fatty, and also quite firm. With a single central bone, they're easy to eat. They take beautifully to fresh herbs and can be baked, broiled, simmered in stew, fried, or poached. One of our favorite breakfast treats is smoked eel, especially when we're lucky enough to find the fat, oversized ones at our island fish store.

Eel are generally available in local fish markets, especially those located in ethnic neighborhoods. No traditional Italian family, for example, would be without a dish of eel on Christmas Eve.

EEL IN GREEN SAUCE

A rich, emerald-colored sauce bathes pieces of firm, delicious eel as an unusual first course.

1 pound fresh spinach, stems trimmed

1 cup parsley leaves, stems trimmed

1 large bunch watercress, stems trimmed

4 large scallions, coarsely chopped

2 fresh large sage leaves, coarsely chopped

2 sprigs tarragon, stems removed, or ½ teaspoon dried tarragon

¼ cup loosely packed fresh dill leaves

2 tablespoons butter

2 tablespoons olive oil

3 pounds thick meaty eel, skinned, gutted, and cut into 3-inch pieces (substitute: ocean pout)

½ teaspoon pepper

Salt to taste

1½ cups boiling Fish Stock (see page 402)

2 egg yolks, lightly beaten

¼ cup light cream

3 tablespoons lemon juice (1 medium lemon)

Using a food processor, finely purée the spinach, parsley, watercress, scallions, sage, tarragon, and dill in several batches. There should be about 2½ cups purée. Put the purée into a saucepan and set aside.

In a large skillet, heat the butter and oil over medium-high heat until bubbly. Season the eel with the pepper and salt, add to the skillet, and sauté, turning often with tongs, until it begins to look opaque. Add the hot fish stock, cover the skillet, lower the heat, and simmer for 8 minutes. Using a slotted spoon, transfer the eel to a deep serving bowl and cool while preparing the sauce.

Pour the fish stock into a medium saucepan and whisk in the egg yolks and cream. Cook, whisking constantly, over very low heat for 1 minute. Stir in the puréed greens and cook, whisking constantly, until it is thick and almost to the boiling point. Do not boil or the eggs will curdle. Add the lemon juice and season with salt and pepper. Pour the sauce over the eel and let cool to room temperature before serving.

GROUP D
Fresh-Water Fin Fish

Pike

Carp

Perch

Trout

Whitefish

Sturgeon

Buffalofish

Sunfish

Catfish

PIKE

Our first taste of pike probably came to us as to many others of our ethnic backgrounds, when our grandmothers and then our mothers cooked for hours to make the well-loved and festive holiday dish gefilte fish (also using carp and whitefish, see page 245). It was not until many years later that we were introduced to its French cousins, quenelles and mousse of pike (see page 242), as well as pike used for stuffing other fish.

Actually, using pike in recipes that require grinding makes very good sense since the flesh of the fish is flaky, very lean, and delicate, and it breaks up easily, while the small bones make it very difficult to fillet. By grinding the fish, the tiny, small bones become pulverized. However, when properly scaled and prepared by your fishmonger, it can also be braised, steamed, poached, baked, or sautéed.

Pike is part of a family of fresh-water fish that also includes pickerel, an especially popular fish with sports people, many of whom fish for it through the winter ice, and muskellunge, the largest member of the family and known as the "king" of the gamefish. Walleye pike is not a member of the family, in spite of its name, but is actually a perch (see page 249).

The entire family is distinguished by long bodies and pugnacious-looking jaws with strong teeth. To sports people, they are the most difficult of fish to catch and land—moody, temperamental, unpredictable, and tricky. There are fisherpeople who have been after them for years and have yet to get their first strike. Pike weigh about 5 to 10 pounds, and the smaller pickerel is usually marketed at 2 to 3 pounds; both are available at the fish market all year round. The giant of the family, the muskellunge can top the scales at 60 pounds and runs 5 to 6 feet in length. However, they are most often brought home only by sports people.

Should you be lucky enough to be given a gift of a fresh-caught member of this fish family, first dip it in boiling water for 30 seconds, then into cold water to cool it. The fresh-caught fish can be somewhat slimy, and this will help make the scales come off more easily.

MOUSSE OF PIKE IN A FISH MOLD WITH RED PEPPER AND TOMATO SAUCE

Mousse of Pike in a fish Mold

MAKES 6 TO 8 FIRST-COURSE SERVINGS

Light, delicate, and served with a sauce that has some zap, this fish-shaped mousse makes a lovely presentation. You can also bake it in a loaf pan, then serve slices with a stripe of sauce spooned over them, garnished with a sprig of watercress.

1½ pounds skinned pike fillets (substitute: sole, red snapper, or salmon)

2 tablespoons butter, softened

3 ounces shallots, finely minced (about 3 tablespoons)

2 tablespoons dry vermouth or dry white wine

2 eggs, separated

1 tablespoon lemon juice

⅛ teaspoon nutmeg

⅛ teaspoon cayenne pepper

¼ teaspoon white pepper

   Salt to taste

1 cup heavy cream, cold

½ cup milk

¼ teaspoon cream of tartar

RED PEPPER AND TOMATO SAUCE:

3	tablespoons butter		2	tablespoons balsamic vinegar
1	tablespoon walnut oil		½	teaspoon dried thyme
3	shallots (about 2 ounces), thickly sliced		¼	teaspoon cayenne pepper
4	red peppers (about 1¼ pounds), stemmed, seeded, and cut into ¾-inch strips			Salt and black pepper to taste
			⅓	cup sour cream
4	plum tomatoes (about ½ pound), cut in quarters			Watercress for garnish

Cut the fish fillets into 1-inch pieces and chill. In a small saucepan, melt 1 tablespoon of the butter over low heat. Add the shallots and sauté, stirring frequently, until soft, 4 to 5 minutes. Add the vermouth, raise the heat to medium, and bring to a boil. Lower the heat again and simmer until the liquid has evaporated, about 5 minutes. Set aside to cool.

Butter a 4-cup mold, preferably fish shaped, or a loaf pan. Preheat the oven to 350° and boil a kettle of water. Using a food processor, purée the fish until smooth. Add the shallot mixture and process until blended. Add the egg yolks, lemon juice, nutmeg, cayenne, white pepper, and salt and process again with a few strokes. Then, with the motor running, gradually add the cream and milk through the feed tube.

In a bowl, using a hand beater, beat the egg whites until foamy, sprinkle the cream of tartar and a few grains of salt over the whites, and continue to beat until stiff but not dry. Scrape the fish mixture from the processor and fold it into the beaten egg whites. Then spoon into the mold and smooth the surface. Cut a piece of waxed paper to fit the top, and butter one side with the remaining 1 tablespoon butter and place it butter side down over the fish.

Place the mold in a larger pan and fill the pan with boiling water two-thirds of the way up the side of the mold. Bake for 25 to 30 minutes until the fish mousse has pulled away from the mold. Prepare the sauce while the fish bakes.

In a large skillet, heat the butter and oil over medium-high heat until the butter melts. Stir in the shallots and sauté for 1 minute, stirring. Add the peppers and tomatoes and continue to sauté, stirring occasionally, for 5 minutes. Add the vinegar, thyme, cayenne, salt, and pepper and continue to cook for 10 to 15 minutes until the peppers are tender. Transfer to a food processor and purée. Keep the mixture in the processor until cool, then add the sour cream and process to incorporate. Scrape into a serving bowl. Cover with plastic wrap and refrigerate. Bring to room temperature before serving.

When the fish mousse is baked, let it stand for 20 minutes before inverting it onto a serving plate. The mold also can be covered with plastic wrap and refrigerated for several hours or overnight but bring it to room temperature before unmolding. If any liquid has accumulated, blot the excess with paper towels. Decorate with watercress and serve with the red pepper and tomato sauce.

CARP

The carp was probably one of the first of the farm-raised fish. Its history goes back to China, where it was cultivated as much as 500 years before Christ and where its exquisite beauty was frequently depicted by the artists of the time. Even today, as a reminder of the ornamental ponds in Asian gardens, we still see live carp swimming in the tanks at the Chinese fishmongers in our city.

After its introduction to Europe, carp began to flourish and become a part of both the recipes and the folklore of both continents. We had heard for years, for example, that carp could be trained to come when you clapped your hands, and this folklore was proven to us just three years ago on a trip through the Costa Brava in Spain.

Near the town of Pals, we came across a most unusual sculptor by the name of Antonio Macia, who boasted amidst his unusual works of art a fully stocked carp pond. In order to show off his prized fish, he clapped his hands. Suddenly a vast school of carp appeared, waiting for him to feed them scraps of bread.

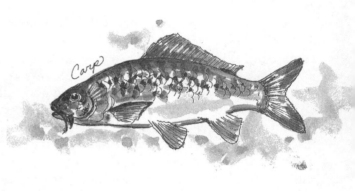

Carp is a fresh-water fish that peppers the history of countries around the entire globe. For the Japanese, the mythical tale of the golden carp is a symbol of courage and bravery and whoever eats it is magically transformed into one who is also brave. Israeli fishermen still cast their nets into the Sea of Galilee (a fresh-water lake, however) in the same way as their ancestors did over a thousand years ago.

Today, carp is found in rivers, lakes, and ponds and cultivated in reservoirs and fish farms. It can best be described as looking like a giant goldfish, with shimmering gold, orange, and reddish brown spots. They're moderately fatty and very bony, with a rich-tasting, firm, but coarse flesh. The average market size ranges from 3 to 10 pounds, although it can grow to a much greater size in the wild, since its normal life cycle is 30 to 40 years. It's sold year round, but we have found that it has the best texture and taste during the winter months. We also find it most available in areas that cater to Middle European, Chinese, and Jewish customers.

The simplest way to buy a carp is to have the fishmonger prepare it for you, but if you should bring home a live fish from the local market, like the pike, the skin and the tough, bony scales will peel off more easily if you plunge the fish into boiling water and lemon juice for about 30 seconds, then into cold water to cool it quickly. If you prefer the milder-tasting white flesh on your fillets, remove the narrow dark lateral meat after cooking. We find the fish a bit bony for baking, steaming, or poaching, but if you marinate, pickle, or grind carp, the bones will soften.

GEFILTE FISH

Although all traditional recipes for this Jewish dish use fresh-water fish, many cooks change the balance of fish according to their preference and family background. When more carp is used, the fish is darker in color, and sometimes a small-mouthed fresh-water bass called buffalofish or buffel is added.

6 pounds fresh-water fish fillets: 3 pounds yellow pike, pickerel, or walleye, 2 pounds whitefish, and 1 pound carp, cut into 1½-inch chunks (reserve the heads with gills and eyes removed, the skin, and bones)

4 large onions (reserve skin of 1 onion, see Note)

½ cup cold water

3 eggs, beaten until foamy

1 teaspoon white pepper

1 tablespoon plus ½ teaspoon sugar

3 tablespoons matzo meal

Salt to taste

2 thin carrots, sliced diagonally ¼ inch thick

In a food processor, purée the fish in 3 or 4 batches to a coarse mixture. Transfer to a wooden chopping bowl. Coarsely chop 3 of the onions in the food processor and add to the wooden bowl. Using a single blade chopper with a handle, chop the fish and onions for 10 minutes, gradually incorporating ¼ cup of the cold water (more may be necessary at the end), the eggs, half the pepper, ½ teaspoon sugar, the matzo meal, and salt until the mixture is gelatinous and sticky in consistency. Place the bowl in the refrigerator to chill while preparing the poaching liquid.

In a fish poacher, a wide deep pot, or turkey roaster, layer any leftover scraps of fish, bones, and heads in the bottom, stretching the pieces of skin flat over the bones (or use a piece of cheesecloth if there is not enough skin). Thinly slice the remaining onion and add it along with the carrots. Slowly pour approximately 8 cups cold water into the pot. Add the onion skin, 1 tablespoon sugar, remaining ½ teaspoon pepper, and salt to taste, cover the pot, and bring to a boil over medium heat. Lower the heat and simmer for 40 minutes.

While the broth is simmering, prepare the fish quenelles: With wet hands (run them under cold running water), form 1½ to 2 tablespoons of the fish mixture into an oval shape about 3 inches long. Keep your hands wet and repeat until all of the mixture is used. As each piece is finished, place it on waxed paper.

Add the ovals to the simmering broth, making sure that the broth covers the fish by two-thirds. Lower the heat, cover the pot, and simmer over very low heat for 2 hours.

Baste occasionally and check to see if additional boiling water needs to be added after about 1 hour.

Let the fish cool in the broth and then transfer to a platter using a slotted spoon. Remove the cooked carrot slices and use them to garnish the fish. Strain the liquid into a separate bowl, pressing the solids against the strainer. Cover both the fish and the broth with plastic wrap. Refrigerate for several hours or overnight. The broth will gel into an aspic.

The gelled broth can be spooned over the fish at serving time or warmed and returned to its liquid state. The traditional accompaniments for gefilte fish are challah and red horseradish (stained beet root).

NOTE: Onion skins color the fish stock a lovely amber shade.

PICKLED CARP

We both remember our grandparents buying carp as it is still sold in Chinatown, live, and they'd keep it swimming in the bathtub until it was time to cook! We loved to visit them, since it was a triple treat: a home aquarium, a delicious dinner—and no bath!

2	cups dry white wine	½	teaspoon celery seeds
1	cup water	½	teaspoon mustard seeds
⅓	cup white wine vinegar	2	dried small hot chiles
2	teaspoons coarse or kosher salt	2	large onions (about ¾ pound), thinly sliced
2	tablespoons light brown sugar	3	pounds (9 to 10) carp steaks, ¾ inch thick, scaled (substitute: salmon steaks)
2	bay leaves		
1	teaspoon whole black peppercorns	1	medium-size red onion (4 to 5 ounces), thinly sliced
2	whole cloves		
4	whole allspice berries		

In a nonreactive 12-inch sauté pan, combine the wine, water, vinegar, salt, sugar, bay leaves, peppercorns, cloves, allspice berries, celery seeds, mustard seeds, chiles, and large onions. Bring to a boil over medium heat and cook, covered, for 10 minutes. Add the fish steaks in one layer and lower the heat to medium-low. Cover the pan and simmer for 15 minutes, then turn off the heat and let the fish cool in the broth for 20 minutes.

Carefully lift out the fish with a slotted spatula, scraping off any spices that might have adhered to the fish. Place the fish in one layer in a flat nonreactive oven-to-table baking dish. Top with the sliced red onion and set aside.

Bring the broth to a boil again and cook over medium-high heat, uncovered, for about 15 minutes to reduce the liquid. Strain the liquid into a bowl, pressing the solids against the strainer. There should be about 2 cups. Discard the solids. Let the broth cool, then slowly pour over the fish and onions. Cover tightly with plastic wrap and refrigerate for at least 24 hours before serving. The broth will gel into an aspiclike consistency. If you wish to liquefy it before serving, place the casserole over very low heat until the aspic melts. In either case, let the fish come to room temperature before serving with buttered pumpernickel bread as a first course or with a green salad as a main course.

NOTE: Carp is fragile and falls apart easily and, although it's a bony fish, the flesh is particularly delicious.

HUNGARIAN CARP IN PAPRIKA *SAUCE* WITH DILL

MAKES 6 SERVINGS

In the Middle East, carp is usually prepared with sesame paste (tahini), while in Asia it's braised with vegetables. Here, as in Eastern Europe, we have smothered it in onions, peppers, and tomatoes with the ubiquitous paprika of Hungary.

2   pounds skinned carp fillets, cut into 6 equal portions, with pin bones removed (substitute: buffalo fish) (see Note)

¼   cup lemon juice

1   teaspoon coarse salt

2   tablespoons corn oil

2   tablespoons butter

2   medium onions, coarsely chopped (about 1½ cups)

2½   teaspoons sweet Hungarian paprika

⅛ to ¼   teaspoon cayenne pepper

2   medium green peppers, cut into ½-inch dice (about 2 cups)

2   medium tomatoes (about ¾ pound), skinned and cut into ½-inch dice (about 2 cups)

2   tablespoons sour cream

1   teaspoon all-purpose flour

2   tablespoons finely minced fresh dill

Place the fish in one layer in a shallow nonreactive dish and sprinkle with the lemon juice and salt on both sides. Let marinate for 20 minutes. Preheat the oven to 350°.

In a medium skillet, heat the oil and butter over medium-high heat until the butter begins to foam. Add the onions, paprika, and cayenne to taste and stir. Lower the heat to medium-low and sauté for 1 minute. Add the peppers and tomatoes, raise the heat to high, bring to a boil, and remove from the heat. Lift the fish out of the marinade and place in one layer in an oiled shallow baking dish. Discard the marinade. Spoon the onion mixture over the fish. Bake, basting occasionally, for about 15 to 20 minutes until the fish flakes when tested with a skewer.

Tilt the pan, spoon out 2 to 3 tablespoons of the liquid, and mix with the sour cream and flour. Spoon this mixture over the fish, carefully turn the pieces of fish over, and bake for another 2 to 3 minutes. Remove from the oven and sprinkle with the dill.

NOTE: For a more delicate flavor, remove the dark brown lateral strip of meat on the carp before cutting it into serving pieces.

PERCH

Although we live near the sea and are most familiar with saltwater fish, one of the treats we always look forward to on our trips to the Great Lakes is the small, tasty fresh-water perch. Mel also remembers his summers as a kid, fishing for perch and sunfish (see page 257) in a Catskill Mountain lake. In fact, most perch are still caught by amateur fisherpeople, many of them through the winter ice.

Small yellow perch as well as its cousin the walleyed pike (or pike perch) have firm, white flesh and are incredibly sweet-tasting fish with a low fat content. Any visitor to the Lake Balaton region of Hungary is informed immediately that the local delicacy is their own pike perch (*fogas*) deep-fried and presented on the platter in the curved shape of a large "U." Frankly we found it quite overrated, with a highly inflated price because of its specialty status.

We might note, as we have before, that the fish world once again has named species "perch" that are not in the family at all. Ocean perch is really a rockfish, and white perch is in the bass family.

The smaller yellow perch usually weighs under a pound; most of the catch is between ½ and ¾ pound. After it's scaled, the very thin skin generally is left on during cooking. They make excellent oven or pan-fried treats, and some cooks like to butterfly them for cooking. They're caught not only in the Great Lakes but also in rivers, streams, and lakes from Canada down to the Carolinas.

The walleye is much larger, sometimes weighing between 15 and 20 pounds, although it's marketed at under 3 pounds. It, too, can be scaled and cooked with the skin left on, and because of its size, it makes excellent fillets. There is also a European relative found in some inland lakes and waters of low salinity, such as the Baltic Sea.

WINE-BAKED YELLOW PERCH WITH ONIONS, TOMATOES, AND MUSHROOMS

This small, delicate, lean-fleshed fish has the ability to nicely absorb the flavorful sauce in which it cooks. Serve it with rice, which also soaks up any remaining sauce.

4	whole yellow perch, about 1 pound each, gutted and scaled (substitute: ocean perch)	5 to 6	medium tomatoes (about 1 pound), skinned and cut into 1-inch cubes (about 2½ cups)
	Salt and black pepper to taste	¼	pound white mushrooms, trimmed and coarsely chopped (about 1 cup)
2	tablespoons olive oil		
2	large onions (about ¾ pound), coarsely chopped (1½ to 2 cups)	1	cup dry white wine
		2	tablespoons finely minced parsley

Preheat the oven to 350°. Rub the outside and inside of the fish with salt and pepper. In a large skillet, heat the olive oil over medium-high heat. Add the onions and sauté, stirring frequently, for 8 to 10 minutes until the onions begin to color.

Spoon the onions evenly over the bottom of a large baking pan. Place the fish over onions, scatter the tomatoes and mushrooms over the fish, then pour the wine over all. Bake, basting occasionally, for 15 to 20 minutes until a skewer inserted in the thickest part of the fish meets with no resistance. Sprinkle with parsley before serving.

TROUT

As seaside fisherpeople who love to stand in the roaring surf and cast our lines out into the ocean, we always have had an affinity for the people who prefer the annual spring ritual of the trout season. About April, just as the streams have begun to break their icy blankets, the waders come out from their winter hiding places, the mail-order and homemade flies that will act as lures take their place in the tacklebox, and the ardent fisherperson sets out on what is to become a delicate and treacherous ballet.

Fishing for trout is performed in slimy rocks amidst swiftly racing currents, while the trout lie in wait under rocks and overhangs. Evaluating the depth and the swiftness of the current, watching for clues as to where the fish might be swimming, guessing at the type and color of fly to use is an intensely consuming, somewhat dangerous, totally involving, and challenging pursuit. It takes skill, it takes patience, and yet most people who engage in it find it totally relaxing.

Rainbow Trout

But there is an added pleasure for those of us who consider ourselves both fisherpeople and environmentalists. Almost all trout in the marketplace are farm raised. The total catch for sportspeople is minimal and not threatening to the trout population. And, best of all, whether by state law or by preference, many trout fisherpeople use hooks without barbs and the catch, after a remarkably tough series of runs and furious leaps for a fish so small, are returned to the stream or river to swim again and to reproduce yet another generation.

The trout is closely related to the salmon family, and indeed some members seem to look and taste more like the latter. A good example is the Arctic char, to which we've given its own small section of this book (see page 224). The rainbow trout is probably the best known and most widely marketed of the family, and it is now farmed all over the United States and Europe. Its flesh can run from white when farm raised to pale orange through deep red when wild. Since the supply is well controlled through aquaculture, size remains fairly constant in the marketplace at about ½ pound.

The steelhead trout is the ocean-going relative of the rainbow, and an anadromous member of the family. It, too, is found both in the wild and on fish farms. Although it can reach a weight of 12 pounds, the smaller fish are usually marketed at 8 to 10 ounces, just as the rainbow.

The brook trout, brown trout, and speckled trout are East Coast varieties and among the most popular with anglers. The lake trout (which is technically a char), is taken commercially in lakes all across Canada and down into the colder regions of the United States, including the Great Lakes. This fish is much larger than its relatives, reaching weights up to 100 pounds, but generally harvested from 10 to 20 pounds. It is also much fattier than other members of the family, and the larger the fish, the fattier it becomes. The flesh varies from white to pink, orange, and red.

Generally, we find that all trout are mild-tasting and easy to prepare. Fresh-caught trout can be boned easily either before or after cooking, and the skin is always left on. They also butterfly easily and take well to poaching, baking, broiling, frying, or steaming. And for those of our readers who love smoked trout, it needs no description from us.

TROUT MEUNIÈRE WITH PECANS AND LEMON SAUCE

MAKES 4 SERVINGS

Meunière is the French word for "miller's wife," probably referring to the simple way of using some of the abundance of flour always available at the mill. When the fish is dredged first in flour, then simply sautéed in butter and seasonings, its delicacy is enriched rather than masked. We have added a few butter-toasted pecans for crunch to add yet another dimension.

4	trout fillets, with skin, about 1½ pounds (substitute: sole, orange roughy, or weakfish/seatrout)	5	tablespoons butter
		1	cup coarsely chopped pecans
½	cup all-purpose flour	1	tablespoon Worcestershire sauce
	Salt and pepper to taste	2	tablespoons lemon juice

Coat the fillets lightly in a mixture of flour, salt, and pepper. In a large skillet, melt 3 tablespoons of the butter over medium heat. Add the fillets and sauté for a total of about 8 minutes, turning once. Transfer to a warm serving dish and keep warm in a low oven.

Add the pecans to the pan and cook, stirring constantly over medium-high heat for 1 minute. Stir in the Worcestershire sauce, lemon juice, and remaining 2 tablespoons butter. When the sauce foams, spoon it over the fish and serve at once.

TROUT GRENOBLAISE (TROUT WITH LEMON AND CAPERS)

MAKES 4 SERVINGS

Adding capers and tiny bits of lemon to a meunière-style butter sauce is the way of preparing this fish dish in Grenoble. So easy and delicious, Grenoblaise sauce can be applied to almost any fish with excellent results.

4 whole trout, 10 to 12 ounces each, gutted and pan-dressed (substitute: skate wings, seatrout/weakfish, or flounder)

¾ cup milk

¼ teaspoon Tabasco

Salt to taste

½ cup all-purpose flour

¼ teaspoon black pepper

¼ cup corn oil

4 tablespoons butter

2 lemons, peel, white pith, and seeds removed, pulp cut into tiny pieces

2 tablespoons nonpareil capers, rinsed and dried

2 tablespoons finely minced parsley

Arrange the trout in a shallow pan. Pour the milk, Tabasco, and salt to taste over the fish. Turn the fish to coat and let stand 20 minutes, turning the fish once.

In a shallow bowl, mix the flour, pepper, and salt to taste. Lift out each fish and roll it in the flour to coat it evenly. Discard the milk mixture. Transfer the fish to waxed paper as each is coated with the flour mixture.

Heat the oil in a large, heavy skillet over medium-high heat. Add the trout and cook for 4 to 5 minutes until the fish is golden on one side. Turn carefully and cook on the other side, tilting the pan and basting with the oil, for 4 to 5 minutes more. Lift the fish out with a slotted spatula to a serving dish and keep warm in a low oven.

Pour off the oil and discard it; wipe out the skillet with paper towels. Add the butter to the skillet and heat over medium-high heat until it foams and begins to turn color. Stir in the lemon bits and capers and sauté, sliding the pan back and forth over the stove burner, for about 15 seconds. Then pour over the fish and sprinkle with the parsley.

WHITEFISH

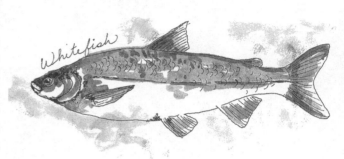

Another member of the large salmon and trout family, the whitefish (also known as lake whitefish) lives in the deep, cold-water lakes and rivers of the northern United States and Canada and is quite popular with winter ice fisherpeople. In fact, the winter catch is considered tastier than the fish caught during the rest of the year, since it then has a higher fat content and the flesh is firmer, with a mild, sweet flavor. Although whitefish can be fried, broiled, or grilled, we prefer to either poach or bake it because of its delicate flavor. It can also be found smoked, and the roe is sold as golden whitefish caviar.

The cisco is a smaller member of the whitefish family and is seldom found fresh, except in the regions in which it is caught, the north-central section of the United States and along the border in Canada. Thus, most of us know cisco as smoked whitefish or chub (or tullibee in Canada). Today, almost every major marketplace offers it in all its small, golden, tasty glory for brunch or Sunday morning breakfast.

For us, the cisco has always carried with it an intriguing story. Each year, out in Utah and Idaho, a winter ritual takes place that lasts only 10 days but which brings as many as 20,000 fisherpeople to the freezing waters of the inland lakes to net the tiny 2-ounce Bonneville cisco. At Bear Lake in Utah along a stretch of shoreline known as Cisco Beach, a busy weekend can bring over 3,000 people down to the water's edge. Dressed in waders, wearing rubber gloves, and wielding dip nets at the end of 10-foot poles, each person is allowed a daily limit of 50 fish. The yearly catch from Bear Lake alone is somewhere around 200,000 cisco. Our friends in Utah claim that there's nothing quite as good as a Bonneville cisco, freshly caught and quickly deep-fried.

SMOKED WHITEFISH SALAD

An attractive summery salad with the smoky taste of whitefish paired with potatoes, vegetables, and fresh herbs.

¾ pound small new potatoes, peeled and coarsely cut into ½-inch pieces

1 egg

Salt to taste

1 small red onion, finely minced (about ⅓ cup)

2 medium ribs celery, finely diced (about ¾ cup)

4 small radishes, sliced paper thin

1 to 1¼ pounds smoked whole whitefish, skinned and boned (there should be about ½ pound of flesh; substitute: smoked sablefish or smoked eel)

½ cup mayonnaise

⅓ cup sour cream

1 teaspoon Dijon mustard

1 tablespoon India relish

1 teaspoon nonpareil capers, rinsed and dried

1 teaspoon finely minced fresh tarragon or ½ teaspoon dried tarragon

2 teaspoons lemon juice

1 tablespoon finely minced parsley

Pepper to taste

Leaf lettuce for garnish

Black olives for garnish

In a medium saucepan, add the potatoes and egg, cover with water, salt it, and bring to a boil over medium-low heat. Cook, covered, for 10 to 12 minutes until the potatoes are tender and the egg is hard cooked. Drain and put the potatoes in a large bowl to cool. Peel and coarsely chop the egg, then add it to the bowl along with the onion, celery, and radishes.

Break the fish into bite-size pieces, carefully removing any stray bones, and add it to the bowl. In a separate small bowl, combine the mayonnaise, sour cream, mustard, relish, capers, tarragon, lemon juice, parsley, salt, and pepper. Spoon over the potato mixture and gently combine.

Make a bed of lettuce leaves on a platter, mound the salad on top, and stud with black olives. Serve or cover with plastic wrap and refrigerate until serving time.

STURGEON

Although today we tend to think of sturgeon only as our major source of prime caviar (see page 233), there was a time when the fish was also highly prized for its fresh, delicate flavor and its firm flesh. King Edward II of England was so fond of sturgeon that he gave it royal status and decreed that all fish caught had to be offered to the court. In addition to caviar, most of us also know it as smoked sturgeon, a fairly expensive treat at that.

By the late nineteenth century, the overfishing of sturgeon, both for the valuable roe and the fresh meat, was responsible for its almost disappearing. Today, however, there has been a slow recovery and the fresh fish is once again available, although the comeback might be considered quite moderate.

Sturgeon is the largest of the freshwater fish, with some reported at over 1,000 pounds; it has an average market weight of about 60 pounds. Some are anadromous, spawning in fresh water and returning to the sea, while others spend their lives in large inland lakes and seas such as the Caspian and the Black Sea. Most American sturgeon are taken in the Pacific Northwest and the southern Atlantic coast.

The most popular variety is white sturgeon, highly protected so that egg-bearing females cannot be taken before spawning. Aquaculture, mostly in California, is helping to renew the supply; in only two years, the farmed fish can reach weights between 8 and 10 pounds.

Sold fresh as steaks and fillets, white sturgeon has a distinctive flavor, compared by some to the taste of veal. And, as we've mentioned, sturgeon is most familiar as a delicacy when smoked, although it can be baked, stir-fried, or grilled and holds its shape well when cut into cubes for kebobs.

Green sturgeon is a smaller, stronger-tasting relative, and usually the catch is smoked.

BUFFALOFISH

We've never seen this one on a restaurant menu, and yet buffalofish is very popular throughout the South, found throughout North America and especially in the Mississippi Valley. Buffalofish is a member of the sucker family. It probably got its name from the large hump on its back, inspiring someone to name it after our native Western herds.

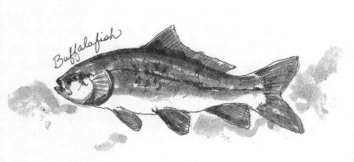

Resembling carp, the flavor and texture of the fish can vary, depending upon the variety, the water quality, and the diet of the particular members of the family. The smallmouth buffalofish is considered to have the best flavor. Marketed between 2 and 12 pounds, it is available year round, usually in ethnic markets. We occasionally have seen some live at our Chinese markets.

The bigmouth and black buffalofish are other members of the family, with some of the former reaching weights of 80 pounds. All have tough skin and scales and some tiny bones very much like the carp and shad. We recommend scaling the fish but keeping the skin on while cooking in order to hold the flesh together, especially with the fillets. It is best to let your fishmonger prepare it for you. This fish has a moist, mild white to pale pink flesh with a fairly high fat content and takes well to baking, frying, broiling, grilling, poaching, steaming, or smoking.

SUNFISH

Any kid who has ever spent a summer at a mountain lake probably has fished for sunfish. Unlike the sophisticated fisherperson who goes to the shore with an expensive 10-foot rod and high-tech spinning reel, the "sunfish child" carries a bamboo pole, a short length of heavy line, a hook, a bobber or float, and a battered can of worms that have been gleaned from the top of the lawn after the nighttime dew. Indeed, almost all of these iridescent beauties are caught by amateurs rather than the professionals who supply our markets with such a vast variety of sea life.

There are many members of the sunfish family caught throughout the United States and Canada, but the bluegill is the best known of the group. All sunfish are rather small, easily scaled and then prepared whole, or butterflied and scaled, with the skin intact. The one drawback for many people when preparing sunfish is that they have small bones, but we think that their taste more than makes up for this slight annoyance. Some cooks dip them in cornmeal or flour, quickly fry them, and then eat them like corn, just nibbling around the bones.

In addition to bluegill, the family includes crappies, pumpkinseed, redear, longear, green, flier, and rock bass. Whichever relative swims in your particular body of fresh water, we think you'll like their sweet smell and mild flavor.

CATFISH

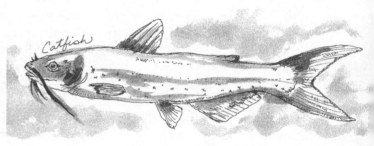

Some years ago we remember reading an article that called catfish a "fish of the future," but not long before that, we might have included it in the chapter of this book titled "The Bizarre Bazaar" (see page 341). It was not that long ago that this most marvelous tasting fish was totally rejected out of hand by almost anyone who lived north of the Mason-Dixon line. When we worked in the South, we had to convince our Northern film crews that catfish and hush puppies were worth trying. Today they devour them by the dozen.

There are about 2,500 species of catfish, most of which live in fresh water, although some inhabit the oceans. Where at one time the catfish that graced our tables were the bounty of local fisherpeople, almost all are now farmed, with the majority coming from the state of Mississippi. In the marketplace, the various members generally are sold under their family name, but you may come across them as bullheads or channel catfish. Years ago, they were so looked down upon that fishmongers would label them "Rocky Mountain trout"!

Catfish are bottom feeders, but their natural habitats have become much too muddy and polluted. Thus the grain-fed aquacultured fish are the ones that are now coming to our markets. Controlled for quality as well as weight, the fish generally are harvested between 1 and 2 pounds; the smaller ones are skinned and left whole, while the fillets of the larger fish are shipped fresh or frozen to markets across the country, including the large supermarket chains. Thus, they're now available year round.

The skins are difficult to take off, because the fish has no scales and a very thick skin at that. Mel learned to skin catfish at the same mountain lake at which he used to catch his sunfish and perch as a kid. But those were the days when bottom feeders were not a polluted species. If you find whole catfish, let the fishmonger prepare it for you. They're best when dipped in cornmeal and fried, but they can also be prepared by baking, braising, sautéing, stewing, and poaching. We think they're among the sweetest-tasting, mild-flavored, and versatile fish in the fresh-water category.

To show how far catfish has come, we recently received a mailing from that favorite town of ours Belzoni, Mississippi. When we wrote our last fish book, we visited their annual Catfish Festival (and also ate about 15 baby catfish with hush puppies). Well, the Catfish Institute, a trade group located in the town, tells us that they've formed a new society for catfish aficionados. Called the Loyal Order of Catfish Lovers, it offers a membership card and button, a bumper sticker, and even a secret handshake (!) with a finger wiggle. The button sports a drawing of the fish and a pseudo-Latin slogan: Sic Semper Whiskers!

CRISP PAN-FRIED PEPPER CATFISH
AND HUSH PUPPIES

MAKES 6 SERVINGS

This traditional Southern specialty of sweet, white, firm catfish uses a light, crisp coating and is always accompanied by tiny puffs of onion-scented cornmeal hush puppies. Try it with coleslaw or black-eyed peas and sautéed greens for a total feast.

HUSH PUPPIES:

- 1 cup all-purpose flour
- 1½ cups stone-ground white cornmeal
- 2 teaspoons baking powder
- 1 teaspoon baking soda
- ½ teaspoon black pepper
- 1 teaspoon salt
- 1 egg
- ½ cup buttermilk, at room temperature
- ½ cup beer, at room temperature
- 1 large onion, grated (about ¾ cup)

PEPPER CATFISH:

- Corn oil for frying
- 1 cup stone-ground white cornmeal
- ½ cup all-purpose flour
- ¾ teaspoon cayenne pepper
- 2 to 2½ pounds catfish fillets, skinned and cut into 3-inch pieces weighing about 4 ounces each, or 6 pan-dressed and skinned whole catfish, about 12 ounces each (substitute: whiting)
- Salt and black pepper to taste

FOR THE HUSH PUPPIES: Whisk together the flour, cornmeal, baking powder, baking soda, pepper, and salt in a bowl. In another bowl, whisk the egg until foamy, then whisk in the buttermilk, beer, and onion. Combine with the dry ingredients. The batter should be slightly stiff; if it is not, add more flour. Set the batter aside while preparing the catfish.

FOR THE PEPPER CATFISH: In a large cast-iron skillet, heat about 1 inch oil to 375°. Combine the cornmeal, flour, and cayenne in a plastic bag. Season the fish with salt and black pepper, then add the fish, a few pieces at a time, to the bag and shake to coat lightly.

Add the fish a few pieces at a time to the hot oil and pan-fry, turning once, for 4 to 5 minutes until golden brown on both sides. Drain on paper towels and keep warm in a low oven. Add more oil if needed to keep the level at 1 inch and return it to 375° before making the hush puppies.

Drop 4 or 5 hush puppies by the teaspoonful into the hot oil. The hush puppies will float to the surface when they are brown and cooked through. Lift them out with a slotted spoon and drain on paper towels. Keep them warm in the oven until all the batter is used. Serve with the catfish.

DEEP-FRIED SESAME CATFISH ORIENTAL-STYLE

The nutty, toasted flavor of sesame seeds permeates each mouthful of sweet catfish that has been dipped into the peppery sauce

½ cup tamari

2 teaspoons rice vinegar

½ teaspoon Oriental sesame oil

½ teaspoon hot chile oil or more to taste

2¼ teaspoons sugar

2 thin scallion greens, thinly sliced on the diagonal (about ¼ cup)

1¼ pounds skinned catfish fillets, cut into 3-inch pieces (substitute: sole or orange roughy)

1 small onion, finely minced (about ½ cup)

1 teaspoon finely minced ginger

½ cup dry sherry

½ teaspoon salt

1 egg, lightly beaten

1 tablespoon water

3 tablespoons all-purpose flour

2 tablespoons cornstarch

1 cup raw sesame seeds

Corn oil for frying

In a small bowl, mix the tamari, vinegar, sesame oil, chile oil, ¼ teaspoon of the sugar, and the scallions together; let this dipping sauce stand while preparing the fish.

Place the fish in one layer in a nonreactive baking pan and set it aside. In a small bowl, combine the onion, ginger, sherry, the remaining 2 teaspoons sugar, and the salt and pour over the fish. Marinate the fish for 30 minutes, turning it once or twice during that time.

When ready to cook, whisk the egg and water together in a bowl. Combine the flour and cornstarch and whisk into the egg, beating until smooth. Put the sesame seeds on a piece of foil.

Heat 2 to 3 inches oil in a deep cast-iron skillet or wok to 375°. When the oil is hot, lift out several pieces of fish from the marinade; dip the fish first in the egg mixture, then roll each piece in the sesame seeds to coat completely. Add to the hot oil, a few pieces at a time, and fry for 1 to 2 minutes. Turn the pieces over with a two-pronged fork and fry for 1 minute more until golden. Drain the fish on paper towels and keep warm on a serving platter in a low oven. Coat and fry the remaining fish a few pieces at a time. Serve with small bowls of the dipping sauce.

GROUP E
Shellfish

Crustaceans

SHRIMP

CRAB

    Blue crab

    Dungeness crab

    Jonah crab

    King crab

    Stone crab

    Snow crab

    Red crab

LOBSTER

CRAYFISH

Mollusks

CLAMS

    Quahogs or hard-shell clams

    Soft-shell clams

    Geoduck clams

    Razor clams

    Manila clams

    Cockles

OYSTERS

SCALLOPS

MUSSELS

For those of us who live near the sea, the receding tide reveals a whole new miraculous world. The shells of sea scallops and periwinkles, snails, starfish, and clams, the detritus of battered crabs, and an occasional reminder of the prehistoric in a dark brown horseshoe crab shell are all laid out in an abstract pattern that changes shape each time the ocean roars over the beach and then makes its way out again. For the lover of seafood, this vast array of shells reminds us of yet another gift from the sea, the pleasure of dining on many of the creatures who make their homes inside the little shell houses.

Essentially, there are two major divisions: crustaceans and mollusks. Crustaceans are distinguished by the presence of legs, and most of them have a jointed shell which is shed from time to time to accommodate the creature's growth. Shrimp, crabs, lobster, crayfish, and Dublin Bay prawns are among the most important members of the group for cookbook readers; other members of the family are generally inedible and actually include both spiders and scorpions! The major rule for cooking edible crustaceans is that it be done very quickly, since the flesh dries out when overcooked.

Mollusks are hard-shelled invertebrates and include many of the creatures described in this chapter (clams, oysters, scallops, and mussels) but also others not generally thought of as belonging to the group. There are three major divisions in the family:

- ❖ *Gastropods:* Those that have a single shell (univalve), such as whelk, abalone, and snails.

- ❖ *Bivalves:* Possibly the most familiar to us, having two shells hinged by a strong muscle, such as the clam and the oyster.

- ❖ *Cephalopods:* The members of the family that have tentacles and ink sacs, such as the octopus, squid, and cuttlefish.

Shellfish and particularly mollusks have been the victims of both natural disasters (such as the red and brown tides) and the continuing and ever-growing pollution of our bays and rivers. And so, with shellfish also go the warnings that we have mentioned earlier. Raw mollusks, such as raw clams and oysters, are no longer an option. And all members of the family should be purchased from reliable sources and fishmongers who do not cut corners. However, with proper caution and by following the rules on page 305, both crustaceans and mollusks should continue to grace your table. They are, indeed, among the most unusual and tasty treasures to come from the sea.

CRUSTACEANS

SHRIMP

Possibly one of the most popular seafood dishes in the entire world, shrimp can be found on menus all across North and South America as well as in the markets of West Africa and India. It's been said that no restaurant or market is too far from the sea to offer shrimp to its customers. The name is one of the more practical ones in the world of seafood, since it comes from both the English description of a puny person, *shrimpe,* and the Swedish *skrympa,* to shrink.

There are hundreds of varieties of shrimp with a vast assortment of names but all are interchangeable in recipes. About 70 percent of our catch is now imported, almost all of it frozen and headless. Although higher in cholesterol than most other seafood, shrimp are low in fat, very mild, and quite firm in texture. They are, perhaps, the prime example of seafood that takes very little cooking to make them ready for the table.

At times we have come across shrimp listed as prawns on restaurant menus or at fishmarkets, especially in the British Isles. Prawns are actually another species and more closely related to the lobster, but the name is applied most often to very large shrimp. Another word frequently used for shrimp is "scampi". In Italy, scampi refers to Dublin Bay prawns (see page 293), but the word has been picked up here, especially in low-priced Italian restaurants, so that shrimp prepared in garlic butter generally appears on the menu as "shrimp scampi" or "shrimp prawns"!

To simplify matters somewhat, shrimp can be divided into two major categories: warm or tropical water shrimp and northern or cold-water shrimp. Our own warm-water varieties are generally caught in the Gulf of Mexico, off South and Central America, and as far away as Australia and Asia. Northern shrimp have traditionally supported the fisheries of Maine and Massachusetts, and some are harvested as far north as Alaska. The northern varieties are sweeter, firmer, and more delicately flavored than their tropical cousins. All shrimp are usually flash frozen at sea, then thawed for sale, something that every buyer must understand in preparing these delicate creatures.

As we've mentioned, the varieties vary, depending upon the season of the year and the area in which they've been caught, but, whether your fishmonger carries brown shrimp or pink shrimp, white shrimp or rock shrimp, just follow the tips on buying them that we give in the next few pages.

However, a variety has begun to appear these last few years that we think surpasses almost all others in terms of taste and handling: tiger prawns. Easily recognized by their black stripes and gray shells, they're being aquacultured now in both Taiwan and Thailand. If you see them and recognize them at your fishmarket, we strongly suggest that you try them.

How to Buy Shrimp

Shrimp are sold by the pound, and thus the number of shrimp to that pound go to make up the designations. However, we have found that many fishmongers change the categories, very much like the toothpaste manufacturer who labels the smallest size as "giant." Thus, the figures we give below may vary slightly, depending upon the market and its attendant hype. A good rule of thumb is that 2 pounds shrimp in their shells will yield about 1¼ pounds when peeled.

How to Prepare Shrimp

Shells can be removed before or after cooking, although shelled shrimp will absorb more of the flavor of any sauce or cooking liquid you use. On the other hand, the shells themselves add flavor if cooked in the sauce. If you're charcoal grilling shrimp, keep-

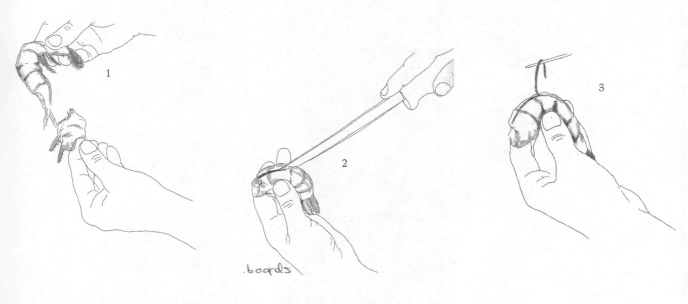

Shrimp

ing them in their shells will prevent them from drying out quickly. Shrimp, of course, are completely edible and only the larger ones need to be deveined.

❖ *Remove the shell and, using a sharp knife, cut down the back about ¼ inch deep and lift out the vein with the point of a knife or with a toothpick.*

❖ *Do not discard the shells (see below).*

TO BUTTERFLY SHRIMP

❖ *Remove the shells.*

❖ *Use any size larger than "medium." Insert the tip of the knife along the back and cut almost all the way through down toward the tail.*

❖ *Leave the tail intact and attached to the shrimp.*

❖ *Open the shrimp and lay it flat like an open book.*

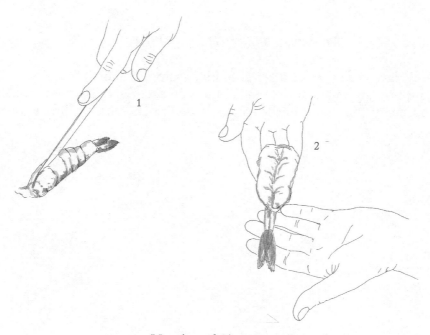

Number of Shrimp per Pound

Colossal or Jumbo	8 to 10
Large	10 to 25
Medium	26 to 40
Small	41 to 60
Tiny	Up to 160 per pound

Allow about ¾ pound headless shrimp in the shell per person; if the shrimp are shelled, figure about ⅛ to ½ pound per person.

The best tip that we can give you about purchasing shrimp is to use your nose and your hands.

- ❖ Fresh shrimp should smell fresh and briny. Since shrimp are high in iodine, a natural outgrowth of its diet at sea, you may detect it when you buy them. Although the iodine smell and taste was once made more pronounced by the addition of a preservative (that is now banned), we try to avoid any shrimp that smell even slightly of iodine.

- ❖ When you touch the shrimp, make sure that the flesh feels firm between your fingers. Discard any shrimp that are soft.

- ❖ Shrimp should be eaten on the day that you buy them. However, if you must hold them for as much as 24 hours, make sure they're refrigerated on ice, covered with damp paper towels to keep them from drying out.

How to Cook Shrimp

If you shell shrimp before cooking, don't throw away the shells, for they're filled with flavor. Rinse them under cold water and cook them in boiling water for 10 minutes. Then strain the liquid and use it to cook the shelled shrimp. Or you can cook the shrimp right in their shells, then peel and devein them afterward.

- ❖ Cook shrimp quickly. Whether shrimp are boiled, grilled, deep-fried in batter, sautéed, stewed, or steamed, we think the biggest mistake that can be made is overcooking.

- ❖ The shrimp should turn from translucent to opaque—just a very few minutes, depending upon the size of the shrimp.

For frozen shrimp that have already been peeled and deveined, do not thaw before cooking but allow a few more minutes of cooking time.

GREEK SHRIMP BAKED WITH FETA CHEESE AND TOMATOES

MAKES 4 SERVINGS

Feta—the briny, Greek goat's milk cheese—adds a lively edge to this anise-perfumed shrimp and tomato dish. It can be prepared in advance, then finished in the oven in just 10 minutes of baking time—just long enough to cook some orzo as an accompaniment.

1	35-ounce can Italian plum tomatoes, drained (about 3 cups)	1	teaspoon dried oregano, preferably Greek
1½	pounds medium shrimp (about 36)	½	teaspoon (scant) hot pepper flakes
1	cup water	2	tablespoons nonpareil capers, rinsed and dried
3	tablespoons olive oil	¼	pound feta cheese, crumbled
1	large clove garlic, finely minced (about 1½ teaspoons)	12	Kalamata or other Greek olives
2	tablespoons Cognac, warmed	½	teaspoon crushed fennel seeds
¼	cup ouzo (Greek anise-flavored liqueur) or Pernod (French anise-flavored liqueur), warmed	2	tablespoons coarsely chopped parsley

In a large nonstick skillet, add the tomatoes, break them up slightly, and cook, stirring occasionally, over medium-high heat until reduced to 2 cups. Transfer to a bowl and set aside. Wipe out the skillet.

Peel and devein the shrimp, leaving the tails intact and reserving the shells. Put the shrimp shells and the water in a medium saucepan and cook over medium heat for 15 minutes. Strain and reserve the shrimp stock and discard the shells.

Preheat the oven to 350°. In the same nonstick skillet heat the oil over medium-high heat. Add the garlic and shrimp. Sauté for 1 minute. Turn the shrimp over and pour the warmed Cognac and ouzo over the shrimp. Ignite with a match to burn off the alcohol.

Remove the skillet from the heat and add the reserved tomatoes, ¼ cup of the shrimp stock, the oregano, hot pepper flakes, and capers. Transfer to an oiled shallow baking pan or individual oven-to-table baking dishes. Sprinkle with the feta, olives, and fennel. Bake for 10 to 12 minutes. Sprinkle with the parsley just before serving.

PAN-GRILLED BUTTERFLIED SPANISH GARLIC SHRIMP WITH SAFFRON (GAMBAS AL AJILLO)

MAKES 4 SERVINGS

A very quick, elegant dish that is particularly good with black beans and perhaps some white rice. To make it complete, serve fruit-filled dry white sangria.

2   tablespoons lemon juice (½ large lemon)

½   teaspoon saffron threads, crumbled

3   tablespoons olive oil

1   tablespoon butter

½   teaspoon paprika

¼   teaspoon hot pepper flakes

3 to 4   cloves garlic, thinly sliced (about 1 heaping tablespoon)

1   teaspoon dried oregano, preferably Greek
     Salt and pepper to taste

1¼   pounds jumbo shrimp, peeled, deveined, and butterflied, tails left on

2   tablespoons dry sherry

1   tablespoon finely minced parsley

Mix the lemon juice with the saffron and let stand for 10 minutes. In a large cast-iron skillet, heat the olive oil and butter over medium-high heat until the butter melts. Stir in the paprika, hot pepper flakes, and garlic and sauté for 1 minute, stirring so that the garlic does not brown. Stir in the oregano and salt and pepper, then place the shrimp in the skillet in one layer (you may need to use 2 skillets or do in 2 batches). Place a plate over the shrimp and weight it with a large can to keep the shrimp from curling. Sauté for 1 minute.

Turn the shrimp over with tongs and replace the plate and weight. Sauté for 1 minute more, then remove the weight and plate. Add the saffron mixture and the sherry. Turn the shrimp quickly in the sauce with tongs for about 30 to 60 seconds. Transfer to a serving dish and sprinkle with the parsley.

JAPANESE FRIED BUTTERFLIED COCONUT SHRIMP WITH WASABI SESAME SAUCE

MAKES 4 SERVINGS

Our favorite local Japanese restaurant serves these shrimp along with an assortment of sushi. Needless to say, they disappear almost immediately, even before our chopsticks dip into the raw fish on our plates.

WASABI SESAME SAUCE:

2 tablespoons wasabi (Japanese mustard) powder

2 tablespoons lemon juice

½ cup soy sauce or tamari

1 teaspoon Oriental sesame oil

1 tablespoon sesame seeds, toasted

COCONUT SHRIMP:

1¼ pounds extra large or jumbo shrimp, shelled, deveined, and butterflied, tails left on

⅛ teaspoon cayenne pepper

½ cup all-purpose flour

1 teaspoon dry English mustard

1 egg, lightly beaten

3 tablespoons light cream

1 cup unsweetened shredded coconut (available in health-food stores)

½ cup fine dry bread crumbs

Corn oil for frying

FOR THE SAUCE: Mix the wasabi powder with enough cold water to form a stiff paste. Cover and set aside for 30 minutes. In a small bowl, whisk together the lemon juice, soy sauce, and sesame oil. Add the wasabi paste a little at a time, whisking after each addition and tasting for the amount of heat you prefer. Stir in the sesame seeds and spoon the sauce into 4 dipping bowls.

FOR THE SHRIMP: Dry the shrimp and sprinkle them with the cayenne. Combine the flour and mustard in one bowl, the egg and cream in another bowl, and the coconut and bread crumbs in a third bowl. Dip each shrimp in the flour mixture first, then the egg mixture, then roll them evenly in the coconut crumb coating.

Place the shrimp on waxed paper and chill in the refrigerator for 10 minutes, uncovered. When ready to fry, pour 2 inches oil in a heavy cast-iron skillet and heat to 375°. When the oil is the correct temperature, fry a few shrimp at a time, turning once during cooking, for 1 to 2 minutes until the shrimp are golden. Remove with a slotted spoon or tongs and drain on paper towels. Keep warm until all are fried. Serve on heated plates with the wasabi sesame sauce for dipping.

SAUTÉED INDIAN SHRIMP WITH YOGURT AND CILANTRO

MAKES 6 SERVINGS

The shrimp marinate for two hours in a tangy mixture of cool and hot spices, imparting a full flavor to them. Then they simmer lightly in an onion and yogurt sauce. Fragrant long-grained basmati rice makes a nice bed to absorb the sauce.

2 pounds medium shrimp, peeled and deveined	2 teaspoons finely minced ginger
½ teaspoon crushed dried mint	Salt and black pepper to taste
¼ teaspoon hot pepper flakes	4 tablespoons butter
2¼ teaspoons turmeric	1 medium onion, grated
½ teaspoon ground coriander	1 cup plain yogurt
¾ teaspoon ground cumin	1 teaspoon mild honey
2 to 3 cloves garlic, finely minced (about 1 tablespoon)	2 tablespoons lemon juice
	2 tablespoons finely minced cilantro

In a bowl, combine the shrimp with the mint, hot pepper flakes, turmeric, coriander, cumin, garlic, ginger, salt, and pepper until well coated, cover with plastic wrap, and refrigerate for 2 hours, stirring once during this time.

In a large nonstick skillet, heat 3 tablespoons of the butter over medium heat. Add the onion and sauté, stirring constantly, until it's fairly dry but not brown. Add the remaining 1 tablespoon butter, add the shrimp and spice mixture, and cook, stirring and turning the shrimp, until they just become opaque, about 30 seconds. Lower the heat to simmer, combine the yogurt and honey with a whisk, and add to the shrimp. Cover the skillet and simmer over low heat for about 3 minutes. Uncover the skillet and simmer for 1 to 2 minutes more. Stir in the lemon juice and cilantro and serve hot.

BROILED SHRIMP STUFFED WITH SHRIMP AND MUSHROOMS

MAKES 6 SERVINGS

Butterflied shrimp are filled with mounds of chopped mushrooms and shrimp scented with thyme and parsley and a crunch of celery for contrast. They're then dusted lightly with Gruyère cheese and bread crumbs and slipped under the broiler to brown just before serving.

1½ to 2	pounds large shrimp
2	tablespoons olive oil
1	medium onion, finely chopped (about ¾ cup)
2	small ribs celery, finely chopped (about ¾ cup)
1	large clove garlic, finely minced (about 1½ teaspoons)
¼	pound white mushrooms, coarsely chopped

1	tablespoon lemon juice
	Salt and black pepper to taste
1	cup plus 2 tablespoons fine dry bread crumbs
½	teaspoon dried thyme
¼	cup finely minced parsley
1	egg, lightly beaten
3	tablespoons grated Gruyère cheese
4	tablespoons butter, melted

Set aside 18 of the shrimp, allowing 3 per person. Peel and butterfly them, leaving the tails intact. Peel and devein the remaining shrimp and coarsely chop them. There should be about ¾ cup. Set them aside.

In a medium skillet, heat the olive oil over moderate heat. Add the onion, celery, and garlic and sauté, stirring frequently, until the vegetables are wilted. Add the mushrooms, lemon juice, salt, and pepper. Cook, stirring constantly, for 3 minutes. Remove from the heat, add 1 cup of the bread crumbs, the thyme, parsley, chopped shrimp, and egg, and combine well. Spoon equal portions of the mixture on top of each butterflied shrimp, mounding it smoothly.

Preheat the broiler. Butter a large oven-to-table baking dish. Arrange the shrimp in one layer in the dish. Mix the grated cheese with the remaining 2 tablespoons bread crumbs and sprinkle over the stuffed shrimp, then trickle the melted butter over all. Broil 5 inches from the heat for about 5 minutes until the shrimp are heated through and the stuffing has browned, basting once with the pan juices that will accumulate. Serve hot.

COLD PICKLED SHRIMP WITH MUSTARD AND DILL SAUCE

The barely poached shrimp are pickled in a citrus, mustard, and dill marinade for two days. It is a wonderful and easy do-ahead dish for a first course, a buffet, or a summer luncheon.

2   large lemons

2   large limes

1   tablespoon strong Dijon-style mustard

½   cup olive oil

⅛   teaspoon hot pepper flakes or more to taste

1   small clove garlic, finely minced (about ½ teaspoon)

2   tablespoons coarsely minced fresh dill, plus a few sprigs for garnish

1   teaspoon freshly ground black pepper
    Salt to taste

1½   pounds medium shrimp, shelled, deveined if necessary

1   large English cucumber, very thinly sliced
    Small lemon or lime wedges for garnish

Using a citrus zester, cut fine shreds of peel from 1 lemon and lime and reserve. Squeeze the juice from both lemons and both limes into a glass or ceramic bowl. This should give you about ¾ cup juice. Whisk in the mustard, olive oil, hot pepper flakes, garlic, dill, citrus peel, pepper, and salt.

Bring a 3-quart saucepan of salted water to a vigorous boil. Add the shrimp and cook for 1 minute when they will lose their transparency. Do not cook them further. Drain at once and add the shrimp to the marinade while they are still hot. Cover with plastic wrap and refrigerate for 48 hours, stirring once after the first day.

When ready to serve, place the sliced cucumber around the outside of a platter in overlapping slices. Drain the shrimp in a strainer and spoon into the center of the platter. Garnish with dill sprigs and small wedges of lemon or lime.

GRILLED *SKEWERED* SHRIMP WITH PROSCIUTTO, SAGE, AND ZUCCHINI

MAKES 4 SERVINGS

Lightly marinated in olive oil and lemon juice, these sage-infused prosciutto-wrapped shrimp are grilled along with zucchini. Try serving them with a Parmesan-laced risotto.

⅔ cup olive oil

3 tablespoons lemon juice

1 large clove garlic, finely minced (about 1½ teaspoons)

2 or 3 drops Tabasco

1 tablespoon finely minced fresh sage plus as many fresh sage leaves as there are shrimp

Salt and pepper to taste

1½ pounds extra large or large shrimp, shelled and deveined, tails left on

6 to 8 scallions, white parts plus 1 inch green, cut into 1-inch lengths

2 small zucchini, about 5 inches long (about ½ pound), trimmed and cut into 1-inch pieces

2 to 3 ounces thinly sliced prosciutto (cut large slices in half)

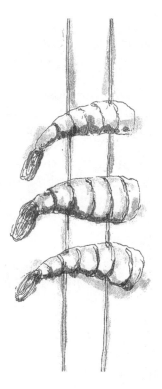

Soak 10-inch bamboo skewers in water for 30 minutes or longer if convenient. In a shallow nonreactive dish, mix the olive oil, lemon juice, garlic, Tabasco, minced sage, salt, and pepper. Add the shrimp, scallions, and zucchini and marinate for 1 hour at room temperature, turning once.

When ready to cook, preheat the broiler or prepare a grill. Thread the zucchini pieces on separate skewers and set them aside. Place a piece of scallion and sage leaf on each shrimp and enclose with a thin slice of prosciutto. Thread them on 2 parallel skewers placed about 1 inch apart.

Broil the zucchini for about 10 minutes total time and the shrimp for about 6 minutes, turning once and brushing frequently with the marinade. Slip the shrimp off the skewers when serving.

CRAB

Although we have devoured crab dinners all over the world, including the most memorable one at Watson's Bay in Australia—a huge Queensland mud crab—the most wonderful thing about this tasty crustacean is that we don't have to wander very far from home to take our choice of the most incredible variety available to both home cooks and restaurant diners.

North America is, by far, the greatest provider of edible crabs than any other place in the world, and those that are found locally are now being shipped to almost every part of the country, many of them available all year long. Thus, along with our Down Under memory, we also remember crab dinners in Baltimore, New Orleans, San Francisco, and Juneau, Alaska. We're certain that many of our readers also can think back to similar seafood experiences, for crab is one of the tastiest and most memorable of dinners.

Crabs vary widely in size and shape, but basically they are all encased in a rigid shell, which they molt at intervals to allow them to grow. It is this shedding of the shell that then yields the famous and tasty soft-shelled blue crab (see below).

Blue Crab

Probably the most common of the East Coast crabs, blue crabs are found all along the Atlantic coast from New England down into the Gulf of Mexico. In spite of their very descriptive name, the crab shell is generally brownish green or dark green, with all white undersides; only the claw tips of the male carry the distinctive blue tint. The female, however, boasts orange claw tips.

Although blue crabs are caught commercially with a variety of sophisticated nets, traps, and "trotlines" (a twisted, long double line with chains, a plastic float and anchor, and baited with chicken heads or beef tripe), it is not at all unusual to see hordes of amateur crab hunters in our region (the authors included) trying to catch their own during the late summer and early fall when the crabs are in season. The rig is simple and ingenious. A long line is tied firmly to a piece of chicken discard or fish and dropped into the water. The crab, clinging firmly to the bait, is then hauled up to be netted quickly. Many of our local children join in, while others prepare the crab boil back in the kitchen.

SOFT-SHELL CRABS: The average female molts 18 to 20 times until she reaches her full size. The immature female is called a "sally" or a "she-crab," and a "sook" when she grows up. The male—called a "jimmy"—molts 21 to 23 times and is slightly larger than his female companion. It is right after a molt that the crab is a "soft shell," and the entire crab is edible at that time. We prefer the smallest soft-shell crabs, since we think they're the tastiest by far. Allow 1 to 3 crabs per person, depending upon size and appetite:

Hotel (smallest)	3 to 3½ inches
Primes	3½ to 4½ inches
Jumbos	4½ to 5 inches
Whales	Over 5 inches

Since they're eaten whole and considered a delicacy, soft-shell crabs are more expensive than those with hard shells, and, we might add, well worth it. In addition, the shell begins to harden within hours of molting, so they must be gathered and shipped to market quickly. We've given instructions on how to prepare soft-shell crabs on page 282.

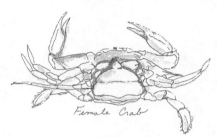

Dungeness Crab

Although the blue crab holds sway on the East Coast, the Dungeness crab is hugely popular on the Pacific Coast, and with good reason. Trapped from the northern coastline up to Alaska, the species has a very high proportion of meat to body weight, and aficionados like them because removing the meat from the shell is much easier than with the blue crab.

Commercial fishing for this delicacy first began in a small fishing village named Dungeness on the Strait of Juan de Fuca in Washington. Since the crab has a cycle of about seven years, there are severe limits on the sizes that can be taken, varying in each area, and generally limiting the catch to males that measure about 6 inches across the shell.

They're sold either live or already cooked and frozen, and sometimes the legs and claws are available separately. The Dungeness is one of the reasons that we envy our friends who live in San Francisco, although occasionally we do find Dungeness crab in the restaurants here in the East as well as live in holding tanks in some Chinese markets.

Jonah Crab

This is a small crab, usually weighing about 1 pound, and caught in the Atlantic from Nova Scotia down to the Southern states. It has been long ignored because of its size and the difficulty of extracting the meat but also because most of the catch is harvested off New England, where the major cash crop is lobster.

The Jonah is a walking crab rather than a swimmer, and thus the body meat is not as developed as with other crabs. However, the claws are well developed and the major portion of the meat is found there. The greater part of the catch is processed and canned in New England, although it is sometimes packaged in small jars. The rock crab is also a member of the family and has similar characteristics.

King Crab

These are among the giants of the crab family and one of Alaska's most valuable resources. The average size of a king is about 10 pounds, but fishermen have reported taking them with a tip-to-tip span of almost 6 feet and a weight of 24 pounds!

Most of the edible meat lies in the long legs, and one of the unusual features of this gangly creature is its ability to drop an injured leg and grow a new one, very much like the stone crab (see below). This regeneration process also allows the crab to escape when it's attacked by an enemy.

Over the past few years, the supply of king crab legs has fluctuated greatly, occasionally creating a severe price rise or disappearing from the marketplace altogether.

However, through stringent conservation methods and the regenerative quality of nature, they have been appearing at our fish markets once again. Usually only the legs are sold, either cooked or uncooked, and split down the length. We think they're one of the tastiest of the crab family.

Stone Crab

Watching tourists (and natives) devouring stone crabs when they were in season, someone once called them "Florida's Messy Marvels," and, although they're best known in that state, they're also available from the Carolinas to Texas and are now being shipped to most parts of the United States. Since only the claws are eaten, the stone crab might well be called a "recyclable" species. When they're caught, one claw is usually twisted off, and the rest of the crab is returned to the sea, where it will grow another claw to replace the one that's missing. The new claw is smaller and called a "retread," but the creature is as good as new, probably promising never to be caught again!

Another unusual aspect of the stone crab catch is that, in order to be of top quality, it must be cooked aboard the boat that harvests it. Since stone crab meat has a tendency to stick to the shell if it's frozen or iced before cooking, the crew cooks the claws and then either delivers them fresh to the marketplace or freezes them for shipment.

Stone crabs are severely limited as to season, with fishing allowed only between mid-October and mid-May, making them an even more special treat. Armed with mallet, nutcracker, and pick, most of us like them cold and dipped in either a hot butter sauce or a mustard sauce.

Snow Crab

Part of a family that includes the tanner crab and the queen crab, all are sold under the name of snow crab. They're mostly found as cooked frozen clusters of the shoulders, legs, and claws, or they can be found as packaged crab meat.

Until a few years ago, the species was underutilized, since most of the northern Pacific and Alaskan fishermen were totally occupied with harvesting Dungeness and king crabs. However, in recent years, commercial fisheries have begun to recognize the potential for this member of the spider crab family. When the catch of king crab declined precipitously, snow crab suddenly was much sought after. It has a delicate flavor and is quite tender and succulent.

Red Crab

These deep sea denizens inhabit the edge of the Continental shelf from the North Atlantic down to the Caribbean. Their yield of meat is high, but at the same time they're quite delicate and difficult to handle whole. Thus, the catch is processed right at sea, and most can be found as frozen crab legs or crab meat. Their taste is quite similar to that of king crab.

The Market Forms

Certainly, when and if a species is sold whole (such as blue or Dungeness crab) and it can be purchased *live,* it should be the first choice for any home cook. And, just as important in a selection of picked crab meat, whether whole lump or flakes, fresh will always be better than frozen. It all depends, of course, upon where you live, the season, the market availability, and your choice of recipe.

LUMP MEAT: The meat from the body of the crab. It comes in large, white chunks, has no waste, and is generally the most expensive of the choices.

BACKFIN: Smaller chunks than the lump meat, some of them broken, and just as good for most recipes.

FLAKED CRAB MEAT: Meat from various parts of the body and usually in very small pieces.

CLAWS: Usually sold as "cocktail claws," cooked with part of the shell removed and marketed frozen.

LEGS: From the Alaskan king crab, they're quite expensive when available but very, very good. Allow about 1½ pounds for 4 persons.

COMBINATIONS: Occasionally, you'll find a combination of both flake and lump crab meat, and since there's no single designation by which they're marketed, it might be called anything from "special" to just plain "mixed crab meat." Read the labels carefully.

PASTEURIZED: Generally sold in 8-, 12-, and 16-ounce sizes, this is crab meat that's been steamed, picked over, and then immersed in a hot water bath. As long as the can is not opened, the meat will remain fresh. However, as soon as you get it home, refrigerate it but don't freeze it. Once opened, it should be consumed within a few hours, and remember, when cooking packaged crab meat, add it to the pot to heat for only a short time since it's already cooked. Handle it gently. Allow 4 to 6 ounces per person.

Some of our friends claim that the pasteurizing process does not alter the flavor of the crab meat. We disagree, however, and prefer crab meat packed in containers instead of cans, even though they're more difficult to find.

FROZEN: Almost all varieties are available frozen and fully cooked.

PREPARING SOFT-SHELL CRAB

If you purchase live soft-shell crabs from the fishmonger, he or she will prepare them for you and all you need do is to sauté them and enjoy. However, if you catch your own or are given some as a gift, the preparation is quite simple.

1. With the crab on a firm surface, cut off the face at the point just behind the eyes. This will kill the crab at once.

2. Find the apron that folds under the rear of the body and, using a sharp knife, peel it off.

3. On the top shell, lift each point of the crab at the sides and, using your fingers, scrape away and discard the soft porous "lungs" or gills underneath the shell.

Cooking Hard-Shell Crab

The crabs should be kept alive before you cook them. The refrigerator or any other cool place will do nicely, but if any of the crabs should die before you cook them, discard them. But crabs are very hardy. In fact, we have noticed that our local Chinese fishmongers keep them in large baskets right outside their stores, yet the casualty rate is practically nil. Just remember, the best time to buy them is the day you're going to prepare your feast.

Use a very large pot, add your favorite seasoning to the water, crab boil (see page 286) for example, or your favorite combination of cayenne pepper, basil, and vinegar or lemon. There are a number of commercial crab boils on the market that are quite acceptable, like Rex Crab Boil and Zatarain's Crab Boil.

When the water comes to a rolling boil, grab the crabs from behind or use a pair of wooden tongs and drop them head first into the water. Let the water come to a boil again and begin timing from this point. Cook the Dungeness crabs for 15 to 20 minutes and smaller blue crabs 10 to 15 minutes.

Hard-shell crabs also can be steamed. You'll need a large pot and a steamer rack. Instead of filling the pot with water, just pour about 2 inches on the bottom, add the crab boil or spices, and bring to a boil. Place the steamer in the pot, put the crabs atop the steamer, and cover the lid. Steam for 20 to 25 minutes.

How to Eat a Crab

It is not a delicate procedure and cannot be done with knife, fork, and demure table manners. It is best to dress appropriately and prepare yourself to dive in and have a good time. We find that most of our guests begin to daintily dismantle the first crab with their fingertips, but by the third one they throw table manners to the wind and quickly imitate the orgiastic eating sequence in the film *Tom Jones.* Just put some newspaper on the table, give your guests a small heavy knife and a wooden mallet, and follow the simple steps we've outlined on the next page.

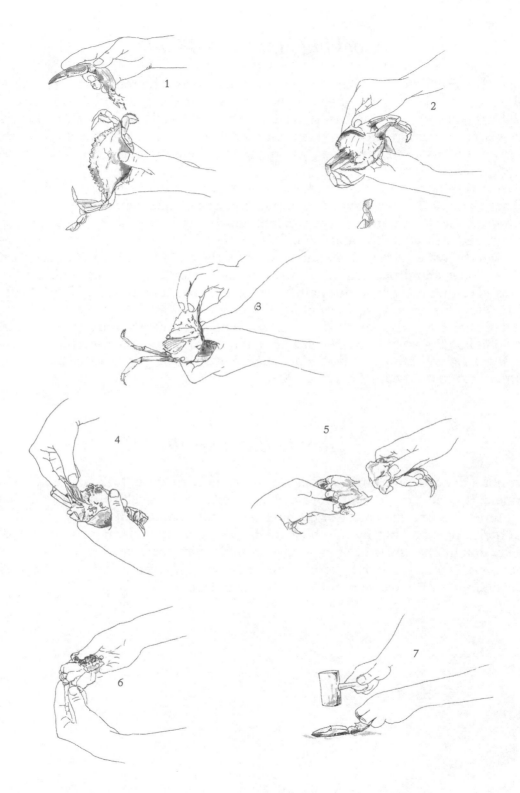

HOW TO EAT BLUE CRAB (see opposite page)

HOW TO EAT BLUE CRAB (illustrated at left)

1. Pull the claws away from the body and remove them. Put them aside or, if you prefer, eat them first.

2. and 3. On the bottom side of the crab, lift up the apron or flap, then take off the top shell, prying it loose with your fingers. Discard the shell and apron.

4. Using your fingers, pull away and discard the spongy white gills on the underside. These are inedible and sometimes called "dead man's fingers" or "devils."

5. and 6. Break the body of the crab in half vertically and, using your fingers, extract the white meat that you find as you peel away the sections. Some people eat them as they pick them out; others accumulate the pieces and consume them all at once.

7. Using the wooden mallet, crack the claws and remove the meat in one piece by pulling on the pincer.

HOW TO EAT DUNGENESS CRAB

1. Turn the crab on its back and pry off the triangular flap on the belly.

2. Turn the crab over and grab the shell firmly from the rear, pulling upward until the shell lifts off. Discard the shell.

3. The top of the crab's body will have a series of spongy gills covering the meat. Twist them off and discard them.

4. Using your hands, twist off the legs right at the edge of the body and put them aside.

5. With a heavy knife, cut the body into halves or quarters.

6. You'll need a cracker or a wooden mallet to crack the leg shells and a metal pick will help you get to the most succulent parts of the body meat.

HOW TO EAT STONE CRABS

1. Place the crab claws in a small bag and gently hit them with a wooden mallet or a meat tenderizer in order to crack the hard shells.

2. Place them on a serving platter or individual plates and pick out the meat with picks or small forks.

3. Dip in the sauce.

HARD-SHELL BLUE CRABS STEAMED IN BEER WITH HOT CHILES

MAKES 6 SERVINGS

A strictly East Coast feast!

6   cans flat strong beer
3   small dried chiles
3   whole bay leaves
⅛   cup whole black peppercorns
1   tablespoon whole mustard seeds
1   teaspoon coarse salt

2 to 3   dozen (depending upon appetite) live, large, hard-shell blue crabs, preferably #1 Jimmys (See Note)

Clarified Butter (see page 65) for serving (optional)

Lemon wedges for serving

Put the beer, chiles, bay leaves, peppercorns, mustard seeds, and salt in the bottom of a steamer and simmer for 20 minutes. Meanwhile, put the crabs in the sink and run cold water over them to clean them. Transfer the crabs (with tongs) to the top of a bamboo or other steamer rack and quickly cover the lid to prevent the crabs from escaping. Raise the heat under the pot, place the steamer rack with the crabs in the pot, and cover. When the steam rises again, steam for 20 to 25 minutes until the crabs are bright red. They must steam without touching the liquid.

Serve on newspapers or brown wrapping paper and give each guest a wooden mallet and a pick, plus lots of paper napkins. Also serve some clarified butter if you wish and some lemon wedges for squeezing at the table. Ice cold beer is usually the beverage of choice in Maryland and wherever else steamed blue crabs are served.

NOTE: In choosing your blue crabs at the market, pick up your choices to make sure they feel heavy with lots of meat inside. Size alone is no measure. And when you get them home, don't enclose them, but keep them cool and remember that they need air to live. Make sure they're still alive when you cook them. We have suggested #1 Jimmys (male crabs) since they seem to have the most meat. See page 277 on how to tell the girls from the boys.

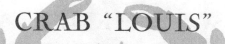

CRAB "LOUIS"

Crab Louis was first served in 1914 at a San Francisco restaurant called Solari's. Our version of a Louis dressing for crab is one that originated in New York. The California version usually contains whipped cream and a lot more mayonnaise; we feel that this less rich version is more in keeping with today's health concerns.

1   large scallion, finely minced (about ¼ cup)

1   small clove garlic, finely minced (about 1 teaspoon)

½   small red pepper, finely diced (about 3 tablespoons)

1   tablespoon nonpareil capers, rinsed and dried

⅔   cup mayonnaise

¼   cup bottled chili sauce

1   tablespoon drained prepared horseradish

⅛   teaspoon hot pepper flakes

¼   teaspoon black pepper

Salt to taste

1   pound lump crab meat, picked over to remove any bits of shell or cartilage

Garnishes: Any combination of leaf lettuce or watercress, cherry tomatoes, quartered hard-cooked eggs, avocado slices, cooked asparagus spears, and small black olives

In a bowl, combine the scallion, garlic, red pepper, capers, mayonnaise, chili sauce, horseradish, hot pepper flakes, black pepper, and salt. Cover with plastic wrap and refrigerate for 2 hours or overnight.

When ready to serve, gently combine only enough sauce to moisten the crab meat. Arrange lettuce or watercress on a platter, top with the crab, and surround with the remaining garnishes. Pass any remaining sauce separately if you wish.

SAUTÉED SOFT-SHELL CRABS WITH BROWN BUTTER AND GARLIC SAUCE

MAKES 4 SERVINGS

The arrival of soft-shell crabs heralds the change of seasons from winter to spring. As the weather warms, the blue crabs molt, shedding their hard shells to grow into their next size. In this vulnerable state, they are consumed with relish in their entirety, not only by other sea creatures but by avid diners as well.

1 cup milk	4 slices peeled and pitted lemon
1 teaspoon Tabasco	3 tablespoons butter
Salt and pepper to taste	1 small garlic clove, lightly crushed
8 prime- or medium-size soft-shell crabs, cleaned (see page 282)	1 tablespoon lemon juice
½ cup all-purpose flour	3 tablespoons finely minced parsley
2 tablespoons olive or corn oil	

In a large shallow dish, combine the milk, Tabasco, salt, and pepper, then add the crabs in one layer. Let them marinate for 10 minutes on each side, turning them over to dampen them. Add the crabs to flour that has been seasoned with salt and pepper, turn to coat them well, then shake off the excess flour.

Heat the oil in a nonstick skillet large enough to hold the crabs in one layer over medium-high heat. When the oil is very hot but not smoking, add the crabs belly side up. Cook for 2 to 3 minutes on each side until the crabs are golden brown. Transfer them to a warm platter with tongs and distribute the lemon slices over the crabs.

Wipe out the skillet, add the butter, and heat over medium-high heat until melted. Add the garlic and cook until the garlic begins to color. Remove and discard the garlic. Continue to heat the butter until bubbling and pale hazelnut in color, then stir in the lemon juice and pour over the crabs. Sprinkle with the parsley and serve.

NOTE: This dish can also be served with some Sauce Provençal (see page 91).

JAPANESE SOFT-SHELL CRABS MARINATED IN PONZU AND SAKE

Small soft-shell crabs are briefly sautéed, then marinated in a combination of ginger and chile-spiked Japanese rice wine and citrus-infused vinegar. It's a refreshing, palate-pleasing combination.

2 cups ponzu (bottled Japanese citrus and vinegar sauce)

1 cup sake (rice wine)

1½ cups light soy sauce or tamari

2 teaspoons finely julienned ginger

1 whole garlic clove, peeled and lightly crushed

1 small dried chile

4 to 6 thin scallions, cut diagonally into 1½-inch pieces

18 prime- or hotel-size soft-shell crabs, about 3½ inches each, cleaned (see page 282)

All-purpose flour for coating crabs

¼ cup corn oil

¼ cup Oriental sesame oil

In a wide, shallow bowl, combine the ponzu, sake, soy, ginger, garlic, chile, and scallions. Dry the crabs very well and coat them lightly in flour.

In a large skillet, heat the corn and sesame oils over medium heat. Add about 6 crabs at a time and sauté for 2 to 3 minutes on each side. As they are cooked, add them to the marinade. Cover and refrigerate for 2 hours.

Before serving, bring the crabs to room temperature. Take them out of the marinade with tongs, arrange 3 on each serving plate, and garnish with the scallion pieces.

JIM REED'S CRAB CAKES

Makes 4 or 5 servings

Crab cakes are especially liked in almost every region of the country, with each area placing its own imprint on the finished product. Most are thickened with lots of bread crumbs and egg. Some include mayonnaise. Our favorite crab cakes are these, bound with a piquant béchamel sauce. Our dear friend Jim Reed, who is a chef, created the recipe and generously gave it to us to share with you.

4	tablespoons butter	1	pound lump crabmeat, picked over to remove any bits of shell and cartilage
¾	cup all-purpose flour		
1	cup hot milk	½	cup dried bread crumbs
¼	teaspoon Tabasco	1	egg, lightly beaten
1	tablespoon Dijon mustard		Corn oil for frying
¼	teaspoon white pepper		Red Pepper Sauce (see page 96) for serving (optional) or lemon wedges or Tartar Sauce (see page 74)
	Salt to taste		
½	cup very finely minced scallions		
¼	cup very finely minced parsley		

Melt the butter in a nonstick saucepan over medium-low heat, whisk in ¼ cup of the flour, then gradually whisk in the hot milk. Cook, stirring constantly, until very thick and remove from the heat. Stir in the Tabasco, mustard, white pepper, and salt and let it cool. Stir in the scallions and parsley, then gently fold in the crab, leaving the lumps as whole as possible. Divide the mixture into 10 equal portions and shape them into patties. Place them on a plate and cover with plastic wrap. Chill for 1 to 3 hours in the refrigerator.

When ready to cook, place 2 pieces of aluminum foil on a work surface and put the remaining ½ cup flour on one and the bread crumbs on the other. Put the beaten egg in a pie plate. Dip each cake into the flour first, then the egg, and then the bread crumbs.

Heat 1 to 2 tablespoons oil in a large, heavy nonstick skillet over moderate heat. Add as many cakes as will fit without crowding and cook about 2 to 3 minutes on each side until golden brown. Drain on paper towels and repeat the process with the second batch, adding more oil if necessary and keeping the first batch warm in the oven. Serve with red pepper sauce if you wish.

BROILED DEVILED CRAB WITH MUSHROOMS AND GRUYÈRE CHEESE

MAKES 6 LARGE SERVINGS (FOR MAIN COURSE)
OR 12 SMALL SERVINGS (FOR FIRST COURSE)

A puffy, peppery blend of crab, mushrooms, and cheese, prepared ahead and slipped under the broiler for a few minutes to brown. It makes a most elegant and welcome main or first course when baked and served in scallop shells.

1 pound lump crabmeat, picked over to remove any bits of shell or cartilage	2 tablespoons dry sherry
4 tablespoons butter	1 teaspoon white wine Worcestershire sauce
2 ounces shallots, finely minced (about 3 tablespoons)	¼ teaspoon Tabasco or more to taste
½ small rib celery, finely minced (about 2 tablespoons)	½ teaspoon black pepper
	Salt to taste
18 very small white mushrooms, trimmed	6 tablespoons mayonnaise
1 tablespoon finely minced parsley	½ cup plus 1 tablespoon grated Gruyère cheese
1 tablespoon lemon juice	

Put the crab in a mixing bowl and set aside. In a nonstick medium skillet, melt the butter over medium-low heat. Add the shallots and celery and sauté, stirring constantly, until wilted, 2 to 3 minutes. Stir in the mushrooms and cook for 2 to 3 minutes more. Set aside to cool.

When the vegetables are cool, add them to the crab meat along with the parsley, lemon juice, sherry, Worcestershire, Tabasco, pepper, and salt. Then add 4 tablespoons of the mayonnaise and ½ cup of the cheese. Combine carefully so as not to break up the lumps of crab.

Preheat the broiler. Lightly oil 6 large scallop shells or 12 to 14 smaller ones or use ramekins instead. Spoon the mixture into the shells. Blend the remaining 2 tablespoons mayonnaise and 1 tablespoon cheese and spoon equal amounts of this mixture over the surface of the crab, smoothing gently with a rubber spatula. Place the shells on a cookie sheet, then broil until golden and bubbly.

LOBSTER

Those lively, lovely lobsters! There's something about the lobster that seems to create intense feelings, among both seafood lovers and animal rights activists, although one can be both (as we are) without contradiction. On the one hand, we have people who can eat lobster for breakfast, lunch, and dinner (plus a midnight snack of leftovers), who "pig out" on any trip to Maine, where the tasty crustacean has its most popular habitat, and who buy it no matter what the current astronomical price at the fish market.

On the other hand, more and more food writers, columnists, and just plain old home cooks have begun debating the question of just how to kill a live lobster humanely and, indeed, is there really a painless way in any case? One of our favorite food writers, Molly O'Neill of the *New York Times,* once made what we think was a mistake by *naming* a lobster she was about to cook, and so, Louie took on a personality. After four struggling attempts, she finally got Louie into the boiling water. She put it quite right for us animal-activist/seafood-lover cooks when she titled her piece "Getting Personal with a Lobster Doesn't Soften a Cook's Heart."

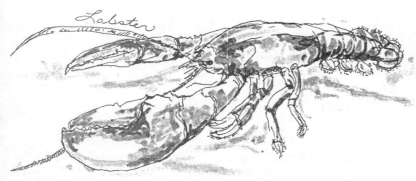

Taking another tack, the test cooks at the now defunct *Cook's Magazine* tried to "hypnotize" their lobster by stroking the upper surface of its tail while the beast was balanced upside down on its nose and claws. It didn't help much, according to their report, because the lobster awoke with a violent start when it was moved toward the boiling water.

Understanding all of this—and it is Mel who does the dirty work while Sheryl joyfully attacks the cooked lobster—we think that everyone would agree that the lobster must be the most popular creature of the entire seafood world. The state of Maine is synonymous with the best lobsters, and the Maine or American lobster holds the unchallenged title as king or queen of its world. With a dark green to black hard shell that turns bright red when cooked, the American lobster has a firm flesh with a distinctive and delicious flavor. It also has the distinction of having two large pincer claws, both of which are repositories of some of the most desired meat. In that way, it differs quite radically from the other species of lobster available.

The clawless variety is called the spiny lobster or rock lobster; this is the species that provides lobster tails, most of them frozen and uncooked. They're found in the warmer waters of the world, including the Caribbean, the Pacific Ocean, and off the coast of

South Africa. Some prefer lobster tails to whole American lobster, possibly because there's no need to work at getting all the wonderful meat from the creature. On the other hand, many (the authors included) prefer the whole live lobster from the New England coast; and we find that its meat is more tender and less stringy, possibly because lobster tails are often frozen. We also find that we especially like the claws, always saving those choice morsels for last.

There are several smaller family members as well, including Dublin Bay prawns, sometimes known as *scampi* or *langostinos* or *lobsterettes*. Usually, they're less than 10 inches in length, meaning that the only practical meat is in the tail, and their taste has been described best as a cross between shrimp and lobster.

Choosing a Live Lobster

SHE OR HE? Some lobster lovers claim that the flesh of the female is more tender than that of the male. Frankly, we have never been able to judge the difference. We love them both. In the female lobster, the tail flanges are much wider than those of the male, "like a woman's hips" according to our fishmonger. And, if you look under the upper section of the belly, you'll find two tiny flippers at the very top which are called "swimmerettes." If they're soft, quite thin, and wispy, the lobster is a girl. If the flippers are long and rigid, it's a boy. On the other hand, we have never bothered to sex our lobsters, preferring instead to choose them by their hyperactivity in the tank.

AT THE FISHMONGER'S: Lobsters are scrappy cannibals. Someone once said that if you put a hundred into a tank without pegging or banding their claws, you'd have one huge lobster in a matter of days! Thus, the activity of the lobster is probably the best gauge in choosing your catch. Make sure the lobster is active and scrappy, because the longer a lobster is kept in captivity, the less it tends to eat, becoming less and less energetic. As a result the flesh has a tendency to shrivel and pull away from the shell.

If the lobster is already cooked, either at the fishmonger or in a restaurant, make certain that you know and trust the place at which you're buying it. The lobster should have been alive before cooking, and the best way to test it is to pull back on the tail and then let it go. If it was alive and fresh when it was cooked, the tail will snap back into a curled position against the body.

WHAT SIZE TO BUY: One of the lobster myths that we have spent years trying to disprove is the story that the larger the lobster, the tougher the meat. When they were more reasonably priced, we experimented with lobsters that ranged in size up to *20 pounds!* The major problem was not the taste or the texture of the remarkable beasts but just finding a pot large enough in which to cook them. Today the problem is compounded in that lobsters are sold by the pound, with the price per pound increasing astronomically as you get to the larger sizes.

We recommend allowing between 1 and 1¼ pounds per person for live lobsters. The yield will be about 3 to 4 ounces of cooked meat. A 2-pound lobster will yield about ½ pound of meat, just about 25 percent of its live weight.

Chicken	About 1 pound
Eighths	1 to 1¼ pounds
Quarters	1¼ to 1½ pounds
Large	1½ to 2¼ pounds
Jumbo	Over 2¼ pounds

BEFORE COOKING: Lobsters must be alive before cooking. Thus, when you get them home, take a large, fairly deep tray or roasting pan and, keeping the lobster in an opened brown paper bag, place it in the container. Cover it loosely with a damp paper towel and put it in the refrigerator. The lobster should manage quite well until cooking time, but check every once in a while. We tend to worry a lot, looking at our future dinner often to check on its condition. If the lobster should die before the time you've set to cook it, cook it at once. In all the time we've been eating them, no lobster has disappointed us.

Cooking the Live Lobster

Many years ago, we settled the controversy that had been brewing in our family whether to boil or to steam. We found that both do equally well, that the lobster tastes almost exactly the same, and that the cooking time is also the same. The only difference that we found is that it takes much less water to steam a lobster, thus condensing the entire cooking process to just a few minutes rather than taking 30 or 45 minutes to boil a huge pot of water. And, for those of us with little strength in our hands and arms, lifting a large pot with a little water takes a lot less energy than moving a filled pot from sink to stove top. The choice, of course, is yours.

BOILING LOBSTER: If you are lucky enough to live or vacation near the sea, you might want to boil your lobster in sea water, just as they do at the docks up in Maine. However, for most of us this is not practical, and ordinary tap water with about 2 teaspoons salt per quart of water added will do.

Some cooks recommend removing the claw pegs or rubberbands, claiming that cooking with them affects the taste. Most lobsters in the marketplace now seem to be bound with rubberbands rather than pegged, and we just leave them on. We have too much respect for the nippers!

To cook the lobster, first bring the water to a rolling boil. Grasp the lobster behind the head and plunge it headfirst into the pot. When the lobster is plunged into the water, the boil will stop. Allow the water to come to a full boil again (about 3 to 5 minutes), then lower the heat slightly to prevent it from boiling over. Begin timing from this point with the water at a brisk simmer. The average lobster of about 1¼ pounds will take about 12 minutes, if the pot is covered. For each additional pound per lobster, add 3 minutes more.

STEAMING LOBSTER: As we've mentioned, this is the method that we prefer, since it just makes life easier—less time, less water, same taste. Take a large covered roasting pan or a Dutch oven and put a rack in it that is raised about 2 to 3 inches from the bottom. We find that a large, narrow fish poacher is just right, and we put crumpet rings under the rack to lift it just enough above the water to steam the lobsters. You can also use empty tuna cans with the tops and bottoms cut out to do the same job.

Fill the pot with water to just below the rack and bring the water to a boil. When steam escapes from the cover, open it and put the lobsters in headfirst, then cover tightly. As soon as steam begins to escape again, begin your timing. Allow 12 minutes for a 1¼-pound lobster, and add 3 minutes for each additional pound per lobster.

BROILING OR GRILLING LOBSTER: In order to broil or grill a lobster, you have to kill it first right before cooking. Therefore, many people prefer to have their fishmonger do the work, then get the lobster home to cook it immediately. However, if you are storing live lobsters in your refrigerator or if it doesn't bother you to kill the lobster, the procedure is quite simple.

About a third to a half of the way down the back of the lobster is a slight crease or indentation where the body meets the tail. Place the lobster on a cutting board or in the sink on a damp towel and, using a large chef's knife or other sturdy kitchen knife, plunge the point into that spot. This will sever the spine and kill the lobster instantly, although reflex action may keep it moving for a few moments.

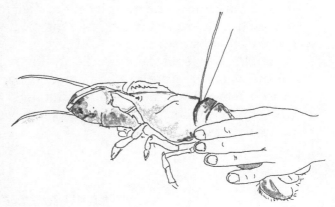

Now turn the lobster over on its back and make a vertical cut through the shell from the top right down to the tail section. Using both hands, just break the lobster apart a bit without separating the sections. Remove the stomach and intestinal vein that's in the tail section close to the shell. Melt a stick of butter and baste the lobster with butter, keeping the melted butter nearby so that you can baste constantly through the broiling or grilling process. There's nothing worse than overcooked, dried-out lob-

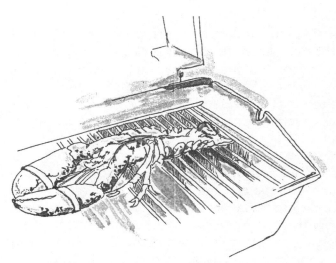

ster, but properly done, broiling or grilling can add a delicious smoky taste to this treat.

For broiling, place the lobster on its back and broil it about 4 to 6 inches from the heat, basting frequently. When it's done, the meat should be tender and opaque. The best way to test it is to crack the tail open slightly and probe with a knife or fork. The process should take 12 to 15 minutes or a bit longer for larger lobsters.

When grilling, prepare the lobster in exactly the same way: Grill the lobster meat side down over the coals for 4 to 5 minutes. Turn the lobster on its back and continue to grill, basting frequently. It's done when the meat turns opaque and is tender when prodded with a knife tip or a fork. This should take 7 to 8 minutes longer.

Cooking Lobster Tails

Lobster tails can be boiled, broiled, or steamed just like their American lobster cousins, or you can remove the meat from the shell for use in other dishes. If you've purchased the tail frozen, thaw it first by running cold water over it and then prepare it just as you would any lobster.

For broiling, split the tail vertically down the middle. When boiling or steaming, wait for the water to return to a boil before beginning your timing. The smaller lobster tails (4 to 5 ounces) will take about 5 minutes. Add 1 minute for each additional ounce. They're done when the meat turns opaque and feels tender when prodded with the tip of a knife or fork.

How to Eat a Lobster

There's very little waste to a lobster. Almost everything is edible, and we even use the leftover shells to make sauces or to add flavor to fish stews and bisques. In addition, the female lobster will frequently offer its roe (or lobster coral), while both male and female yield the tomalley (the greenish yellow liver). However, some recent advisories have warned against eating the tomalley, because it has a higher concentration of PCBs than the rest of the lobster.

HOW TO EAT A LOBSTER (see next page)

One of the things that we always do when the lobster comes out of the pot, shiny red and dripping, is to place a kitchen towel in the sink and then put the lobster on it, shell side down. In that way, when we make the first cut, the water and foam that spurts out is absorbed by the towel. It also keeps the lobster from slipping while being cut.

HOW TO EAT A LOBSTER (see preceeding page)

1. Before placing the lobster on a plate, take a heavy, sharp knife and cut through the entire length of the lobster (top side up) from head to tail. Grasp both halves with paper towels (the lobster will be very hot) and break it apart. Remove the intestinal vein from the tail and the stomach. The tail meat will be exposed. Put each lobster on a plate and serve.

2. Grasp the lobster firmly in one hand and, using your other hand, twist the claws off right down to the body. Place these aside on your plate, unless you are one of those lobster lovers who eats the claws first.

3. Within the body cavity, the lobster is divided into small armored segments, with a leg coming from each one. Break each segment apart, discarding the feathery material clinging to it. You'll find small morsels of meat in each part, reachable with a lobster pick or a small pronged fork.

4. Remove the legs one at a time, break them with your fingers, and suck out the meat.

5. Using a nutcracker or mallet or even a small clean hammer, crack the shell around the claw section, peel it off, and remove the meat with your fingers, a pick, or small fork.

POACHED LOBSTER WITH AROMATIC VEGETABLES AND HERBS

Contrary to the opinion of many other cooks, we feel that hard boiling toughens lobster meat and makes it rubbery. When it's poached, the liquid exchanges flavors with the lobster as it simmers gently, and the meat is more tender, sweeter, and more flavorful.

2	medium onions	8	quarts water
2	medium carrots	2	tablespoons salt
2	medium ribs celery	4	live 1¼- to 1½-pound lobsters
5	sprigs parsley		Clarified Butter (see page 65) for serving
1	large bay leaf		Lemon wedges for serving
4	sprigs thyme		
3	cups dry white wine		

Chop the onion, carrot, and celery coarsely in a food processor and transfer to a 12-quart stock or pasta pot. Tie the parsley, bay leaf, and thyme together and add to the pot, then add the wine, water, and salt. Bring to a boil, cover, and simmer for 15 minutes. Raise the heat and return to a boil.

Leave the rubber bands on the claws intact. Holding the top of the lobster from behind the claws, plunge the lobster headfirst into the boiling liquid. Cover, lower the heat immediately, and poach at a brisk simmer for approximately 10 minutes per pound (1¼ pounds—about 12 minutes; 1½ pounds—about 15 minutes).

Line the sink with a dish towel and, when the lobsters are cooked, remove them with tongs to the sink to drain. The towel will keep the lobster from slipping while you split it. Cut down the center either through the back or the underbelly for ease of eating (see page 297). Serve hot with clarified butter and lemon wedges.

GRILLED LOBSTER
WITH BASIL BUTTER

MAKES 4 SERVINGS

Soak some unhusked ears of corn in water and grill them Native American style to accompany this lobster, perfumed with basil butter. Put them together and you have a perfect summertime and very American feast.

2	live 1½- to 2-pound lobsters	15 to 20	fresh basil leaves, coarsely chopped
2	tablespoons olive oil	⅛	teaspoon cayenne pepper
	Salt and black pepper to taste	2	tablespoons lemon juice
6	tablespoons butter		

To kill the live lobsters, plunge them headfirst in boiling salted water. Cover, then lower the heat immediately and simmer 4 minutes until the shell turns bright red (see Note). Remove the lobsters with tongs and cool them until they are comfortable enough to handle. Cut the lobsters in half lengthwise and remove the intestinal vein that runs the length of the tail and the papery textured sac behind the eyes. The lobsters may be prepared several hours ahead up to this point.

When ready to cook, prepare hot coals to the proper cooking temperature (see page 52). Cut the claws off the lobsters and set aside. In a small saucepan, add the olive oil, salt and pepper, butter, basil, cayenne pepper, and lemon juice and heat until the butter is melted. Brush the lobster flesh with this mixture and place the lobsters flesh side down along with the claws on the grill. Grill for about 3 minutes, then turn over and grill, basting with the basil butter 4 to 5 minutes more until the flesh is just opaque and firm but not tough. Allow an extra minute or two for the claws. Serve half a lobster to each person, spooning on additional butter sauce over each half.

NOTE: Another option for preparing the lobster for grilling is to let your fishmonger kill and split them lengthwise with a cleaver. If you choose this method, eliminate the boiling of the lobster and increase the grilling time accordingly, another 1 or 2 minutes on each side.

CRAYFISH

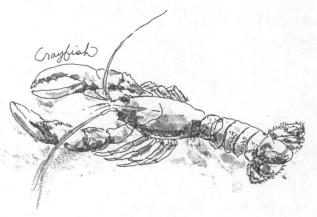

Crayfish

Although the lobsterlike crayfish is found in fresh-water streams, lakes, and rivers across the country, most of the catch comes from Louisiana and the West Coast, with the greater number now being farmed. They're about 3 to 5 inches long, and no visitor to the city of New Orleans would ever return home without regaling listeners about the taste of this bayou treat. In fact, during the season, which begins in a trickle in late fall and then grows to a bonanza in early summer, a madness takes over in Louisiana, and it is not uncommon to find festivals that include eating marathons of crayfish (or crawfish or crawdaddies as they are sometimes called). They also have become a part of the local language, since they scurry backwards when trapped. Thus, the expression "to crawfish" means "to back out of a deal."

The best way to taste crayfish (aside from a trip down to New Orleans) is to buy them live, although you may have to order them from your fishmonger. They're also sold frozen and cooked whole with shell and vein removed, but we don't think they taste quite as good. Allow about one pound of live crayfish per person.

If you're fortunate enough to get them live, put them in a large bowl and run cold water over them, stirring with a wooden spoon. Don't use your bare hands—they are quite capable of nipping your fingers. Drain and discard any silt or dirt at the bottom of the bowl and then rinse the crayfish under cold water again. If any have died, discard them.

We've given some crayfish recipes in the pages that follow, but you can use your imagination in adding spices or seasonings to the boiling water. Friends in New Orleans use everything from cayenne pepper, garlic, lemons, onions, to prepared blends of seasonings. After cooking them, remove the heads from the tail section and then, grasping the crayfish behind the claws, turn them stomach side up and twist the tail section. The shell will break, and the sand vein can be pulled out easily.

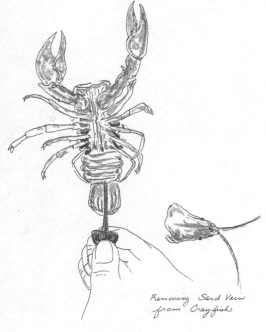

Removing Sand Vein from Crayfish

LOUISIANA CRAYFISH IN A MUSHROOM MADEIRA SAUCE ON TOAST POINTS

MAKES 4 SERVINGS

A most elegant, light supper or luncheon dish or a first course for a special dinner party.

1 ounce dried porcini mushrooms	2 tablespoons all-purpose flour
2 tablespoons Madeira wine	½ cup heavy cream
10 slices white bread, crusts removed	¼ teaspoon Tabasco
1 cup Fish Stock (see page 402)	½ teaspoon dried thyme
1 cup water	¼ teaspoon dried oregano
2 pounds crayfish (substitute: shrimp or lobster tails, about 1½ pounds)	Salt to taste
2 tablespoons butter	1 teaspoon lemon juice
1 large shallot, finely minced (about 2 tablespoons)	

Louisiana Crayfish in Mushroom Madeira Sauce on Toast Points

In a small cup, soak the mushrooms in the Madeira for 45 minutes. Cut 10 slices of white bread in half diagonally, toast them, and set aside. When the mushrooms have finished soaking, strain them through a dampened coffee filter, pressing the mushrooms against the side. Reserve the liquid. Mince the mushrooms and reserve as well.

In a large saucepan, bring the fish stock and water to a boil over medium heat. Add the crayfish and return to a boil, then cook for 30 seconds and remove the pot from the heat. Scoop up the crayfish with a slotted spoon and place them on a plate to cool. When they are cool to the touch, twist off the tails from the bodies. Squeeze the sides of the tails until the shell cracks and extract the tail meat. Pull out the vein from the back as you would from a shrimp. Set the tail meat aside and return the bodies with attached claws to the fish stock. Return to the stove and simmer over medium-low heat for 20 minutes to intensify the flavor and reduce the stock. Strain the stock into a bowl and set it aside. Reserve 8 crayfish bodies for garnish and discard the rest. Then stir the reserved mushrooms and liquid into the stock.

Wipe out the saucepan, add the butter, and melt over medium heat. Add the shallot and sauté for 1 minute, stirring. Then stir in the flour and cook, stirring constantly, for 2 to 3 minutes until golden in color. Slowly add the fish stock mixture and cook for 1 minute. Add the cream, Tabasco, thyme, oregano, and salt and bring the sauce to a boil. Lower the heat to medium-low and simmer, stirring constantly, for 2 to 3 minutes until slightly thickened. Stir in the reserved crayfish tail meat and the lemon juice and continue to cook only until heated through.

To serve, arrange 5 toast triangles on the outsides of 4 serving plates to form a star pattern with the center square reserved for the seafood and sauce. Distribute the seafood among the plates and decorate each serving with 2 of the reserved heads and claws placed in opposite directions. Serve hot.

Crayfish

WILD RICE AND CRAYFISH SALAD WITH SUGAR SNAP PEAS AND RED PEPPERS

MAKES 6 SERVINGS

Whether you refer to them as crayfish, crawfish, or crawdaddies, these 3- to 5-inch crustaceans, the small fresh-water version of a lobster, make an elegant first course when paired with wild rice and crunchy, sweet sugar snap peas.

6   ounces wild rice, rinsed
4   cups boiling water
1   large bay leaf
1   teaspoon salt
    Black pepper to taste
3   tablespoons butter
1   tablespoon olive oil
1   teaspoon dried thyme

12 live crayfish (substitute: unshelled jumbo shrimp)
¼   pound sugar snap peas, tips and strings removed, blanched
2   medium red peppers, roasted, skinned, seeded, and diced
2   tablespoons lemon juice
4   tablespoons finely minced parsley

To a medium saucepan, add the rice and stir frequently for 3 to 5 minutes over low heat, toasting the grains. Add the boiling water, bay leaf, salt, and pepper. Bring to a boil, then reduce the heat to low, cover the pot, and cook for about 45 minutes until the rice is tender. Drain the rice and discard the bay leaf. Slip a paper towel between the pot and the lid to absorb any excess moisture and let stand for 10 minutes.

Heat the butter and oil in a large skillet over medium-high heat until hot. Stir in the thyme and add the crayfish. Cover the skillet and cook, shaking the pan frequently, for about 5 to 6 minutes, until the shells turn deep pink. Lift out the crayfish with tongs, then stir the rice into the butter mixture in the skillet. Stir in the blanched sugar snap peas, the red peppers, lemon juice, and parsley. Cut the crayfish in half lengthwise and place them on the surface of the rice and vegetable mixture. Adjust the seasoning and distribute among 6 serving plates. Serve warm or at room temperature and provide picks or small forks to extract the crayfish meat.

MOLLUSKS

In the introductory section of this book, we gave some shellfish guidelines, stating rather firmly that the cardinal rule about them, particularly with reference to mollusks, is to eat them and enjoy them, but *don't eat them raw.* We're certain that most of our readers have seen, as we have, the barrage of articles that might be summed up in one word: Beware. But then again, we also have been inundated with frightening information about our polluted planet as well as with warnings about salmonella contamination of eggs and poultry. However, statistically, seafood is still ten times safer than eating the ubiquitous bird or an egg cooked insufficiently.

On the other hand, the evidence also tells us that 85 percent of all illnesses caused by eating seafood (about 1 in 250,000 servings) comes from eating *raw* oysters and clams. Bivalves tend to be the troublemakers because they lie on the bottom of the ocean or cling to the docks, filtering the water through their systems, not only pulling in the nutrients but also the ambient pollutants as well. If harmful bacteria or viruses are present, they're passed on to us—but only if the bivalve is eaten raw. Perhaps the most succinct statement on the subject comes from Anthony Guarino, director of the FDA fishery research branch at Dauphin Island, Alabama: "What other animal do we eat, digestive tract and all, without cooking it first?"

But all of this doesn't mean that you have to give them up forever. The primary rule about all seafood still holds: know your supplier. Louisiana and California require warning labels about eating raw shellfish, but the wise consumer shouldn't need a printed warning. If you're in doubt, ask to see the tag that certifies that the mollusks have come from safe water.

Once you get the live mollusks home, make sure they're refrigerated immediately on a bed of ice. Keep them damp by covering them with a damp paper towel and don't allow fresh water to come in contact with them. Never place them in an airtight container or in plastic or they'll die.

Scallops are shucked at sea, so the best test for them is your nose. They should smell fresh and of the sea. Mussels, oysters, and clams keep their shells tightly shut while alive. When they come out of the refrigerator, if some shells seem to be slightly open, sharply tap the bivalve on the counter and if they close, they're still alive. Discard any that are dead.

The rule is exactly the opposite for cooked mollusks. If they *don't* open after cooking, discard them. There are three exceptions in the clam family: the soft-shell clam, razor clam, and the geoduck (pronounced "gooeyduck"), all of which keep their shells open naturally.

We'd like to make one other point for those of you who live close enough to the saltwater shallows and the sea so that you can hunt for your own clams, mussels, and scallops. Check with your local Environmental Protection Agency or local or federal authorities to be certain that, first of all, the waters are not polluted, and second of all, just what permits or licenses are needed before you can legally harvest them.

Above all else, we return to our first warning: *Cook them thoroughly,* and enjoy them. They're another of the great treasures of the sea.

CLAMS

Although found in many parts of the world, clams are essentially an American delicacy. Even for the amateur clamdigger, towing a large basket that sits in an inflated inner tube and struggling with a long rake, the treasures that lie half buried in the tidal sands and in the bays are ours to harvest: quahogs and steamers on the East Coast, razor clams and geoducks on the West Coast. Coming home with our catch, indeed, can make us "happy as a clam!" And almost all the varieties—Atlantic and Pacific—are now available at the local fishmonger.

The American Indians used the largest shells both as sharpening utensils and hoe blades and as a medium of exchange (wampum), with the inner purple section of the clam shell being more valuable than the white. At the same time, it was they who taught the colonists how to eat the strange creatures, plentiful and free for the taking, the forerunner of what was to become a great American passion.

There are two basic categories of clams: hard shell with their tightly closed hinges, and soft shell, more delicate and recognized by their long necks that extend past the shell.

Quahogs or Hard-Shell Clams

These are the most popular on the Atlantic Coast, with some species now being aquacultured and harvested in the Pacific. Occasionally, we find some confusion among consumers, since many fishmongers sell and label them by their descriptive sizes rather than by their proper names. All the clams listed below are quahogs, and their market names depend only upon size.

LITTLENECK CLAMS: These are the smallest of the quahogs and the most tender. They get their names not from their anatomical description but from the area in which most of them are harvested in the waters on Long Island in New York. When clams were more often eaten raw, these were the choice of the group. They're about 1½ inches long. There is also a Pacific variety called littleneck, generally cultivated along with some that are harvested wild in the Northwest, but they are slightly tougher than their East Coast cousins and usually are used for chowder.

CHERRYSTONE CLAMS: A bit larger than the littlenecks, these are about 2 inches long and usually sold at a lower price than their smaller cousins.

CHOWDER CLAMS: Larger and tougher than the cherrystones, these are perfect for just the dish that the name indicates—chowders—or fritters when chopped.

OCEAN QUAHOGS: A deep sea clam, about 3½ to 4 inches long and sometimes referred to as mahogany clam or black clam because of its shell color. It has a stronger flavor and aroma than the others in the family and, thus, is used mostly for chowders or is chopped and canned or frozen.

SURF, SEA, OR BAR CLAMS: Most canned clams are made from the varieties that are found on the sandy, surf-pounded shoreline of the Atlantic Ocean. They range from 4 to 7 inches in size, and unlike the other varieties of clams which can be eaten whole, only the two adductor muscles are eaten, while the rest of the clam body is discarded.

Soft-Shell Clams

These go by a variety of nicknames, the most common of which is "steamer." Those of us who live on the East Coast know them by this name and try to find those seafood restaurants where steamed clams are the specialty, served with hot clam broth and melted lemon butter. Others love them dipped in batter and then deep-fried, as they do up in New England, where they're dubbed "Clam Rolls Ipswich Style."

They have the peculiar habit of spitting out a stream of water when something comes too near them, also giving them the nickname of pisser clam or squirt, plus longneck or belly clam.

Geoduck Clams

The giant in the clam family, the geoduck (pronounced "gooey-duck") is harvested in the Northwest at sizes that range from 2 to 5 pounds, with necks that can extend as much as 2 feet. Although related to the East Coast soft shells, the siphon of the geoduck more closely resembles that of an elephant's trunk. They're usually available fresh in Oriental markets, although recently we've begun to see them at our local fish market.

The peeled trunk and the strip of flesh that runs around the belly are the parts that are eaten, with the firm meat cut into steaks and then tenderized by tapping them lightly with a wooden mallet.

If you purchase geoducks fresh, dip them into hot water for 3 to 5 minutes to open the shell and loosen the skin. Discard the skin and the stomach, then rinse the remainder of the clam in cold water. You can probably get 3 steaks from one average-size clam—two from the neck and one from the breast. You can also mince the meat to make fritters or chowder. Allow about ¼ pound of clam per person.

Razor Clams

The American Indians are said to have shaved with the shells of these clams (hence the name), for the shells can be very sharp, although they are also quite fragile and break or chip easily. Their fragility also makes them difficult to harvest, for they live vertically in the soft sand and are quite capable of burying themselves deeply when they're disturbed.

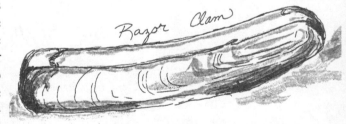

The East Coast variety is not often seen at the fishmonger, although we occasionally do come across them at our Chinese markets and at some of the specialty fish markets. East Coast razor clams run about 4 to 10 inches in length, are generally steamed or minced, and used in fritters. On the West Coast, the clams are a bit shorter, and cooks fry them or use them in chowders.

Manila Clams

A very small hard-shell Pacific clam, usually 1¼ to 1½ inches long, very round and with light brown striated ridges. We first came across them—you guessed it—in Manila in the early 1970s, but we were very wary of the waters in which they were harvested, so we didn't really taste them until they became more popular and were cultivated commercially near the Puget Sound in the Pacific Northwest. We find them to be our primary choice among the hard-shell clams, since they all seem to open at the same time when they're steamed and their small shells make them quite decorative and tasty in a variety of dishes that call for clams, such as pastas, risottos, and shellfish soups and stews.

Cockles

Distinguished by their tiny size and their very distinctive ridged shells, most of our cockles now come from New Zealand, although there are many varieties around the world, including some from our own Pacific Coast and the shoreline of Europe. They have a tendency to be sandy, so put them in a container with salted water for several hours to let them filter out the sand before you cook them. They can be prepared in very much the same way as the other hard-shell clams.

Preparing the Clams

Clean the clams thoroughly by scrubbing them under cold running water with a nylon scrub pad. Make sure all the silt and dirt clinging to the clam shells have been removed. If you harvest your own clams, place them in cold, salted water to cover and sprinkle either cornmeal or oatmeal on top. Since clams feed by filtering water through their systems, the grains act as an irritant, and the grit inside will be flushed out in several hours. Make certain that the water is salted or from the sea; fresh water will kill the clams. Afterwards, rinse them again under cold running water, scrubbing them with a stiff brush or nylon pad.

Shucking the Clams

The soft shells are easy, since they are slightly open naturally. Hard-shell clams require a bit more deftness. One trick that we suggest is to put the raw clams in the freezer for about 5 minutes to relax them. This should be done right before you plan to shuck them. Then, be sure to use a clam knife rather than a sharp kitchen knife. Opening a stubborn clam can sometimes be tricky and you could easily cut yourself using a kitchen knife. Also open them over a bowl so that you don't lose any of the juices. However, if you're going to use the clams for a dish such as clam chowder, there's no need to go through the shucking process. Just steam the clams until they pop partly open, then pry them fully open and remove the clam.

Hold the clam between your palm and thumb, with the hinge placed firmly toward the back of your hand. Hold the clam knife between your palm and fingers, leaving the thumb free to rest on the shell. Place the blade in the crease between the shells toward the narrow part of the clam, resting the thumb on the other end. Close your fingers over the blade.

Squeeze down with your fingers and press the blade downward to separate the shells. Twist the point of the clam knife to open completely, and cut the muscles that hold the shell together.

To free the meat, run the knife completely under it so that you can lift it easily from the shell. Do not wash the clams once they are opened. Keep the meat in its own broth or on the half shells for baking.

CLAMS WITH COUSCOUS, ZUCCHINI, TOMATOES, AND BASIL

Couscous is steeped in the broth that the clams have given up, then tossed with shredded zucchini, tomatoes, and basil and studded with tender morsels of clams.

24 cherrystone clams, scrubbed well	4 plum tomatoes (about ¾ pound), quartered
2 tablespoons butter	1 teaspoon finely minced lemon peel
1 medium clove garlic, finely minced (about 1 teaspoon)	3 tablespoons lemon juice
4 sprigs parsley	3 tablespoons finely shredded fresh basil
1 cup instant couscous, preferably medium granulation	⅛ teaspoon cayenne pepper
½ pound small zucchini, shredded	¼ teaspoon black pepper
	Salt to taste

Put the clams in one layer in a large skillet or a Dutch oven. Add 1 inch cold water and cover the pot tightly. Bring to a boil over medium-high heat and steam for 5 to 8 minutes until the clams open, sliding the pan back and forth a few times during cooking. Lift the clams out with a slotted spoon, discard the ones that haven't opened, and remove the meat from the shells. Reserve the clams and strain the clam broth through a strainer that is lined with a man's cotton handkerchief. Measure the broth and add enough water to make 1½ cups liquid.

In a medium saucepan, melt 1 tablespoon of the butter over low heat. Add the garlic and sauté, stirring constantly, until soft, 1 to 2 minutes. Add the clam broth and parsley sprigs and bring to a boil. Remove from the heat and slowly stir in the couscous. Cover the pot and let it stand for 5 minutes, then remove and discard the parsley.

Fluff the couscous with a fork to separate the grains. Stir in the remaining butter, zucchini, tomatoes, lemon peel, lemon juice, basil, cayenne, black pepper, and the reserved clams. Taste for salt (clam broth is salty and none may be necessary) and serve hot or at room temperature.

AMÊIJOAS NA CATAPLANA
(PORTUGUESE PORK AND CLAMS)

In Portugal's southern Algarve province, this traditional dish is cooked in a cataplana, *a hinged, hammered copper pot shaped like 2 shallow bowls clamped together to seal tightly so that no steam can escape. It is used on top of the stove, and when the dish is finished, the* cataplana *is presented dramatically at the table, as the top half is removed in a puff of ambrosial steam.*

1½ pounds pork tenderloin, cut into ¾-inch thick slices

1 tablespoon paprika

¼ teaspoon cayenne pepper

⅛ teaspoon salt

¼ teaspoon black pepper

3 large cloves garlic, lightly crushed

1 bay leaf

2 whole cloves

⅔ cup dry white wine

⅔ cup all-purpose flour

5 tablespoons olive oil

2 medium onions, thinly sliced

1 large shallot, finely minced (about 1½ tablespoons)

2 medium cloves garlic, finely minced (about 2 teaspoons)

4 to 5 plum tomatoes (about 1 pound), peeled and diced

24 small littleneck or 36 Manila clams, scrubbed well

2 tablespoons finely minced cilantro or parsley

6 lemon wedges

In a shallow nonreactive dish, mix the pork with the paprika, cayenne, salt, pepper, crushed garlic, bay leaf, cloves, and wine. Cover tightly with plastic wrap and marinate for 6 hours or overnight, stirring once or twice during that time.

When ready to cook, remove the pork with a slotted spoon and dry on paper towels. Reserve the marinade, discarding the crushed garlic, the cloves, and the bay leaf. Dredge the pork lightly with the flour.

Heat 3 tablespoons of the oil in a large nonstick skillet and brown all sides of the pork over high heat. Pour the reserved marinade over the meat, lower the heat, and simmer for 8 to 10 minutes until there is very little marinade left.

While the pork is cooking, heat the remaining 2 tablespoons oil in another large skillet over medium-high heat. Add the onions and sauté, stirring constantly, for 2 to 3 minutes. Then add the shallot and minced garlic and continue to sauté for 1 to 2 minutes more. Stir in the tomatoes and bring to a boil (see Note). Add the clams in one layer to the tomato-onion mixture, cover tightly, and cook for 5 minutes until the clams open, sliding the pan back and forth a few times during the cooking. Discard any clams that do not open.

Spoon the clams and sauce over the pork, stir, and transfer to a serving platter. Sprinkle with the cilantro and tuck in the lemon wedges to be squeezed over all at the table. Serve with rice or thick slices of sourdough bread to mop up the sauce.

NOTE: If you own a *cataplana,* transfer the cooked pork from the pan to the *cataplana* and spoon the tomato sauce over. Then tuck in the raw clams, close tightly, and cook over medium-high heat on top of the stove. When serving, place the round bottom of the *cataplana* on a damp cloth to steady it before you unhinge the top.

JALAPEÑO CORN AND CLAM CAKES

MAKES ABOUT 18 CAKES

Peppery tongue-tingling clam cakes are paired with fresh corn kernels and a cornmeal base, then baked briefly on a griddle. They are crusty on the outside and creamy on the inside with morsels of clams and corn.

1½ cups coarsely chopped chowder clams, with clam juice reserved	1 teaspoon white wine Worcestershire sauce
1 medium ear fresh corn, shucked	3 cups stone-ground yellow cornmeal
3 tablespoons butter	1 teaspoon salt
1 medium onion, chopped (about ½ cup)	1 teaspoon sugar
1 fresh jalapeño chile, seeded and finely minced	3 tablespoons heavy cream
¾ teaspoon black pepper	2 tablespoons finely minced chives or scallion greens
	Corn oil for griddle

Have your fishmonger shuck the clams. There should be about 2 cups before chopping and 1½ cups after chopping them. Strain the broth into a bowl. There should be about 2 cups clam broth; if not, add water. Set the clams and the broth aside.

Put the corn into a pot of boiling water, turn off the heat, cover, and let stand for 10 minutes. Remove the corn and let cool. When cool enough to handle, scrape off the kernels. There should be about 1 cup. Stir the corn into the chopped clams.

In a medium skillet, melt the butter over medium heat. Add the onion and sauté, stirring frequently, until wilted but not brown. Stir in the jalapeño, black pepper, and Worcestershire. Let cool, then add to the bowl with the clams and corn.

Heat the clam broth to a boil. Skim off the foam and strain it into a cup.

In a large mixing bowl, combine the cornmeal, salt, and sugar, then slowly, without stirring, pour the hot clam broth over the cornmeal. Stir in the cream and chives. The cornmeal should absorb the liquid, but if it's too dry, add some water. Add the clam mixture to the cornmeal and combine well. Cover the bowl and refrigerate for 15 minutes.

When ready to cook, oil a heated griddle. Using about ¼ cup of the mixture for each cake, form and flatten the cornmeal mixture into 3½-inch cakes. Brown both sides over medium heat for about 3 minutes on each side. Serve hot.

BROILED LITTLENECK CLAMS CORSINI

These broiled little clams became a favorite of ours when we first sampled them at the venerable New York restaurant La Grenouille and created our own version at home.

48	littleneck clams	½	teaspoon white wine Worcestershire sauce
2	cloves garlic, peeled		
1 or 2	large shallots (about 1 ounce), peeled	2 or 3	drops Tabasco
1	cup flat-leaf parsley, tightly packed		Salt and black pepper to taste
¼	pound butter, softened	1	cup dry white wine

Have the fishmonger open the clams, leaving them on the half shell and packing them on a bed of ice. Keep the clams refrigerated this way, covered with a dampened paper towel, until ready to use.

In a food processor, process the garlic, shallots, and parsley together until very finely minced. Scrape the mixture into a piece of cheesecloth and twist the cloth to remove as much moisture as possible. Return to the food processor, and add the butter, Worcestershire, Tabasco, salt, and pepper, and process until well combined.

Preheat the broiler. Place the clams in one layer in a baking dish. Spread some of the butter mixture evenly on the clams, and then trickle some wine over them all. Broil just until the butter is sizzling. Do not overcook or the clams will be tough.

CLAMS AND POTATOES PROVENÇAL

The potatoes and licorice-infused vegetables can be prepared in advance. The clams are then added and in fifteen or twenty minutes dinner is ready. A boon for the cook!

1½	pounds new very small potatoes
4	tablespoons olive oil
4 to 5	large cloves garlic, finely minced (about 1½ tablespoons)
2	medium onions (about ½ pound), thinly sliced and separated into rings
1	large red pepper, cut into ½-inch strips
1	large green pepper, cut into ½-inch strips
1	large fennel bulb (about 1¼ pounds), trimmed and thinly sliced, a few feathery tops reserved for garnish
1	teaspoon dried oregano, preferably Greek

¼	teaspoon hot pepper flakes
	Salt and pepper to taste
8	large plum tomatoes (about 1¼ pounds), quartered
¾	cup dry white wine
3	tablespoons Pernod or Ricard
⅓	cup coarsely chopped parsley
8 to 10	large black olives, Kalamata or Alfonso, pitted and quartered
36	small littleneck clams, all the same size if possible (see Note)
2	scallions, thinly sliced (about ½ cup)
	Lemon wedges for serving

Boil the potatoes in salted water to cover until tender. Drain and cool, then peel them and set aside. In a 12-inch sauté pan, heat the olive oil over medium heat. Add the garlic and onions and sauté, stirring constantly, for 1 minute. Stir in the red and green peppers and sauté, stirring frequently, for 4 to 5 minutes. Add the fennel, oregano, hot pepper flakes, salt, and pepper and continue to cook, stirring occasionally, for 2 to 3 minutes more. Add the tomatoes, wine, and Pernod, raise the heat, and bring to a boil. Then lower the heat, cover the pan, and simmer for 5 minutes. Stir in the parsley and olives and remove from the heat. At this point, you can continue the recipe or set the vegetables aside until ready to serve.

Preheat the oven to 500°. In a large, shallow oven-to-table baking dish, add the cooked potatoes and the clams and spoon the hot vegetables over them. Cover with aluminum foil and bake for 10 minutes. Uncover, stir, cover again, and bake for 8 to 10 minutes more, until the clams have opened. Scatter the scallions over the top, along with the reserved fennel tops, and tuck in the lemon wedges to be squeezed over all at the table.

NOTE: Any larger clams will take a bit longer to open when cooking.

OYSTERS

When it comes to discussing oysters, there are two myths that have to be put to rest at once. The first, that oysters are a potent aphrodisiac, has yet to be proven, in spite of the fact that Casanova was supposed to have devoured somewhere around 4 dozen each day, dubbing them "a spur to love." The other is that oysters should only be eaten during the months that contain the letter "R." The owners of a famous seafood restaurant maintain that the "Oysters R In Season" slogan was invented by a public relations person at the end of the nineteenth century. However, we have been able to trace it back as far as the year 1599, when William Butler wrote: "It is unseasonable and unwholesome in all months that have not an *r* in their name to eat an oyster." However, these days, with twenty or more varieties of oysters available from both the Atlantic and Pacific coasts as well as from Europe, oysters are in season all year long. The rule of the "R" months probably came about because some oysters spawn during the other months, making them taste a bit mushy and look milky. Another reason may have been the fact that the only months without an "R" are the warmer ones, when shipping raw oysters could lead to spoilage and food poisoning.

At one time, oysters were so plentiful that in the nineteenth century poor people consumed them as a cheap substitute for meat. Baltimore, to this day, still has some roads that are paved with crushed oyster shells, and a trip to New Orleans would not be complete without sampling the ubiquitous oyster bars that dot the French Quarter. The popularity of oysters dates far back in history, and long before the Christian Era they were cultivated by both the Chinese and the ancient Romans. Our own forty-niners devoured them by the ton during the Gold Rush days in California.

Over the years, however, overfishing and industrial pollution have taken their toll, along with the mysterious "red tide" and a series of oil spills. Thus the oyster has become more of a luxury than a plentiful bounty, in spite of its continuing popularity. To fill some of the gap, the process of cultivation and aquafarming has taken hold, with a large part of today's catch coming from properly supervised beds.

In a way, that's probably the best thing that could have happened, for the oyster, like the clam, is subject to some risk when it's consumed raw. And *raw* seems to be the favored way of eating these superb mollusks. The Oyster Bar in New York City's Grand Central Station sells over 2 million oysters a year, with almost all of them served raw.

Only a small part of the problem has to do with pollution, although it's certainly a factor. Oysters also are subject to spoiling by a bacteria that thrives in warmer waters

(*Vibrio vulnificus*) and is especially threatening to anyone with a pre-existing liver or immune system disorder. Some states now require a warning label for all oysters that are to be consumed raw. The solution, though, is quite simple. If you are in doubt, cook them thoroughly and eliminate all risk. For those who love raw oysters and cannot do without, one of our earlier warnings serves just as well here: Know your supplier. You can also ask to see the tag that accompanies all mollusks that are harvested in waters considered safe.

Although there are a hundred varieties of oysters around the world, only twenty to twenty-five are of economic and culinary importance. Once only the local species was available at the fishmonger's or on restaurant menus, but now it is not at all unusual to see four, five, or more varieties being offered, all delivered fresh and by air. Their tastes and textures vary, with cold water oysters tending to be briny and smelling of the sea, while the oysters from warmer waters are sweeter and somewhat softer.

Richard Lord of the Fulton Fish Market claims that he's heard oysters described as metallic, briny, mild and sweet, but also like the taste of copper, cream, cucumbers, and melon. The selection of a favorite oyster is very subjective, although we tend to prefer the briny, such as our local bluepoint. The best advice we can give is to try many different oysters, raw if you wish, or cooked as we have suggested in our recipes that follow.

Here are the varieties that may be available currently both in your local fish market or on the menu of a specialty seafood restaurant. The name of the oyster is frequently also the name of the area in which it is harvested, and market sizes run anywhere from 3 to 5 inches.

ATLANTIC OYSTERS
Alabama Gulf
Apalachicola
Bluepoint
Chatham
Chesapeake Bay (or Kent Island)
Chincoteague
Cotuit
Florida Gulf
Long Island
Louisiana Gulf (or New Orleans)
Malpeque
Pemaquid
Texas Gulf
Wellfleet

PACIFIC OYSTERS
Golden Mantle
Hog Island Sweetwater
Kumamoto
Lasqueti
Penn Cove
Quilcene
Rock Point
Shoalwater Bay
Westcott Bay
Willapa Bay
Yaquina Bay

OLYMPIA OYSTERS: These are our own delicious native oysters, originally found in the Puget Sound area but almost entirely lost through pollution. They are now being cultivated off the coast of Washington State.

EUROPEAN FLAT OYSTERS: Called "Belon" oysters, they have been imported from the French coast but are now also being farmed both on the Atlantic and Pacific coasts of the United States.

Buying the Oysters

Oysters are highly perishable, especially once they've been shucked. If your fishmonger shucks them for you or you eat them at a "raw bar," make sure that they're tightly closed specimens and that the shucking is done while you watch. All oyster shells should be tightly closed, but if one is gaping open just slightly, tap the shell. If the oyster is alive, the shell will snap shut. If it doesn't, discard it.

- ❖ Never buy an oyster that has a damaged shell.

- ❖ Oysters should never be buried in ice but should be displayed cup side down on a bed of ice. Unlike clams, oysters have a flat side and a rounded shell.

- ❖ Oysters can be cleaned in very much the same way as clams by brushing them thoroughly under running water, using a nylon pad or a strong brush.

- ❖ If you are buying fresh shucked oysters, make sure that the oysters have been packed in their own juices and that the liquid is clear. If the liquid is milky, find another jar.

❖ If the fishmonger shucks the oysters, make sure that they're plump and that they smell of the sea. Oysters give off a foul odor when they're spoiling, so use your nose.

Keeping the Oysters

Oysters in their shells will keep in the refrigerator for 3 to 4 days. However, if they're shucked in advance, they should be consumed as soon as possible. This also holds true for oysters on the half shell, eaten raw. The process (see Box) should be done right before you plan to serve them.

❖ Place the unshucked oysters in a flat dish cup side down in a single layer and cover them with a damp towel or paper. Refrigerate. They will be at their best and most flavorful for 1 to 2 days but will keep for a week unshucked.

❖ Never put oysters in fresh water or in a plastic bag or they will die.

❖ If you can't eat shucked oysters at once and you have to keep them for a short time, put some ice on a flat plate, cover the ice with a damp, thick towel, then place the oysters on the towel. You can refrigerate them for up to 1 hour. After that time, they'll degenerate rather quickly.

SHUCKING YOUR OWN

You should use a specially designed oyster knife, a firm-handled instrument with a short blade and, occasionally, a guard to protect your hand. Actually, some home cooks have successfully used an ordinary "church key," and others claim success with a screwdriver! However, if you use the latter two, you'll still need a knife to loosen the oyster body from its shell. We suggest using the "real McCoy."

❖ Scrub the oysters thoroughly under cold running water. Some experts suggest that the oysters then be immersed in carbonated water for about 5 minutes before attempting to open them. The carbon dioxide in the water will get them "drunk" enough to relax their adductor muscles, making them much easier to open.

❖ Shuck over a bowl. Use a kitchen towel or several layers of paper toweling with which to hold the oyster in one hand. (The shells can be very sharp.)

❖ Place the oyster on the towel or paper, cup side down, and hold it firmly. Insert the oyster knife into the space nearest the hinge, moving it back and forth until it goes into the body of the oyster. Some shuckers prefer to just find any space along the oyster shell into which the point of the knife will fit and then move it along from there. Both methods will work. Just choose the one you like best.

❖ Twist the knife from side to side to force the shells apart. Slide the blade along the top shell to loosen the body and remove the shell.

❖ Place the knife under the body and cut along the bottom to sever the adductor muscle and loosen the oyster from the shell.

❖ Before serving your oysters on the half shell, inspect them to be certain that there are no stray bits of shell floating around.

Cooking the Oysters

Never wash the meat in anything except the liquid from the oyster itself, and remember that regardless of the cooking method that you use, oysters toughen considerably when they're heated too long. Thus, cook them just long enough to plump them up, with the edges just curled slightly.

❖ Oysters can be poached, baked, sautéed, or batter-fried (for only 1 minute).

❖ You also can grill oysters right in the shell, by placing them close to the coals, cup side down. When they pop open, twist off the top shell, add your selected sauce, and return them to the grill for only 1 minute more. (We suggest that you try the Romesco Sauce on page 388.)

CRISP-FRIED DEVILED OYSTERS WRAPPED IN BASIL LEAVES

MAKES 4 SERVINGS

Herb-wrapped oysters are dipped first in a fiery Tabasco-spiked mustard base, then rolled in a flour, bread crumb, and cornmeal mixture. The result is crisp and hot but tempered by the sweetness of the basil with a creamy oyster prize within.

24	large basil leaves		¼	cup stone-ground cornmeal
24	oysters, shucked and drained		½	cup all-purpose flour
1	egg			Salt and black pepper to taste
½	cup Dijon mustard			Corn oil for frying
½	teaspoon Tabasco or more if you like it hot			Lemon wedges for serving
¼	cup fine dried bread crumbs			

Freeze the basil leaves for a few minutes to make them pliable, then wrap 1 leaf around each oyster.

In a small bowl, lightly beat the egg with a whisk; add the mustard and Tabasco and whisk to combine. In another bowl, combine the bread crumbs, cornmeal, flour, salt, and pepper.

Heat about 1½ inches corn oil in a cast-iron skillet until very hot. Dip each wrapped oyster first in the egg mixture, then in the flour mixture and gently lower into the hot oil. Fry for 4 to 5 minutes, until golden, turning once.

Lift out with a slotted spoon to paper towels to drain. Serve at once with lemon wedges to be squeezed at the table.

BROILED OYSTERS WITH BACON, TOMATO, AND VODKA

MAKES 4 APPETIZER SERVINGS

A scattering of tiny nuggets of crisp bacon tops a peppery tomato sauce spiked with the elusive kick of vodka.

12	oysters, scrubbed, shucked, and returned to the half shell (see page 321)
	Rock, coarse, or kosher salt
1	large tomato, skinned, seeded, finely diced, and drained in a strainer
2	tablespoons tomato paste

2 tablespoons vodka
1 teaspoon white wine Worcestershire sauce
⅛ teaspoon hot pepper flakes
Pinch of table salt
1 slice bacon, finely minced

Place the oysters in their half shells in one layer on a bed of salt that has been poured into a baking pan. Preheat the broiler.

In a small bowl, combine the tomato, tomato paste, vodka, Worcestershire, hot pepper flakes, and salt. The sauce should not be too watery. If it is, add additional tomato paste. Spoon equal amounts of the sauce over the oysters and scatter the minced bacon on top.

Broil just long enough for the bacon to become crisp and golden. Watch carefully so that the oysters don't overcook. Serve hot.

BAKED OYSTERS ROCKEFELLER WITH SPINACH AND FENNEL

Oysters Rockefeller were so named by Jules Alciatore of Antoine's Restaurant in New Orleans in the 1800s because of the dish's richness. There's a half pound of butter plus a quarter pound of bacon in the original recipe. Our pared-down, lower-fat version might be called Oysters Rockefeller, Nineties-Style!

4	cups coarse kosher salt or rock salt
24	large oysters, scrubbed (see page 319)
2	slices bacon
4	tablespoons butter
2	ounces shallots, finely minced (about ⅓ cup)
1	medium clove garlic, finely minced (about 1 teaspoon)
1	large scallion, finely minced (about ¼ cup)
½	small fennel bulb with feathery tops, finely chopped (about ⅛ cup)

2	cups finely shredded trimmed spinach (½ to ¾ pound)
¼	cup finely minced parsley
3	tablespoons coarse dried bread crumbs
2	tablespoons Pernod or Ricard
⅛	teaspoon cayenne pepper or more to taste
1	tablespoon Parmesan cheese
	Salt to taste

Using a lasagna or jelly-roll pan or individual ovenproof serving plates, cover the bottom with the coarse salt to steady the oyster shells. Shuck the oysters or have them done at the fishmonger, keeping only the bottom concave shells and any oyster broth. Tuck the oysters in the bed of salt, cover with dampened paper towels, and refrigerate while preparing the rest of the recipe.

In a medium skillet, fry the bacon, drain on paper towels, crumble, and set aside. Pour off almost all the bacon fat, leaving only a thin film on the bottom of the skillet. Melt the butter in the same skillet over medium-low heat. Add the shallots and sauté for 2 minutes, stirring. Add the garlic, scallion, and fennel and continue to cook, stirring, for 2 to 3 minutes more. Stir in the spinach and parsley and cook, stirring, until the spinach is wilted. Remove from the heat, transfer to a food processor, and chop coarsely. Scrape the mixture into a bowl and add the bread crumbs, Pernod, cayenne, Parmesan, reserved bacon, and salt to taste.

When ready to serve, preheat the oven to 450°. Spread about 1 tablespoon of the spinach mixture over each oyster, covering the oyster completely. Bake for 6 to 8 minutes, only until hot and bubbly. Serve at once.

SCALLOPS

Scallop

There was a time when the tastiest bay scallops came from areas right off our island in the bays of Long Island—the Great South Bay, Peconic Bay, and Gardiner's Bay. During the late fall, we joined the professional scallop fishermen by rigging our little boat with a cleaning board and hauling a much-too-heavy dredge along the sandy bottom. As each dripping load was taken aboard our tiny craft *Piccolo Mondo* (Small World), we would separate the scallops, still clacking like castanets, quickly shuck them, and drop the fresh, shining jewels into a small bucket for a well-deserved dinner for that evening. But then, alas, we became the victims of yet another natural disaster of the sea: the brown tide algae that suffocated the maturing scallops right in their beds. And the "true" bay scallop of Long Island is no more.

Although they have been replaced by scallops from Nantucket and the Chesapeake Bay as well as the cultivated catch from New England and Canada, we still miss the late fall search. To make matters worse, too often the calico scallops dredged off the coast of Florida, although they have an acceptable taste, are mislabeled as bay scallops. To the true believer, there will only be one bay scallop and, temporarily, it is gone. We still have hopes that it will return.

In spite of the fact that scallops have the most exquisite shells of the mollusk family, they are shucked at sea, and thus we probably never see them in the market places here in North America, although occasionally we do find some washed up on the shores of our local beaches. Scallops are very active swimmers, moving freely through the water and over the ocean floor by snapping their shells together. The constant action results in the development of the adductor muscle (called the "eye"), and this sweet-flavored drum-shaped tidbit is the only part of the scallop that we eat.

The Europeans consider the entire scallop a delicacy, and since this mollusk is a hermaphrodite, what we discard is actually both roe and testes as well as the rest of the body. However, there is another pragmatic reason that the scallop is shucked at sea. Since it is very perishable, taking only the adductor muscle maintains the body moisture and the freshness of the catch for a longer period of time.

There are over 400 varieties of scallops throughout the world, and the fact that it is so plentiful has led to a history that includes the use of the shell as both a symbol and a practical tool. The Christian martyr Saint James, who was beheaded by Herod Agrippa (A.D. 44), wore the scallop shell as his symbol, and when the exquisite cathedral in the Spanish city of Santiago de Compostela was built, the decorations around the entire square were those of scallop shells. Even the hospital built by Queen Isabella and King Ferdinand (now a *parador*) carries the shell symbol above its doorways, and all pilgrims who made their way to that small city were give scallop shells as proof of their journey.

The French honored St. James with their *coquille St. Jacques*, scallops baked in their shell. Botticelli's famous Venus is perched on a scallop half shell, and even today it is a decorative motif for sculpture, furniture, and fabrics. On a more commercial level, need we point out that a well-known oil company uses the distinctive shape for its logo?

Although there are many varieties, we generally see only a few popular species in our country:

BAY SCALLOPS: Among the tiniest and certainly the sweetest of the scallop family, usually found only on the Atlantic Coast in the inshore saltwater bays and ponds, bay scallops are now of very limited supply because of the problems with the brown tide algae. Their meat varies in color from creamy white to pale pink and range from 50 to 100 per pound.

CALICO SCALLOPS: Found along the Carolina coastline down into Florida and the Gulf Coast, calico scallops have been the most popular substitute for the disappearing "true" bay scallops. They're not quite as flavorful as the bays, are whiter in color, slightly smaller, and run between 150 and 250 per pound.

SEA SCALLOPS: The most common variety, generally ranging up to 2 inches in length, and not as tender as the other two major varieties, sea scallops average about 30 to a pound.

Buying the Scallops

Again, it comes down to two things: your nose and your fishmonger! Scallops should be firm and smell fresh, with each one standing out like a shiny jewel. The color, as we've mentioned, should be cream or beige, possibly ranging to pink. If scallops are too white, it is possible that they've been soaked in water to increase their weight.

Allow about 6 ounces per person and get them home at once to be placed in the refrigerator. Use them the same day, if possible, although they'll still be fit to eat within a day or two later.

PINK SCALLOPS
~~/LB

Preparing the Scallops

Inspect the scallops first for any stray shell bits and pull off the tough connective tissue on one side of each scallop. Also, if the sea scallops vary in size, cut off a small slice crosswise to make them all the same size and thus allow for even cooking.

Dry them well on paper towels and then make sure that you cook them quickly. Scallops can overcook in a very few minutes, making them give up their moisture. They then shrivel up and toughen. Even undercooking them slightly is better than drying them out.

Scallops keep their shape quite well and can be skewered and grilled, sautéed, or baked in a shell. They also can be eaten raw (see the warnings earlier in this chapter) in salads or they make excellent seviche.

SAUTÉED BAY SCALLOPS WITH GINGER, RED PEPPER, AND CHIVES

MAKES 4 SERVINGS

Dinner that cooks in under 3 minutes! Prepare some rice first and mix with tiny green peas for a perfect accompaniment.

¼	cup Clarified Butter (see page 65)	2	tablespoons finely minced chives
½	large red pepper, finely diced (about ⅓ cup)	1	tablespoon lemon juice
2	teaspoons finely minced ginger	⅛	teaspoon ground cloves
1	pound bay scallops, picked over for bits of shell		Salt and pepper to taste

Heat the clarified butter in a large skillet over medium heat until very hot. Add the red pepper and sauté, stirring constantly, for 1 minute. Add the ginger and scallops and sauté, stirring, for about 1 minute, just long enough to heat through. Do not overcook or the scallops will give up their juices and become tough. Toss with the chives, lemon juice, cloves, salt, and pepper. Serve at once.

PAN-SEARED SEA SCALLOPS WITH MIXED HERB SAUCE

MAKES 4 SERVINGS

Sea scallops are quickly pan-seared just long enough to form a golden surface, then sit in a verdant herb sauce dotted with tomato.

2	tablespoons olive oil	1	teaspoon lemon juice
2	medium shallots, finely minced (about 1 tablespoon)	½	teaspoon fresh thyme leaves
1	small clove garlic, finely minced (about ½ teaspoon)	¼	cup finely shredded fresh basil leaves
1¼	cups Fish Stock (see page 402)	1	tablespoon finely minced fresh chives
¼	cup dry white wine	1	teaspoon minced fresh chervil
1	tablespoon white wine vinegar	1	teaspoon finely minced fresh parsley
1	medium tomato, skinned, seeded, and finely diced (about ¾ cup)	½	teaspoon finely minced fresh tarragon
3	tablespoons butter		Salt and pepper to taste
		28 to 30	small sea scallops (about 1 pound), picked over for bits of shell

Heat the oil in a nonstick skillet over medium heat. Add the shallots and garlic and sauté, stirring frequently, for about 2 minutes until soft. Add the fish stock, wine, and vinegar and simmer for 5 minutes. Add the tomato and continue to cook for 5 minutes more. Strain; reserve the solids and return to the skillet. Pour the liquid into a food processor and add the butter, lemon juice, half the herbs, the salt, and pepper. Process with a few strokes until the butter melts, then return the sauce to the skillet with the tomato mixture. Keep warm over very low heat.

Heat another large nonstick skillet until very hot and almost smoking. Add the scallops in one layer and sear them on both sides, 1 to 2 minutes on each side. The scallops should be brown on the top and the bottom, with the center just cooked through. Spoon the sauce among 4 serving plates and arrange the scallops in the center. Distribute the remaining herbs over the sauce only and serve.

COQUILLES ST. JACQUES WITH ENDIVE, RADICCHIO, AND MUSHROOMS

MAKES 6 TO 8 FIRST-COURSE SERVINGS

This dish owes its name to the scallop shell emblem of St. James (St. Jacques in French, Santiago in Spanish) and the medieval Christian pilgrimage to Santiago de Compostela in Galicia, Spain.

5	tablespoons butter		2	tablespoons all-purpose flour
2 to 3	large shallots, finely minced (about ⅓ cup)		1	egg yolk
3	ounces small white mushrooms, thinly sliced		½	cup heavy cream
			⅛	teaspoon cayenne pepper
1¼	cups dry white wine		½	teaspoon crushed dried tarragon
	Bouquet garni: 2 sprigs parsley, 1 bay leaf, and 1 sprig thyme tied together		1	teaspoon lemon juice
	Salt and pepper to taste		1	small endive, cut into fine julienne (about 1 cup)
1½	pounds bay scallops, or sea scallops quartered or halved depending upon size, picked over for bits of shell		3 to 4	small radicchio leaves, shredded
			3	tablespoons grated Gruyère cheese

In a medium nonstick saucepan, heat 1 tablespoon of the butter over medium-low heat. Add the shallots and sauté, stirring frequently, for 1 to 2 minutes. Stir in the mushrooms and sauté for 1 minute more. Add the wine, bouquet garni, salt, and pepper and bring to a boil. Lower the heat and simmer for 3 minutes. Add the scallops and poach for 30 seconds. Lift out and discard the bouquet garni, then strain, reserving the poaching liquid. Set the scallop mixture aside.

Measure the liquid. If there is more than 1 cup, return it to the saucepan and reduce it to that amount. In another nonstick saucepan, heat the remaining 4 tablespoons butter and whisk in the flour. Cook over low heat for 1 to 2 minutes, whisking constantly, then remove from the heat and slowly whisk in the reserved poaching liquid.

In a small bowl, mix the egg yolk, cream, cayenne, tarragon, and salt and pepper to taste. Return the saucepan to very low heat and, stirring constantly, slowly add the egg mixture. Cook, stirring, for about 2 minutes until the sauce is thickened; do not let the sauce boil. Stir in the lemon juice. If the sauce seems too thick, thin it a bit with milk. Pour off and reserve one-third of the sauce.

Stir the reserved scallop mixture into two-thirds of the sauce, then stir in the endive and radicchio. Butter or oil 6 to 8 large scallop shells or individual ovenproof gratin dishes. Divide the scallop mixture evenly among the shells and spoon the remaining sauce on the surface. Sprinkle the tops with cheese. The recipe can be prepared well ahead up to this point. Just cover the shells with plastic wrap and put them in the refrigerator until serving time.

When ready to serve, preheat the oven to 375°. Unwrap the shells and place them on a jelly-roll pan. Bake for 5 minutes, then heat the broiler and broil 4 to 5 inches from the heat for 2 to 3 minutes until the tops are brown and bubbly. Serve hot.

GRILLED JAPANESE SCALLOPS AND SALMON KEBOBS

MAKES 6 MAIN-COURSE OR 12 APPETIZER SERVINGS

Coral-colored salmon is wrapped around a creamy scallop, separated by spikes of scallion on a skewer, and quickly grilled. Cold soba (buckwheat noodles) can be prepared in advance to be served alongside.

¾ pound center-cut skinned salmon fillet, pin bones removed

36 small sea scallops (about 1 pound), picked over for bits of shell

4 scallions, cut into 2-inch pieces

3 tablespoons light soy sauce

2 tablespoons mild honey

1 tablespoon mirin (sweet rice wine)

1½ teaspoons finely minced ginger

⅛ teaspoon hot pepper flakes

Soak twelve 10-inch bamboo skewers in water for 30 minutes. Thinly slice the salmon so there are 36 strips 3 to 4 inches long and 1 inch wide. Wrap a strip of salmon around each scallop, then thread 3 wrapped scallops onto each skewer, alternating with pieces of scallion.

Combine the soy, honey, mirin, ginger, and hot pepper flakes. Place the skewers on a plate and spoon the soy mixture over them. Cover with plastic wrap and refrigerate for 40 minutes, turning once during that time.

When ready to cook, preheat the broiler or prepare a grill. Lift the skewers onto an oiled rack, reserving the marinade. Grill the skewers about 4 inches from heat, basting frequently with the marinade, for 2 to 4 minutes on each side. Serve at once.

MUSSELS

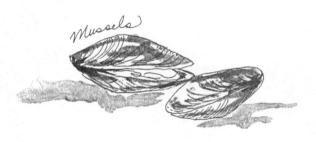

Mussels

Many years ago we found the solution to keeping our Fire Island visitors "happy as clams" by involving them totally in that night's dinner. For many years (until the powers that be in our little Fire Island village decided that our docks needed replacing and then proceeded to do the job using arsenic-treated lumber so that nothing can now grow on it safely) we used to wander down to the bay with our clam rakes and, in one or two large lifts of the basket, garner enough mussels to feed a small army. Growing wild that way, the mussels were covered with small barnacles and some seaweed, all of which had to be cleaned. And that, of course, is where the guests came in.

Given a few small stools, a nylon scrubbing pad, and a couple of buckets (along with as much wine as was needed to keep them happy), our guests would spend the late afternoon busily and happily cleaning, scrubbing, and pulling out the "beards" of the fresh blue mussels that *they* had harvested themselves. Needless to say, the dinner was always a delightful, joyful, memorable affair. Tired, glowing, full, and fulfilled, our guests would then stumble off to bed.

Although mussels have been much sought after and harvested in large quantities in Europe, they are only just beginning to catch on here and never seem to match the sales figures of both clams and oysters. We remember seeing farmed mussels in France being grown on poles driven into the ocean floor, while in Spain they cultivate them on ropes suspended from rafts. The mussels, clinging to their perches with their ropelike beards (or byssus), seemed to do rather well.

In North America, blue mussels, the most common variety, grow on pilings, bulkheads, piers, and even on some bridge anchorages, where most of us who harvest our own find them. The aquacultured mussels (like those in Europe) are grown on ropes suspended in the water. Blue mussels are harvested from the clear sea waters off the New England coast, while a relative also grows in the northern waters of the Pacific. However, the West Coast mussels have been quite severely limited by the "red tide," and there are a number of limitations on commercial harvesting, since the disease renders the shellfish toxic. Our Pacific Coast friends are warned, therefore, not to eat any shellfish from May into September.

Large commercial dealers on both coasts are strictly monitored as to safety standards. Market sizes range from 1 to 3 inches, and a good healthy blue mussel should be shiny ivory (male) to deep orange (female). There is no difference in flavor. If you should be lucky enough to gather your own from the wild, be sure to check with your local or county game or fish wardens about possible health hazards, restrictions, or permit requirements.

Recently other varieties of mussels have come into the fish markets and we find them quite good. New Zealand greenlips are larger than blue mussels, with a shell color that ranges from brown to green. We find that their flavor is more pronounced than our local blues. Prince Edward mussels are also at our fish markets. They're aquacultured in Canada and Nova Scotia, smaller than the New Zealand variety, and seem to have a more delicate flavor. Whichever variety you choose or you find at your market, the mussel body is completely edible.

Buying the Mussels

Mussels are sold alive and in their shells. Some will open slightly but still be quite active and alive. When buying them, tap them lightly or slide your fingers across both shells; if the mussel is alive, it will snap shut. Don't purchase any mussels that won't close. If a mussel feels too heavy, it may be filled with mud; too light and it may be dead.

Keeping and Cleaning the Mussels

The fishmonger will probably pack the mussels in a plastic bag, but take them out of the bag just as soon as you return home. They're best stored in the refrigerator lying flat on a dish or a platter on a bed of ice and covered with a damp towel, paper or cloth. Depending upon the price, mussels bought at the fishmonger are generally quite clean—and the more you pay for them, the cleaner they seem to get! However, they should still be scrubbed under running water with a firm brush or a nylon pad. Then beard them by grasping the wiry byssus "hairs" with thumb and forefinger and pulling down and out toward the thinner part of the closed shell. However, don't pull the beards off until just before cooking, since they die more quickly once they're bearded.

Try sorting the mussels according to size, since they'll cook more evenly that way, then fill a pail or the sink with cold running water, add the mussels, and gently swish them around in the water. *Lift* them out so the silt settles to the bottom and repeat the process two or more times until the water is clear.

Use a dull knife to scrape off any barnacles and then a nylon pad to scrub the mussels thoroughly under cold running water. The same rules hold true here as they do with your store-bought purchases. If a mussel stays open after sliding your fingers across the shell or if it feels light and empty inside, discard it.

Cooking the Mussels

We have given several recipes for mussels in the pages that follow, but the general rule is that the very best way to prepare mussels is to steam them open. After steaming, any mussels that do not open should be discarded. In addition, they take much less time to cook than clams, so if you are planning to combine them in a recipe, steam the clams first, then add the mussels so that the latter are not overcooked.

Mussels can be roasted, fried, broiled, or stuffed, but the warnings about eating them raw hold here too. You'll also find mussels dried, smoked, pickled, canned, and frozen.

Don't chop mussels or put them in a blender. They'll turn to mush. And keep cooked mussels covered in their own broth so they don't dry out or shrivel up.

A MUSSEL "SHELL GAME"

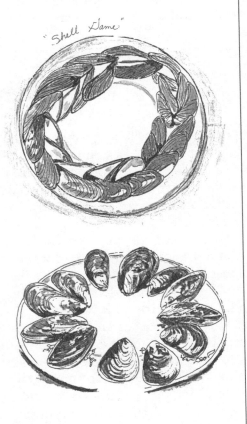

Until we began to work extensively in Belgium, we used to devour our mussels and pile the shells high helter-skelter in a nearby dish. If we were lucky, the dish was emptied from time to time in order to make room for still more shells.

One day, sitting in Ostend on the north shore of Belgium and absolutely going insane over the best *moules marinière* we'd ever tasted, we watched an elderly gentleman at the next table as he, too, enjoyed the same dish. However, when he finished eating each mussel, instead of haphazardly tossing the shell into a dish, he neatly put it on the edge of his plate, then took the next one and nested it inside the first. Within ten or fifteen minutes, he had neatly circled the platter in a wreath of nested shells. We have discarded mussel shells in just that way ever since!

MOULES VINAIGRETTE EN COQUILLES (MUSSELS IN THEIR SHELLS WITH VINAIGRETTE SAUCE)

MAKES 4 TO 6 FIRST-COURSE SERVINGS

Tiny capers and bits of hard-cooked egg are part of this very French vinaigrette spooned over warm, steamed mussels—a bistro favorite in France.

1 tablespoon Dijon mustard

2 tablespoons red wine vinegar
Salt and pepper to taste

6 tablespoons light olive or canola oil

1 small onion, finely minced (about 3 tablespoons)

1 large shallot, finely chopped (about 1 tablespoon)

2 teaspoons finely minced parsley

1 hard-cooked egg, peeled and finely chopped

1 teaspoon nonpareil capers, rinsed and drained

3 pounds (2 quarts) mussels, scrubbed and bearded (see page 335)

In a small bowl, whisk together the mustard, vinegar, salt, and pepper. Gradually whisk in the oil, then stir in the onion, shallot, parsley, egg, and capers. Set it aside.

In a steamer with 2 inches water, steam the mussels over high heat until they open, 3 to 5 minutes. Discard any that do not open. Transfer the mussels with a slotted spoon to a bowl to cool. When the mussels are cool enough to handle, remove and discard the top shell, leaving the mussels on their bottom shells and loosening them a bit for easier eating. Arrange the mussels on a serving platter and spoon the sauce over them. Serve warm or at room temperature.

ARMENIAN STUFFED MUSSELS

Glistening black poached mussels are filled with a lemony rice mixture, simmered in the poaching liquid, and cooked along with onions, sweet spices, currants, pine nuts, and fresh herbs. A refreshing and delightful first course.

1	cup dry white wine	¼	teaspoon cinnamon
1	cup water	⅛	teaspoon ground cumin
3	pounds (about 2 quarts) large mussels, scrubbed and bearded (see page 335)		Salt and pepper to taste
		⅓	cup lightly toasted pine nuts
⅓	cup olive oil	2	tablespoons finely minced parsley
2	large onions, finely chopped (about 2 to 2½ cups)	2	tablespoons finely minced fresh dill
		2	tablespoons lemon juice
1	cup long-grain white rice		Lemon wedges and dill sprigs for garnish
⅓	cup currants		
¼	teaspoon ground allspice		

In a wide, shallow pan with a tight-fitting lid, bring the wine and water to a boil over high heat. Add the mussels, cover the pot tightly, and steam for 3 to 5 minutes until the mussels open, sliding the pot back and forth a few times over the burner. Lift the mussels out with a slotted spoon to cool, discarding any that do not open. Strain the broth through a paper coffee filter and reserve. Let the mussels cool while preparing the filling.

In a large skillet, heat the olive oil over medium-high heat. Add the onions and sauté, stirring occasionally, for 4 to 5 minutes until wilted. Add the rice and stir until the rice is coated with the oil. Stir in the currants, allspice, cinnamon, cumin, salt, and pepper, then add 2½ cups of the reserved mussel broth. Bring to a boil, then cover the pan and lower the heat. Simmer for 17 to 18 minutes. Turn off the heat and let the rice mixture stand for 5 minutes. Stir in the pine nuts, parsley, dill, and lemon juice and let the rice cool completely.

When the rice stuffing is cool, taste and adjust the seasoning. Stuff between 1 teaspoon and 1 tablespoon of the rice mixture into each mussel, depending upon size. Arrange on a large serving platter and garnish with lemon wedges and dill sprigs. (Any leftover rice mixture can be used to stuff a fish.)

MUSSEL AND POTATO SALAD WITH PARSLEY AND CAPERS

MAKES 8 TO 10 FIRST-COURSE SERVINGS

Moules Françillon is a French mussel and potato salad which calls for Champagne and black truffles—two prohibitively priced ingredients. Here is our version—without the costly additions, but just as good.

¼	cup dry white wine	1	rib celery, finely diced (about ½ cup)
3	tablespoons white wine vinegar	2 to 3	small Kirby cucumbers, diced (about 1 cup)
1	bay leaf		
8	whole black peppercorns	1	tablespoon Dijon mustard
3	pounds mussels, scrubbed and bearded (see page 335)	1	teaspoon anchovy paste
			Pepper to taste
2	pounds small new red potatoes	½ to 1	cup mayonnaise
	Salt to taste	¼	cup finely minced parsley
3	medium scallions, white parts with 2 inches green, thinly sliced (about ⅔ cup)	2	tablespoons capers, rinsed and drained

In a large shallow skillet, bring the wine, 1 tablespoon of the vinegar, the bay leaf, and peppercorns to a boil over high heat. Add the mussels and cover tightly. Cook for 4 to 5 minutes until the mussels open, sliding the pan back and forth occasionally. Turn off the heat, uncover, and cool the mussels in their liquid. Discard any that do not open.

In a 3-quart saucepan, add the potatoes with water to cover and salt to taste. Bring to a boil, then reduce the heat and simmer until tender, 15 to 20 minutes. Drain and let cool. When they are cool enough to handle, cut the potatoes into ¾-inch pieces. (If the potatoes are very small, cut them in half only.) Place them in a large bowl.

Remove the mussels from their shells, reserving several empty double shells for garnish. Strain ¼ cup of the mussel liquid through a paper coffee filter and reserve. Add the shucked mussels to the potatoes in the bowl (there should be between 1½ and 2 cups mussel meat), then add the scallions, celery, and cucumbers to the bowl. Do not stir.

To a small bowl, add the remaining 2 tablespoons vinegar, the mustard, anchovy paste, salt, and pepper to taste. Add ½ cup of the mayonnaise or more if needed to make a thickish creamy sauce. Thin, if necessary, with some of the reserved mussel liquid for the proper consistency. Pour the sauce over the salad and fold gently to blend, sprinkling with parsley and capers as you combine the ingredients. Taste and adjust the seasoning. Spoon the salad onto a serving platter. Garnish with the reserved empty shells nested one inside the other.

MUSSELS STEAMED IN ORANGE JUICE WITH BASIL

MAKES 6 FIRST-COURSE SERVINGS

A colorful first course with a dipping sauce that's made from the mussels' own cooking broth.

1 large navel orange

2 tablespoons finely minced fresh basil plus a few leaves for garnish

2 tablespoons olive oil

⅓ cup water

1 large shallot, finely minced (about 1 table-spoon)

Salt and black pepper to taste

18 large mussels, such as New Zealand greenlip, scrubbed and bearded (see page 335)

Grate the outer skin of the orange and reserve. Cut 1 thin slice from the center of the orange, peel the skin, and cut the flesh into tiny triangles to use as a garnish and set aside. Squeeze the juice from the remaining orange; there should be about ¼ cup.

In a large skillet, bring orange juice, half of the grated orange peel, the basil, oil, water, shallot, salt, and pepper to a boil. Add the mussels in one layer, cover, and steam over high heat for 3 to 5 minutes until the mussels open, sliding and shaking the pan occasionally over the burner. Lift out the mussels with a slotted spoon, discarding any that have not opened. Strain the broth through a coffee filter into a bowl and set aside.

Remove the top half of each mussel shell and discard. Loosen the mussel from the bottom half of the shell. Finely shred 1 or 2 of the basil leaves for garnish and distribute the shreds among the mussels, along with the remaining orange peel. Arrange on plates, allowing 3 per person. Garnish with a whole basil leaf and the tiny triangles of reserved orange. Serve with small cups of the strained broth as a dipping sauce.

GROUP F
The Bizarre Bazaar
Or, the Cinderellas of Tomorrow?

Blowfish

Frogs' Legs

Mahi-Mahi

Monkfish

More Misunderstood Mollusks
  Abalone
  Conch
  Gooseneck barnacles
  Periwinkles
  Whelk

Ocean Pout

Octopus

Opah

Sea Robin

Sea Urchin

Skate

Squid

Cuttlefish

Tilapia

Wolffish

We always have been amused at the peculiarly unfortunate American disposition having to do with the marketing and consumption of our foods. If it looks ugly, or if it has a head on it, or there are bones within, even if it has an ugly name, we reject it out of hand. We reject it, that is, until we grudgingly and tentatively taste it, smack our lips, and wonder, "Where has this been all our lives?"

The history of seafood is not only an example, but it may be the *prime* case in point. While Europeans and Asians have been partaking of delicacies from the sea for centuries, most of us Americans have been slow to accept that the world of fish and shellfish extends far beyond fluke and flounder, sole and lobster. Bit by bit, we have begun to adopt more of that vast variety that exists in our bountiful waters, as witness the explosion of Japanese sushi bars across the United States. And fish that we once considered second rate for totally illogical reasons (such as catfish and tilefish) are now quite common both at the fish market and on restaurant menus.

Although some of our island neighbors are beginning to accept whole fish rather than wincing and asking for fillets, we still find that some species are given the label of "trash" fish, while some are lovingly used by ethnic groups (such as squid) and disregarded by almost everyone else. One of our favorite stories to prove this point took place at a local Spanish restaurant in Manhattan to which we took one of our dear friends, usually a very conservative eater. We ordered the *pulpo,* deliciously served in the owner's special sauce, and our friend devoured it without stopping to breathe. Finally, he looked up, a heavenly grin on his face and asked, "What do you call this in English?" With a straight face we answered, "Octopus." His face fell and his eyes opened wide in horror, as he muttered, "Tell it to me again in Spanish, please!"

Certainly we can understand the aversion to fish that carry names such as lizardfish or brotula or morwong or toadfish. But this prejudice has carried through to seafood with very ordinary names (at least until quite recently) like ocean pout and monkfish, as well as skate and sea robin. The most wonderful thing, as we found out when we wrote our earlier fish book, is that today's pariah can very well be tomorrow's elegant and popular choice. As a result, the seafood we cover in this chapter may well be species that will be among the most requested in a very short time. For example, we've found that skate wings are beginning to appear more often, and it's a fish we love.

You may be sure of one thing, however. As some of these fish move into the category of "common," others will take their places in "The Bizarre Bazaar." And, as over-fishing takes its toll of tuna and the other species that are fast disappearing because of pollution, and as the prices rise accordingly for those varieties that we've become so used to, other "future fish" will take their place. Then, we'll just have to get used to names like kingklip (already coming to the marketplace), guitarfish, kahawai, and file-fish. If they have ugly heads, we'll just sell them as fillets. If the name is off-putting, the marketers will change it to something beautiful, just as blowfish are now sold as sea squab. And we'll all end up saying, "Where has this fish been all of my life?"

BLOWFISH

The fishmongers, ever sensitive to the likes and dislikes of the American marketplace, usually display blowfish as "sea squab," although they're also known by the name above as well as puffer fish, northern puffer, chicken of the sea, toadfish, and globefish. The one common peculiarity in the species, found throughout the world, is that they  inflate when they sense danger. Thus, we love to see reactions of the local fisherpeople, especially the children, as they hoist one onto the dock, only to see the little fish expand to three times its size. Unfortunately, the end result is that the disappointed Izaak Waltons throw them back into the water, unaware that they contain some of the most delicate morsels of any saltwater fish.

Only the meat along the spine is edible, and four or five thin triangular-shaped sections of meat per person can make one of the rarest and most memorable dinner feasts. Anyone fishing for blowfish should be aware that there is a strong toxin in every part of the blowfish except for the meat along the back. The skin, the roe, and the entire digestive system of the blowfish should *never* be eaten. Fishmongers usually sell them already skinned, with only the backs for sale. If, on the other hand, you should catch some on your Sunday fishing expedition, we've given instructions below on how to clean and prepare them.

The Japanese, as many of us already know, play a form of "seafood roulette" with a particularly toxic variety of blowfish, and stories about people dying from eating *fugu* abound. Prepared only by specially trained chefs who are licensed to prepare the dish and sold in small restaurants that display the special sign of *fugu,* it still occasionally claims a victim or two. Luckily, the North American consumer need not worry. Sea squab, especially when sold by your local fishmonger, is totally safe after preparation. Sautéed, braised, or grilled and ranging in size from 3 to 8 inches, we highly recommend it as a good example of one of the lesser-known species, tasty and unusual.

If You Catch Your Own

Use gloves when you prepare blowfish, since the fish has powerful teeth and a very prickly skin. Use a sharp knife and, if you don't have gloves, make sure the fish is held firmly with a towel or a heavy piece of cloth.

Grasp the blowfish firmly in your left hand and cut through the spine in back of the head and down past the front fins. Using the knife, insert the blade between the skin and flesh just enough so that you can grasp the skin between your thumb and forefinger (using the cloth for protection). Pull the skin back from the flesh, a movement similar to removing your glove. When the skin has been pulled back, hook the forefinger of one hand right under the fin bone and pull hard. The fleshy back, looking much like a chicken thigh, will be pulled loose from the rest of the body. *Discard the head and entrails.* Remember that nothing is edible but the back tail meat along the spine.

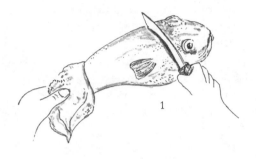

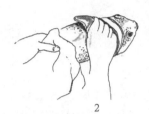

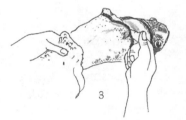

BLOWFISH TAILS GRILLED
WITH HERBS

Simply grilled or broiled with a shower of fresh herbs, this underutilized, delicious treat has a taste that is similar to chicken.

16 to 20 blowfish tails, allowing 4 to 5 per person, depending upon size (substitute: large shrimp)

½ cup corn oil

3 tablespoons white wine vinegar

2 teaspoons fresh thyme leaves or 1 teaspoon dried thyme

1 small sprig rosemary

2 medium shallots, finely minced (about 1 heaping tablespoon)

½ teaspoon freshly ground black pepper

Salt to taste

1 tablespoon finely minced chives

1 tablespoon finely minced parsley

Place the blowfish tails in one layer in a nonreactive pan. Mix the oil, vinegar, thyme, rosemary, shallots, pepper, and salt together, pour over the blowfish tails, and marinate at room temperature for 1 hour, turning the fish once.

Preheat the broiler or prepare a grill. Line a baking sheet with aluminum foil and place the tails on the foil, reserving the marinade. Broil or grill for 4 to 5 minutes on each side, basting with the reserved marinade (see Note). Mix the chives and parsley together and sprinkle over the tails just before serving.

NOTE: If you substitute shrimp for the blowfish tails, reduce the broiling time to a minute or two, just until the shrimp turn opaque.

FROGS' LEGS

With very rare exception and even in titles that carry the word "complete," fish cook-books omit what we think is a rare culinary delicacy. The legs of this jumping amphibian are the only edible parts, and when they're broiled or sautéed, they're probably the only seafood whose taste can be legitimately described as "a cross between chicken and lobster." They also make a perfect marriage of seafood and garlic.

Frogs' legs are harvested and marketed all across the country, and some species are imported. Choose them fresh if you can find them, since we think that they're more delicate than the frozen frogs' legs found in supermarket freezer cases and at some fish markets. However, if frozen is the only way you can get them, defrost the legs by soaking them in milk to improve the flavor, color, and texture.

Allow three pair of frogs' legs per person, and after they're cooked, don't be afraid to pick them up and eat them like chicken legs.

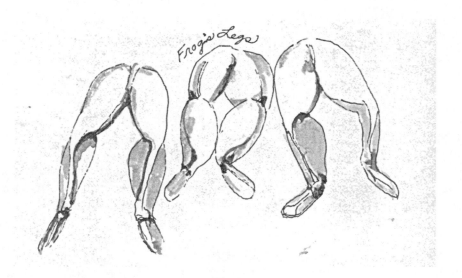

FROGS' LEGS CAFÉ BRITTANY

MAKES 4 SERVINGS

We first tasted frogs' legs at the tender age of 17 at the long-defunct New York bastion, Café Brittany. We vividly recall asking after our first bite, "Where have these been all our lives?"

12	pair medium frogs' legs, frozen or fresh (see Note)	4	tablespoons olive oil
2	cups milk	6	tablespoons butter
½	teaspoon Tabasco	4	large cloves garlic, finely minced (about 1½ tablespoons)
1	teaspoon coarse or kosher salt	2	tablespoons lemon juice (about ½ lemon)
¾	cup all-purpose flour	⅓	cup finely minced parsley
½	teaspoon freshly ground black pepper		Salt and pepper to taste

Place the frozen frogs' legs in the milk, Tabasco, and salt and let them thaw at room temperature. If they're not frozen, soak them in the milk/Tabasco mixture in the refrigerator for a few hours before cooking.

About 10 to 15 minutes before serving, combine the flour and pepper on a piece of aluminum foil. Lift the frogs' legs from the milk and turn them in the flour mixture to coat evenly.

In a large skillet, heat the oil over medium-high heat until very hot. Add the frogs' legs a few at a time and sauté for 3 to 4 minutes on each side, turning so they brown quickly. Drain on paper towels and keep them warm in a low oven until all are done.

While the frogs' legs are sautéing, melt the butter in a small skillet over medium-low heat. Add the garlic and sauté, stirring constantly, only until the garlic begins to turn golden, then stir in the lemon juice, half the parsley, and salt and pepper to taste. Pour over the frogs' legs when they are ready and sprinkle with the remaining parsley.

NOTE: Although not a true substitute for the delicate frogs' legs, monkfish can be cooked in the same manner.

MAHI-MAHI

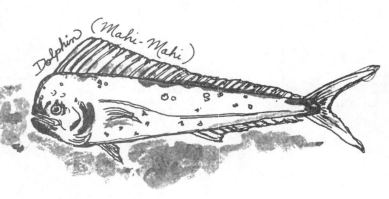

Dolphin (Mahi-Mahi)

Another rising star on the menus of seafood restaurants, but only after the public became fully aware that this dolphinfish was no relation to the mammal that has been in danger of eradication by being trapped accidentally in the nets of tuna fishing fleets, nor akin to the dolphins of myth, song, and story or even William Shakespeare, who "heard a mermaid on a dolphin's back."

Mahi-mahi (also known as dolphinfish and dorado) is one of the most beautiful fish in the sea. However, only sports fisherpeople can admire its bright, yellowish green beauty and its strong, sloping, squarish head, for its color quickly fades to a silvery gray after it's been out of the water a while. Sports fisherpeople also love it because it's one of the toughest of fighters, with a dazzling display of acrobatics when it's hooked. The Hawaiian translation of its name, incidentally, is "strong strong," a title it obviously richly deserves.

Mahi-mahi is found in warm waters around the world and ranges in size from 5 to 40 pounds, with the average market weight at about 15 pounds. The flesh is firm, sweet, and flaky, with a low fat content. It's usually available as fillets with the rather tough skin still on. About 6 to 8 ounces per person is the proper portion for serving. It can be broiled, grilled, stewed, baked, or braised, and its dark flesh will lighten as it cooks.

ORIENTAL MAHI-MAHI SALAD WITH NAPA AND RED CABBAGE

Delicate pale-green Napa cabbage and crisp red cabbage are tossed with mild flavored mahi-mahi in a gingered herb sauce in which the fish is first marinated.

1	large clove garlic, peeled		Salt to taste
1	1½-inch piece ginger, peeled	1¼	pounds mahi-mahi fillets, cut into 1 inch cubes (substitute: tuna)
⅓	cup fresh cilantro leaves		
¼	cup fresh mint leaves plus a sprig for garnish	½	pound red cabbage, thinly sliced
		1¼	pounds Napa cabbage, cored and cut into fine chiffonade
½	cup canola oil		
3	tablespoons orange juice	2	carrots, cut into thin julienne or shredded (about 1½ cups)
5	tablespoons rice vinegar		
1	teaspoon Oriental sesame oil	6	scallion greens, thinly sliced on a diagonal (about 1⅛ cups)
1	teaspoon sugar		
¼	teaspoon hot pepper flakes	4	tablespoons corn oil

In a food processor, finely chop the garlic and ginger until fine. Add the cilantro and mint and process until coarsely chopped. Add the canola oil, orange juice, vinegar, sesame oil, sugar, hot pepper flakes, and salt and process until blended. Scrape out with a rubber spatula into a large nonreactive bowl. Add the mahi-mahi to the marinade, stir, cover, and refrigerate for 40 to 60 minutes.

Lift the fish out of the marinade with a slotted spoon. Stir the red and Napa cabbages, carrots, and scallions into the marinade and set aside.

In a large nonstick skillet, heat 2 tablespoons of the corn oil over medium-high heat. Add half the fish at a time and cook and stir for 1 minute just to sear the fish. Add more oil if necessary for the second batch. Transfer the fish and any juices that accumulate to the cabbage mixture. Stir gently to combine. Cover with plastic wrap and chill in the refrigerator for 2 to 3 hours before serving. When ready to serve, taste and adjust the seasoning and garnish with a sprig of mint.

GRILLED SPICED MAHI-MAHI WITH MANGO JALAPEÑO BUTTER

A Creole-style spice rub flavors the grilled fish, which is served with a spicy jalapeño butter tamed with soothing sweet mango and a touch of honey and vinegar.

1½ to 2   pounds mahi-mahi fillets, about 1 inch thick, cut into 4 portions (substitute: tuna)

1   tablespoon finely minced onion

1   small clove garlic, minced (about ½ teaspoon)

2   teaspoons freshly ground black pepper

½   teaspoon cayenne pepper

¾   teaspoon paprika

1   teaspoon dried oregano

1   teaspoon dried thyme

1   tablespoon finely minced fresh basil

½   teaspoon salt

MANGO AND JALAPEÑO BUTTER:

1   teaspoon olive oil

½   small jalapeño chile, seeded and finely minced

½   medium red pepper, seeded and finely diced (about ⅔ cup)

1   medium shallot, finely minced (about 2 teaspoons)

3   tablespoons red wine vinegar

½   teaspoon mild honey

⅛   teaspoon cayenne pepper

1   ripe large mango, peeled and pitted

6   tablespoons butter, softened

Place the fillets in a flat dish. To a food processor or spice grinder, add the onion, garlic, pepper, cayenne, paprika, oregano, thyme, basil, and salt and blend well. Rub about 1½ tablespoons of this mixture over both sides of each fillet and marinate for 30 minutes.

Prepare a grill and make the mango and jalapeño butter.

In a small skillet, heat the oil over medium-low heat. Add the jalapeño, red pepper, and shallot, and sauté, stirring constantly, for 1 to 2 minutes until soft. Stir in the vinegar, honey, and cayenne and simmer until the liquid evaporates, about 2 minutes. Let cool. To a food processor, add the mango, butter, and the cooled mixture and process until smooth. Set aside.

When the grill is ready, oil the grill rack and grill the fillets for 3 to 4 minutes on each side. Spoon some of the mango butter on top of the fish and serve at once.

NOTE: You can broil the mahi-mahi in this recipe, 4 to 5 inches from the heat, instead of grilling it.

MONKFISH

This is probably the true "Cinderella fish," once considered a trash fish here in the United States and even questioned by the authors in a previous book: "How Can Anything That Ugly Taste That Good?" However, the French have consumed it for years as *lotte*. The Italians also have utilized it for centuries, and travelers have eagerly eaten it as *coda di rospo,* while in Spain it's called *rape*. Only here has it been so late in arriving, almost always called by its market name of monkfish, although it carries many, many others, such as goosefish, anglerfish, frogfish, and bellyfish.

The monkfish has a large, ugly, bizarre head with a huge mouth which reflects its insatiable appetite. Lying on the bottom of the sea, it waves its thin antenna as a lure, capturing baitfish, crustaceans, water birds, and anything else that wanders into its path, including some nipping at the toes of ocean waders, according to reports. But it is just this diet that gives the monkfish its texture and taste; it's often referred to as "poor man's lobster."

Much like the blowfish, only a part of the monkfish is eaten—the firm, sweet, lean, and slightly chewy tail; the rest of the fish is discarded at sea. Although the fish can reach weights of up to 50 pounds, only the two boneless tail fillets between 2 and 10 pounds each are brought in to the market.

After you purchase the fillets, they must be skinned of their purplish outer membrane. Use a sharp knife and slip the blade under the membrane, pulling it off slowly to leave only the pearl-white flesh. Also cut away and discard the outer fiber that is on the side nearest the backbone. Allow about 8 to 10 ounces per person, since the fish will shrink and lose some of its moisture after cooking. Monkfish holds its shape very well, and it can be steamed, stir-fried, oven roasted, poached, cut into kebobs, added to soups and stews, and even eaten as ersatz lobster dipped in a buttery sauce. Another advantage of monkfish is that it can be found year round.

GRILLED MONKFISH AND *SWEET* PEPPER BROCHETTES WITH ORANGE-CILANTRO BUTTER SAUCE

MAKES 6 SERVINGS

A buttery citrus sauce acts as a basting liquid to keep the lean monkfish moist while grilling. The basting liquid then becomes a colorful, flavorful sauce with the addition of tiny specks of tomato and cilantro.

3 pounds monkfish fillets, outer membrane removed, cut into 2-inch pieces (substitute: large shrimp)

1 large yellow pepper (about ½ pound), cut into 1½-inch squares

1 large red pepper (about ½ pound), cut into 1½-inch squares

2 tablespoons olive oil

Coarse salt and pepper to taste

2 cups orange juice

2 medium scallions, sliced diagonally ¼ inch thick (about ½ cup)

5 tablespoons cold butter, cut into 5 pieces

¼ teaspoon ground cumin

⅛ teaspoon hot pepper flakes

2 large plum tomatoes, skinned and finely diced (about ¾ cup)

2 tablespoons coarsely chopped cilantro

Soak 24 bamboo skewers, 8 to 10 inches long, in water for 30 minutes or longer if convenient. Prepare a grill 45 minutes before you are ready to cook or preheat the broiler 15 minutes before cooking.

Thread 3 pieces of fish, alternating with 2 slices of yellow pepper and 2 of red pepper, on parallel skewers about ¾ inch apart so the brochettes will be easier to turn and the food will stay in place while cooking. Brush with olive oil and season with salt and pepper. Set aside.

In a 2-quart nonreactive saucepan, cook the orange juice and scallions over medium heat until the liquid is reduced to half the amount, about 25 minutes. Lower the heat to very low and whisk in the butter one tablespoon at a time only until melted. Stir in the cumin, hot pepper flakes, and additional salt if you wish. Keep warm over very low heat.

When the grill or broiler is ready, grill the brochettes 4 inches from the heat, turning occasionally and basting with some of the orange butter sauce, for 10 to 12 minutes until the fish is opaque and slightly brown on the outside. Stir the tomatoes and cilantro into the remaining sauce. Place the brochettes on serving plates and spoon some of the sauce over each brochette.

MEDALLIONS OF MONKFISH WITH THYME AND LENTILS

Firm medallions of monkfish are quickly sautéed and then fanned out around a bed of lentils that have been cooked with leeks and tomatoes.

LENTILS:

2 cups green lentils, picked over and rinsed

4 cups water

1 large onion, peeled, stuck with 2 whole cloves

1 bay leaf

½ teaspoon dried thyme

Salt to taste

2 tablespoons olive oil

3 thin leeks, white part and 1 inch green, chopped (about 1¼ cups)

1 large clove garlic, finely minced (about 1 teaspoon)

1 large tomato (about ½ pound), skinned and cubed (about 1 cup)

Pepper to taste

MONKFISH:

2½ to 3 pounds monkfish fillets, outer membrane removed, sliced diagonally ¾ inch thick (substitute: grouper or mahi-mahi)

2 teaspoons dried thyme

4 tablespoons olive oil

4 tablespoons butter

1 clove garlic, thinly sliced

½ cup Fish Stock (see page 402)

2 tablespoons lemon juice

¼ cup finely minced parsley

PREPARE THE LENTILS FIRST: In a 3-quart saucepan, combine the lentils and water and bring to a boil. Lower the heat and add the onion, bay leaf, and thyme. Simmer, covered, for 15 to 20 minutes until the lentils are tender but maintain their shape. Add salt to taste and set aside.

While the lentils are cooking, heat the oil in a medium skillet over medium heat. Add the leeks and garlic and sauté, stirring frequently, until soft but not brown. Stir in the tomato, pepper, and additional salt if you wish; simmer over low heat for 5 minutes.

When the lentils are tender, lift out the onion and bay leaf and discard them. Drain the lentils in a strainer and stir them into the tomato mixture. Set aside while preparing the fish. The lentils can be prepared the day before and rewarmed over very low heat when ready to serve.

FOR THE MONKFISH: Season the fish with the thyme and salt and pepper to taste. In a large skillet, heat the olive oil and 2 tablespoons of the butter over medium-high heat. Add the garlic and sauté for 1 to 2 minutes. Remove the garlic with a slotted spoon, add the slices of fish in batches to avoid overcrowding, and sauté, turning once, over medium-high heat for 4 to 5 minutes total until the fish is lightly brown. Transfer the fish to a plate, cover with aluminum foil to keep warm, and sauté the remaining fish.

Wipe out the skillet with paper towels. Add the fish stock and lemon juice and bring slowly to a simmer. Whisk in the remaining 2 tablespoons butter, 1 tablespoon at a time. Spoon the lentils off center on each serving plate and arrange a portion of fish around the lentils. Trickle a bit of sauce over the fish, then sprinkle the parsley over the fish and lentils.

MONKFISH, DILL, AND CUCUMBER MOUSSE TIMBALES

Delicately flavored with dill and cucumber, these airy timbales make an easy and elegant first course.

2   medium Kirby cucumbers, peeled and seeded, plus 1 cucumber sliced paper thin for garnish

1   pound monkfish fillet, outer membrane removed, cut into small pieces (substitute: catfish)

2   eggs
    Butter for the molds

¾   cup Crème Fraîche (see page 66), chilled

⅛   teaspoon cayenne pepper

1   tablespoon finely minced fresh dill, plus 6 small sprigs for garnish

⅛   teaspoon ground cumin

¼   teaspoon salt or to taste

¼   teaspoon white pepper

Finely chop the 2 cucumbers in a food processor. Transfer to a strainer and press with the back of a spoon to drain them very well. Return them to the food processor along with the fish and eggs and process to a smooth purée. Scrape the purée into a small bowl, cover, and chill for 1 hour.

Preheat the oven to 425°. Butter 6 timbale molds or custard cups. Boil a kettle of water. Add the crème fraîche, cayenne, dill, cumin, salt, and pepper to the purée and combine by folding it lightly into the fish mixture with a rubber spatula. Place the molds in a shallow baking pan and distribute the mousse equally among the 6 buttered cups. Pour boiling water into the baking pan so that it reaches two-thirds of the way up the sides of the molds.

Bake for 15 minutes, then lift the molds from their water bath and put them on a wire rack to cool for 5 minutes. Slip a thin knife around the inside of each mold, top with a plate, and invert the timbale onto the plate. Decorate each timbale with a ring of overlapping paper-thin cucumber slices and a tiny sprig of dill on top. Serve warm or at room temperature. If any liquid accumulates after unmolding, blot the excess with paper towels.

MORE MISUNDERSTOOD MOLLUSKS: ABALONE, CONCH, GOOSENECK BARNACLES, PERIWINKLES, AND WHELK

We have discussed the more popular mollusks in the section of the book beginning on page 305, but there are some members of the family that, unfortunately, are not quite as accepted by seafood eaters. Whereas clams and scallops are on the list of the top ten favorite American seafoods, the orphans listed above have gone mostly unloved and untried or at best underutilized. In some cases, as with abalone, its popularity might be greater if the supply had not been almost devastated by overfishing, making it one of the more expensive mollusks. So, here are five that we think are special if slightly unusual.

Abalone

Found in the Pacific from the central coastline of California up to British Columbia and Alaska, the abalone is an unusual single-shelled mollusk with a very muscular, tough "foot" that allows it to cling to rocks while it feeds on a diet of seaweed. In addition to overfishing, there has been a severe dwindling of their seaweed supply, adding to their diminishing harvest as well as to their increasing price. However, they now are being farm raised in both Hawaii and California and possibly will soon become more available at our markets.

Their shells are beautiful, reflecting a rainbow of iridescent colors, and they've been used universally for the manufacture of mother-of-pearl trinkets and decorations. The flesh of abalone closely resembles an ivory colored human ear and is very firm, almost tough, unless it's tenderized before cooking by using a wooden mallet. However, the cooking time itself must be quite short or abalone will toughen.

When buying abalone live (certainly preferred over the frozen variety), touch the flesh lightly with a toothpick or your finger. If the "ear" wiggles, it's okay. To shuck them, just use a strong oyster knife to detach the flesh. Cut off any dark portions, slice the abalone about ⅛ inch thick, tenderize it with the mallet, and cook it gently by sautéing or steaming. A few seconds on each side will be quite sufficient.

Conch

We should begin by stating that conch (pronounced "conk") are not whelk, although often the two are confused. Conch are herbivorous, while whelk (see page 359) feed on any other mollusks that happen to get in their way. Conch are very popular in the South from North Carolina down to the Florida Keys and into the Caribbean; only a small crop eventually reaches northern markets for the lovers of this large, tasty, edible snail.

Many years ago, we first tasted the incredible conch chowder at a little, seedy, out-of-the-way restaurant on a highway in Florida. A well-kept secret by the locals, it was an experience for any seafood lover, and the chowder was served with large loaves of Bimini bread and a pitcher of beer.

The shell is spiral shaped with an iridescent inside pink or rose color. Down in the Bahamas and Jamaica, the fishermen remove the meat by pounding the shells together until they break, releasing the inside flesh. However, if you buy whole conch in their shells at the fishmonger's, an easier way is to drop them into boiling water for 3 to 5 minutes to relax the flesh, then, holding the shell with a potholder, use a knife or a clean screwdriver to pull the meat down and away from the shell and remove it. Cut away the "claw" and the soft, inedible portions, leaving a milky-white edible section that's encased in a tough outer layer. Peel the layer off with a knife, revealing the edible inner meat. Then slice and tenderize the conch meat with a wooden mallet or chop it in a food processor if you're going to make fritters.

Conch is, by nature, chewy in texture and is best used in chowders or fritters, or you can sauté or braise the meat. Bahamians and Jamaicans also use conch to make a tasty, chewy, and unusual seviche.

Gooseneck Barnacles

In spite of their unpretty name, they're incredibly popular in Spain and Portugal (as *percebes*) as well as in North Africa, but they have yet to achieve the popularity of the clam or mussel here in the United States. They're extraordinary creatures, found at the base of rugged sea cliffs where they cling to the ocean-swept rocks and live in large groups. They also can be found near piers, on boats, and wherever they can latch on. We have noticed an increase in their availability in our local markets, but they are still quite rare except for the harvest taken by people in the Pacific Northwest who go on their own "barnacle hunt." If you do decide to take them on your own, it's a good idea to check with your local authorities about the rules and regulations as well as checking that they're fit to eat in that particular area.

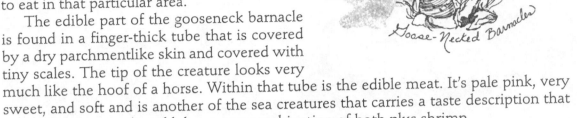

Goose-Necked Barnacles

The edible part of the gooseneck barnacle is found in a finger-thick tube that is covered by a dry parchmentlike skin and covered with tiny scales. The tip of the creature looks very much like the hoof of a horse. Within that tube is the edible meat. It's pale pink, very sweet, and soft and is another of the sea creatures that carries a taste description that ranges between crab and lobster or a combination of both plus shrimp.

To cook it, pinch off the outer skin and pry the hoof off with your fingers. Steam it or lightly poach it in its shell for a few minutes, allowing ½ to ¾ pound per person.

Periwinkles

These tiny—about 1 inch long—convoluted dark gray snail-like mollusks are found up and down the Atlantic coast as well as in the waters off northern Europe. They're called *willicks* in Ireland, *winkles* in England, and *bigorneau* in France and Belgium. Mel remembers his first taste of them while stationed near Brussels right after World War II. They were being sold fresh from a wooden, wheeled pushcart, steamed right in front of the passersby, and sold by the small packetful. After getting up his courage, he tried them by removing the small bodies with a pin, then popping them into his mouth. The experience was, to say the least, memorable, and it was many years later that both of us learned to love them as the Chinese prepare them, with a strong salted black bean sauce and eaten out of hand by prying them out with toothpicks. They have a nutty, smoky taste and can be steamed or cooked in garlic, hot pepper sauce, or black beans.

Periwinkle

Periwinkles are sold fresh and alive in the Chinese markets and that, of course, is the best way to buy them. When you get them home, soak them in salted water along with a bit of cornmeal to purge them of any grit. Then rinse them in cold water. Boil them in their shells for about 3 minutes—the water can contain hot pepper or cayenne or crab boil if you like—then immediately rinse them under cold water to stop them from cooking.

To eat the periwinkles, pull off the hard lid that sits at the opening of the shell (operculum), then remove the meat with a toothpick or lobster pick. Dip them in a sauce of melted butter and lemon or vinegar and pepper. They come about 60 to a pound. Allow about 6 to 8 ounces in the shell per person.

Whelk

Since a conch is not a whelk, a whelk is also not a conch. They are similar, but, as we've mentioned, the whelk feeds on other mollusks, while the conch is a vegetarian, so to speak.

As we remember many of our first tastes of unusual dishes, so do we remember whelk. We were working in Hong Kong in the early 1960s, and our local customs broker took us to our first "welcome" Chinese feast. Among the six or seven overwhelming dishes served that hot, sticky day was whelk, the conical shells lying in all their glory on a sterling silver tray that was covered with a whelk-shaped top. The mollusks had been blended with chicken livers and various spices, then stuffed back into their shells and steamed. We remember staggering into the summer streets afterward, stuffed to the brim with an enormous amount of food, and coming close to a dead faint when the hot, humid air hit us.

The whelk lives in a shell that can reach 6 inches or more, and the meat is a rich orange yellow with a chewy texture and a smoky flavor. In addition to being very popular with Asian communities, whelk is also familiar to those of us (if not all of us) who have eaten Italian *scungilli.*

Whelk is usually available in ethnic markets partially cooked, frozen, or fresh. Our local Chinese merchants open them for us in the same way as the fishmongers in Hong Kong—by smashing the front end with a brick and then crushing the shell to remove the meat in one piece. If you buy whelk in the shell, remove the body in the same way as the conch (page 357), then discard the tough skin and the intestines, leaving the meat. If you do buy it uncooked and in the shell, soak it in salted water for an hour or two, adding some cornmeal to purge it of dirt. Whelk also should be pounded with a mallet to tenderize it, and, like squid, it should not be overcooked; it requires either quick cooking or low heat slow cooking.

More Misunderstood Mollusks

ABALONE CHINESE-STYLE WITH ASPARAGUS AND BEAN CURD

MAKES 4 SERVINGS

At times, abalone is eaten raw as sushi or sashimi, and even when it's cooked, it requires only a few seconds of heat or it toughens. Stir-fry dishes are perfect for controlling the length of cooking time. This one offers a contrast of textures, with crisp asparagus, meltingly tender bean curd, and firm abalone.

12   ounces abalone (substitute: whelk or squid) (see Note)

2   tablespoons corn oil

1   medium clove garlic, finely minced (about 1 teaspoon)

1   teaspoon finely minced ginger

¼   teaspoon hot pepper flakes

½   pound thin asparagus, cut diagonally into 1½-inch pieces

2   tablespoons tamari or light soy

2   tablespoons rice wine

1   teaspoon sugar

1   teaspoon tomato paste

¼   pound firm bean curd (tofu), cut into ¾-inch cubes

2   tablespoons green scallion, diagonally sliced into ¼-inch pieces

Rinse and dry the abalone on paper towels. Slice ¼ inch thick with a very sharp knife, then place the pieces between 2 sheets of plastic wrap, and pound gently with a wooden mallet or meat pounder to tenderize until the slices are limp.

In a skillet or wok, heat the oil over medium-high heat. Add the garlic, ginger, and hot pepper flakes and stir-fry for 30 seconds, until fragrant. Add the abalone and stir-fry for 20 seconds only or they will toughen. Remove the abalone to a plate using a slotted spoon. Add the asparagus to the skillet and stir-fry for 1 minute. Add the tamari, rice wine, sugar, and tomato paste and bring to a boil, then lower the heat, add the bean curd, and simmer for 1 minute. Return the abalone to the pan and heat for no more than 10 seconds. Transfer to a serving dish and sprinkle with scallion. Serve at once.

NOTE: Abalone is a rare West Coast specialty, hard to come by at times in the Midwest and on the East Coast. However, we have seen an increasingly large supply in the East, since they are now being farmed on the West Coast.

FLORIDA CONCH SALAD WITH ROASTED RED PEPPERS AND ANCHOVIES

MAKES 4 TO 6 SERVINGS

When captured live off the Florida Keys or in the Caribbean, conch are sometimes cracked open with a hammer to allow easier access to the white flesh. These are the shells that we held up to our ears as kids to "hear" the sounds of the sea—much too beautiful to be carelessly broken.

1 pound conch meat, fresh or thawed frozen (substitute: squid; see page 375)

2 large red peppers, roasted, peeled, seeded, and cut into ½-inch strips

1 tablespoon large capers, rinsed and drained

6 flat anchovies, rinsed, drained, halved lengthwise and then crosswise

2 large cloves garlic, finely minced (about 1 tablespoon)

¼ cup lemon juice

2 tablespoons coarse-grain mustard

Salt and black pepper to taste

¼ cup canola oil

¼ cup light olive oil

3 tablespoons finely minced parsley

Frilled green lettuce leaves

With a sharp knife, peel away the tough outer skin of the conch and pull off the operculum (the thin hard disk covering at the opening of the shell) and discard, leaving only the interior white, firm flesh. Cut into paper-thin slices, place between 2 sheets of plastic wrap, and pound the slices with a wooden mallet or meat pounder until tenderized and somewhat velvety in texture. Cut the conch into needle-thin julienne and place the strips in a strainer.

Boil a small saucepan of water, submerge the conch and the strainer in the water, and blanch for 30 seconds. Lift out and place the blanched conch in a medium serving bowl. Add the peppers, capers, anchovies, and garlic and set aside.

In a small bowl, whisk the lemon juice, mustard, salt, and pepper together, then gradually whisk in both oils until combined. Pour over the conch mixture, add the parsley, and mix well. Cover with plastic wrap and chill in the refrigerator from 2 to 6 hours before serving. Taste and correct the seasoning; more lemon or pepper may be needed. Spoon the salad onto frilled lettuce leaves and serve at room temperature.

GOOSENECK BARNACLES WITH GARLIC SAUCE

MAKES 4 APPETIZER SERVINGS

In Spain, these extraordinary creatures, which look like the long neck of a goose ending in a hoof, are called percebes. *It was there that we gathered our courage to taste them, since we were at first put off by their bizarre appearance.*

GARLIC SAUCE:

- 8 garlic cloves, peeled
- 2 small slices white bread, crusts trimmed
- 2 tablespoons milk
- ½ cup mayonnaise
- ½ teaspoon each salt and black pepper
- ⅛ teaspoon cayenne pepper
- 1 tablespoon white wine vinegar
- 1 teaspoon lemon juice
- ¾ to 1 cup olive oil

BARNACLES:

- 3 quarts water
- 1½ tablespoons coarse salt
- 1 small onion
- 2 bay leaves
- ½ lemon
- 1 pound gooseneck barnacles, rinsed thoroughly (substitute: crab claws or shrimp)

Leaf lettuce

Lemon wedges for serving

FOR THE GARLIC SAUCE: Finely mince the garlic in a food processor. Add the bread and milk and process a few more seconds. Add the mayonnaise, salt, pepper, cayenne, vinegar, and lemon juice and process again for a few more seconds.

With the motor running, pour the olive oil in a steady stream through the feed tube and process until the mixture is thick and homogenized. You may need a bit more oil. Scrape it out into a bowl, cover, and set aside at room temperature. If it's made well in advance, chill in the refrigerator but bring it to room temperature before serving.

FOR THE BARNACLES: To a large nonreactive pot, add the water, salt, onion, and bay leaves. Squeeze the juice of the lemon into the water and drop in the lemon shell as well. Bring to a boil over high heat, add the barnacles, stir, and reduce the heat to medium. Cook for 3 to 4 minutes until the base of the barnacles turns a deep pink color. Drain and put the barnacles into a bowl, then cover with ice cubes to chill them rapidly.

When ready to serve, arrange equal portions of barnacles over lettuce leaves on serving plates; add the lemon wedges. Spoon the garlic sauce into small scallop shells or sake cups (or a similar small dish) and serve alongside as a dip.

PERIWINKLES WITH GARLIC, GINGER, AND FERMENTED BLACK BEAN SAUCE

Their smoky, nutty taste makes these tiny morsels worth digging out of their shells, even though they're messy to eat. The sauce in this recipe can also be used with lobster that has been cut into chunks with a cleaver and left in its shell.

2 pounds live periwinkles	1 tablespoon cornstarch
1 tablespoon cornmeal or oatmeal	3 tablespoons cold water
1 tablespoon Chinese fermented black beans	2 tablespoons corn oil
1 tablespoon finely minced ginger	1 teaspoon Oriental hot chile oil
1 tablespoon plus 1 teaspoon tamari or light soy	1 clove garlic, crushed
2 tablespoons sherry or rice wine	½ cup chicken stock
1 teaspoon sugar	2 scallions, green parts only, finely minced

Thoroughly rinse the periwinkles in several changes of cold water, then soak them for 1 hour in salted water mixed with 1 tablespoon cornmeal to purge any grit. Lift them out with a slotted spoon and rinse them again. Soak the black beans in cold water for 10 minutes, then rinse them to remove any excess salt.

In a small cup, combine the ginger, 1 tablespoon tamari, the sherry, and sugar. In another cup, blend the cornstarch, water, and the remaining 1 teaspoon tamari to a paste.

In a wok or skillet, heat the corn oil and hot chile oil over medium-high heat. Add the garlic and cook, stirring constantly, for 1 minute. Add the periwinkles and cook, stirring for 2 minutes. Add the ginger mixture and cook for 30 seconds. Stir in the black beans and chicken stock, cover the skillet, and cook for 3 minutes. Add the cornstarch paste to thicken the sauce and stir for a few seconds. Transfer to 4 serving bowls and sprinkle with the scallions. Serve with toothpicks or lobster picks, finger bowls with a wedge of lemon, lots of paper napkins, and hot rice for any remaining sauce. To eat, pick out and discard the hard disk-shaped cap (the operculum) of the periwinkle, then pick out the flesh.

WHELK (SCUNGILLI) WITH LINGUINE AND DIAVOLO SAUCE

MAKES 4 SERVINGS

Whelk is not only favored in Chinese cuisine, but it is also relished in the Italian communities in the United States, where it is known as scungilli. A peppery tomato-based sauce is lightly and quickly cooked with the scungilli and served over pasta, as in this very traditional recipe.

1 pound whelk meat, out of shell (*scungilli*), rinsed well (substitute: squid)	¼ cup dry red wine
	2 tablespoons tomato paste
¾ to 1 pound linguine, depending on appetite	1 teaspoon dried oregano
3 tablespoons olive oil	½ teaspoon dried rosemary
2 to 3 large cloves garlic, coarsely chopped (about 1 tablespoon)	½ teaspoon fennel seeds
	1 small bay leaf
1 small onion, finely chopped (about ⅔ cup)	¼ teaspoon hot pepper flakes
	¼ teaspoon sugar
1 14-ounce can Italian plum tomatoes, with liquid	Salt and pepper to taste
	¼ cup finely shredded fresh basil

With a sharp knife, lift off and discard the operculum of the whelk and cut off the tough outer skin and intestines. Slice the whelk paper thin, place the slices between 2 sheets of plastic wrap, and pound them with a meat pounder or a wooden mallet to tenderize. Set aside.

Boil a large pot of salted water and add the linguine. In a large skillet, heat the oil over medium heat. Add the garlic and the onion and sauté, stirring constantly, for 4 to 5 minutes until tender but not brown. Add the tomatoes, wine, tomato paste, oregano, rosemary, fennel seeds, bay leaf, hot pepper flakes, sugar, salt, and pepper. Bring to a boil, then lower the heat and simmer, uncovered, stirring occasionally, for 10 minutes while the linguine cooks.

Remove the bay leaf from the sauce and discard. Add the whelk to the sauce and simmer for about 1 minute (see Note). Stir in the basil. Drain the linguine and combine with the sauce. Transfer to a warmed large serving dish and serve at once.

NOTE: Do not overcook whelk; like squid, it requires either very quick cooking or slow cooking over low heat so it will not become tough and chewy.

OCEAN POUT

Although commercial fishermen have been landing ocean pout for years, it has remained a terribly underutilized fish. We've included it here, since we occasionally spot it in our fish market and we just never know when the "bizarre" will become the "rising star." It's a most unusual looking species, more closely resembling an eel than a fin fish, since it has no tail and, indeed, is a member of the eelpout family.

The major market for ocean pout is in the New England area, usually lasting from late winter into early spring, with some of the fresh fish trickling down the coast to the New York area. The flesh of the ocean pout is quite dense and chewy, making it perfect for stews and soups since it holds its shape well. We have also found it to be a mild-tasting fish which also does well as fillets. However, if you buy fillets, they will have to be tenderized—the easiest way is by pounding with a wooden mallet.

OCTOPUS

This shy, retiring creature has been the victim of bad press! We remember as kids sitting in the darkened local movie palace and watching as the deep sea diver, bubbles rising from his windowed steel helmet, made his way along the ocean bed, probably in search of Captain Kidd's buried treasure. Suddenly, from the murky depths, a long, wavering tentacle came from the sunken wreck, grabbed the hapless diver by his neck and slowly strangled him, his agonized face showing through the glass plate as the enthralled and terrified audience gasped in horror.

Aside from the fact that the octopus is terribly bashful and would probably slink into the darkest corners of the wrecked ship when it first sighted the intruder, it seldom reaches a size large enough to put a tentacle around the neck of a diver. All that aside, it is probably a sea creature that is avoided by many of us because of the way it *looks,* while the populations of Greece and the other Mediterranean countries, China, and Japan have been selfishly keeping this culinary secret to themselves. We personally think it's one of the greatest treats of the ocean.

The octopus is a shell-less mollusk (cephalopod) that is related to the squid. It's found world-wide, both in temperate and tropical waters, and it boasts over 140 species, which vary in size and weight but generally range from 3 to 5 pounds. During the fall months, we sometimes find tiny baby octopus at our local ethnic markets, with about 20 of the little creatures in a single pound.

Since the octopus feeds mostly on shellfish, its flesh is quite firm; its taste, sweet and mild. We strongly suggest that you have your fishmonger cut away the tough beak and separate the head and tentacles. Since it can be quite rubbery in its natural state, it has to be tenderized before cooking: Precook it in simmering salted water for 1 hour, then let it cool in the liquid until the skin can be rubbed or scraped off. If you like, you can add aromatic spices, vegetables, and/or wine to the water in which you precook it. Then use the octopus for frying, braising, baking, or sautéing. It also can be added to stews as well as cold salads.

You may find octopus in your local ethnic markets partially cooked or frozen. On the East Coast, they're available fresh in the winter, usually imported from Portugal. We also find that they've become more and more popular on the menus of our local Greek and Italian restaurants.

Octopus

PULPO (SPANISH-STYLE OCTOPUS WITH GARLIC AND PAPRIKA)

MAKES 6 TO 8 FIRST-COURSE SERVINGS

This octopus specialty hails from Galicia, the region of Spain that lies to the north of Portugal. Tender morsels of cooked octopus are served in an insinuating, peppery sauce redolent of garlic, sherry, and saffron.

OCTOPUS:

1   small whole onion, peeled
1   small carrot, cut in half
1   small rib celery, cut in half
1   large clove garlic
1   small lemon, cut in half
1   bay leaf
½   teaspoon whole black peppercorns
1   teaspoon salt
2   cups dry white wine
1   tablespoon dry sherry
1   tablespoon white wine vinegar
2   2-pound octopuses, cleaned and rinsed
     (see page 366)

SAUCE:

⅔   cup olive oil
4   tablespoons butter
3   cloves garlic, finely minced (about 1 table-
     spoon)
2   medium onions, coarsely chopped (about
     1 cup)
½   teaspoon cayenne pepper
¼   teaspoon saffron threads, crumbled
⅓   cup dry sherry
1   bay leaf
⅓   cup lemon juice
1   tablespoon paprika
½   teaspoon salt
¼   cup finely minced parsley

FOR THE OCTOPUS: To a 6-quart nonreactive Dutch oven, add all the ingredients plus enough water to cover and bring slowly to a simmer over medium-low heat. Cover and simmer for 45 minutes to 1 hour, testing the octopus with the tip of a sharp knife until the octopus is tender but still slightly resistant. Remove from the heat and cool in the liquid for 40 minutes. When cool enough to handle, lift out the octopuses, cut off and discard the body, and scrape and rub as much skin as possible from the tentacles. Rinse and cut into ¾-inch pieces.

While the octopus is cooling, prepare the sauce. In a medium skillet, heat ⅓ cup of the olive oil and 2 tablespoons of the butter. Add the garlic and onion and sauté for 3 to 5 minutes, stirring frequently. Stir in the cayenne, saffron, sherry, and bay leaf and simmer over medium-low heat for 5 minutes. Add the remaining olive oil and butter, the lemon juice, paprika, and salt; cook and stir over low heat for 1 minute. Remove and discard the bay leaf, then stir in the parsley. Add the octopus and warm over low heat, stirring frequently, until hot. Serve in individual ramekins or in a flat earthenware casserole.

OPAH

Those of us who live on the East Coast are often convinced that we are the first to try anything new, the first to discover a new species, an underutilized treat, a rare and tasty delicacy. And we are just as often *wrong!* Our first discovery of opah came through our sister-in-law, Elaine, who lives in Chicago and telephoned to say that she had tasted a new fish in a local restaurant, and it was called by a name that she had to spell over the phone. Since then, we're happy to say, the fish has appeared on the ice beds of our fishmonger, and we have had an opportunity to try it.

Opah is also called moonfish because of its almost bloated shape, as well as Jerusalem haddock. We overheard one wag call it the "Mussolini fish" because it has a definite underslung jaw, but we don't think the name will stick. It is an exotic and colorful fish, caught both in the Atlantic and the Pacific, but most of our catch here in the United States comes from Hawaii and California. The opah is a large fish, averaging about 100 pounds, and, looking at the entire fish, some have described it as resembling the shape and size of a garbage can lid!

One of the most curious things about the opah is that it actually contains four types of flesh, each one a different color and taste. We remember the first time we purchased it, our fishmonger showed us the four very distinctive cuts and sliced a large fillet off each one of them.

The flesh near the breast plate is ruby red, and it maintains most of its color after cooking. It tastes a bit like veal, although it has some of the fibrous texture of flank steak. The other parts, from the loin (the most tender and expensive part), the belly, and the cheeks, all range from pink to rosy red flesh, and all turn white during cooking. The skin is thick with heavy scales and should be cut away before cooking. In addition to being sold as thick fillets, it can also be cubed or scalloped, then grilled, broiled, or braised.

OPAH BAKED WITH VEGETABLES

This recipe uses the pinkish part of this very large fish, which has several types of flesh, each a different color, taste, and texture.

3 tablespoons butter

1 pound skinned opah fillet, belly part (substitute: halibut or grouper)

  Salt and pepper to taste

1 small leek, white part plus 1 inch green, julienned (about ⅓ cup)

1 small fennel bulb, trimmed and cut into julienne

1 large plum tomato, finely diced (about ½ cup)

16 small Niçoise olives, pitted and halved

1 teaspoon finely minced lemon peel

¼ cup dry white wine

1 tablespoon coarsely chopped parsley

Preheat the oven to 400°. Melt the butter in a medium skillet, dip the fish in the butter on both sides, sprinkle with salt and pepper, and set the fish aside. In the same skillet, add the leek and fennel and sauté over low heat for 2 to 3 minutes, stirring occasionally. Add the tomato, olives, and lemon peel and cook, stirring, for 1 minute. Add the wine and bring to a boil.

Transfer the vegetable mixture to a baking pan and place the fish on top. Bake, uncovered, for 10 to 12 minutes until the fish flakes when tested with a skewer. Tilt the pan while baking and spoon some sauce over the fish. Sprinkle with parsley just before serving.

OPAH GRILLED WITH CILANTRO PESTO, ORANGE, AND PINE NUTS

For the adventurous diner, the opah is a surprisingly delicious fish, since its color is even darker than the tuna. The cilantro pesto makes this dish even more unusual, while the pine nuts add an interesting crunch.

1 pound dark pectoral opah fillet, cut into 2 equal portions (substitute: swordfish)

3 tablespoons olive oil

¼ teaspoon ground cumin

¼ teaspoon Tabasco

Salt to taste

3 teaspoons pine nuts

⅔ cup orange juice

2 teaspoons finely minced orange peel

⅔ cup cilantro leaves

Pepper to taste

1 navel orange, cut into wedges, for garnish

Place the fillets in a flat dish. Mix the olive oil, cumin, Tabasco, and salt together and rub the mixture on both sides of the fish. Let stand at room temperature for 30 minutes.

Meanwhile, prepare a grill and the cilantro pesto: In a food processor, coarsely chop 2 teaspoons of the pine nuts. Add the orange juice, orange peel, cilantro, and salt and pepper to taste and process until a thick purée is formed.

When the fish has marinated, tilt the pan and spoon off 1 tablespoon of the marinade and add it to the pesto along with about 1 tablespoon of water to thin it a bit. Grill the fish, turning once, for 8 to 10 minutes until it flakes. Divide it into 4 portions, spoon some of the cilantro pesto over each portion, scatter with the remaining 1 teaspoon pine nuts, and tuck in a wedge or two of orange for garnish.

SEA ROBIN

This prehistoric-looking mini-monster is actually the *grondin,* celebrated by many French chefs, yet probably the fish most often thrown back by disgusted bay and surf fisherpeople here in the United States. Its reputation as a "trash fish" comes first from looking the way it does, with huge wings that flap when it's caught and a bug-eyed Neolithic face, and secondly because it's truly a tough-skinned very bony fish.

In spite of all this, the sea robin is quite edible (just ask the French) and can occasionally be found in ethnic fish markets. It has a firm texture, low fat content, and a sweet, delicate taste and can be steamed, poached, or stewed. If you catch one, the skin can be pulled off with a pliers after cutting it around the head, very much like a catfish. Fillet the sea robin by cutting down along the backbone and then feel for bones when you have finished. Pull the pin bones out with a pair of long-nose pliers or strong tweezers.

SEA URCHIN

Since we have all become quite familiar with the "other names" given to seafood to make them more marketable or more descriptive, our nomination for this creature would be "the pin cushion," for that is exactly what it looks like. A ball-shaped cephalopod that ranges in size from 3 to 6 inches and sporting spines that might be compared to a porcupine or hedgehog, the sea urchin actually got its name from the hedgehog, or urchin as it was once called in ancient England.

Sea urchin is far more popular in Europe and Asia than it is in the United States, and, in fact, the only times we've seen them sold here have been on visits to Asian markets. Purple, green, and red, they grow on the rocky shores of both the Pacific and Atlantic coasts and are always sold live, then eaten raw right out of the shells. Since they spoil quickly, to make certain that they're alive, test them by gently touching the spines to see if they move.

To prepare sea urchins and eat them is to, first of all, wear work gloves or heavy kitchen gloves. Hold the sea urchin with the "mouth" or "eye" side up and cut a circle into the shell with a sharp knife. The only edible portion of the sea urchin, the bright golden triangular ovaries or roe that forms a five-pointed star, will then be visible. The rest of the urchin—the brown intestines—are discarded.

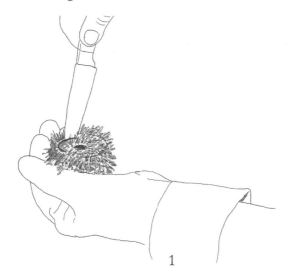

If you prefer, remove the sea urchin roe and put it on a slice of a good baguette as the French do, topped only with a squeeze of lemon. Allow from 3 to 5 per person. They also can be cooked as an omelet, with 1 urchin per egg, or mixed into a hollandaise sauce. And, on your next visit to the local Japanese restaurant, if you find *uni* on the sushi menu, know that you'll be eating sea urchin.

1

2

SKATE

This is yet another fish that may well move out of the "bizarre" category very soon to take its place in North America with the more popular seafood selections. Although this diamond-shaped creature with its whiplike tail and kite-shaped wings has been popular in Europe for centuries, it has been subjected here to the same bad press as the octopus and its cousin the shark. The Hollywood motion pictures of the thirties and forties presented the sting ray as a denizen of the deep, a threat to underwater explorers and the subject of nightmares. Certainly, it will never win a prize in an oceanic beauty contest, although we find its placid, graceful floating movement through the water a joy to behold.

Since skate (also called a ray) is a mollusk eater, it has an excellent flavor quite similar to scallops, is low fat, with tender shreds or strands of sweet-tasting white meat. Only the wings are edible. They have pale skin on their undersides and a darker grayish brown skin on top, with the meat sandwiching a center cartilage, and thus making the wings perfect either for fillets or to be cooked whole. Because they are members of the shark family, skates carry urea, giving them an ammonia smell unless they are bled immediately after landing.

After buying your skate wings, blanch them in acidulated water or marinate them in salted water, milk, or lemon juice in the refrigerator for 2 to 3 hours before cooking. In the recipes that follow, we have called for skate already skinned and filleted. Ideally, you might have the fishmonger do the job for you. However, if you bring home the entire wing, skin and all, you can remove the skin 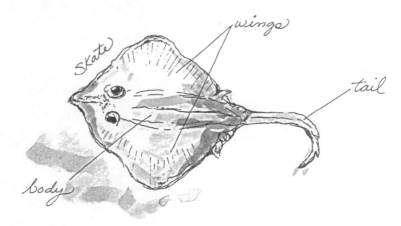 easily by putting the wings into a pot of rapidly boiling water, lowering the heat, and simmering for only a minute or two. Remove the skate, put it on a board or on paper towels, and scrape the skin away with a sharp knife. Turn the wing over and repeat the procedure on the other side. Then fillet the meat off the center cartilage.

Skate can be baked in parchment, poached, steamed, braised, or sautéed. Most of the wings now being sold weigh about 1½ pounds each, enough to serve two.

RAIE AU BEURRE NOIRE (POACHED SKATE WITH BLACK BUTTER AND CAPER SAUCE)

MAKES 4 SERVINGS

Sweet and delicate, with deeply ridged flesh, skate wings are much prized in France, where they are teamed with a dark burned butter sauce containing vinegar and capers, just as we have presented it here.

2	1½-pound skate wings, skinned, filleted, and cut into 4 portions (substitute: flounder)	1	cup water
½	cup lemon juice	1	small onion, stuck with 2 whole cloves
1	medium clove garlic, slivered (about 1 teaspoon)	2	strips lemon peel, about 2 inches long
½	teaspoon dried oregano	½	teaspoon whole peppercorns
1	bay leaf	6	tablespoons butter
½	teaspoon dried thyme	2	teaspoons balsamic or red wine vinegar
	Salt to taste	1	tablespoon nonpareil capers, rinsed and dried on paper towels
½	teaspoon freshly ground black pepper		Dash of cayenne pepper
½	cup dry white wine	1	tablespoon finely minced parsley

Place the skate fillets in a nonreactive dish along with the lemon juice, garlic, oregano, bay leaf, thyme, salt, and pepper. Cover with plastic wrap and marinate in the refrigerator for 1 hour, turning once. Transfer the fillets to a plate and strain the marinade.

To a wide skillet, add the strained marinade, the wine, water, onion with cloves, lemon peel, peppercorns, and skate wings. Bring just to a boil over medium heat, then lower the heat at once and simmer for 2 minutes. Turn the fillets over in the liquid, cover the skillet, and let stand in the poaching liquid for 5 minutes while preparing the sauce.

In a small heavy skillet, heat the butter over medium-high heat, skimming any foam as it rises to the top, until it reaches a very dark brown color; remove from the heat and away from the flame. Add the vinegar, capers, and cayenne. Transfer the fish with a slotted spatula to serving plates, spoon some of the black butter sauce over the fish, and sprinkle with parsley.

SQUID

Possibly the greatest error that can be made in preparing squid is that of overcooking it, making it tough. And yet, a great many ethnic family recipes surprisingly call for at least 2 hours up to all day simmering of squid—as an ingredient in pasta sauces, for example. Thus, the best advice we can give is that squid be cooked very quickly (about 1 minute) to keep it from turning tough and rubbery.

Overcooking this unusual cephalopod may be one of the reasons that it is not overly popular here in the United States, but certainly another explanation is the way it looks, although that has not stopped our Mediterranean and Japanese cousins from devouring most of the world's catch.

Squid is available all year round, sold at various weights and sizes. Although squid can reach up to 30 feet in the wild, its market size is usually no more than a ½ to 1 pound. When we can get it, we prefer the baby squid, 2 to 3 inches in length. Whatever the size, there's very little waste, and since squid is plentiful and not terribly popular, its price is generally much, much lower than most of the other seafood displayed at the fish market.

The rocket-shaped tube has a transparent cuttlebone or "quill" which is removed (see below), while the head contains the ink sac, the contents of which are squirted forcefully outward to discourage predators. This is the ink that is used to make black pasta and the sauce for black risotto. You may also find the ink sold in packets in some specialty or ethnic markets. The head has eight thick tentacles with suction cups attached as well as two thinner tentacles. All are entirely edible, and they along with the body turn bright white after cooking.

Squid can be poached, stuffed, baked, fried, added to pasta sauces, and used as a base for cold seafood salads.

How to Clean a Squid

If the squid is frozen, let it thaw under cold running water. Grasp the squid firmly by the head and pull the body gently. This will separate the head from the body. Scrape or rinse off the thin outer membrane on the body.

Cut through the arms near the eyes, using a sharp knife. Then, with your thumb and forefinger, find the small beak on the section with the tentacles and squeeze it out. It feels like a hard pea. Discard it. Hold the tentacles under running water and rub off the dark skin with your fingernails. The tentacles can be left whole or cut up for your recipe.

Grasp the body (mantle) and reach inside to pull out the thin cartilaginous quill and the attached viscera, then wash the mantle under running water. You can cut it into rings or strips, or stuff it, or score it for "squid steaks." If you want the ink sac, you'll find it near the head and inside the eyes.

Some squid can be purchased already prepared by the fishmonger and will need very little work with the exception of a good, thorough rinsing under running water before cutting it up to recipe specifications. And remember—quick cooking is the secret!

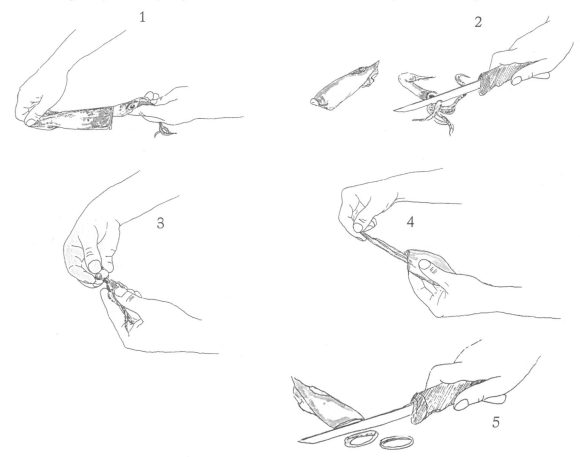

CUTTLEFISH

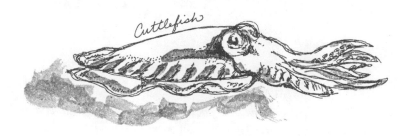

These are the smallest of the cephalopods, oval in shape, and about no more than 10 inches in length, with the tiniest ones most desirable. Just as the squid, it has eight short tentacles plus two that are somewhat longer. One of the most interesting stories about this small fish is that the old Italian masters used their dark brown ink for their sepia drawings—*seppia* being the Italian name for the cuttlefish.

They should be prepared and dressed in exactly the same way as the squid, although the choice in Italy is a tiny version of the fish, about 1 to 1½ inches in length, that is fried whole after cleaning and popped into the mouth all in one sweep. And, just as with squid, they should be cooked very quickly or they toughen and turn rubbery.

BROILED SQUID STUFFED WITH PANCETTA AND RADICCHIO

Squid, with their torpedo-shaped mantles, are filled with a bit of Italian bacon and flavored radicchio, then bound with wine-scented bread crumbs and a touch of anchovy. They then are rolled in a bit of lemon butter and quickly grilled for a smoky, heavenly taste.

2 ounces pancetta, finely diced

2 medium cloves garlic, finely minced (about 1½ teaspoons)

2 anchovy fillets, rinsed

1 small head radicchio, finely chopped, 4 small leaves reserved for garnish

1¼ pounds squid with 4-inch mantles (about 4), cleaned (see page 376), tentacles removed and finely chopped

4 tablespoons fresh bread crumbs

2 tablespoons dry white wine

1 teaspoon lemon juice

1 tablespoon finely minced parsley

Pinch of cayenne pepper

Salt and pepper to taste

1 tablespoon olive oil

2 tablespoons butter

Lemon wedges

Soak about 12 toothpicks in water for 15 to 20 minutes so that they don't burn while grilling the squid.

In a medium saucepan, sauté the pancetta over medium heat until it takes on a golden color. Add the garlic and anchovies and sauté, stirring constantly, for 1 to 2 minutes. Add the radicchio, raise the heat to medium-high, and cook, stirring, for 1 minute. Stir in the chopped squid tentacles and continue to cook, stirring constantly, for 30 seconds more. Remove from the heat and stir in the bread crumbs, wine, lemon juice, parsley, cayenne, salt, and pepper. Let cool.

Fasten the narrow ends of the squid bodies with a soaked toothpick and fill them about two-thirds full with stuffing (the squid will shrink a bit and the stuffing will expand). Fasten the top with 1 or 2 more toothpicks to enclose the filling.

Preheat a broiler or prepare a grill. Heat the oil and butter together in a small skillet. Squeeze a wedge of lemon into the butter and oil, then roll each stuffed squid in the mixture. Grill or broil close to the heat for 1 to 2 minutes on each side until the squid is opaque and slightly dappled with brown.

Serve one squid per person, garnished with a lemon wedge and radicchio leaf. Sharp knives will be welcome to slice the stuffed squid without squeezing out the filling.

FRIED SQUID WITH GARLIC ANCHOVY SAUCE

Immaculately fried, crisp little nuggets of squid are dipped lightly in a delicate garlic mayonnaise with a whiff of anchovy.

GARLIC ANCHOVY SAUCE (ABOUT 1½ CUPS):

- 1 cup mayonnaise
- 1 teaspoon sweet pickle relish, drained
- 2 teaspoons mashed anchovy fillets
- 1 teaspoon lemon juice
- 2 teaspoons finely minced parsley
- 2 cloves garlic, finely minced (about 2 teaspoons)
- ⅛ teaspoon cayenne pepper

FRIED SQUID:

- 2 pounds small squid, cleaned (see page 376) (substitute: shucked oysters or clams)
- ½ cup buttermilk
- ¼ teaspoon Tabasco
- 1½ cups all-purpose flour
- ½ cup stone-ground yellow or white cornmeal
- ½ teaspoon salt or to taste
- ½ teaspoon black pepper or to taste
- Corn oil for frying
- Lemon wedges for serving

FOR THE GARLIC ANCHOVY SAUCE: Whisk together all the ingredients in a medium bowl. Cover and refrigerate until serving time.

FOR THE FRIED SQUID: Slice the cleaned squid bodies ⅛ inch thick and slice the tentacles into bite-size pieces. Put the squid into a bowl and mix with the buttermilk and Tabasco.

Combine the flour, cornmeal, salt, and pepper in a large dish and blend to combine. Heat 2 to 3 inches of the corn oil in a deep cast-iron skillet or deep fryer to 370° (use a thermometer). Dip a few pieces of the squid in the flour mixture until coated and drop them into the oil without crowding in order to maintain the temperature of the oil. Stir and fry for 30 to 60 seconds until lightly golden. Lift out with a slotted spoon to drain on paper towels, then transfer to a serving dish to keep warm in a low oven until all the squid is done. Serve with lemon wedges, a sprinkling of additional salt if you wish, with the garlic anchovy sauce.

MARINATED SQUID SALAD WITH TOASTED PINE NUTS AND SCALLIONS

Rings of squid marinate for 24 hours in a flavorful poaching liquid with a touch of olive oil. Then the squid is tossed with scallions and golden pine nuts before serving.

2	pounds small squid, cleaned (see page 376), bodies cut into ¼-inch rings, larger tentacles cut into bite-size pieces, keeping the smallest ones whole (substitute: shrimp)	12	whole black peppercorns
		8	sprigs parsley, tied together
		2	large lemons, both juiced and the peel of one finely minced (about ¼ cup juice, 2 teaspoons minced peel)
2	cups water	2	tablespoons olive oil
1	medium onion, thinly sliced		Salt and pepper to taste
1	rib celery with leaves, thinly sliced	3	medium scallions, diagonally sliced (about ⅔ cup)
1	bay leaf		
1	small dried chile		Lettuce leaves
1	clove garlic, crushed		Lemon wedges
½	teaspoon whole fennel seeds	1	teaspoon butter
1	teaspoon whole coriander seeds	1½	tablespoons pine nuts

Tie all the squid in a cheesecloth bag. Set aside. To a 5-quart Dutch oven, add the water, onion, celery, bay leaf, chile, garlic, fennel and coriander seeds, and peppercorns and bring to a boil. Add the parsley and lemon juice and peel. Cover the pot and simmer for 25 minutes. Lower the cheesecloth bag of squid into the simmering liquid and simmer for about 1½ minutes, only until the squid becomes opaque. Lift the bag out to drain. Open the cheesecloth and transfer the squid to a bowl.

Raise the heat and boil the poaching liquid, uncovered, until reduced to about ¾ cup. Strain the liquid, discarding the solids. Mix the strained liquid, the olive oil, salt, and pepper and toss with the squid. Cover the bowl with plastic wrap and marinate for 24 hours.

When ready to serve, stir the squid, taste for additional lemon juice or salt and pepper, and toss with the scallions. Spoon onto lettuce-lined individual plates and add the lemon wedges to the plates. In a small skillet, heat the butter over medium heat. Add the pine nuts and cook, stirring constantly, until lightly golden. Distribute evenly over portions of the salad.

CALAMARI MARINARA WITH BLACK SQUID INK PASTA

This rustic, spicy tomato sauce has just a touch of sweet grated carrot to take the acidic edge off the tomatoes. Rings of creamy white squid are briefly cooked in the sauce, then combined with black squid-ink–tinted pasta. Paradiso!

3	tablespoons olive oil	1	tablespoon tomato paste
3 to 4	large cloves garlic, finely minced (about 1½ tablespoons)	¼	cup dry white wine
1	medium onion, coarsely chopped (about ¾ cup)	1	small bay leaf
			Salt and black pepper to taste
1	medium carrot, shredded (about ¾ cup)	1	pound black squid-ink pasta, linguine or fusilli
½	teaspoon dried thyme	2	pounds medium squid, 4 to 5 inches long, cleaned (see page 376), bodies cut into ¼-inch-thick rings, tentacles cut into ½-inch pieces (substitute: shrimp)
1	teaspoon dried oregano		
⅛	teaspoon hot pepper flakes		
2	pounds fresh tomatoes, skinned and cut into large pieces, or 2 14-ounce cans Italian plum tomatoes, with liquid	6	large fresh basil leaves, finely shredded
		1	teaspoon finely minced lemon peel
		2	tablespoons coarsely chopped parsley

In a large, heavy skillet, heat the oil over medium heat. Add the garlic, onion, and carrot and sauté, stirring frequently, until the onion begins to color, about 4 to 5 minutes. Stir in the thyme, oregano, and hot pepper flakes, then the tomatoes, tomato paste, wine, bay leaf, salt, and pepper. Bring to a simmer and cook, uncovered, over medium-low heat for 15 minutes, stirring occasionally.

Raise the heat to medium-high to reduce the sauce for 5 minutes. While the sauce is cooking, cook the pasta in lots of boiling salted water until *al dente.* When the pasta is almost cooked, add the squid to the tomato sauce. Cook, stirring, for only 1 minute. Remove the sauce from the heat and stir in the basil, lemon peel, and parsley. Drain the pasta and add it to the sauce, tossing to coat it well. Transfer to a large serving bowl or platter and serve at once.

TILAPIA

Tilapia

There will always be a warm spot in our hearts for this African native and, although we didn't actually discover it, we always have felt that we were involved in its American introduction as a "future fish." In the late 1970s we became quite excited with the experimental fish farming then taking place at the Organic Gardening and Farming Research Center in Maxatawny, Pennsylvania. Developed by Bob Rodale and his scientists, the farm contained almost fifty tanks, all filled with a fish that was fifty times cheaper to produce than beef, thirty-five times cheaper than chicken, and even four times cheaper than soybeans. Most impressive of all was the fact that one mating pair could produce up to 100,000 fish in six months! The fish, of course, was tilapia.

Today tilapia has become a reality in the marketplace, and we see it not only in our Chinese fish markets but also packaged in the local supermarkets. They are being farmed in Israel as well as in the United States, and since they grow equally well in salt as well as fresh water, fed on duckweed, lettuce, coffee pulp, or algae, their price has remained moderate as other species have become more and more expensive. The best-tasting are those that are raised on grain or fish meal and in clean, fresh water.

Tilapia have a mottled salt-and-pepper skin and grow to about 3 pounds before being sent to the market. The fillets weigh from 4 to 6 ounces, so you should allow two per person in planning your recipes. Their flavor is similar to that of catfish, and they're quite versatile in the kitchen—you can pan-poach, steam, roast, grill, or sauté them.

We've also noted recently that tilapia are occasionally sold live at ethnic markets, along with such species as catfish and carp. Needless to say, it's the best way to buy them.

POACHED TILAPIA WITH CHAMPAGNE AND MUSHROOM SAUCE

If you ever have such a thing as leftover Champagne—and sometimes there is after a special party—save some to prepare this very elegant Champagne and mushroom sauce with just a whiff of tarragon, to spoon over gently poached, sweet, firm-fleshed tilapia.

3 tablespoons butter

3 large shallots, finely minced (about ¼ cup)

⅛ pound whole small mushrooms, trimmed, or larger mushrooms, thickly sliced

½ teaspoon dried tarragon

Salt and white pepper to taste

2 cups Fish Stock (see page 402)

½ cup Champagne or dry white wine

8 tilapia fillets with skin, about 3 ounces each (substitute: skinned catfish, sole, orange roughy, or skinned skate wings)

½ cup heavy cream

1 tablespoon lemon juice

Heat 2 tablespoons of the butter in a small skillet over medium heat. Add the shallots and sauté, stirring constantly, until soft, about 2 minutes. Add the mushrooms, season with the tarragon, salt, and pepper, and continue to sauté until the mushrooms give up some of their liquid. Turn off the heat and reserve.

In a large nonstick sauté pan, bring the fish stock and Champagne to a boil. With a sharp knife, lightly score the skin of the fillets in a crosshatch pattern to prevent them from curling. Add the fillets in one layer, lower the heat to medium-low, and simmer, covered, for 4 to 5 minutes or more, depending upon the thickness of the fish. Test for doneness with a skewer after 4 minutes.

Transfer the fillets, 2 per person, to warmed serving plates, cover with aluminum foil, and set aside. Reduce the poaching liquid over high heat to 1¼ cups, about 10 minutes. Stir in the cream and continue to reduce the sauce to 1 cup or until the sauce has thickened a bit. Stir in the reserved mushroom mixture and continue to cook until the sauce is bubbly and the mushrooms are hot. Lower the heat to low and stir in the remaining 1 tablespoon butter and the lemon juice. Spoon some of the sauce over each fillet and serve.

STEAMED TILAPIA WITH WATERCRESS MOUSSELINE

MAKES 4 SERVINGS

Small, thin fillets of moist, sweet, slightly earthy tasting tilapia are steamed lightly and served with a cloud of peppery watercress sauce.

¾ cup trimmed watercress sprigs

1 medium scallion, cut into large pieces

1 tablespoon lemon juice

1 teaspoon anchovy paste

Pinch of cayenne pepper

½ cup heavy cream

8 tilapia fillets with skin, 3 to 4 ounces each (substitute: orange roughy, flounder, or catfish)

1 large scallion, sliced diagonally into 1-inch pieces

1 medium carrot, cut into needlelike julienne

Pinch of dried tarragon

2 small bay leaves

Salt and pepper to taste

In a food processor, coarsely chop the watercress and scallion. Add the lemon juice, anchovy paste, cayenne, and 2 tablespoons of the cream and process until puréed. Refrigerate the remaining cream. Cover and refrigerate the watercress mixture for 1 hour.

When ready to serve, whip the chilled cream and fold it into the watercress purée. With a sharp knife, lightly score the skin of the fillets in a crosshatch pattern to prevent them from curling. Arrange the fish on a heatproof plate or platter that will fit into a large pot with at least 1 inch to spare, so that the plate can be removed easily. Sprinkle the fish with the sliced scallion, carrot, tarragon, bay leaves, salt, and pepper.

Place a rack in the large pot and pour 1 inch of boiling water into the bottom. Put the plate of fish on the rack, cover the pot tightly, and steam over high heat until the center of the fish is slightly translucent, 3 to 8 minutes depending upon the thickness of the fillets. Test with a skewer after 3 minutes.

Lift the plate out with potholders. Discard the bay leaves and serve on the same plate on which the fish was steamed. Allow 2 fillets per person. Pass the watercress mousseline separately.

WOLFFISH

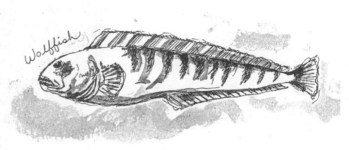

It's possible that you'll find wolffish more often marketed as ocean catfish, perhaps as a balm to consumers who shudder at its fierce name and its absolutely terrifying look, a likely candidate for the next Hollywood horror movie. The fish has huge eyes and frightening canine teeth that are just perfect for crunching clams and mussels as well as any other shellfish it happens to come across. Commercial fishermen who bring it in (usually by accident) report that it snaps and bites like a vicious animal when caught.

On the positive side, wolffish has no scales and a firm, white, lean sweet flesh that is particularly tasty and probably due to its diet. Yet it has still not made its solid mark either in the restaurant world or in home kitchens. It can be baked, braised, broiled, steamed, or used in soups or salads.

Even after our vivid description of the way it looks, if you do find wolffish, your fishmonger already will have prepared fillets. Try them. We think you'll be pleasantly surprised.

WINE-POACHED WOLFFISH WITH RED PEPPER, ZUCCHINI, SQUASH, AND THYME CREAM

MAKES 4 SERVINGS

The fierce-looking wolffish is a crustacean eater, which gives its flesh a delicious flavor. After all "you are what you eat," no? Served on a quickly sautéed tangle of colorful vegetables and moistened with a rich, creamy sauce redolent of fresh thyme, this fish dish is a winner.

1 cup dry white wine	1 small zucchini (about ¼ pound), cut into very long thin julienne
1 cup plus 6 tablespoons water	1 small yellow squash (about ¼ pound), cut into very long thin julienne
2 sprigs parsley	
1 sprig thyme	1 small red pepper, cut into very long thin julienne
½ bay leaf	
2 whole cloves	Salt and pepper to taste
6 whole peppercorns	½ cup heavy cream
1 rib celery	1 egg yolk
1 small carrot	3 or 4 drops Tabasco
1½ pounds wolffish fillets, cut into 4 portions (substitute: halibut)	2 tablespoons fresh thyme leaves
2 tablespoons olive oil	

To a large nonreactive skillet, add the wine and 1 cup water. Tie the parsley, thyme, bay leaf, cloves, peppercorns, celery, and carrot in cheesecloth for easy removal and drop it into the skillet. Bring the liquid to a boil, then lower the heat to medium and simmer for 15 minutes. Add the fish fillets, cover the pan tightly, and simmer for 6 to 8 minutes (or more depending upon the thickness of the fillets) until the fish is slightly translucent at the center when tested with a skewer.

Meanwhile, heat the olive oil in another large skillet over medium-high heat. Add the zucchini, yellow squash, and red pepper and sauté, stirring constantly, for 1 minute. Season with salt and pepper to taste and add the remaining 6 tablespoons water. Cook, stirring frequently, until the water evaporates. Transfer the vegetables to a warm serving platter. When the fish is cooked, transfer it with a slotted spoon over the vegetables. Cover with aluminum foil and keep warm.

Lift the cheesecloth bag from the poaching liquid and discard it. Increase the heat under the liquid and reduce liquid by half. Mix the cream, egg yolk, Tabasco, thyme leaves, and salt and pepper to taste and gradually whisk it into the poaching liquid. Lower the heat to medium-low and cook, stirring constantly, for about 5 minutes, until the sauce is slightly thickened. Spoon over the fish and vegetables and serve at once.

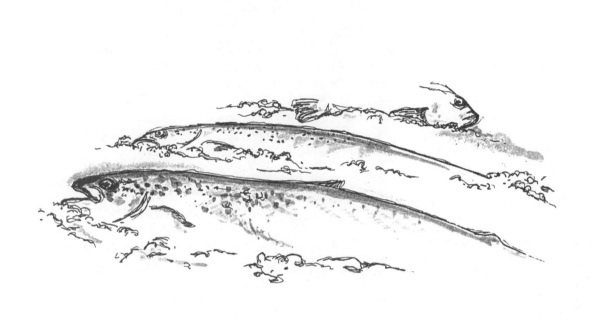

MIXED SEAFOOD

PARILLADA WITH ROMESCO SAUCE

The Spanish often grill their seafood, a method of cooking that preserves and enhances the delicate flavors. Each region of Spain has its own version of Romesco sauce; this one dates back almost a thousand years.

ROMESCO SAUCE (MAKES ABOUT 2 CUPS):

- 2 large red peppers (about ½ pound) cut into ½-inch strips
- ⅓ cup red wine vinegar
- 2 tablespoons dry white wine
- 1 bay leaf
- 2 ½-inch-thick slices French baguette or sourdough bread, crusts trimmed
- 3 cloves garlic, peeled
- 1 small dried chile, such as japonés
- 18 almonds or hazelnuts
- ½ teaspoon paprika
  Salt and pepper to taste
- ½ cup plus 1 teaspoon olive oil

PARILLADA:

- 3 tablespoons lemon juice
- 2 tablespoons dry white wine
- ½ teaspoon coarse salt
- 1 teaspoon freshly ground black pepper
- ½ teaspoon dried green peppercorns, crushed
- 1 large clove garlic, crushed
- 1 tablespoon fresh rosemary leaves
- ½ cup olive oil
- ¾ to 1 pound large shrimp in their shells
- ¾ pound dense meaty fish, such as grouper, monkfish, pollack, or sea scallops, cut into 1½-inch pieces
- 3 live jumbo blue crabs, cleaned (see page 283)
- 6 cherrystone clams, scrubbed well
- 3 live 1¼-pound lobsters
- 6 oysters, scrubbed well

PREPARE THE SAUCE FIRST: Place the peppers in a nonreactive bowl. Add the vinegar, wine, and bay leaf and marinate at room temperature for 3 hours. Drain the peppers and reserve the marinade, discarding the bay leaf. Dry the peppers on paper towels. In another bowl, soak the bread in water and set aside. To a blender (not a food processor), add the garlic, dried chile, nuts, paprika, salt, and pepper and process until very finely chopped.

In a large skillet, heat 1 teaspoon of the olive oil over medium heat. Scrape the nut mixture into the pan and sauté, stirring constantly, for 2 minutes. Then return the mixture to the blender. To the same skillet, add 3 tablespoons of the olive oil and heat over medium-high heat. Add the peppers and sauté, stirring frequently, until tender-crisp. Transfer to the blender and blend for 30 seconds.

Squeeze the bread between your hands to extract the water; the bread should be damp and not soaking wet. Add the bread to the blender and blend, adding the remaining olive oil a little at a time until the consistency is light and creamy. Taste and add a bit of the reserved marinade if you prefer a more tart taste.

FOR THE PARILLADA: In a large bowl, mix the lemon juice, wine, salt, both peppers, garlic, rosemary, and oil and set aside. Soak about 24 bamboo skewers (10 inches long) in water for 30 minutes. Thread the shrimp onto 2 parallel skewers and about 1 inch apart—one to the left of the center of the shrimp, the other to the right of the center—allowing 5 shrimp per double skewer. Place the shrimp, the fish, and the crabs in a large nonreactive baking pan and spoon the marinade over.

Wrap the clams individually in pieces of aluminum foil. To prepare the lobster for grilling, drop them headfirst into a large pot or roasting pan of boiling salted water. Cover the pot and cook for 4 minutes only. Then lift them out with tongs, cool slightly, split them in half lengthwise, and remove and discard the sac behind the eyes and the intestinal vein that runs down through the tail. Pull off the claws and set aside. Brush the flesh with some of the marinade.

Prepare the fire about 45 minutes before cooking so there are hot embers. Use an oiled mesh or "Griffo" grill, placed over the grate to prevent the seafood from falling through the grids (see page 52 for grilling advice). When the fire is ready, place the grill 3 to 4 inches from the source of the heat. Take into account the different amounts of time the seafood takes to cook and transfer to the serving platter to keep warm as they are cooked. Shrimp take about 2 to 3 minutes on each side, lobster takes about 4 minutes on each side, oysters may take a little longer. Lift the shrimp, fish, and crab out of the marinade and place them on the grill. Using the marinade as a basting liquid, grill the fish and shrimp about 2 to 3 minutes on each side and, as the seafood is cooked, place it onto a large serving platter and keep warm, covered with aluminum foil. The crab may take 1 or 2 minutes longer, depending upon size.

Place the foil-wrapped clams directly on the embers. Put the lobster halves flesh side down on the grill, then place the lobster claws and the oysters, cup side down, around the lobsters. Grill the lobsters and claws 4 minutes on each side. The oysters and clams are done when they open slightly, 8 to 12 minutes depending upon their size. To test the clams after the cooking time, unwrap only one clam to see if it has popped open.

Serve with the Romesco sauce as a dip and provide picks, claw crackers, and lots of paper napkins.

LAYERED TERRINE OF SALMON, COD, AND SORREL

MAKES 8 FIRST-COURSE SERVINGS

Delicate, yet having the bite of green peppercorns and the sprightly tart taste of sorrel, this green, pink, and white layered terrine makes a very attractive presentation when sliced, particularly with a few salmon caviar eggs strewn over the surface.

3 ounces sorrel (12 to 13 leaves), with stems and center ribs removed

4 medium scallions, finely minced (about ¾ cup)

1 cup tightly packed parsley leaves

Salt and pepper to taste

1 tablespoon butter, very soft, plus additional butter for terrine and aluminum foil

1½ pounds cod or scrod fillets, with pin bones removed

2 eggs

1 tablespoon lemon juice

1 teaspoon dried whole green peppercorns, crushed (about 2 teaspoons)

½ cup fine fresh bread crumbs

⅛ teaspoon freshly grated nutmeg

½ cup heavy cream, chilled

½ pound salmon fillet, cut into ¼-inch-thick slices

2 sprigs tarragon

1 ounce fresh red salmon caviar (optional)

To a large saucepan of boiling water, add the sorrel, scallions, and parsley; stir, remove from the heat, and let stand for 2 minutes. Strain and purée in a blender. Scrape the purée out into a double layer of slightly dampened cheesecloth; twist and squeeze out the excess moisture. Scrape into a bowl, season with salt and pepper, beat in the butter, and set aside.

Butter a 1½-quart Pyrex or ceramic terrine and one side of a piece of aluminum foil cut to fit the top of the terrine. Preheat the oven to 350°. Boil a kettle of water. Cut the codfish into 1-inch pieces and add to a food processor along with the eggs and the lemon juice; process with a few strokes until combined. Add the peppercorns, salt to taste, the bread crumbs, and nutmeg and process with a few more strokes. With the motor running, add the cream through the feed tube and combine.

Pack half the codfish purée into the buttered terrine, smoothing it even with a rubber spatula. Then cover with the sorrel mixture and smooth it. Lay the salmon strips evenly on the sorrel and top with the remaining codfish purée. Place the aluminum foil butter side down on the surface.

Place the terrine in a larger baking pan and fill the pan with enough boiling water to come halfway up the side of the terrine. Bake for 30 minutes. Remove and discard the foil; cool on a wire rack.

When the terrine is cool, cover with plastic wrap and refrigerate for at least 4 hours. Unmold onto a serving platter and blot up any excess moisture with paper towels. Garnish with sprigs of tarragon. Serve thin slices and scatter about ¼ teaspoon of the salmon caviar over each slice.

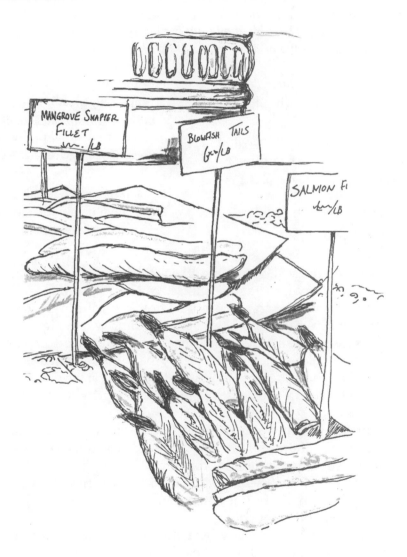

SEAFOOD SAUSAGE

MAKES 6 TO 8 SERVINGS

Created in the years of nouvelle cuisine, seafood sausage has managed to survive several food fads since that time. You can make the sausage in advance and reheat it in a steamer or slice and sauté it in a bit of oil until brown, then serve with a lightly sauced pasta or risotto or as a first course with a Beurre Blanc.

½ pound sea scallops, cut into quarters

½ pound sole fillet, cut into 1-inch cubes

3 egg whites

1½ tablespoons finely minced fresh chervil

2 teaspoons finely minced fresh tarragon

2 teaspoons finely minced chives, plus 1 tablespoon for garnish

⅛ teaspoon cayenne pepper

⅛ teaspoon ground nutmeg

Salt and white pepper to taste

½ cup heavy cream

½ pound shrimp, shelled, deveined, and coarsely diced in ¼-inch pieces

6 feet of sausage casings (see Note)

Beurre Blanc (see page 56)

1 tablespoon canola oil

1 or 2 medium plum tomatoes, finely diced (about ½ cup)

To a food processor, add the scallops, sole, and egg whites and process until thoroughly puréed. Then add the chervil, tarragon, chives, cayenne, nutmeg, salt, pepper, and cream; process until combined. Scrape out into a bowl and stir in the diced shrimp.

Thoroughly rinse the sausage casing with cold running water. Lightly oil a large pastry tube and fit the sausage casing over the tube, tying off the bottom end tightly with string and making a double knot. Fill the pastry bag with the seafood mixture and squeeze the bag until all the fish has been pushed into the casing. Tie off the other end tightly with string, then tie off the sausages in 6-inch lengths with the string, making double knots.

In a large pot, bring enough water to cover the sausages to a boil, then reduce to a slow simmer (about 190°). The water must not boil. Add the sausage and weigh it down with a plate to keep it submerged; simmer for 20 to 25 minutes. After 5 minutes, while the sausage is poaching, remove the plate and prick the casings all over with a needle to prevent them from bursting; continue to simmer, with the plate holding the sausages down. Lift out the sausages and let cool.

Cut the sausage links at the points where they were tied and remove the strings. The sausage can be prepared several hours in advance up to this point and refrigerated until ready to serve. When ready to serve, prepare the beurre blanc sauce and keep it warm. Sauté the sausages in the oil in a large skillet over medium-low heat until lightly browned all over. Spoon about 2 tablespoons of the sauce on a small serving plate, scatter a few tomato bits plus a sprinkle of chives over the sauce, and place a sausage on top.

NOTE: If you cannot find sausage casings, make individual 6-inch sausages and wrap tightly in plastic wrap, following the same procedure as for the casing and tying both ends tightly using double knots. Steam over boiling water on a rack, covering the pan tightly. Remove the plastic wrap after steaming and sauté the sausages as directed in the recipe.

ITALIAN SEAFOOD SALAD

MAKES 6 TO 8 SERVINGS

Prepared the day before, bite-size pieces of tender seafood marinate in a light, lemony dressing that is crisped with a touch of celery and scallions. It's a perfect salad for a light luncheon or first course.

1	pound monkfish (see Note)	1	tablespoon white wine vinegar
1½	pounds mussels (about 1 quart)	⅛	teaspoon Tabasco
1½	pounds littleneck clams		Pinch of sugar
1	pound small squid, cleaned (see page 376)		Salt and black pepper to taste
1	pound large shrimp in shells	6	tablespoons canola or light olive oil
1	cup dry white wine	2	medium scallions, thinly sliced (about ½ cup)
3	cups Fish Stock (see page 402)	1	rib celery, thinly sliced (about ½ cup)
1	teaspoon finely minced lemon peel	3	tablespoons finely minced parsley
2	tablespoons lemon juice	6	cups mixed greens, loosely packed

Pull off the membrane from the monkfish and cut the fish into ¾-inch cubes. Scrub and beard the mussels. Scrub the clams. Rinse and dry the squid and cut the bodies into ¼-inch rings, leaving the tentacles whole if the squid are small or halve them if they are larger. Keep the shrimp in their shells.

In a Dutch oven or a wide skillet, bring the wine and fish stock to a boil. Add the monkfish, lower the heat, and simmer for 2 minutes. Lift the fish out with a slotted spoon and transfer to a large mixing bowl. Cover the bowl and set it aside. Bring the liquid to a boil again, add the clams, cover the pot tightly, and cook for 3 minutes. Then add the mussels, cover the pot, and cook for 3 to 5 more minutes until the mollusks open. Slide the pot over the burner a few times while cooking. Lift the shellfish out with a slotted spoon, discarding any that did not open.

Add the squid to the stock and cook until just opaque, less than 1 minute. Again, lift out with a slotted spoon and add to the monkfish. Add the shrimp to the same boiling stock and cook for 2 to 3 minutes. Lift out and let cool. When cool enough to handle, remove the mussel and clam meats first and add them to the monkfish and squid. Then shell and devein the shrimp, cutting them in half along the back, and add them to the bowl. Cover with foil and keep warm.

Strain and freeze the broth for a sauce or for poaching other fish. In a small bowl, whisk together the lemon peel, lemon juice, vinegar, Tabasco, sugar, salt, and pepper, then gradually whisk in the oil. Add the scallions and celery to the seafood, then pour the sauce over all and mix gently to combine. Cover and refrigerate for 6 hours or overnight. Taste and correct the seasoning. Stir in the parsley and serve on a bed of greens.

NOTE: One-half pound cooked, cubed lobster meat can be used instead of, or along with, the monkfish.

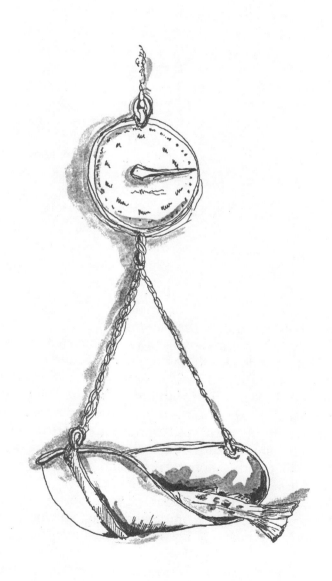

RISOTTO DI FRUTTI DI MARE (SEAFOOD RISOTTO)

MAKES 4 TO 6 SERVINGS

Toothsome, yet creamy, short-grain Arborio rice is laden here with luscious lemony seafood. The Italians do not use Parmesan cheese with any seafood dishes, and in fact many risottos of all types are better without it, because the delicate flavors of the ingredients are easier to appreciate.

2 to 3 shallots, finely minced (about ⅓ cup)

1 small onion, quartered

1 bay leaf

1 cup dry white wine

1½ pounds mussels, scrubbed and bearded

4 tablespoons butter

1 pound medium or small shrimp, shelled and deveined

¾ pound bay scallops, or sea scallops cut into ½-inch pieces

3 tablespoons lemon juice

1 small onion, minced (about ⅓ cup)

1 small fennel bulb, trimmed and finely chopped (about 1 cup)

2 cups chicken broth, homemade or canned

2 cups Arborio or Vialone rice (short-grain Italian rice)

½ teaspoon saffron threads

⅓ cup pine nuts, lightly toasted

⅓ cup finely minced parsley

Salt and freshly ground black pepper to taste

Put half the shallots, the quartered onion, the bay leaf, and ½ cup of the wine into a wide skillet. Add the mussels, cover tightly, bring to a boil, and steam, covered, for 4 to 5 minutes until the mussels have opened, sliding the pan over the burner a few times. Discard any that do not open. Cool slightly and remove the mussels from their shells, reserving a few shells for garnish. Strain the broth into a 2-quart saucepan and reserve.

Wipe out the skillet and melt 2 tablespoons of the butter over medium-high heat. Add the shrimp and scallops, sprinkle with 2 tablespoons of the lemon juice, and sauté, stirring frequently, just until the shrimp turn pink and the scallops are opaque, about 1 minute. Remove from the skillet with a slotted spoon and add to the shelled mussels. Add any pan juices to the mussel broth.

In a 3-quart saucepan, melt the remaining 2 tablespoons butter over medium heat. Add the remaining shallots and the minced onion and sauté, stirring constantly, for 1 minute. Add the fennel, lower the heat, cook, stirring occasionally, for 2 to 3 minutes until softened.

While the fennel is sautéing, add the chicken stock and remaining ½ cup of wine to the mussel broth; add water, if necessary, to bring volume of liquid up to 5 to 6 cups all together. Bring to a simmer over medium-low heat and keep it hot over low heat. Add the rice and saffron to the fennel mixture and stir over medium heat. The rice will turn transparent and then opaque in color. When the rice is opaque, add ⅓ cup of the hot liquid to the rice and simmer gently, stirring frequently. Continue to add the liquid ⅓ to ½ cup at a time as the liquid in the pan is absorbed. Keep to a low simmer and cook until the rice is tender and creamy—test a kernel after 25 to 30 minutes. When the rice is tender, stir in all the seafood and cook for about 1 minute only until the seafood is reheated.

Stir in the pine nuts, parsley, remaining 1 tablespoon lemon juice, salt, and pepper. Serve hot in wide soup bowls and garnish with a few mussel shells.

Mixed Seafood

SEAFOOD IN GREEN SAUCE

The emerald green sauce is prepared several hours before serving to allow the flavors to blend. Poached scallops and shrimp are then stirred into the sauce and placed on a bed of ruby red radicchio. It's a festive and colorful presentation in addition to being delicious.

1 small clove garlic, peeled	Salt and black pepper to taste
6 large spinach leaves	3 tablespoons minced chives
12 sprigs parsley	4 cups water
½ large bunch watercress, stems removed	1 teaspoon tarragon vinegar
3 sprigs dill, stems removed	2 tablespoons mixed whole pickling spices
2 teaspoons lemon juice	1 pound medium shrimp in shells
¾ cup sour cream	1 pound sea scallops
2 tablespoons mayonnaise	Radicchio or red leaf lettuce

Prepare the sauce first: In a food processor, mince the garlic first, then add the spinach, parsley, watercress, and dill and process until finely minced. Add the lemon juice, sour cream, mayonnaise, salt, and pepper, and process until smooth. Transfer to a bowl and stir in the chives. Cover and refrigerate for several hours or overnight.

In a nonreactive pot, bring the water and vinegar to a boil, along with the pickling spices tied in cheesecloth for easy removal later on. Add the shrimp and scallops, cover the pot, and return to a boil. Remove from the heat, uncover, and let the seafood cool in the liquid for 5 minutes.

Drain the seafood and discard the liquid and the spice bag. Let cool a bit for easier handling, then peel and devein the shrimp and cut the scallops horizontally into 2 or 3 slices depending upon their thickness. Toss the seafood with the green sauce and serve on a bed of radicchio.

SEAFOOD AND VEGETABLE TIMBALE WITH TOMATO VELOUTÉ

MAKES 6 TO 8 SERVINGS

A creamy, pink-tinged tomato velouté is spooned over layers of spinach pasta, mixed seafood, and vegetables. When assembled in advance, it's ready to serve in 30 minutes.

½	pound spinach lasagna ricci (ruffled edge)	1	teaspoon dried thyme
3	cups uncooked seafood, cut into ¾-inch pieces: a combination of shelled shrimp, monkfish with membrane removed, and cleaned squid in any proportions that you prefer	½	teaspoon dried oregano
		2	teaspoons finely minced lemon peel
		2	tablespoons finely minced parsley
			Salt and pepper to taste
4	cups mixed raw vegetables, such as string beans, zucchini, and broccoli florets, cut into ¾-inch pieces	6	tablespoons butter
		4½	tablespoons all-purpose flour
2	tablespoons olive oil	1	cup Fish Stock (see page 402)
2	large shallots, finely minced (about ¼ cup)	1½	cups milk
1	medium clove garlic, finely minced (about 1 teaspoon)	½	cup heavy cream
		2	tablespoons tomato paste

Cook the lasagna in boiling salted water, drain, and then spread out on a tea towel to absorb any excess moisture. Press a piece of plastic wrap over the lasagna and set aside.

Put the seafood in one mixing bowl and all the vegetables in another bowl. Butter a round 12- by 2-inch baking pan and set it aside. In a small skillet, heat the oil over medium heat. Add the shallots and garlic and sauté, stirring frequently, until wilted, and mix the thyme, oregano, lemon peel, parsley, salt, and pepper together; divide these seasonings and toss half with the seafood and half with the vegetables.

In the top of a double boiler over medium heat, melt the butter and whisk in the flour. Stir and cook for 2 minutes. Mix the fish stock, milk and cream together and whisk into the butter/flour mixture. Cook, while stirring with a wooden spoon, for 10 to 15 minutes until thickened and smooth with no floury taste. Stir in the tomato paste and season with salt and pepper to taste. Assemble the dish as follows: Using half the pasta, make a layer on the bottom of the prepared pan. Layer all the seafood over the pasta layer. Pour half the tomato velouté sauce over the seafood, top with another layer of pasta, and follow with a layer of all the vegetables. Pour the remaining sauce over the vegetables. Cover with aluminum foil and, at this point, refrigerate until ready to serve or bake at 450° for 10 minutes, then remove the foil and bake for 10 minutes more until hot and bubbly around the edges. Remove from the oven and let rest for 10 minutes before cutting into pie-shaped wedges.

SOUPS FROM THE SEA
Soups, Stews, Chowders, and Bisques

The greatest and most delectable, the traditional and most memorable of fish soups and stews of the world have always developed spontaneously from the basic indigenous ingredients of the region. Every country that touches a bay or ocean shore, inland lake, inlet or running steam or river has taken the yield to develop its own classic specialty. And all are usually composed of a triad of fish, fish stock, and a sauté of aromatic vegetables, herbs, and flavorings. Once the seafood is added to the vegetables and stock, the cooking time can be measured in minutes because of the very delicacy of fish and seafood. Certainly, this is quite unlike meat stews, which require long cooking times to tenderize the tough cuts.

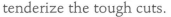

Many travelers who have tasted local fish soups and stews, both here and abroad, bring back memories of a very special treat.

There are many fish soups from the south of France alone and myriad versions of each one: the regal Marseilles bouillabaisse is made with what locals call a "netful of fish"—at least eight different kinds to be authentic. *Bourride,* another from the same region of France, is the color of sunlight, laced with aïoli, that unctuous garlic-laden mayonnaise. Or possibly you've tried *aigo-sau,* a simple fish version of a *pot-au-feu,* where the fish and vegetables are eaten separately and the broth is served in bowls. The *cotriade,* another simple yet substantial fish and potato stew, is from Brittany, and *pauchouse,* made from eel and fresh-water fish, is a gift from the Burgundy region.

The Italian *cacciucco,* from Livorno, is a fish stew cooked in red wine. There is no doubt that this is the recipe that was brought to the shores of the United States by Italian immigrants to become the famous cioppino of California.

Then there are the Spanish soups and stews: *Suquet* is from Catalonia and thickened with a paste of bread and almonds and then flamed with Cognac. And, of course, there's *zarzuela,* a sherry-laced fish and shellfish combination.

In a veritable "League of Nations" of fish soups and stews, we cannot discount the contributions of the Middle East—of dark, firm-fleshed king mackerel and bright sweet red peppers, cumin, and a fiery *harissa* hot pepper sauce. Or, think of the licorice-scented

Greek fish stew with the gorgeous garlic, almond, bread, and potato sauce called *skordalia.*

Not to be outdone, our American offerings are equally delectable. Since we are a nation composed of immigrants, we have adapted the French bisques and chowders and have made them our very own. Silken bisques are made from a purée of crustaceans—shrimp, lobster, crayfish—with a basic recipe that has remained unchanged for 200 years. They are prepared with a technique that is designed to extract every last bit of flavor from the seafood, then reduced to intensify it even more.

And, oh, the chowders! They derive their heartiness from totally straightforward and simple ingredients, and they carry their name from the French pot called the *chaudière,* a sort of cauldron or kettle. Both in Newfoundland and later, when they migrated down the coast of New England, each fisherman contributed part of his catch to the *chaudière,* sometimes adding vegetables to complete the soup. Somewhere along the way, with every "recipe" evolving from a serendipitous contribution of seafood and vegetables, the great "chowder dispute" of the region eventually evolved—and it continues to this day. The early French chowders contained neither milk (which the French viewed as a beverage to be imbibed only by small children) nor tomatoes (which were considered poisonous). But it was these two ingredients that became the crux of the dispute, clearly and geographically defined. Generally, above the Connecticut line, people dismiss the tomato-sparked Manhattan clam chowder as nothing more than vegetable soup with clams. On the other hand, the tomato-based chowder rooters below the Connecticut border claim that the milk-based New England chowder is nothing more than bland potato soup with clams. We love them both which, of course, maintains our position of unbending neutrality.

And, finally, what of Louisiana by way of Africa: seafood gumbos, stews of shellfish thickened with tiny pods of okra and filé powder with a woodsy scented base of dried sassafras leaves.

What follows, then, are only a few of our favorites touching on just a few places in this vast world of seafood, and given to other lovers of fish and seafood who have fond memories of that very special dish taken at a small restaurant that overlooked the Bosporus or the Mediterranean Sea or the Atlantic Ocean at Cape Cod.

MAKING YOUR OWN FISH STOCK
AND FUMET

Considering the minimal amount of time involved in preparing it, fish stock can add the most phenomenal flavor to many of your recipes. It serves as a base for all soups and stews, and when reduced to a concentrated form (fumet—page 403), it can be used for sauces.

Although frozen prepared fish stock can now be purchased in some gourmet shops, the cost runs about $4 per cup at this writing. Thus, the 14 cups that can be made with the following recipe would be worth over $50! Some cookbooks do suggest that you use bottled clam juice as a substitute for fish stock. However, we feel that it's an over-salted, very pallid replacement that gives an "off taste" to the recipes in which it is used.

We suggest that you try the recipe that follows. Freeze half of it in 1-quart containers, then reduce the remainder to make fish fumet, which then can be frozen in either 1-cup portions or in ice cube trays. When the cubes are solidly frozen, transfer them to larger containers to use as you need them, so that you'll always have some on hand. One or two melted cubes of fish fumet will add exquisite flavor nuance to many sauces, while the fish stock will be available for all your soups and stews.

FISH STOCK

MAKES ABOUT 14 CUPS

Ask your fishmonger for fish skeletons (fish racks), including a scaled fish head with eyes and gills removed. Any lean white-fleshed fish—flounder, weakfish, striped bass, or tilefish—will do. Rinse well under cold running water.

3	pounds fish racks and head as described above	4	sprigs thyme
1	tablespoon olive oil	4	sprigs parsley
2	large onions (about 1 pound), coarsely chopped	1	bay leaf
		¾	teaspoon whole black peppercorns
2	whole thin leeks, white and green parts, trimmed, rinsed, and coarsely chopped	2	whole cloves
		12	cups water
2	large ribs celery, coarsely chopped	1½	cups dry white wine

Loosely tie the fish head and racks in cheesecloth for easy removal later on and set aside. In a 7- to 8-quart heavy nonreactive pot (aluminum will discolor the stock), heat the olive oil over medium-low heat. Add the onions and sauté, stirring frequently until transparent, about 4 minutes. Stir in the leeks, celery, thyme, parsley, bay leaf, peppercorns, and cloves. Set the cheesecloth-wrapped fish rack and head on the bed of vegetables and herbs, then add the water and wine. Cover and bring to a boil over medium heat. It might take as long as 25 to 30 minutes to reach the boiling point. Lower the heat and simmer, covered, for 25 minutes. Cool slightly.

Put the pot in the sink, lift out the cheesecloth bag containing the fish, and tie it around the water spigot to allow the broth to drip back into the pot. When it's cool, gently squeeze the remaining liquid from the cheesecloth and into the pot. Strain the stock, pressing the solids against the strainer to extract as much of the stock as possible. Discard the solids.

If you like, you can untie the cheesecloth package to pick off the flesh from the fish head. Many times, a large head, such as that of a tilefish, contains enough fish to make a cold salad. In the meantime, let the stock stand until the sediment settles, then pour off the clear stock into 1-quart containers and freeze them or use half to make fish fumet, a concentrated form of fish stock used mostly to flavor sauces.

TO MAKE FISH FUMET

Bring the strained fish stock to a boil over high heat, then lower the heat to medium and cook, uncovered, until it is reduced by half. Season with salt and freeze in either 1-cup containers or in ice cube trays. When the cubes are frozen, transfer them to freezer containers to use when you need them. Most sauces require only small amounts of concentrated fish fumet.

NOTE: If you plan to make fish fumet, do not add salt to the fish stock. Season both *after* cooking. If the fish stock is salted and then reduced, it will become overpoweringly salty. If fish scales are left on the skin, the stock will become cloudy, while not removing the gills and eyes will turn the stock bitter.

Soups from the Sea

CRAB AND SHRIMP GUMBO

MAKES 8 TO 10 SERVINGS

This seafood gumbo is a robust Creole dish with many layers of flavor. Typically, in Louisiana, gumbo refers to any stew that contains okra, as this one does.

¾	pound chaurice, andouille, or kielbasa sausage, cut into ¼-inch slices
1	large onion, finely chopped (about 1½ cups)
3 to 4	large cloves garlic, finely minced (about 1½ tablespoons)
3	large shallots, finely minced (about ⅔ cup)
1	medium green pepper, finely diced (about 1 cup)
1	medium red pepper, finely diced (about 1 cup)
2 to 3	large ribs celery, finely diced (about 1 cup)
1	pound fresh okra, preferably small pods, trimmed and left whole; if large, cut into ¾-inch pieces; or one 10-ounce package frozen okra
¾	pound coarsely diced plum tomatoes (about 2 cups), or one 14-ounce can Italian plum tomatoes, undrained
5	cups Fish Stock (see page 402)
2	cups water
3	pounds shrimp, shelled and deveined, shells reserved

2	tablespoons tomato paste
1	tablespoon ground cumin
½	teaspoon dried oregano, preferably Greek or Mexican
¼	teaspoon black pepper
½	teaspoon cayenne pepper
3	whole allspice
2	whole cloves
2	bay leaves
4	tablespoons butter or combination butter and oil
4	tablespoons all-purpose flour
⅛	teaspoon grated nutmeg
	Salt to taste
½	pound fresh lump crab meat, picked over for bits of cartilage
2	tablespoons lemon juice
1 to 2	tablespoons filé powder (optional, see Note)
2	tablespoons coarsely chopped parsley
	Cooked white rice for serving

In a 7-quart heavy Dutch oven, sauté the sausage, stirring frequently, over medium-low heat until lightly browned; transfer to a bowl with a slotted spoon. Add the onion, garlic, shallots, green and red peppers, and celery to the sausage drippings and cook, stirring frequently, for 3 to 5 minutes until the vegetables are wilted. Stir in the okra and cook for 3 to 5 minutes more. The mixture should be fairly dry. Add the tomatoes and turn off the heat under the pot.

In a 3-quart saucepan, bring the fish stock, water, and shrimp shells only to a boil; lower the heat and simmer for 10 minutes. Strain the liquid into the Dutch oven. Add

Soups from the Sea ❖ 404 ❖

the tomato paste, cumin, oregano, pepper, and cayenne. Tie the allspice, cloves, and bay leaves in a piece of cheesecloth and add it to the pot. Cook over low heat for 15 minutes.

While the soup is simmering, heat the butter in a small heavy skillet over very low heat. Whisk in the flour and cook, stirring frequently with a wooden spoon, until the roux takes on a caramel color. Do not burn it or it will be bitter. The cooking time should be 10 to 15 minutes. When the roux is finished, gradually ladle 1 cup of the soup into the pan, stirring constantly, then return this mixture to the Dutch oven. Lift out and discard the cheesecloth bag of spices. Add the nutmeg and salt to taste, then stir in the shelled shrimp, crab meat, and reserved sausage. Simmer for 3 to 5 minutes until the shrimp are opaque. Stir in the lemon juice, filé powder if using, and the parsley. Cook over medium-low heat for 3 minutes, then correct the seasoning to your taste. Serve over hot cooked rice in deep bowls.

NOTE: Filé powder is a sassafras-based herb that thickens the gumbo and gives it an authentic Louisiana taste. Do not cook longer than 3 minutes or allow it to boil or it will become stringy.

Soups from the Sea

PROVENÇAL SEAFOOD RAGOUT WITH ROUILLE

The flavors of Provence are combined in this ragout, accompanied by the fiery scarlet sauce rouille, which is also served traditionally with bouillabaisse.

ROUILLE:

2 to 3	thick slices French or Italian bread, crusts trimmed, torn into small pieces
¼	cup Fish Stock or Fish Fumet (see page 402) or more if necessary
3	large cloves garlic, peeled
1	large sweet red pepper, cut into pieces
½	teaspoon Tabasco or less if you prefer, or 1 to 2 seeded fresh jalapeño or small red chiles
¾	teaspoon paprika
6	tablespoons olive oil
1	teaspoon lemon juice
	Salt and pepper to taste

TOASTS:

6	¾-inch-thick slices sourdough or Italian peasant bread
2	tablespoons olive oil

RAGOUT:

¼	cup olive oil
1	large onion, thinly sliced (about 1¼ cups)
4 to 5	large cloves garlic, finely minced (about 2 tablespoons)
1	large carrot, cut into julienne (about 1½ cups)
2 to 3	ribs celery, cut into julienne (about 1 cup)

1	medium green pepper, cut into thin strips (about ¾ cup)
2 to 3	leeks, cut into julienne (about 2 cups)
½	teaspoon loosely packed saffron threads, crushed
2	tablespoons water
¾ to 1	pound plum tomatoes, peeled and cut into quarters
1	tablespoon fresh thyme leaves or 1 teaspoon dried thyme
1	bay leaf
1	teaspoon fennel seeds
	Salt and pepper to taste
2	tablespoons tomato paste
1	cup dry white wine
2	cups Fish Stock (see page 402)
1	3-inch strip orange peel
½	cup sliced pitted oil-cured black olives
2	tablespoons finely shredded fresh basil
2	tablespoons finely minced parsley
2	pounds skinned fish fillets: any white-fleshed, firm fish or a combination of them, such as pollack, snapper, sea bass, blackfish, or tilefish, cut into 1½-inch pieces
12	small littleneck clams, scrubbed well
18	mussels, scrubbed and bearded
18	sea scallops, quartered or halved depending upon size
18	large shrimp, peeled and deveined
2	tablespoons Pernod or Ricard

FOR THE ROUILLE: Prepare the rouille at least 1 hour before using it to allow it to develop its full flavor. Put the torn bread into a small bowl, pour the fish stock over, and soak. Squeeze out any excess liquid from the bread into a bowl and reserve it. The bread should be slightly mushy. Set aside.

To a blender or food processor, add the garlic and process until finely minced. Add the red pepper, Tabasco, paprika, and the bread; process for 1 to 2 minutes until thick. With the motor running, slowly trickle the oil through the feed tube. Add the lemon juice, some of the reserved fish stock, and the salt and pepper; process until combined. The consistency should be creamy; a bit more fish stock may be necessary. Taste and add Tabasco if you want more heat. Scrape into a bowl and set aside.

FOR THE TOASTS: Place the bread on a baking sheet, brush with olive oil, and broil, turning once, until both sides are golden. Set aside.

FOR THE RAGOUT: In a large heavy Dutch oven, heat the oil over medium heat. Add the onion, garlic, carrot, celery, green pepper, and leek and sauté, stirring occasionally, for 3 to 4 minutes. Mix the saffron and water together and let stand for a few minutes until the water takes on the saffron color. Then add it to the vegetables along with the tomatoes, thyme, bay leaf, fennel seeds, salt, and pepper and cook for 5 minutes more.

In a small cup, mix the tomato paste and wine until smooth. Add it to the pot along with the fish stock and orange peel. Bring to a boil, then lower the heat and simmer, covered, for 8 minutes. Stir in the olives and 1 tablespoon each basil and parsley. Add the fish, cover the pot, and simmer for 1 minute. Add the clams and mussels; cook, covered, until they begin to open. Add the scallops and shrimp and cook only until the clams and mussels are completely opened.

Remove and discard the bay leaf and orange peel. Sprinkle with the Pernod and remaining 1 tablespoon each basil and parsley. Serve in deep bowls, spooning some of the stock over all, and accompany with the rouille, dolloped on soup, and the oven-baked toasts.

WEAKFISH (SEATROUT) BISQUE

MAKES 6 TO 8 SERVINGS

Although firm fish is the kind to use for most soups, the soft, tender flesh of the weakfish is perfect for a puréed bisque, thickened with potato and flavored with just a touch of thyme and tomato paste.

3   tablespoons diced bacon

3   medium onions, coarsely chopped (about 2 cups)

1   large potato (about ¾ pound), peeled and cut into ½-inch dice

2   cups Fish Stock (see page 402)

1   small dried chile

3   cups milk

3   tablespoons tomato paste

1   teaspoon dried thyme
    Salt and white pepper to taste

2½ pounds weakfish (seatrout) fillets, cut into 1½-inch pieces (substitute: flounder or sole)

1   tablespoon finely minced chives

2   tablespoons finely minced parsley

In a 6-quart Dutch oven, fry the bacon over medium heat until crisp. Lift it out with a slotted spoon, drain on paper towels, and reserve. Add the onions to the Dutch oven and sauté, stirring occasionally, until wilted but not browned, 3 to 4 minutes. Add the potato, fish stock, and chile and bring to a boil. Lower the heat and simmer for 15 minutes until the potato is tender.

Add 1½ cups of the milk, the tomato paste, thyme, salt, and pepper and continue to simmer until hot. Then add the fish and cook until the fish is opaque and tender, about 10 minutes. Remove the pot from the heat and discard the chile. Lift out half the fish with a slotted spoon and set aside.

Add the remaining 1½ cups milk to the soup and simmer for 5 minutes more. Purée the soup in batches in a blender and return to the Dutch oven. Taste and adjust the seasoning. Simmer over low heat for 2 minutes, add the reserved fish, and simmer until the fish is heated through. Sprinkle with the chives, parsley, and reserved bacon and serve.

ZUPPA DI PESCE (ITALIAN FISH SOUP WITH PASTA AND LETTUCE)

MAKES 6 TO 8 SERVINGS

Use leafy salad greens, such as sweet romaine or slightly bitter escarole, or a green vegetable such as Swiss chard or spinach, and any kind of firm, white-fleshed fish available at the market for a delightful and hearty whole-meal soup/stew.

3 tablespoons olive oil	4 cups Fish Stock (see page 402)
2 to 3 large cloves garlic, finely minced (about 1 tablespoon)	2 cups water
1 medium onion, finely chopped (about ½ cup)	1 bay leaf
	½ teaspoon hot pepper flakes
1 medium carrot, finely chopped (about ½ cup)	Salt and black pepper to taste
1 medium rib celery, finely chopped (about ½ cup)	¼ pound tubettini or other small macaroni pasta
1 small leek, white part and 1 inch green, finely chopped (about ½ cup)	1 pound fish fillets, such as striped bass, sea bass, or scrod, cut into 1½-inch pieces
1 large potato (about ½ pound), peeled and cut into ½-inch cubes	2 cups shredded romaine lettuce, escarole, Swiss chard, or spinach
10 fresh large plum tomatoes, quartered, or 2 14-ounce cans Italian plum tomatoes	½ cup finely minced flat-leaf parsley
	½ cup grated Parmesan cheese

Heat the oil in a heavy 6- to 7-quart Dutch oven over medium heat. If you have a food processor, you can use it to chop the garlic, onion, carrot, celery, and leek together. Add them to the oil and sauté, stirring frequently, for 5 minutes until the vegetables are wilted.

Add the potato, tomatoes, fish stock, water, bay leaf, pepper flakes, salt, and pepper and bring to a boil. Lower the heat and simmer for 10 minutes. Add the pasta and cook for 10 minutes more, then add the fish and continue to cook for 5 minutes. Add the shredded greens, stirring carefully, and cook for an additional 3 minutes.

Serve in large soup bowls and sprinkle each portion with parsley and cheese right before serving. Pass additional cheese at the table along with a pepper mill if you wish.

RAGOUT OF RED SNAPPER AND SEA SCALLOPS

MAKES 4 SERVINGS

*A delicate blend of orange and fennel plus the woodsy taste of wild mushrooms
give this ragout a lovely subtlety.*

2	cups Fish Stock (see page 402)			Salt and black pepper to taste
8	small new red potatoes, peeled		1	sprig sage
4	tablespoons butter		2	sprigs parsley
6	shiitake mushrooms (about 3 ounces), trimmed, wiped clean with damp paper towels, and thickly sliced		2	bay leaves
			2	3-inch pieces orange peel
6	shallots (about 3 ounces), peeled and cut in half lengthwise		1	pound red snapper fillets with skin, cut into ¾-inch strips (substitute: sea bass)
1	medium red onion, thinly sliced		½	pound sea scallops, cut in half horizontally
1	small fennel bulb (about ½ pound), trimmed and cut into small wedges		½	cup heavy cream
1	medium carrot, cut into julienne		2	tablespoons orange juice
4	tablespoons dry white wine		1	tablespoon coarsely chopped parsley

In a small saucepan, boil the fish stock, uncovered, over high heat until reduced to 1 cup; set aside. In another saucepan, cook the potatoes in boiling salted water to cover for 10 minutes; drain and set aside. In a large sauté pan or Dutch oven, heat 1 tablespoon of the butter over medium-high heat. Add the mushrooms and sauté, stirring frequently, for 2 to 3 minutes. Lift out the mushrooms with a slotted spoon and set aside on a plate.

In the same sauté pan, heat the remaining 3 tablespoons butter over medium-high heat. Add the shallots and sauté, stirring frequently, for 1 minute. Add the red onion; sauté 3 minutes. Add the fennel, the carrot, 2 tablespoons of the wine, salt, and pepper and cook for 2 minutes more. Stir in the reserved mushrooms and potatoes. Tie the sage, parsley, bay leaf, and orange peel together and lay them over the vegetables. Top with the strips of red snapper, then spoon on the remaining 2 tablespoons wine and the reduced fish stock.

Cover the pan and cook over medium-high heat for 5 minutes. Add the scallops and cook for 3 minutes more. Transfer the fish and vegetables with a slotted spoon to a serving platter. Discard the tied herbs. Stir the cream into the sauce in the pan and boil vigorously over high heat for 5 to 6 minutes, until thickened. Stir in the orange juice, taste and adjust the seasoning, and pour over the fish and vegetables. Sprinkle with the parsley and serve.

CACCIUCCO ALLA LIVORNESE

MAKES 6 TO 8 SERVINGS

The name of this celebrated spicy fish stew is derived from a Turkish word for small fish. It is traditionally filled with crustaceans and as many varieties of fin fish as there are C's in cacciucco. *It is so similar to the San Francisco version of cioppino with its Dungeness crab that the addition of crab or lobster could easily make it pass for the California version of this stew.*

TOASTS:

- 8 ¾-inch-thick slices sourdough or Italian peasant bread
- 2 tablespoons olive oil
- 1 clove garlic, halved

STEW:

- 6 tablespoons olive oil
- 1 large onion, quartered
- 2 medium carrots, cut in 1½-inch pieces
- 2 to 3 medium ribs celery, cut in 1½-inch pieces
- 3 to 4 large cloves garlic, peeled
- 2 tablespoons coarsely chopped parsley
- 1 large bay leaf
- ½ teaspoon dried thyme
- ½ teaspoon dried rosemary
- 1 14-ounce can Italian plum tomatoes with liquid

- ¼ teaspoon hot pepper flakes
- Salt and pepper to taste
- 1 cup dry red wine
- 2 cups Fish Stock (see page 402)
- 1 teaspoon finely minced lemon peel
- 2 pounds assorted firm, white-fleshed fish fillets, such as sea bass, halibut, pollack, tilefish, and/or ocean perch depending upon region and seasonal availability, cut into 2-inch pieces
- ¾ pound sea scallops, sliced horizontally if large
- ¾ pound medium shrimp, shelled
- ½ pound small squid, cleaned (see page 376), bodies cut into rings, tentacles left whole
- 3 tablespoons finely shredded fresh basil

PREPARE THE TOASTS FIRST: Place the bread on a baking sheet, brush both sides with olive oil, and toast them under the broiler on both sides until golden. While the toasts are warm, rub the surfaces with the cut clove of garlic. Wrap the toasts in aluminum foil to be rewarmed later. Set aside.

FOR THE STEW: Heat the oil in a 12-inch nonstick sauté pan over medium heat. In a food processor, finely chop the onion, carrots, celery, and garlic; add them to the pan and sauté, stirring occasionally, for 2 minutes. Add the parsley, bay leaf, thyme, and rosemary. Sauté, stirring frequently, for 3 more minutes. Stir in the tomatoes, pepper flakes, salt, and pepper and simmer for 10 minutes until reduced a bit.

Add the wine, raise the heat to medium-high, and heat for 3 to 4 minutes more. Remove and discard the bay leaf. Purée the sauce in a food processor and return to the sauté pan. You may prepare the sauce up to this point well ahead of time and continue the recipe 15 minutes before serving.

When ready to continue, reheat the garlic toasts and your serving bowls or plates in a low oven. Add the fish stock to the puréed sauce and heat to a boil over medium heat. Stir in the lemon peel and add the pieces of fish in one layer. Cover and cook gently for 5 minutes. Tuck in the scallops and distribute the shrimp among the fish. Tilt the pan and, using a baster or spoon, moisten the surface with the sauce. Cover and cook for 3 more minutes, then add the squid, baste, and cook for 1 to 2 minutes until the seafood is opaque. The sauce should not be watery but have some body. Do not stir to avoid breaking up the fish.

To serve, place a toast in a warmed bowl or plate and ladle equal portions of fish, shellfish, and sauce over the toasts. Sprinkle with the basil and serve hot.

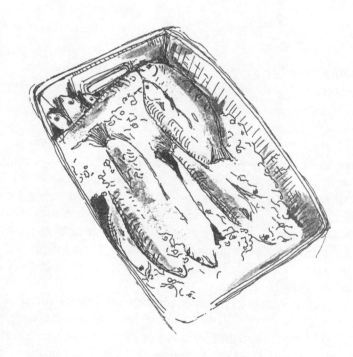

SPANISH CODFISH STEW WITH ORANGE, SAFFRON, AND PARSLEY

MAKES 4 SERVINGS

The bitter oranges of Seville are used to perfume and flavor many dishes in Spain. Here, we have combined sweet domestic oranges with tart lemon juice to approximate the flavor in this Spanish saffron fish stew thickened with bread crumbs.

½ teaspoon saffron threads, crumbled

¼ cup boiling water

2 tablespoons olive oil

1 medium onion, chopped (about ⅔ cup)

½ small fennel bulb, finely chopped (about ½ cup)

2 to 3 cloves garlic, finely minced (1 tablespoon)

1½ pounds codfish steaks or scrod fillets

Salt to taste

¼ teaspoon freshly ground black pepper

½ teaspoon fennel seeds

1 tablespoon fresh thyme leaves

1 14-ounce can Italian plum tomatoes with liquid, tomatoes cut in half crosswise

1 cup water

¾ cup dry white wine

2 bay leaves

2 teaspoons finely minced orange peel

¼ cup plus 2 tablespoons coarsely chopped parsley

½ cup fresh bread crumbs

⅔ cup orange juice

1 tablespoon lemon juice

⅛ teaspoon cayenne pepper

Steep the saffron in the boiling water for 15 minutes. In a 5-quart heavy Dutch oven, heat the oil over medium heat. Add the onion, fennel, and garlic and cook, stirring frequently, for 3 to 4 minutes. Add the fish and cook on each side for 1 minute. Sprinkle with the salt, pepper, fennel, and thyme. Then add the saffron liquid, tomatoes, water, wine, bay leaves, and orange peel. Bring to a boil and stir in ¼ cup of the parsley and the bread crumbs. Lower the heat and simmer, covered, for 5 minutes. Remove the fish with a slotted spoon and set it aside on a plate to cool. Continue to simmer the soup, covered, for 20 minutes more.

When the fish is cool enough to handle, remove and discard the skin and bones if using fish steaks. At the end of the 20-minute simmering period, return the chunks of fish to the soup and add the orange and lemon juices and cayenne. Continue to simmer for 5 minutes more until the fish flakes when tested with the point of a knife. Just before serving, remove and discard the bay leaves and sprinkle with the remaining 2 tablespoons parsley.

NEW ENGLAND SCROD AND CORN CHOWDER

MAKES 6 TO 8 SERVINGS

A humble trio of New England ingredients—scrod, corn, and potatoes—are gently simmered in a rich and creamy broth.

3	strips bacon		½	cup heavy cream
1½	cups coarsely chopped onions		2	cups frozen corn kernels, thawed, or fresh kernels cut from 4 ears of corn
1	tablespoon all-purpose flour		1	teaspoon dried thyme
3 or 4	large potatoes, peeled and cut into ½-inch cubes (2½ cups)		¼	teaspoon cayenne pepper or more to taste
2	pounds scrod fillets, cut into 2½-inch pieces (substitute: other firm, white-fleshed fish such as cod, haddock, or halibut)		½	teaspoon white pepper
				Salt to taste
			1	tablespoon butter, softened
3	cups Fish Stock (see page 402), boiling			Paprika for garnish
3	cups milk			

In a 6- or 7-quart heavy Dutch oven, fry the bacon until crisp. Lift out the bacon, crumble, and set aside. Add the onion to the bacon fat and sauté over medium heat, stirring frequently, for 2 to 3 minutes until wilted. Sprinkle with the flour and stir. Add the potatoes and stir. Layer the fish over the onions and potatoes, then slowly pour the boiling fish stock over all. Bring to a boil, then reduce the heat and simmer, covered, for 5 minutes.

Stir in the milk, cream, corn, thyme, cayenne, pepper, and salt. Cover and simmer for 10 to 15 minutes until the potatoes are tender. Add the butter and taste and adjust the seasoning.

Serve the chowder in individual bowls, topped with crumbled bacon and a dash of paprika for color.

COTRIADE
(A BRITTANY FISHERMAN'S STEW)

MAKES 6 SERVINGS

A simple, substantial fin fish and potato stew from the French coast of Brittany.
It's sometimes referred to as "Breton bouillabaisse," particularly when
lobster is added for special guests.

6   1-inch-thick slices peasant or sourdough bread, toasted

2   medium shallots, halved

½   cup parsley leaves

3   tablespoons red wine vinegar

1   teaspoon strong Dijon mustard
    Salt and black pepper to taste

½   cup olive oil

4   tablespoons butter

2   large onions (about 1 pound), cut into 1-inch pieces

1   medium leek, white part and 1 inch green, sliced ½ inch thick

1   large clove garlic, finely minced (about 2 teaspoons)

4   cups Fish Stock (see page 402)

1   cup dry white wine

1½ pounds small potatoes (12 to 14), peeled

6   sprigs fresh thyme

2   large bay leaves

4   sprigs parsley

8   whole peppercorns

1   1¼-pound lobster (optional; have your fishmonger kill, clean, and cut the lobster into chunks, keeping meat in shell)

½   teaspoon dried marjoram

½   teaspoon freshly ground black pepper

2½ pounds assorted firm-fleshed fish fillets, such as scrod, grouper, snapper, bass, parrot fish, halibut, tilefish, or monkfish—any combination of 3 varieties, cut into 2-inch pieces

1   tablespoon coarsely chopped parsley

⅜ to ¾   cup heavy cream (optional)

Place the toasted bread in a basket and set aside. In a food processor, finely chop the shallots, then add the parsley and process until finely minced. Add the vinegar, mustard, salt, and pepper and process with a few strokes until combined. With the motor running, slowly add the oil through the feed tube and process until a slightly thickened emulsion is formed. Scrape into a small bowl and reserve.

In a heavy 7½-quart Dutch oven, melt the butter over medium heat. Add the onions and sauté, stirring frequently, for 2 to 3 minutes. Then add the leek and garlic and sauté, stirring occasionally, for 3 to 4 minutes. Add the fish stock, white wine, and potatoes and bring to a boil. Tie the thyme sprigs, bay leaves, parsley sprigs, and peppercorns in a cheesecloth bag and add to the pot. When the stock returns to a boil, lower the heat and simmer for 10 minutes. Tuck in the chunks of lobster if using, add the marjoram, pepper, and salt to taste and continue to simmer for 5 minutes. ·

Lay the pieces of fish fillets over the top. Cover the pot and simmer for an additional 8 to 10 minutes, tilting the pot and ladling the stock over the fish occasionally as it cooks. Cook until the fish is opaque, testing it with a skewer. With a slotted spatula, transfer the fish and lobster to a large serving casserole. Add the potatoes and ladle the onion mixture and some broth over all. Sprinkle with parsley. Pour the remaining hot broth into a separate serving bowl.

To serve, place a piece of the toasted bread on the bottom of an individual serving bowl. Spoon a tablespoon or two of the parsley vinaigrette over the bread, then ladle some of the broth over that. Add some fish, lobster, onion mixture, and potatoes. If you wish, you may add 1 to 2 tablespoons of heavy cream per serving to the broth, something that is occasionally done in Brittany.

Soups from the Sea

ARABIC FISH STEW WITH SWEET RED PEPPERS AND ONIONS

MAKES 6 SERVINGS

Try this firm, meaty, distinctively flavored stew served with quickly cooked couscous and tiny green peas for a colorful and compatible combination.

4 tablespoons olive oil

6 king mackerel steaks, about ¾ inch thick, 2½ to 3 pounds (substitute: Spanish mackerel, bluefish, jackfish, or mahi-mahi)

Salt and pepper to taste

1 large sweet onion (about 1 pound), such as Bermuda, Vidalia, or Oso, sliced about ¼ inch thick

3 to 4 cloves garlic, finely minced (1½ table-spoons)

2 large red peppers, cut into ½-inch strips (about 1 pound)

½ teaspoon ground cumin

½ teaspoon *harissa* or cayenne pepper (see Note)

1½ cups Fish Stock (see page 402)

¼ cup coarsely chopped cilantro

2 tablespoons lemon juice

1 teaspoon finely minced lemon peel

In a 12-inch sauté pan, heat the oil over medium-high heat until very hot. Season the fish with salt and pepper and sauté for 3 minutes on each side until almost cooked. Remove to a plate with a slotted spatula and set aside. To the same skillet, add the onion and garlic and sauté, stirring constantly, for 1 minute. Add the peppers and continue to sauté for 5 minutes more, stirring frequently. Sprinkle with cumin, *harissa,* and additional salt and pepper if you wish.

Add the fish stock and bring to a boil. Return the fish steaks to the pan, tilt the pan, and spoon some of the sauce over the fish. Lower the heat, cover, and simmer for about 5 minutes until the fish is cooked.

Transfer the fish steaks to a serving platter. Stir the cilantro and lemon juice into the sauce and spoon it around the fish. Scatter the lemon peel over all. You also can serve this fish at room temperature or chilled if you wish.

NOTE: *Harissa* is a fiery paste of chiles and spices. It can be found in a tube in gourmet or Middle Eastern food shops.

VEGETABLE AND CRAB CHOWDER WITH BLACK BEANS

Fresh sweet corn, zucchini, crab meat, and black beans are presented in a thick, colorful chowder inspired by the flavors of the Southwest.

2 ounces bacon or pancetta, diced

2 thin leeks, white part and 2 inches pale green, coarsely chopped (about 1 cup)

1 large potato (about ¾ pound), peeled and cut into ¾-inch pieces

½ cup diced roasted red pepper

1 medium jalapeño chile, seeded and minced

3 cups chicken stock, homemade or canned

1 pound zucchini, cut into ¾-inch pieces (about 2 cups)

2 cups fresh corn kernels (3 to 4 ears fresh corn) or thawed frozen kernels

1 teaspoon ground cumin

2 teaspoons sugar

Salt and pepper to taste

1 cup milk

2 tablespoons masa harina flour

1 cup cooked or canned black beans, rinsed and drained

½ pound lump crab meat, picked over to remove any stray cartilage

Cayenne pepper to taste

2 tablespoons coarsely chopped cilantro

In a 5-quart Dutch oven, sauté the bacon over low heat until crisp. Lift out with a slotted spoon and reserve on paper towels. Raise the heat to medium, add the leeks to the bacon fat, and sauté, stirring frequently, until wilted, about 3 minutes. Add the potato, red pepper, jalapeño, and chicken stock. Cook for about 10 minutes, then stir in the zucchini, corn, cumin, sugar, salt, and pepper; cook for 5 more minutes.

Stir in the milk, masa harina, and beans and continue to cook until slightly thickened and hot, about 5 minutes. Stir in the crab and cook for 1 minute only, until the crab meat is hot. Add cayenne if you wish more heat and taste and adjust the seasoning. Sprinkle with the cilantro and bacon just before serving.

BOURRIDE WITH AÏOLI

MAKES 6 TO 8 SERVINGS

Unlike its relative bouillabaisse from Marseilles, sun-colored bourride *never includes crustaceans or shellfish. It traditionally incorporates aïoli, the mayonnaise sauce redolent with garlic, which thickens and flavors the broth while gently cooking the egg.*

AIOLI:

3 large cloves garlic

½ teaspoon coarse salt, or more to taste at end

2 egg yolks, at room temperature (see Note)

1 teaspoon Dijon mustard

Black pepper to taste

¾ cup olive oil

¼ cup canola oil

2 teaspoons lemon juice

BOURRIDE:

2 large baking potatoes, peeled and cut into ½-inch slices

1 sourdough baguette, sliced ½ inch thick

Olive oil for the bread plus 3 tablespoons

1 garlic clove, halved

1 large onion, coarsely chopped (about 1 cup)

2 thin leeks, white and green parts, coarsely chopped (about 1 cup)

1 small fennel bulb (⅛ pound), coarsely chopped (about 1¼ cups)

1 medium clove garlic, finely minced (about 1 teaspoon)

1 teaspoon loosely packed saffron threads, crumbled

¼ cup boiling water

4 cups Fish Stock (see page 402)

1 cup dry white wine

1 cup water

3 to 4 sprigs fresh thyme

1 large bay leaf

1 strip each lemon and orange peel, about 1 by 3 inches

¼ teaspoon cayenne pepper

⅛ teaspoon turmeric

Salt to taste

1 cleaned fish head or rack (optional)

3½ pounds white-fleshed, firm fish fillets, such as scrod, halibut, tilefish, pollack, or ocean perch—any combination of 3 or 4 varieties—pin bones removed and cut into 2-inch chunks

PREPARE THE AÏOLI AHEAD OF TIME: Using the side of a large knife, smash the garlic cloves to release the flavor, peel, and finely mince. Add to a mortar and pestle along with the coarse salt and pound into a smooth purée. Set aside.

In a food processor, process the egg yolks, mustard, and black pepper for about 10 seconds. Combine the olive and canola oils. With the motor running, slowly trickle half the oil through the feed tube. Add 1 teaspoon of the lemon juice and then the remaining oil, keeping the processor running while you do so. Process until thick. Add the remaining 1 teaspoon lemon juice and the garlic paste and process with a few more strokes to combine. Transfer to a small bowl, cover with plastic wrap, and refrigerate for a few hours or overnight.

FOR THE BOURRIDE: Peel and cook the potatoes in boiling salted water to cover for 10 minutes. Drain and set aside. Preheat the oven to 375°, place the sourdough slices on a baking sheet and brush both sides of the bread lightly with olive oil, reserving 3 tablespoons of the oil for later on. Toast in the oven until golden, turning the slices once, then rub the slices with a cut clove of garlic. Wrap the toasts in aluminum foil to be reheated just before serving.

In a 6- to 7-quart Dutch oven, heat the 3 tablespoons olive oil over medium heat. Add the onion, leeks, fennel, and minced garlic and sauté, stirring occasionally, until soft but not brown, about 5 to 8 minutes.

While the vegetables are sautéing, add the saffron threads to ¼ cup boiling water and let steep for 10 to 15 minutes. Add the fish stock, wine, and water to the vegetables. Tie the thyme, bay leaf, and citrus peels together and add to the pot along with the saffron liquid, cayenne, and turmeric. Bring to a boil over medium heat. At this point, if you have a fish head or rack of bones, tie them loosely in cheesecloth and add to the pot for extra flavor. Lower the heat, cover the pot, and simmer for 20 minutes.

Remove and discard the cheesecloth bag and the herbs. Cool the stock slightly, add salt to taste, and purée in a blender (not a food processor) in several batches. The recipe can be made up to this point ahead of time and refrigerated.

When ready to continue, bring the stock to a boil, add the pieces of fish, and cook over medium heat for 3 minutes. Add the cooked potatoes and heat until the fish is just cooked through and the potatoes are warmed. Lift out the fish and potatoes with a slotted spoon and transfer them to a serving tureen; cover with foil to keep warm.

Slowly whisk 1 cup of the hot broth into 1 cup of the aïoli. Lower the heat and whisk the mixture into the pot. Cook, stirring constantly, over very low heat for about 5 minutes until thickened. Do not let it boil or the soup will curdle. Then ladle over the fish and potatoes and pass the toasts in a basket. To serve, place a piece of toast in the bottom of individual bowls, ladling the soup over them, and follow with the fish and potatoes.

NOTE: Although there has been some concern over the use of raw eggs in recipes, there is no need for anxiety in this one. When the aïoli is added to thicken the hot soup, the 2 egg yolks called for will cook slowly.

CREAM OF CLAM AND MUSSEL SOUP WITH THYME AND OREGANO

MAKES 4 SERVINGS

A creamy, pink shellfish soup redolent with thyme and oregano. A sauté of diced vegetables is added at the end along with tiny, briny clams and mussels.

3	tablespoons butter		½	medium carrot, cut into ¼-inch dice (about ¼ cup)
1	small onion, thinly sliced (about ⅔ cup)		¼	cup tomato paste
4	medium ribs celery, 2 ribs thinly sliced (about ½ cup) and 2 ribs cut into ¼-inch dice (about ⅓ cup)		1	teaspoon dried oregano, preferably Greek
1½	large cloves garlic, ½ clove minced and 1 clove peeled but kept whole		1½	teaspoons dried thyme
1	large bay leaf		¼	teaspoon saffron
1½	cups dry white wine		½	cup heavy cream
1	cup water		2	cups milk
24	very small littleneck clams, scrubbed well		½	teaspoon sugar
24	medium mussels, scrubbed and bearded		2 to 3	drops Tabasco
2	large shallots, coarsely chopped (about ¼ cup)			Salt and pepper to taste
			4	sprigs fresh thyme for garnish

In a 5-quart Dutch oven, heat 1 tablespoon of the butter over low heat. Add the onion, the sliced celery, the whole garlic clove, and the bay leaf. Cover the pot and cook over low heat for 3 minutes. Add ½ cup of the wine and the water and bring to a boil over medium-high heat. Add the clams, cover, and cook for 5 minutes. Then add the mussels, cover, and cook just until the shellfish open, about 5 minutes more. Lift out the shellfish with tongs and place them in a bowl to let them cool slightly. Lower the heat, cover the pot again, and simmer the broth for 15 minutes more.

Line a strainer with a man's handkerchief and strain the cooking broth into a bowl, gathering up the handkerchief and pressing the solids with a wooden spoon to extract as much of the broth as possible. Discard the solids and return the broth to the Dutch oven.

In a small skillet, heat the remaining 2 tablespoons butter over medium heat. Add the shallots and sauté, stirring frequently, for about 2 minutes. Spoon half the shallots into the broth and leave the rest in the skillet. Add the diced celery and carrots to the skillet and sauté over low heat for 2 minutes. Turn off the heat and reserve the diced vegetables.

Combine the tomato paste with the remaining 1 cup wine and stir it into the shell-fish broth. Bring to a boil. Stir in the oregano and thyme, cover the pot, lower the heat, and simmer for 20 minutes. Stir in the saffron threads along with the minced garlic and simmer for 10 minutes more.

While the soup is simmering, remove the mussel and clam meats from their shells; reserve 4 whole mussel shells for garnish. Mix the cream and milk together, add to the soup, and continue to simmer until hot. Stir in the clams and mussels along with the reserved diced vegetables and simmer for 1 to 2 minutes until heated through. Add the sugar, Tabasco, salt, and pepper. Ladle into large soup bowls; garnish with the mussel shells and thyme sprigs if you wish.

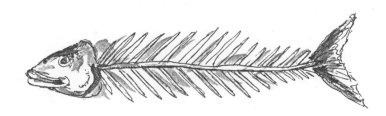

Soups from the Sea

INDEX

appetizers

Tapenade 168
Pickled Shrimp 273

Sauces

Charmoula 174
Tropical Salsa 190
Orange juice - mint 195
Cucumber mint caper 197
Puttanesca Sauce 213
Leek - Sorrel Sauce 232
✓ Romesco Sauce 388

Firm Fish

Baked Swordfish - mustard glaze 189
Baked Fish - tomato + feta 200

Tender Fish

Trout Lemon caper - 253

Shell fish

Shrimp baked with feta and tomato 268
Shrimp in Garlic s. 269
Coconut shrimp 270
✓ Sauteed Indian Shrimp 271
mushroom stuffed shrimp 272
✓ crab salad + sauce 287
Crab cakes 290
✓✓ crab in scallop shell 291
Scallops ginger, red pepper 329
Scallops - herb sauce 330
Shrimp in Green Sauce 398
✓ Shrimp in Gumbo 404